# Primary *Ousia*

# Primary *Ousia*

## An Essay on Aristotle's *Metaphysics* Z and H

MICHAEL J. LOUX

Cornell University Press

ITHACA AND LONDON

First published 1991 by Cornell University Press.

International Standard Book Number 0-8014-2598-0
Library of Congress Catalog Card Number 90-25775

Printed in the United States of America

*Librarians: Library of Congress cataloging information appears on the last page of the book.*

♾ The paper in this book meets the minimum requirements of the American National Standard for Information Sciences–Permanence of Paper for Printed Library Materials, ANSI Z39.48-1984.

*To Timothy O'Meara*

# Contents

# Preface

My interest in Z and H goes back more than twenty-five years to my sophomore year in college. I was taking a required course in metaphysics, and the text for the first half of the semester was Aristotle's *Metaphysics*. As it turned out, the teacher spent almost all the allotted time on the first six books, focusing on the great controversy over the subject matter of first philosophy, and we were left with only one class to cover all of Z and H. I made the mistake of putting off the reading assignment until the night before. It was a frustrating struggle. I would read a paragraph, dismayed that I could not understand any sentence in it, depressed that I could not remember a thing from the paragraph I had just completed, and painfully conscious that there were many such paragraphs to go. I went to bed in a state of utter confusion, and our whirlwind survey of the text the next day did little to dispel that confusion.

But however little I understood of Z and H, I must have become convinced by that first experience that this was an important text; two years later I asked the teacher of the required metaphysics course to direct me in a reading course on Z and H and Saint Thomas's commentary on them. My second experience with the text was even more frustrating than the first. On this reading, I had the time to work my way through the text at a more leisurely pace; but, however often I returned to Z.1, I would have the experience of thinking I had a particular body of the text under control only to lose it as I tried to master what followed. Things became worse rather than better as the semester wore on, and I can remember the depressing thought, at semester's end, that I did not understand anything at all of the middle books.

My third experience with Z and H came in my second year in graduate school when I was preparing to write a dissertation on the *Categories*. In my naivete, I supposed that the corpus constituted a vehicle for expressing a single unchanging body of doctrine, and I approached Z and H to find what they would tell me about Aristotle's "theory of categories." This time, I thought I understood some of what I was reading, but I was anything but comforted by what I was finding there. How can form be primary *ousia* when concrete particulars are supposed to play this role? How can the idea of a basic subject of predication be wanting as a guide to picking out the *ousiai* when that idea just tells us what *ousiai* are? How can a primary *ousia* be identical with its essence when primary *ousiai* are things like Socrates which share their essences? Unable to make any headway with these and other questions, I dodged them by choosing a "safe" topic for the dissertation, Ockham's interpretation of Aristotle's *Categories*.

I had, however, been bitten by the Z–H bug. Not long after coming to Notre Dame, I began giving a graduate seminar on the middle books on the questionable premise that, if you do not understand something, you should teach it to graduate students. I continued to give that seminar, often on an annual basis, over the next fifteen years. Little that transpired in the course found its way into print, in part because there were other topics on which I wanted to have my say, and in part because I found, paradoxically, that the deeper I went into the text, not just my understanding but also my puzzlement grew.

In 1983, I was appointed Dean of the College of Arts and Letters at Notre Dame. On accepting the appointment, I knew that I would have to put Z, H, and all other things philosophical aside for a time. I assumed, however, that once I mastered the routine of the job I would be able to keep up with philosophy; but after five years as dean, I had the frightening realization that since accepting the appointment I had done no philosophy at all. So, in the spring of 1988, I requested a year's leave to catch up on the discipline. Happily, the leave was granted. My plan was to write nothing at all, but merely to spend the year reading the journals and recent book-length studies on the topics that had been the focus of my published efforts—individuation, abstract entities, modality, and so on. But before I went to the most recent issue of *Philosophical Review*, I decided to spend a week reading through Z and H. The week became a month; the month, a semester; and the semester, an academic year.

This time, however, things were different. The time away from philosophy had evidently been liberating. From the earliest rereading of the text, I realized I had something to say about Z and H as a whole. After going through the body of critical literature that had accumulated in my years away from philosophy, I had a clear sense of how my views on Z and H related to the work of others. And the business of writing it up seemed easy, easier than any philosophical writing I had done before; when I returned to the dean's office in August of 1989, I had a full draft of a manuscript on Z and H. My retrospective sense of the project was not that I had written it, but that it had written itself.

Although what I wrote over that year is a study of Z and H as a whole, it is only a partial study since there is much in the text I do not yet understand. Having been under the spell of the middle books for more than a quarter of a century, I know I will be unable to resist the temptation to go back; having had at least ten different opinions on virtually every sentence of the text, I am not naive enough to suppose that the views I express here will be my final ideas on Z and H. Perhaps I will see things differently five years from now, and I will be compelled to write a series of retractions. Z and H are like that. In any case, what follows is an account of the middle books as I now understand them.

I said that writing the book was easy. In part it was easy because so many individuals helped. At the beginning of my leave, I asked several people for advice on the secondary literature I needed to read, and many of them gave me their counsel. I was especially helped by an excellent bibliography of recent work on the themes of the middle books that Daniel Devereaux had compiled. Others who were extremely helpful include John Ackrill, Jonathan Barnes, Sheilah Brennan, William Charlton, Alan Code, Marc Cohen, Sheldon Cohen, Montgomery Furth, Jonathan Lear, Frank Lewis, Ernan McMullin, Mohan Matthen, D. K. Modrak, Kenneth Sayre, Michael Wedin and Christopher Williams. Michael Frede, Philip Quinn, and David Burrell all read the first draft of the book and provided the kind of advice that helps transform a half-baked idea into something more, and an anonymous reader for Cornell University Press gave me extremely detailed suggestions for revising the second draft. Albert Wimmer helped me with the German text of the Frede–Patzig commentary. Margaret Jasiewicz and Kay Herrick did yeowomen's work on the typing of the manuscript. While I was on leave, Nathan Hatch and Roger Skurski kept the house in order and made sure that I was never once bothered by the worries of the dean's office. My family gave me more support than they had on any project I had previously undertaken. They realized how important it was for me, at that stage of my career, to get back to the life of the scholar, and they made sure that our house was a place where I could do it. Especially supportive was the tolerance of Ann and Julie, who were forced to endure nightly progress reports at the dinner table. They never once let on that something other than primary *ousia* might be an appropriate topic of mealtime conversation. I thank all of these people and, especially, Edward Malloy, C.S.C., Notre Dame's president, and Timothy O'Meara, our provost, for allowing me the freedom of a leave. When I became dean, Tim assured me that the job would make me a better philosopher. I do not know whether he was right, but I do know that in my years as dean I have learned many things I would never have known had I not accepted the appointment. Since Tim taught me most of these, I have dedicated the book to him.

Parts of my "Form, Species, and Predication in *Metaphysics* Z, H, and Θ," *Mind* (1979), 1–23, appear in the second section of Chapter 4. The final section of Chapter 7 includes several paragraphs from my "*Ousia*: A Prolegomenon to *Metaphysics* Z and H," *History of Philosophy Quarterly* (1984), 241–225. These pieces of text appear here with the permission of the editors of the relevant journals.

Unless otherwise indicated the translations of Aristotle in what follows are my own.

Michael J. Loux

*Notre Dame, Indiana*

# Primary *Ousia*

# Introduction

In what follows I attempt to make sense of the very difficult *Metaphysics* Z and H, and I address two quite different audiences in doing so.[1] First, I have tried to write a philosophical essay on Z and H for the nonspecialist in Greek philosophy. I have in mind the reader who approaches the middle books in the hopes of finding there Aristotle's mature views on what we nowadays call the problems of substance, but who finds the often obscure text and tortuous argument of Z and H a source of frustration rather than philosophical insight. With this reader in mind, I lay out the main contours of the theory Aristotle develops in the middle books and reconstruct the line of argument supporting that theory. But I also use the occasion to have my say on some of the central disputes dominating the extensive literature on Z and H; in this connection, what I say is aimed at a specialist audience.

The attempt to speak to two such different audiences can result in

---

[1]The idea that Z and H constitute a single treatise would not generally be challenged. It is, however, customary to lump Z and H together with Θ under the title "the middle books." But, although there certainly are themes in Θ that are relevant to the discussions of Z and H, much of what happens in Θ is tangential to the central themes of Z and H. Book Θ just does not provide us with materials that can be understood only as parts of a single unified argument of which Z and H are earlier components. It is, however, difficult to read Z and H except in terms of each other, and pretty clearly H.6 represents the finale of a dialectic that goes back to Z.1. I ask readers with initial doubts about this contention to suppress them, since I believe (or hope) that by the end of my Chapter 7 those doubts will have been dispelled. For an exegetical argument for the idea that Z and H constitute what was originally intended as a single treatise, see Michael Frede and Gunther Patzig, *Aristoteles "Metaphysik Z"* (Munich: Verlag C. H. Beck, 1988), vol. 1, 21–26.

failure on both fronts. In addressing the nonspecialist, one runs the risk of saying things the specialist takes to be obvious or to involve over-simplification; in joining the controversies that animate the specialist's literature, one is in danger of losing the nonspecialist reader. In the present case, the former risk is less serious. There is just not enough agreement among commentators on Z and H for any particular inter-pretation of the middle books to count as the received view. Although my attempt to delineate the theory Aristotle advances in Z and H is certain to be challenged by some or even most scholars of the middle books, it is unlikely that the attempt will result in an account that is viewed as too obvious to warrant formulation. The second danger is, however, more real. For someone unfamiliar with the disputes and controversies surrounding Z and H, the strategies required to defend a particular interpretation of this or that text might seem unnecessary detours that hinder rather than advance our understanding, and the result of relating one's reading of the middle books to those of other commentators can appear a tangled mess only marginally more accessi-ble than the middle books themselves.

The middle books are difficult, and no book on Z and H is likely to make for easy reading. So, in the interests of helping the nonspecialist, I want to provide here a kind of overview of what I am trying to do. The overview is not meant as a substitute for the chapters that follow, nor is it presupposed by them. The aim is rather to abstract the key themes of my interpretation from the detailed textual and philosophical argu-ments by which they are supported, to relate these themes to each other and to the main divisions of Aristotle's text, and to situate my own reading within the secondary literature on the middle books.

All commentators would agree that one important aim of Z and H is to provide an answer to the question, Which things are the primary *ousiai*? Although they variously translate *'ousia'* as 'substance', 'reality', 'entity', 'being' (I choose to leave the term untranslated), scholars would agree that, for Aristotle, the primary *ousiai* are the ontologically basic entities. They are the things by reference to which we explain why other things exist, but whose existence itself stands in no need of explanation. Scholars would also agree that the question Aristotle poses for himself in Z and H is precisely the question dominating the much earlier *Categories*, and it turns out that the Z–H attempt to identify the ontologically basic entities is undertaken with an eye to that earlier work. The answer Z and H propose to the question, Which things are the primary *ousiai*? is at variance with that developed and defended in the *Categories*, and much of Z and H is concerned with the tension between its own answer to that question and that found in the earlier work. Accordingly, in the first chapter I lay out the background of the discussions of the middle books by delineating those features of the *Categories* account that function as foil for the theory advanced in Z and H.

The intuition at work in the *Categories* is that the familiar concrete particulars of common sense (the paradigms of which Aristotle takes to be particular living beings like a "certain man" and a "certain horse") are the primary *ousiai*; what makes them ontologically privileged, Aristotle wants to say, is the fact that they are what I call basic subjects. They are the things of which universals are predicated or which instantiate universals, but they are not themselves predicated of or instantiated by anything else. The idea that this fact about familiar concrete particulars underwrites their status as primary *ousiai* or ontologically basic items has its roots in the anti-Platonic assumption that the existence of a universal presupposes the existence of one or more objects that instantiate it.

But while the Aristotle of the *Categories* insists that the existence of all universals presupposes or depends on the existence of basic subjects, he draws a distinction among the universals instantiated by or predicated of the familiar particulars he calls primary *ousiai*. In rough terms, the distinction is that between universals that mark out primary *ousiai* as *what* they are and those that merely characterize particulars antecedently so marked out. The former include the species and genera under which a primary *ousia* falls as well as the universals (differentiae) included in their definition; Aristotle tells us that these universals are "said of" the primary *ousiai* that are their subjects. The latter include such things as the qualitative and quantitative determinations of a primary *ousia*, the actions it performs, and the ways it is related to other primary *ousiai*. The tradition has lumped these universals together under the label "accidents," and Aristotle tells us that they are "present in" primary *ousiai*.

This distinction turns out to be central to the *Categories* account of primary *ousiai*. There is a kind of essentialism at work in that account. Aristotle argues that the concept of a primary *ousia* is given by the universals that mark it out as what it is, and, although he concedes that we can identify a primary *ousia* by reference to universals of varying levels of generality, he claims that we most fully articulate what a primary *ousia* is when we identify it by reference to the lowest-level kind or infima species to which it belongs. What primary *ousiai* are, he wants to say, are particular instances of their species; to be for them just consists in being instances of those species.

So two themes are pivotal in the *Categories* account of primary *ousiai*:

the idea that the things that are ontologically fundamental are basic subjects, and the idea that the ontologically basic entities are instances or members of their infimae species. The intersection of these two themes yields a third theme that is a critical component in Aristotle's early thinking on *ousia*. This theme, which I call the Unanalyzability Thesis, is just the idea that a primary *ousia*'s belonging to or falling under its infima species must be a primitive or irreducible fact about it, a fact that is not susceptible of further ontological analysis. Just how this thesis emerges is a complicated story; in short compass, the idea is that if basic or ultimate subjects of predication are ontologically fundamental and if the very concept of these subjects is given by their infimae species, then it cannot be the case that a primary *ousia*'s belonging to its species rests on or is analyzable in terms of some prior case in which a universal is predicated of some more fundamental or lower level subject. Were that to be the case, the more fundamental subject would have a better claim to status as primary *ousia*. But the only materials for ontological reduction or analysis the Aristotle of the *Categories* has at his disposal are those provided by the notion of a universal's being predicated of (either by being said of or present in) a subject. So the relation between the universals that mark out the basic subjects as what they are and the basic subjects they so mark out must be primitive, unanalyzable, or irreducible.

It turns out that there are pressures from two different directions on Aristotle's early attempt to identify the primary *ousiai*. There are pressures internal to the account itself, pressures having their origin in Aristotle's essentialist emphasis on the infimae species under which basic subjects fall. That emphasis calls into question the idea that an inventory of familiar particulars exhaustively delineates the ontologically fundamental things. Primary *ousiai* are things on which all other things depend for their existence, but things which do not, in the same way, depend on anything else for their existence. Although the anti-Platonic assumption that the existence of a universal presupposes the existence of something of which it is predicated serves to show that the existence of infimae species turns on the existence of Aristotle's basic subjects, the essentialist interpretation of basic subjects entails that basic subjects, in turn, depend on their infimae species for their existence. So if we judge the early theory on its own terms, we have to question its claim that basic subjects alone constitute the primary *ousiai*; the universals that provide basic subjects with their essences have as good a claim to the title 'primary *ousia*' as do those basic subjects.

External pressures also come to bear on the early theory. In texts written later than the *Categories*, Aristotle confronts the fact that the basic subjects of the early theory have temporally bounded careers, that they are things that come to be, exist for a while, and then pass away;[2] and his account of this fact involves the idea that things like the man and the horse of the *Catégories* have an internal structure, that they are composites of what Aristotle calls matter and form. The elaboration of this idea involves two claims that turn out to wreak havoc for the account of the *Categories*. First, Aristotle claims that the matter–form constitution of familiar particulars must enter into our account of their coming to be things like men and horses and their continuing to be men and horses once they have come to be these things; second, he construes the relation between the matter and form making up the basic subjects of the early theory as that between a subject and a universal predicated of it. But these claims call into question the Unanalyzability Thesis. They also suggest that familiar particulars are not the most basic or fundamental subjects of predication, and they point to items (the matter and form making up an ordinary object) that seem to be ontologically prior to the man and the horse of the *Categories*.

These two clusters of concern about the early theory play a crucial role in Z and H. Both the idea that universals expressing essences deserve status as primary *ousiai* and the idea that as hylomorphic composites familiar particulars cannot be ontologically fundamental function as constraints on the theory Aristotle develops in his attempt to answer anew the question, Which things are the primary *ousiai*? Indeed, the convergence of these two ideas results in the central thesis of that theory, the thesis that it is the substantial forms of ordinary objects that are the primary *ousiai*.

*Metaphysics* Z opens with a pair of chapters in which Aristotle attempts to show the continuity between his own concern with the problems of *ousia* and the metaphysical inquiries of his predecessors. Then, in Z.3, the first substantive chapter of the middle books, Aristotle confronts his own early attempt at identifying the primary *ousiai*. The assessment in Z.3 of that early attempt provides the material for my Chapter 2. The centerpiece of Z.3 is the *Categories* claim that the concept of a basic subject provides us with a principle for identifying the ontologically fundamental entities, and the pressures generated by the hylomorphic analysis play a major role in Aristotle's assessment of this

---

[2]I assume that the development of the hylomorphic analysis is subsequent to the formulation of the early theory of *ousia* in texts such as the *Categories* and *Posterior Analytics*. If it were to turn out that texts in which we initially meet the notions of matter and form have to be allocated to an earlier time, this would not severely undermine my account since the fact would remain that in the relevant logical works Aristotle is unwilling to take the kind of internal structure the hylomorphic model reads into the primary *ousiai* of the *Categories* to enter into our analysis of their being the kinds of things they are.

claim. His contention is that, because familiar particulars are matter–form composites, the Unanalyzability Thesis is falsified in their case. Their being what they are (i.e., particular instances of their infimae species) rests on a prior relation between a more basic subject (the matter out of which they are composed) and something predicated of it (their substantial form). But, then, the idea that basic subjects constitute the primary *ousiai* leads to the conclusion that matter is ontologically fundamental, which for Aristotle is an unsatisfactory result. If something is to be ontologically basic, it must be both separable and a "this something"; matter, he claims, fails on both counts.

It turns out, however, that there are interpretative problems surrounding Z.3. Commentators disagree about the force of Aristotle's claim that matter provides us with the best candidate for status as basic subject. Some insist that he has in mind the matter making up things like the man and the horse of the *Categories*. But Aristotle holds that the matter making up those things itself fails the test provided by the Unanalyzability Thesis. He wants to claim that what functions as matter for familiar objects (things like flesh and bones) is itself susceptible of the same pattern of analysis as the familiar objects into whose constitution it enters: it is a composite of a prior, lower level matter that functions as subject for its own form, and there is reason to believe that Aristotle took the same pattern of analysis to be successively repeatable until we reach a matter (traditionally called prime matter) that has no essence at all. Some commentators contend that the Aristotle of Z.3 has this matter in mind. The disagreement between these commentators enters into my account of the Z.3 assessment of the early theory; I try to show that it makes no difference which matter we have Aristotle take to play the role of basic subject in Z.3. Whether we take Aristotle to be talking about the familiar matter making up ordinary objects or about prime matter, we can make sense of the claim that matter cannot be said to be separable and a "this something." The idea that we must look beyond the notion of subjects of predication in our attempt to identify the primary *ousiai* stands; and it is the task of Z and H to tell us where to look.

In Z.4–6, Aristotle makes a start in this direction; those three chapters are the focus of my Chapter 3. The suggestion motivating the discussion in Z.4–6 is the idea (implicit already in the *Categories* account) that universals expressing essences deserve status as primary *ousiai*; the culmination of the discussion is the claim (I call it the Z.6 Identity Thesis) that each primary *ousia* is necessarily one and the same as its essence.

For Aristotle, the essence of a thing is what we identify in giving the correct definition of the thing; it is what being that thing amounts to or consists in. Since only universals are definable, only universals have essences in the strict sense. But Aristotle would insist that there is an extended sense in which particulars can be said to have essences. Where a universal $U$ marks out a particular $x$ as what $x$ is, the essence of $U$ can be said to be $x$'s essence. So there is both a strict and an extended sense in which a thing can be said to have an essence, and the metaphysical project surrounding the attempt to identify the primary *ousiai* can be thought of as the project of explaining why things have (whether in the strict or the extended sense) the essences they do. We have said that to identify the primary *ousiai* is to identify those things that depend for their existence on nothing else, but on which everything else depends for its existence. But from his earliest writings onward, Aristotle denies that there is any such thing as just existing or being. He insists on an essentialist reading of 'to be', so that to be for a thing is to be a thing of a certain kind, to have a certain essence. Accordingly, to identify the primary *ousiai* is to identify things whose being what they are (whose having the essences they do) depends on nothing else, but are such that by reference to what they are we can explain why everything else is what it is or has the essence it does.

The relations of priority we seek to display in our identification of the primary *ousiai* are thus the relations in virtue of which things have the essences they do. But if we understand the metaphysician's project in these terms, we must provide an account of the relationship between the primary *ousiai* and their essences. Although the Aristotle of the *Categories* never explicitly speaks of essences, the Unanalyzability Thesis of the early theory represents one attempt at characterizing that relation. The force of endorsing that thesis was to construe the relationship between a primary *ousia* and its essence as one of predication, but to insist that the predicative tie here is unique in being irreducibly primitive or unanalyzable. A central claim of Z.6 is that, however we supplement it, talk of predication fails to capture the intimacy that must obtain in the relationship between a primary *ousia* and its essence. The identification of the primary *ousiai* is supposed to provide a terminus to questions about why things are what they are, and things that are what they are only because something else is predicated of them fail to do this. Only things that are necessarily one and the same as their essence provide the kind of terminus presupposed by the attempt to identify the primary *ousiai*, so the primary *ousiai* must be their own essences.

It is, however, easy to misunderstand the force of the Z.6 Identity Thesis and to construe it as an idiosyncratic feature of Aristotle's later theory of *ousia*. In fact, Aristotle means the discussion of Z.4–.7 to be theory-neutral. That discussion is meant to delineate the form or structure for any theory of *ousia*, and the Z.6 Identity Thesis represents a constraint on any attempt at identifying the primary *ousiai*. A theory of *ousia* represents the attempt to display the priority relations in virtue of which things have the essences they do; if an attempt of this sort is to be genuinely explanatory, there can be no gap between the items it takes to be basic or fundamental and the essences in virtue of which they are what they are.

It is only in Z.7–9, where he provides us with detailed analyses of the concepts of matter, form, and composite, that Aristotle turns to the elaboration of his own theory of *ousia*. Although some of the key tenets of that theory are implicit in the Z.3 critique of the early theory, their detailed presentation is found in Z.7 and after. My Chapter 4 takes Z.7–9, together with several closely related passages from elsewhere in Z and H, as its focus.

Aristotle claims that there are two kinds of substance-predications. There is the sort of predication that is central in the early theory. In this case, a substance-species is predicated of one of its instances. But corresponding to each species-predication there is what I call a form-predication. Here, the substantial form associated with a given species is predicated of the parcel of matter making up or constituting the relevant instance of the species. Aristotle concedes that the linguistic expression of these two forms of substance-predication is by way of sentences in which a single substance term functions as linguistic predicate, but he claims that the term has distinct senses or meanings in the two cases. In the former case, he tells us, the term signifies a substance-kind and functions as what we nowadays call a sortal or individuative predicate. In the latter case, it signifies or expresses a form; although the surface grammar of the term is substantival, its depth logic is that of an adjective rather than a count noun.

Aristotle marks the contrast between these two forms of predication by reference to a pair of pronomial schemata. Species-predications, he wants to say, exhibit a "this something" structure. In a species-predication the concrete particular that is "this" or subject is marked out as a countably distinct member of its substance-kind, and the predication is a case of essential or what-predication. Form-predications, on the other hand, exhibit a "this such" structure. A form is not essentially predicated of its matter. It is not what its matter is but only how it is, so we have merely accidental or adjectival predication.

But Aristotle takes a form-predication to be more basic or fundamental than the corresponding species-predication; in Chapter 5, I focus on this idea. The crucial texts here are Z.17–H.2, in which Aristotle argues that substantial form is primary *ousia*, and Z.10–.12, in which he tries to show that form exhibits the categorial features required of what is to play the role of primary *ousia*. The central idea is that the very existence of a concrete particular (like the man or the horse of the *Categories*) is grounded in the form-predication that relates its matter and its substantial form. As we have seen, however, there is no such thing as just existing or being. To be, for a concrete particular like Socrates or Bucephalus, is to be a member of its proper kind. So the existence of a thing is expressed in its species-predication, and it is because the appropriate form-predication obtains that that species-predication obtains. Accordingly, Aristotle tells us that the matter and form constituting a familiar particular are its *ousiai*, or the causes of its being.

Although Aristotle concedes that a reference to the matter of which it is composed must enter into our explanation of the existence of a concrete particular, the dominant thesis of Z and H is that substantial form is primary *ousia* and *the* primary *ousia* of concrete particulars. As we have seen, what plays the role of primary *ousia* has to provide a terminus to questions about why things are what they are or have the essences they do. But the matter making up any familiar particular is itself subject to the same pattern of analysis as that particular. It is the kind of thing or stuff it is because some more basic thing or stuff functions as matter or subject for the predication of its form, and the same pattern presumably repeats itself until we reach a matter (prime matter) that has no essence or is essentially no kind of thing at all. So among the things that function as matter, it is only prime matter that does not have a cause for its being what it is or its having the essence it does. But prime matter has no essence, and we know from Z.6 that what plays the role of primary *ousia* must be an essence; it must be something that is necessarily one and the same as its essence. So nothing that functions as matter can be primary *ousia*.

But Aristotle holds that substantial forms are suited to play the explanatory role associated with the notion of a primary *ousia*. Forms are potential objects of definition, so they count as essences. However, unlike familiar particulars and the matter out of which they are composed, forms do not come to be or pass away. Accordingly, they lack the internal structural complexity of things that have something else as their *ousia*. Forms are simples, and this fact is expressed in their definition. They are the only things that can be defined without reference to prior things; despite the linguistic complexity of a definition of a form, what we articulate in such a definition is something that is "one thing" par excellence. So forms are the *ousia* of other things, and there is nothing distinct from a form that is its *ousia*. As Aristotle puts it, each form is its own *ousia*. But, then, substantial forms have the explanatory status of primary *ousia*. And since they pass the Z.6 test by being essences, they qualify as the primary *ousiai*.

Forms are essences, but they are not the essences of the composite particulars into whose analysis they enter. The essence of a particular is provided by the relevant substance-species; what the particular is is a member of the species. The form is not even predicated of the particular; its subject is the matter making up the particular, and a form is predicated of its matter accidentally, not essentially. Indeed, Aristotle wants to claim that, although the existence of a particular hinges on the form-predication relating its form and its matter, the relevant form- and species-predication belong to distinct ontological levels. A form-predication operates within a framework one level below that at which we have countably distinct members of substance-kinds, and Aristotle claims that any attempt to assimilate the framework constituted by form-predications to that constituted by particulars under substance-kinds can only result in the kind of confusion we nowadays mark by talk of category mistakes.

The most significant dispute in the literature on Z and H hinges on the interpretation we give to substantial form.[3] Along with some commentators, I develop and defend the view that for each species there is a single substantial form which, in virtue of being predicated of numerically distinct parcels of matter, gives rise to the numerically distinct particulars falling under that species. Many commentators, however, claim that according to the theory of Z and H substantial forms are particulars and there is a numerically distinct substantial form for each member of a species. Those who take Aristotle to hold to a theory of particular forms point to a variety of claims from Z and H to support

---

[3]Two other issues that have divided commentators on the middle books are (a) the extent to which the claim that form is primary *ousia* represents a reversion on the part of the mature Aristotle to some form of Platonism, and (b) the relationship between Z and H, on the one hand, and the theology of Λ, on the other. Neither of these issues plays a central role in my reading of Z and H. As regards (a), I believe that, although there are themes in Z–H that can appear more Platonistic than the doctrine of the *Categories*, we misrepresent Aristotle's philosophical development if we construe it in terms of his endorsement or rejection of the views of his teacher. It is fairly clear that the apparently Platonistic themes of the middle books derive from a dialectic that is so thoroughly unique to Aristotle's way of looking at things that those themes bear nothing more than a superficial resemblance to views Plato might have held. The themes must be understood in terms of the framework that Aristotle himself invokes in approaching metaphysical problems. By the time we reach Z and H, that developing framework has so transformed and altered things that the claim that substantial form is primary *ousia* fails to have a sense that makes it any more than a distant relative of claims found in the Platonic dialogues. As regards (b), I hope that the views expressed in Z–H are consistent with the theology of Λ, but it is not a part of the present project to show this.

their reading of the middle books; in passing, I deal with the relevant claims as they enter into my presentation of Aristotle's account in Chapters 3–5. But the crucial piece of evidence in the case for particular forms is the claim (defended at length in Z.13 and elaborated in Z.14–16) that no universal is *ousia*. In Chapter 6, I examine this claim in detail. Although this chapter will likely provide the focus for the attention of the specialist in Aristotle, the reader unfamiliar with the secondary literature on Z and H will find it less accessible than the earlier chapters. I try to show that it is only if we endorse a whole panoply of deviant readings of the text that we have any grounds at all for taking what I call the Z.13 thesis (the claim that no universal is *ousia*) to run counter to the idea that there is a single substantial form that functions as the *ousia* of all the members of a given species. After showing that no defensible reading of Z.13 and its immediate successors supports the idea that there are particular forms, I identify the kinds of view the slogan of Z.13 and the arguments supporting it are meant to counter.

Finally, in Chapter 7, I address two problems associated with the theory of Z and H. The first is one that is not considered explicitly in Z and H but bears on the concept of prime matter. I argue that the notion of a matter that is essentially no kind of thing at all is one Aristotle almost certainly endorsed and that it presents difficulties for his essentialist reading of 'to be', according to which to be is to be some kind of thing or other. I contend as well that revisionist readings denying that Aristotle endorses a doctrine of prime matter fail to provide much help, since they succeed in eliminating the appeal to prime matter only at the expense of denying claims central to the rest of the theory of *ousia* developed in Z and H.

The second problem I discuss in Chapter 7 focuses on a tension that might seem to exist between the account defended in Z and H and the everyday conception of the world championed in the *Categories*. It is tempting to read the theory of Z and H as a reductionist account that calls into question our commonsense view of the world, for the theory seems to deny both the reality and unity of familiar particulars. It tells us that at the metaphysically basic level there are no objects like the man and the horse of the *Categories*, and it denies that the universals providing object concepts for these things are a part of the preferred framework of form-predication. According to the theory, the status of commonsense objects is merely derivative; in characterizing these objects and their kinds in terms of talk about composites and complexes, the theory seems to rob ordinary objects of the kind of overriding unity implicit in our practice of singling them out as the central focus for our thought and talk about the world.

The tension between the everyday conception of the world and the later theory is the focus for the concluding chapters of H, and in particular for H.6; but it is on Aristotle's mind throughout the middle books. Although Aristotle finds the *Categories* answer to the question, Which things are the primary *ousiai*? unsatisfactory, he is reluctant to give up the intuitions motivating the early theory, and he is anxious to show that his new answer to that question does not undermine those intuitions. I indicate how many of the central themes of the later theory are formulated with an eye to this tension and, then, how H.6 mobilizes characteristic Aristotelian doctrines about the notions of being and unity to show the groundlessness of worries about this tension. Those doctrines, Aristotle concludes, entail that we can endorse both the metaphysical account of Z and H and the idea that familiar particulars falling under substance-species are genuine realities and genuine unities.[4]

---

[4]Terence Irwin's *Aristotle's First Principles* (Oxford: Oxford University Press, 1989) and Charlotte Witt's *Substance and Essence in Aristotle* (Ithaca: Cornell University Press, 1989) were published as I was completing the final draft of this book, so I was able to register my reactions to their respective attempts to defend the view that substantial forms are particular rather than general in the footnotes. Unfortunately, I did not have access to the Frede–Patzig commentary on Z until the final stages of my work on the manuscript. It turns out that many of the philosophical moves their commentary deploys in support of the particular-form interpretation are continuous with those found in Frede's earlier writings on the middle books, but the commentary develops those moves and supplements them by detailed exegesis. Although I had already devoted considerable attention to Frede's earlier work, reading the introduction and crucial parts of the commentary led me to make last-minute revisions in Chapter 6 as well as in those parts of Chapters 3 and 4 that bear on texts pivotal in the controversy over forms as particular or universal. But I had concluded that the basic issue separating their interpretation from my own was, not the issue of particular versus general forms, but their assumption that one and the same thing—form—is both the *ousia* and essence of familiar objects. Since their defense of this assumption is so articulate and so detailed, I added a long section to Chapter 5 in which I criticize their use of that assumption. As regards other issues, had I access to the commentary as I composed the original manuscript, I would certainly have been anxious to express my agreement or disagreement with the Frede–Patzig reading of other texts in Z. But given the format of that work (as a line-by-line commentary on Z) and my own concern with the more general interpretative and philosophical issues associated with the middle books, prior access to the commentary would not have altered, in any significant way, what follows here.

# Chapter 1

# The Background

I

It is tempting to think that Aristotle takes the expression *'ousia'* to be something analogous to a natural kind term. For one thing, *'ousia'* marks one of the categories, and the categories presumably represent the summa genera, or highest kinds.[1] For another, Aristotle characterizes kind terms (terms signifying species and genera) as expressions

[1]See, e.g., *Topics* A.9 (103b20), H.1 (152a38), *Posterior Analytics* A.32 (88b1–3), *Physics* A.6 (189b24), and *Metaphysics* Δ.6 (1016b33–34). I follow the traditional reading of these texts. For doubts about this reading, see Michael Frede, "Categories in Aristotle," in his *Essays in Ancient Philosophy* (Minneapolis: University of Minnesota Press, 1987), 29–48. Frede points out, quite correctly, that *'kategoria'* has a variety of senses in Aristotle, and he argues that few of Aristotle's references to categories point unequivocally to the idea that the categories are a classification of nonlinguistic entities according to their highest kinds. In most contexts, he wants to say, the categories represent a classification of the kinds of things we can say about objects; he takes *'ousia'* to mark one of these—saying what a thing is, where the thing in question can be virtually anything that can function as a subject for discourse. Frede pretty clearly establishes that Aristotle sometimes uses *'ousia'* in this sense. Despite Frede's arguments, I am not convinced that *Topics* A.9 is such a context. It seems to me, in any case, that *Metaphysics* Z.1 (1028a10ff) shows that Aristotle's willingness to concede that the What is it? question applies to qualities, quantities, and the like does not threaten the idea that there are things (men, gods, and whatever admits the "this something" epithet) for which that question applies in a primary way and that these constitute a kind of nonlinguistic entity. Indeed, before conceding that the What is it? question applies to these accidents, Aristotle shows how we can have doubts about their status as beings, doubts that do not arise for the things he wants to call *ousiai*. Such a position presupposes that we have already segregated kinds of things, and the kind marked by *'ousia'* is identified by the "this something" schema and the What is it? question in its primary use.

that enable us to identify an object in terms of what it is; and just as he insists that lower-level kind terms serve as the correct answers to the What is it? question for each of the things of which they are true, he implies that 'ousia' provides the most general available answer to the What is it? question for the things that are *ousiai*.[2] So 'ousia' seems to mark out a certain nature and provide its own principles for classifying objects,[3] and the traditional translation of the term as 'substance' reinforces this understanding. It reads into the meaning of 'ousia' the *Categories* idea of something that "stands under" or is subject for its attributes, as though that idea captures the nature marked out by the term.

Understanding 'ousia' as a kind term does not, however, enable us to accommodate all Aristotle's uses of the term. In works later than the *Categories*, we meet the term in contexts in which it functions not as a concrete general term but as an abstract singular term. Even in the *Categories*, we find an ancestor of this use when Aristotle talks of "the formula (*logos*) of the *ousia*" (1ª2, 4, 7, 9). Nonetheless, the idea that 'ousia' functions as something analogous to a kind term seems to underlie one important (in the *Categories*, certainly, the most important) use of the term.

Unfortunately, not even Aristotle's use of the expression as a concrete general term is consistent with the idea that 'ousia' carries its own pretheoretical principles for identifying and classifying objects. In works subsequent to the *Categories*, he frequently suggests that the attempt to isolate the *ousiai* is something common to the theoretical accounts provided by his predecessors;[4] but if things as different as

---

[2]As I read it, *Topics* A.9 (103ᵇ23–27) portrays the categories as answers, the most general answers available, to the What is it? question posed of the items falling under them. This text might, I fear, mislead us into thinking that one could formulate a theory of categories simply by taking sample objects and pressing, at successively more general levels, the What is it? question. The idea would be that, once we have reached an answer to this question such that the only more general answer available is some term like 'thing', 'object', 'entity', 'being', we have reached a term marking an Aristotelian category. Then, by reiterating the procedure again and again until we reach a point at which new category terms cease to turn up, we would, subject to normal inductive constraints, generate a system of categories. There is much that is philosophically problematic in this account. In any case, I do not think that the passage in *Topics* A.9 is any evidence that Aristotle himself held this view of his categories. Although it may be a mistake to suppose that a theory of categories could be generated in this simplistic way, once we have (by other means) generated and articulated a theory of categories as highest kinds, we certainly can view the categories constitutive of the theory as the most general answers to the What it is? question; I take Aristotle to be envisioning this retrospective interpretation of his own list of categories in the *Topics*.

[3]See *Metaphysics* Δ.26 (1023ᵇ27–32), where Aristotle defines a sense of '*holon*' that nicely expresses the idea of a kind.

[4]See, e.g., *Metaphysics* Z.1 (1028ᵇ2–6) and Z.2 (1028ᵇ8–27). For an account of '*ousia*' that agrees with what I develop here, see Frede and Patzig, *Aristoteles "Metaphysik Z,"* vol. 1, 36–37.

Pythagorean numbers, Platonic Forms, and Democritean atoms all count as candidates for the label 'ousia', the idea that 'ousia' is a term expressing anything like a natural kind becomes suspect. And in the middle books of the *Metaphysics*, Aristotle expresses doubt about his own earlier view that things functioning as subjects of predication are *ousiai*.[5] Skepticism on this score would be incongruous were that view nothing more than an expression of the semantic underpinnings of the term; and Aristotle gives us no reason to suppose that what appear to be doubts about a substantive claim are really the expressions of a decision to associate a new sense with a familiar term.

The Aristotle of the *Categories* certainly believes that, in the final analysis, the term 'ousia' can be used to identify what we could call a summum genus or highest kind, but even he does not believe that there is some nature or kind that is pretheoretically expressed by the term, a nature or kind we could isolate by successively pressing, at ever more general levels, the What is it? question; nor does he see his own remarks about subjects as having the effect of stipulating a sense for a technical term he idiosyncratically wants to introduce into philosophical jargon. He takes those remarks rather to express his own attempt at identifying the criteria for the application of an antecedently understood term. Thus we find him presenting arguments to show that the things satisfying the criteria he outlines deserve the title 'ousia' ($2^a34$–$2^b6$), and arguments would be out of place were he merely recording the established meaning of a familiar term or stipulating a sense for a term he wanted to introduce into the philosophical lexicon.

Although we may never find anything like an explicit account of the meaning of 'ousia', the term is not without a fixed sense in Aristotle.[6] In part, that sense is given by the term's occasional use in Plato to express the idea of an ontologically privileged entity, and certainly the term's connections with the verb 'to be' figure prominently in that use. *Ousiai* are, so to speak, the paradigmatic "to be-ers," the best examples of genuine, full-fledged beings. But apart from the inelegance resulting from an attempt to translate 'ousia' in terms of 'to be', Aristotle's skepticism about the Platonic idea that there is a determinate content expressed by that verb suggests we look elsewhere for a translation. Several recent translators and commentators have rendered the term 'reality', and that rendering does a good job of capturing the force of 'ousia' where it functions as a concrete general term. *Ousiai* are the genuine realities. But we also have to accommodate uses of 'ousia' as an

[5]See *Metaphysics* Z.3 ($1029^a1$–30). I devote most of Chapter 2 to a discussion of the implications of this text.

[6]For a slightly different account of the notion of *ousia*, see Witt, *Substance and Essence in Aristotle.*

abstract term. When it functions as an abstract term, 'reality' is just too close to 'being' to be a suitable translation,[7] and since Aristotle employed a single term for both uses we should try to do the same in our translation. The traditional translation of *'ousia'* as 'substance' is certainly well entrenched, and although nothing compels us to read its etymology into its meaning, the history of empiricist thinking about substance makes the temptation here strong. The best course, I think, is simply to leave the term untranslated. I occasionally gloss Aristotle by way of such expressions as 'genuine realities', and I follow current philosophical usage and speak of substance-species, substance-kinds, substance-predication, and so on, but I am content to treat *'ousia'* itself as an English word, one that appears in italics and has an irregular plural form—*'ousiai'*.

Since it deprives us of any familiar English counterpart to Aristotle's term, this strategy only gives added urgency to the task of finding a sense for the expression *'ousia'*. A claim we meet early in *Categories* 5 is helpful here. Aristotle has been attempting to justify his own selection of candidates for status as the primary *ousiai*, and he concludes by telling us that, if the things he wants to construe as "the primary *ousiai* were not to exist, it would be impossible for any other things to exist" ($2^b4$–6). That he is prepared to press the truth of this conditional in behalf of his own account suggests that he takes the concept of a primary *ousia* to be a kind of functional notion, the concept of something that plays a certain explanatory role. The underlying idea is that a metaphysical theory represents the attempt to delineate very general patterns of ontological priority and dependence; it seeks to identify entities whose existence stands in no need of explanation and to show how the existence of all other things depends on the existence of these ontologically basic entities. The entities a given ontological theory characterizes as basic in this way represent its candidates for status as primary *ousiai*, and the primary *ousiai* of a correct picture of the world are those things that belong to that smallest set such that we can truly say of its members, If none of these things existed, nothing else would either.

Although he takes the phrase 'primary *ousia*' to be functional, Aristotle assumes that the primary *ousiai* of any credible ontological theory constitute a single category or summum genus. Accordingly, he believes that the criteria a theory invokes in its attempt to identify the

---

[7]This point about 'reality' as an abstract term was brought to my attention by Montgomery Furth's discussion of *'ousia'* in *Substance, Form, and Psyche: An Aristotelian Metaphysics* (Cambridge: Cambridge University Press, 1988), 14–15.

primary *ousiai* should make reference to features of objects that can plausibly be thought to yield something analogous to a natural kind, albeit a very general kind; he thinks further that those criteria should carry their own justification. It must be clear just how, in virtue of satisfying those criteria, objects are fitted out for the explanatory role marked by the label 'primary *ousia*'.

So, while Aristotle is confident that the primary *ousiai* of a correct theory constitute a natural kind, there is no kind that is, antecedent to the identification of the primary realities, expressed by the term '*ousia*'. On this score, '*ousia*' might seem to be unique among the terms marking the categories. The other category terms are all plausibly thought to express natures things might be said to exhibit and to signify what we might prephilosophically want to call kinds or sorts. It might seem, for example, that it is a theory-independent fact about colors that they are qualitative features of the world, that our concepts of numbers are in themselves quantitative or mathematical concepts, and that things like running and cutting are, regardless of the theory we might choose to formulate, properly classified as actions. And, in his early writings, Aristotle may have viewed things this way. But in his more mature writings, where the doctrine that 'being' has focal meaning looms large, he seems committed to the idea that there is no theoretically neutral way of fixing the extension of any of the terms marking the categories. In *Metaphysics* Γ.2 (1003b 7–10) and Z.1 (1028a 18–20), for example, Aristotle suggests that we must treat terms such as 'quality' and 'quantity' as incomplete expressions. Things other than *ousiai*, he tells us, can be said to be only with reference to what is said to be in the core sense of that term, so there is no such thing as just being, say, a quantity. Things are said to be quantities because they are quantitative features of what exists in the core sense; in a similar vein, our concepts of other things from the accidental categories are concepts of what is inherently related to *ousia*: concepts of what is an action *performed by an ousia*, of what is a place *occupied by an ousia*, and of what is an affection *in an ousia*.[8] Accordingly, the identification of an extension for each of these concepts presupposes the identification of the *ousiai*; if the latter is not prephilosophically fixed, then neither is the former.

[8]The demand that we attach the supplementary phrases expressing the relation to *ousia* might strike us as gratuitous. Aristotle's point comes out better when we think of the accidental categories as identified, not by a list of abstract terms like *poiotes*, *posotes*, etc., but, as they often are, by a sequence of concrete forms like *poion*, *poson*, *pros ti*. Introduced in this way as the how, the how much, the to something, to do, to suffer, accidents cry out for a subject. When we supply it, we get the idea of the accidental categories as how (an) *ousia* is, how much (an) *ousia* is, how (an) *ousia* stands with respect to other things, where (an) *ousia* is. There is nothing otiose in the reference to *ousia* in this context.

II

Whatever he may have thought about the dependent categories, the early Aristotle construes the idea of a primary *ousia* or genuine reality as a functional concept, a concept of something that plays an explanatory role in a certain kind of account of the world. For anyone seeking to develop an account of that kind, the central task is to specify criteria, the satisfaction of which fixes, in the desired way, the extension of the phrase 'primary *ousia*'. The definitive test we meet in the *Categories* makes use of two notions, that of being said of a subject and that of being present in a subject. Although the language Aristotle uses may suggest otherwise, the phrases 'being said of' and 'being present in' express metaphysical relations between nonlinguistic entities, and these relations are construed as primitive ties that cannot be reduced to more basic notions.[9] But if Aristotle resists reductive analyses of these notions, he tells us enough to identify the relations he has in mind. In rough terms, it is the entities by reference to which we identify *what* an object is that are said of it. Thus, Socrates is a subject of which the species *man* is said, and both Socrates and *man* are subjects of which the genus *animal* is said. Attributes that characterize an object in some way but do not figure in an account of what it is (often called accidents)[10] are present in that object. Socrates is the subject in which his complexion and character traits are present; these characteristics, in turn, are subjects of which other things are said. Thus, color is said of Socrates' complexion, and virtue is said of the courage present in him.

[9]Those who find the term 'relation' problematic on the grounds that it carries with it the specter of a vicious regress, that it suggests that the application of the notion of being present in a subject to the category Aristotle labels '*pros ti*' is circular, or that it implies that that category is somehow prior to the category of *ousia* can substitute 'nonrelational tie' for 'relation' throughout my rough and ready formulations. The sense in which these two notions are relations is not that operative in translations of '*pros ti*' as 'relation', and Aristotle's own familiarity with the problems associated with the Third Man tell against any interpretation of the said-of or present-in ties that would generate Bradley-style regresses. For a discussion of this aspect of the two notions, see Daniel Graham, *Aristotle's Two Systems* (Oxford: Oxford University Press, 1988), 20–24.

[10]I follow the practice of calling things outside the category of *ousia* accidents, but I should enter the traditional caveat here that 'accident' is a term with many senses. We must distinguish predicamental accidents (where these are things from one of the dependent categories) from predicable accidents (as in *Topics* A.5 and 8). Although predicamental accidents can be predicable accidents (as, for example, when they are predicated of an *ousia*), what Aristotle calls properties are also predicamental accidents not predicable as accident (in the *Topics* sense) of *ousiai*. Further, items from the accidental categories can be genera for less general items from the same category. This fact, among others, points to the need to distinguish both of the above senses of 'accident' from that operative when we speak of accidental predication in the sense of how-predication or nonessential predication. Predicamental accidents (predicable of *ousai* as accidents) can be nonaccidentally predicated of things from the same category.

Although he construes them as ontological relations between non-linguistic objects, Aristotle's characterization of these two notions appeals to the linguistic machinery in terms of which they are expressed. He wants to claim that, where a thing $x$ is said of a thing $y$, both the name and definition of $x$ are true of $y$. Both the name of the species ('man') and its definition ('biped animal') are true of Socrates. As Aristotle puts it, Socrates and the species are *synonyms*: a single name applies to both, and there is a single account of what is expressed by the use of the name—that given by the definition of the species.[11] Aristotle denies, however, that where one thing is present in another the two are synonyms. Typically, he claims, neither the name nor the definition of an attribute is true of a subject in which it is present.($2^a27$–29). It is true neither that Socrates is courage nor that he is such and such a virtue. But if courage is present in him, Socrates is what Aristotle calls a paronym of courage ($1^a12$–15; $10^a26$–$10^b11$). Although the name of the virtue does not apply to him, a closely related term (one built out of or derived from the relevant name) does. 'Courageous' is true of Socrates if the relevant virtue is present in him; and the effect of applying 'courageous' to him is just to assert that the virtue is present in him.

Aristotle is aware, however, that language sometimes runs roughshod over the distinction operative in the case of 'courage' and 'courageous'. A single term does double duty as name of an attribute and predicate of the objects in which the attribute is present. Color words (in both Greek and English) provide a notorious example. As Aristotle himself points out, both the color and an object in which it is present are called white, but he calls these homonyms: although the name is common, there is a different account or definition of what being white amounts to in the two cases ($2^a29$–33; $1^a1$–6; $3^a15$–17). When the accounts are spelled out, what we find is that, functioning as a predicate, a term like 'white' exhibits precisely the semantics of a derivative or paronymous form like 'courageous': to apply the predicate 'white' to a thing is just to say that the relevant color is present in it.

It is clear that Aristotle construes the things said of a subject as universals; it is the species and genera under which a thing falls as well as the items mentioned in their definitions (differentiae) that are said of the thing. It is less clear how he understands the things present in others. He tells us that there are things that are both present in a subject and said of a subject. His example is the determinable *knowledge*; it is present in the soul and said of a determinate piece of grammatical

[11]$1^a6$–12; $2^a19$–26; $3^a32$–$3^b9$. See also *Topics* B.2 ($109^b5$ff.), $\Gamma$.3 ($123^a27$–29), and H.4 ($154^a18$.)

knowledge ($1^a29$–$1^b3$). So some of the things present in others are universals. He also tells us, however, that things present in others are subject to an inseparability condition. As he puts it, "it is impossible for them to exist apart from that in which they are" ($1^a29$–$1^b3$). Some commentators have taken this requirement to entail the existence of particular attributes, each unique to the particular in which it is present.[12] The idea is that where a particular like Socrates is the subject in which an attribute is present, only a particular attribute (the kind of thing that in our time has been called an abstract particular, a trope, a unit property, a case, or an aspect) is inseparable from its subject in the way the condition seems to require. Aristotle tells us that some things are present in others but not said of others, and his examples include "a certain white" and "a certain piece of grammatical knowledge" ($1^a26$–28). The examples, these commentators tell us, are precisely the particular attributes or accidents Aristotle's account requires.

Unfortunately, Aristotle also tells us that things said of others, universals like the determinable *knowledge*, are present in particulars ($2^b1$–3). Some defenders of particular attributes shrug off this claim as "compressed and careless";[13] others take it as evidence that Aristotle has several distinct ontological relations in mind when he speaks of things present in a subject.[14] But some commentators have taken the claim to show that particular attributes are not a part of the ontological machinery of the *Categories*.[15] They argue that Aristotle's references to "a certain

---

[12]See, e.g., J. L. Ackrill, *Aristotle's Categories and De Interpretatione* (Oxford: Oxford University Press, 1963), especially 74–76; G. E. M. Anscombe, "Aristotle: The Search for Substance," in Anscombe and Geach, *Three Philosophers* (Oxford: Basil Blackwell, 1963), especially 14–19; G. B. Matthews and S. M. Cohen, "The One and the Many," *Review of Metaphysics* (1968), 630–655; R. E. Allen, "Individual Properties in Aristotle's *Categories*," *Phronesis* (1969), 31–39; Edwin Hartman, *Substance, Body, and Soul* (Princeton: Princeton University Press, 1977), 12–21; Robert Heinaman, "Non-Substantial Individuals in the *Categories*," *Phronesis* (1981), 295–307; and Daniel Graham, *Aristotle's Two Systems*, 27–30.

[13]Ackrill, *Aristotle's Categories and De Interpretatione*, 83.

[14]See, e.g., James Duerlinger, "Predication and Inherence in Aristotle's *Categories*," *Phronesis* (1970), 179–203.

[15]See G. E. L. Owen, "Inherence," *Phronesis* (1965), 97–105; Michael Frede, "Individuals in Aristotle," in *Essays in Ancient Philosophy*, 49–71; and Montgomery Furth, *Substance, Form, and Psyche*, 15–21. See also Russell Dancy, "On Some of Aristotle's First Thoughts about Substance," *Philosophical Review* (1975), 338–373. Dancy sides with Owen but offers an account of the attributes present in others that is different from that found in the other opponents of particular attributes. For a view that takes the particular/general dichotomy to be inconstant as we move through the various accidental categories, see J. M. E. Moravscik, "Aristotle on Predication," *Philosophical Review* (1967), 80–96. Finally, for a view that prefers not to see Aristotle as engaged in deeply theoretical issues in the *Categories* and hence as not having an official line on this problem in that treatise, see Mohan Matthen, "The Categories and Aristotle's Ontology," *Dialogue* (1978), 228–243.

white" and "a certain piece of grammatical knowledge" pick out fully determinate but recurrent attributes (a determinate shade of white such as winter white and a determinate piece of grammatical knowledge such as knowledge of the genitive plural of '*anthropos*') rather than particular attributes unique to their possessors. They tell us that, since they are fully determinate, the attributes Aristotle has in mind have no more specific attributes or accidents of which they are said; nonetheless, they can be present in more than one subject. Furthermore, they insist that what can be called the inseparability requirement must be understood in a looser sense than defenders of particular attributes would claim. We need not take Aristotle to be claiming that for each thing present in another, there is some one subject such that the former cannot exist apart from the latter. He may merely be telling us that nothing present in another can exist without some subject or other.[16] Or, if he is insisting that for each accident there is some one subject on which it depends for its existence, there is no reason to suppose that the subjects he has in mind here are particulars. There is no particular body such that winter white cannot exist apart from it, but surely that shade of color is inseparable from the universal *body*, in the sense that were no body at all its subject there would be no such thing as winter white.[17]

These commentators, then, see the distinction between being said of and being present in as a distinction between two ways universals can be related to their subjects. All parties to this dispute agree that a distinction between two forms of metaphysical predication (what have been called strong or essential predication and weak or accidental predication)[18] is operative in the *Categories*. The former is a relationship between a subject and a universal that marks out that subject as *what* it is; the latter, one in which a universal determines *how* its subject is. Those who deny that Aristotle embraces an ontology of abstract particulars identify the distinction between these two forms of metaphysical predication with that marked by the expressions 'said of' and 'present in', and they construe Aristotle's discussion of synonyms and homonyms/paronyms as the attempt to show how the metaphysical contrast between these two forms of predication is reflected in the linguistic contrast between predicate terms that do and predicate terms that do

[16]This is the interpretation suggested by Owen in "Inherence."

[17]See Frede, "Individuals in Aristotle" in *Essays in Ancient Philosophy*, for this account of the inseparability requirement.

[18]For the terms 'strong' and 'weak' here, and an account of the distinction, see G. E. L. Owen, "The Platonism of Aristotle," reprinted in J. Barnes, M. Schofield, and R. Sorabji, eds., *Articles on Aristotle* (London: Duckworth, 1975), vol. 1, 14–34.

not have their sense exhaustively determined by the definition of the universal they express.[19]

Because it has totally dominated recent literature on the *Categories*, this debate over particular attributes must be familiar to even the most casual reader of that treatise. So much has been written on the topic that it is difficult to add anything, and I do not try here.[20] Although I believe that the evidence is not completely conclusive, I tend to side with those who deny that abstract particulars or tropes are part of the ontology of the *Categories*, taking the two relations of being said of and being present in as two forms of predication. I find little evidence to support the claim that several different ontological relations are marked by the expression 'present in a subject',[21] and I take the following claim from *Categories* 5 to provide fairly solid evidence that Aristotle did not endorse an ontology of particular accidents:

> Just as the primary *ousiai* are related to *all other things*, so are the species and genera of primary *ousiai* related to *all the remaining things*. For *all the remaining things are predicated* of these. (3ª2–4, emphasis added)

[19]Presumably the defender of particular accidents denies that the pattern of linguistic predication operative in Aristotle's account of the homonymy/paronymy of accidental predication applies to all cases of one thing being present in another. In the case of a particular attribute being present in a subject, the application of Aristotle's analysis is, at best, indirect. The linguistic expression of the fact that a certain white (where this is construed as particular) is present in Socrates is by way of a sentence like 'Socrates is white'. That sentence applies to Socrates, not the name of the particular color present in him (that color is named by the expression 'the white of Socrates'), but the name of something said of that color—the species to which it and all paticular colors qualitatively indistinguishable from it belong. Likewise, the fact that a particular instance of courage is present in Socrates is not expressed by a sentence whose linguistic predicate is a derivative or paronymous form of the name of that instance, but by a sentence like 'Socrates is courageous' whose predicate term is derived from the name of the universal under which Socrates' proprietary courage falls.

[20]Frede has managed to introduce a novel point into the debate. It has been argued that we need particular accidents on the grounds, for example, that "it is my negligence, not someone else's, which caused the accident" (*Essays in Ancient Philosophy*, 62–63). Frede points out that this line of argument mistakenly construes expressions that function as stand-ins for the nominalizations of sentences as names of particular accidents. To speak of my negligence is a shorthand way of referring to the fact that I was negligent and not to refer to an accident unique to me.

[21]This is not to deny that certain cases of one thing's being present in another might rest on other more basic cases. The principle I dub (iii) in the following section likely implies that some cases of inherence are more basic than others; but to say this is not to say that we have categorically different metaphysical relations operative in the fundamental and nonfundamental cases. As I understand Aristotle, there is just one relation or tie at work in all cases of one thing being present in another. The same point holds as regards the said-of relation.

This passage assumes a number of ideas we are not yet prepared to deal with, but it makes two things clear: first, all the things present in particulars are present in the universals said of those particulars, so the so-called inseparability condition cannot have the force defenders of particular accidents have read into it; second, all the things present in particulars are things predicated of others, so it is plausible to infer that they are universals.

III

Whatever our views about the debate over particular accidents, we must agree that Aristotle takes the two notions of being said of and being present in as crucial to his own attempt to identify the primary *ousiai*. He tells us initially that all and only those things that are "neither said of a subject nor present in a subject" ($1^b12$-$13$) are primary *ousiai*. The first clause excludes things said of others—species, genera, and their differentiae—so that we are left with (a) particulars like Socrates and Plato and (b) fully determinate attributes like winter white and the knowledge of the genitive plural of *'anthropos'*. The second clause excludes the attributes under (b). So the criterion has the effect of identifying the familiar concrete particulars of common sense as the primary *ousiai*.

Despite its ready application, a criterion both of whose conditions are stated in the negative and which is therefore merely exclusionary is not quite what we would expect or want in an attempt to identify the primary *ousiai*. A thing has status as a primary *ousia*, we want to say, because of properties it has and not because of properties it lacks. The fact is that Aristotle agrees; although he initially presents the criterion in strictly negative terms, it is clear that the initial formulation abbreviates a criterion that is not strictly negative. Let us say that a thing $x$ is subject for a thing $y$ just in case $y$ is either said of or present in $x$, and that a thing is a *basic subject* just in case it is the subject for something else but nothing is its subject. If we assume that there are no unpropertied particulars, then we can agree that all and only the things that satisfy the strictly negative criterion are basic subjects. Pretty clearly, Aristotle makes this assumption. In subsequent works, he formulates the criterion of the *Categories* as the claim that all and only the things I have called basic subjects are primary *ousiai*,[22] and, although we never meet

---

[22]See, e.g., *Metaphysics* Δ.8 ($1017^b12$–$14$) and Z.3 ($1028^b36$–$37$); and *Physics* A.7 ($190^a36$–$37$). Cf. *Posterior Analytics* A.2 ($71^b23$–$24$).

with an explicit definition of the notion of a basic subject in that early work, it is assumed throughout and treated as the pivotal concept for identifying the genuine realities. What makes the notion so critical is the fact that, taken cumulatively, basic subjects turn out to be subjects for everything that has a subject:

> all the other things are either said of the primary *ousiai* as subjects or are in them as subjects. This is clear from particular examples. For example, *animal* is predicated of *man*; therefore, *animal* is also predicated of the particular man; for if it were not predicated of the particular man, it would not be predicated of *man* at all. Again, *color* is in *body*, so it is also in a particular body; for if it were not in some particular, it would not be in *body* at all. Therefore, all the other things are either said of the primary *ousiai* or are in them as subjects. (2ª34–2ᵇ5)

Aristotle is obviously relying here on a number of principles that relate universals to the subjects of which they are predicated. Two bear on the said-of relation:

(i)   For any object $a$, if $a$ is a kind, then there is some object $b$ such that $a$ is said of $b$.

(ii)  For any objects $a$, $b$, and $c$, if $a$ is said of $b$ and $b$ is said of $c$, then $a$ is said of $c$.

A third bears on the present-in relation:

(iii) For any universal $a$, if there is some entity $b$ such that $b$ is present in $a$, then there is some entity $c$ such that $a$ is said of $c$ and $b$ is present in $c$;

Aristotle is telling us that the relentless application of these principles shows that every universal is predicated of one of the things we have called basic subjects; every universal is either said of or present in some concrete particular. But he takes this fact to justify his attempt at identifying the primary *ousiai*, for he goes on to say that, if the things his account isolates did not exist, "it would be impossible for any other things to exist" (2ᵇ6). But why should he have thought that this fact about basic subjects has the consequence that they are suited to play the explanatory role ingredient in the concept of a primary *ousia*? The answer, as many commentators have said, is to be found in a deep-seated belief on Aristotle's part, one he remains committed to throughout his career. If we say that a universal is *concretely instantiated* just in case it is predicated of (either by being said of or by being present in) some concrete particular, then we can make a rough approximation at expressing this belief by saying that the existence of a universal at any given time presupposes its concrete instantiation at that time.[23] We meet with expressions of this belief over and over again. In a frequently cited passage from *Categories* 11, for example, Aristotle says: "In the case of contraries, it is not necessary that, if one exists, the other one does as well. For if all things are healthy, then health will exist, but sickness will not. And likewise, if all things are white, whiteness will exist, but blackness will not" ($14^a7-9$). And in the later *Metaphysics* Λ.3, he tells us: "When the man is healthy, then health exists; and the shape of the bronze sphere also exists at the same time as the bronze sphere" ($1070^a$ 22–24). This same intuition lies at the core of Aristotle's recurrent criticism of Plato that Forms cannot have an existence separate from the particulars whose Forms they are[24] as well as his own view that the eternality of the universals that constitute the subject matter of a science precludes a time at which those universals fail to be exemplified. Whatever we make of the intuition, it lies at the heart of Aristotle's thinking in general and of the *Categories* identification of primary *ousiai* in particular. It has the consequence that universals require basic subjects for their existence; but since basic subjects are not themselves predicated of anything, there is nothing on which they are, in the same way, dependent. Aristotle finds in these facts grounds for concluding that basic subjects can play the explanatory role associated with the notion of a primary *ousia*. Since an inventory of familiar particulars (of which individual living beings are taken to be paradigmatic) serves to pick out the basic subjects, concrete particulars are such that, if none of them existed, nothing else would either.

[23]This is only a first approximation; the claim can apply only in the case of first-order universals or what the medievals called first intentions. The defender of the view would contend that, if the insight applies in their case, then, despite its failure for higher-order universals (like *being a species*), we can easily tell a story of just how higher-order universals presuppose the existence of familiar particulars. This same qualification obviously holds for the claim that (i–iii) establish that every universal is said of or present in a basic subject; (i–iii) only show this for first-order universals. While I believe that one can articulate the dependence of second-order universals on primary *ousiai*, I am uncertain about just where in the categorial hierarchy Aristotle would place those universals.

For a nice account of the intuitions at work in these various principles of instantiation as they apply to accidents, see Furth's discussion of what he calls the "no toehold situation"; *Substance, Form, and Psyche*, 25–27.

[24]See, e.g., *Metaphysics* A.9 ($991^a11-13$ and $991^b1-2$); B.3 ($999^a17-21$); Z.8 ($1033^b19-24$); Z.16 ($1040^b25-30$); M.4 ($1078^b30-32$); M.5 ($1079^b15-20$ and $1079^b35-1080^a2$); M.9 ($1085^a23-27$ and $1086^a32-38$); M.10 ($1087^a5-7$).

IV

I have said that Aristotle assumes that there are no unpropertied particulars. His examples of things that are neither said of nor present in a subject are "a certain man" and "a certain horse" ($2^a13$); and he construes the sortals here as critical in identifying the things he takes to be primary *ousiai*. At this stage in his career, he stoutly denies that talk of subjects of predication leads to the "something I know not what" of Locke or the "bare particular" of Bergmann.[25] The basic subjects are things falling under kinds. By reference to their kinds, we can say what those subjects are; the intuition that guides Aristotle here is the idea that, for each object, the concept of that object is provided by the appropriate answer to the What is it? question. He concedes that when posed of a primary reality the question can be answered by reference to both its genera and species, but he insists that by identifying their infimae species we most fully "reveal," "make known," or "express" what primary realities are ($2^b30$–37; $2^b7$–14). Since the kinds under which basic subjects fall are branches in the categorial tree, Aristotle feels compelled to call them *ousiai*, secondary *ousiai*,[26] but he insists that species are more real or have a better claim to the title '*ousia*' than the genera to which they are subordinated on the grounds that they are "nearer the primary realities" and so provide more appropriate or more informative answers to the What is it? question posed of the primary realities.[27] Indeed, when he tells us that the said-of-relation is transitive, he implies that substance-genera are properly said of the individuals at the bottom of the categorial tree only because the species subordinated to them are said of those individuals ($1^b9$–15).[28] So he takes the fact that the infimae species are said of their instances to be prior to or to underlie the fact that the genera they subordinate are predicated of those same things. The idea is that an individual is an animal, say, just

[25]John Locke, *An Essay Concerning Human Understanding*, Bk. 2, chap. 23, sec. 2, John Yolton, ed., (London: Dent, 1947), vol. 1, 245. The actual Locke passage puts the phrase in third person. See, e.g., Gustav Bergmann, "Particularity and the New Nominalism" and "Individuals," chaps. 4 and 7 of Bergmann's *Meaning and Existence* (Madison: University of Wisconsin Press, 1959).
[26]The qualifying phrase is introduced at $1^b13$–18. It is not clear to me just what the force of the qualifier is in *Categories* 5. I suspect that Aristotle waffles a bit with the term.
[27]See, especially, $2^b7$–14, but also $2^b32$–34.
[28]The transitivity of the said-of relation appears again at $2^a37$–$2^b2$. See also *Topics* B.4 ($111^a33$ff.) and Γ.1 ($121^a26$ff.). If my interpretation of the implications of this account is correct, then it may be that there is something in the *Categories* that logically commits Aristotle to the claim that Montgomery Furth correctly points out was intended but never explicitly stated, viz., that every primary *ousia* falls under some substance-species. See Furth's "Transtemporal Stability in Aristotelian Substances," *Journal of Philosophy* (1978), 624–646, and his *Substance, Form, and Psyche*, 33–40.

because it is a horse, a dog, a giraffe, or something similar. And although the *Categories* never spells out this priority, it is tempting to understand it in the terms Aristotle invokes in later works, where genera are mere determinables that get their reality from the species that are their determinates [as in *Metaphysics* Z.12 (1038$^a$6–7)], genera are nothing over and above their species [as in Z.13 (1038$^b$30–33)], or there is no such thing as just being an animal, but only the particular ways of being an animal expressed by the species [as in I.8 (1058$^a$3–4)].

Toward capturing the relation between a primary *ousia* and its infima species, I have said that the concept of an object is given by its lowest-level kind. This is Kantian language. A more characteristically Aristotelian way of putting the point is to say that to be for a concrete particular is to be a member of its proper kind. In the *Categories*, Aristotle does not offer us anything like a philosophical analysis of the concept of being. But in works from roughly the same time, we find him denying that 'being' expresses a genus,[29] and it is clear that he does not merely mean to deny that 'being' or 'existent' serve as informative answers to the What is it? question. He means to deny that there is a single character or feature of things that we pick out when we refer to them as beings. On this score, his reactions to the Platonic account of being are pretty much what we find in later works, in which he insists that there is no such thing as just being a being or just being a thing.[30] He wants to replace the idea that 'being' expresses or signifies a single universally exemplified character or nature with the idea that 'being' applies homonymously,[31] and there is strong evidence that, even early in his career, Aristotle took the categories to provide the parameters for disambiguating the term.[32] So 'to be' means something different for an

---

[29]*De Sophisticis Elenchis* 11 (172$^a$12–14). Although the classic texts for the thesis that being is not a genus are *Metaphysics* B.3 (998$^b$21–26) and K.1 (1059$^b$31–34), the materials required to reconstruct the argument presented there are found in *Topics* Z.6 (144$^a$32–144$^b$1). Presumably, then, Aristotle knew of the B.3 argument when he wrote the *Topics*. For a discussion of this passage, see my "Aristotle on the Transcendentals," *Phronesis* (1973), 225–239; although I stand by the interpretation of the passage in question and the account of the relationship between that passage and the doctrine that being and one are not genera, I believe that virtually all the arguments raised in that paper against the multivocity thesis are misdirected. If anyone held that thesis in the form I state it, then the objections stand. But I am now convinced that Aristotle's account bears little resemblance to the characterization outlined there. This point was urged by S. Marc Cohen, commentator on a version of the paper at an APA symposium in 1972. Unfortunately, I only came to appreciate the force of his remarks much later.

[30]*De Sophisticis Elenchis* 11 (172$^a$37–39). See also *Topics* Γ.6 (127$^a$26–35); cf. *Metaphysics* B.4 (1001$^a$4 ff.) and I.2 (1053$^b$17–23).

[31]*De Sophisticis Elenchis* 7 (169$^a$22–24); 10 (170$^b$22); 33 (182$^b$22–31). See also *Posterior Analytics* B.7 (92$^b$13). Compare with *Metaphysics* I.2 (1053$^b$23–24 and 1054$^a$13–19).

[32]See *Eudemian Ethics* A. (1217$^b$25–35). The classic discussion of Aristotle's developing views on this issue is G. E. L. Owen's "Logic and Metaphysics in Some Earlier Works of

*ousia* and a quality. For the one, 'to be' means 'to be an *ousia*'; for the other, 'to be a quality'.

Talk about the being of a thing, then, becomes talk about what the thing is. In later works, we find Aristotle extending this idea beyond the case of the categories to infimae species themselves, so that 'to be' means something different for a dog and a giraffe.[33] Although we never find talk about the homonymy of 'to be' in the *Categories*, it is not implausible to think that, even in that early work, Aristotle held to the general idea that to be for a thing is to be a member of its lowest-level kind. If we concede that in the *Categories* Aristotle took the highest kinds to fix the various senses of 'to be', then we must agree that the transitivity of the said-of relation points to just this consequence. For anything in the category, to be is to be an *ousia*; since its extension has been fixed by the notion of a basic subject, *'ousia'* expresses a genus. Given the transitivity of the said-of relation, that genus's being said of any particular hinges on the fact that one of the kinds at the bottom of the categorial tree is said of that particular. The particular's being an *ousia*, then, just consists in its being a member of that infima species; but, since for that particular to be is to be an *ousia*, for it to be is for it to be a member of its lowest-level kind.[34]

We are not surprised, then, to find the idea that primary *ousiai* fall under substance-species at the core of some of the central claims Aris-

---

Aristotle" in Owen and During, eds., *Aristotle and Plato in the Mid-Fourth Century* (Goteburg: Studia Graeca et Latina Gothoburgensia 11, 1960), 163–190. I rely heavily on Owen's references here. I do not, however, mean to suggest that the claim that 'being' is said in many ways bears exclusively on its homonymy over the categories. See *Metaphysics* Δ.7, where the complex semantical structure of 'to be' includes, but is not exhausted by, homonymy over the categories.

[33]*Metaphysics* H.2 ($1042^b24$ff.). This text actually makes the meaning of 'to be' hinge on the predication of a form. But that predication determines membership in a species, so that we get the result that 'to be' means something different for things from different species.

[34]My line of argument represents an attempt to provide an alternative route to some of the conclusions of G. E. L. Owen's "Aristotle on the Snares of Ontology" in Renford Bambrough, ed., *New Essays on Plato and Aristotle* (London: Routledge and Kegan Paul, 1965), 69–95, and to show that we can locate the essentialist reading of 'to be' as early as the *Categories*. As Owen points out, the essentialist reading works best in the case of singular existential claims about particulars, its application to the case (among others) of general existential claims being obviously problematic. Although the account I am defending bears on the semantics of 'to be', it meshes nicely with the syntactic primacy of the copulative 'to be' defended by Charles Kahn. See Kahn's *The Verb 'Be' in Ancient Greece* (Dordrecht: Reidel, 1974), and his "On the Theory of the Verb 'To Be'" in Milton Munitz, ed., *Logic and Ontology* (New York: New York University Press, 1973), 1–20. For a view that takes the existential use of 'to be' as basic, see Wilfrid Sellars, "Aristotle's Metaphysics: An Interpretation," in his *Philosophical Perspectives* (Springfield, Ill.: Charles Thomas, 1967), 73–124, especially 93–100. The best support for a reading such as Sellars' is provided by *Posterior Analytics* B.1, especially $89^b32$–35.

totle makes about *ousia*. From the *Categories* onward, a recurrent theme is that *ousia* is "this something" (*tode ti*).[35] Initially one wants to parse the idea as the claim that the expression 'this something' is true, in turn, of each primary *ousia*. But I think we better capture the point of the "this something" epithet if we understand it as a kind of schema, where the term 'something' functions as a placeholder for predicates expressing the species under which primary *ousiai* fall. Since the kinds that most definitely express what primary *ousiai* are are substance-species, the fully articulated application of the schema in particular cases yields expressions like 'this man', 'this giraffe', and 'this oak tree'. It is the applicability of expressions like these that Aristotle has in mind when he invokes the "this something" epithet, and the force of the epithet is just to underline the idea that every primary *ousia* is a particular instance of a substance-kind.

Another recurrent theme is the tight connection between the What is it? question and the category of *ousia*. We have already noted the weight Aristotle attaches to this question. Although he concedes that the question plays a role in each of the categories, he stresses its role in the case of *ousia*. What he finds significant about its role in that category is the fact that the question serves to collect those universals that provide us with object concepts for the genuine realities, concepts that identify what to be consists in for the primary *ousiai*. Aristotle frequently uses the question as a label for the category. Sometimes he couples the question with the "this something" epithet, calling the category the "What is it?" and "this something."[36] Commentators have suggested that there is a kind of tension between these two labels;[37] but, although it is true that the What is it? question has as its answers general terms

---

[35]3ª10–13. My view that the "*tode ti*" epithet typically functions as a schema whose actual application to particular cases yields expressions of the form 'this *K*', for appropriate *K*, may be controversial. For contexts in which '*ti*' functions as a placeholder for substance terms, see Z.3 (1029ª20 and 24) as well as Z.12 (1037ᵇ27), where '*hen ti*' is coupled with '*tode ti*.' Much has been written on the "*tode ti*" formula. A classic discussion is found in J. A. Smith, "*Tode Ti* in Aristotle," *Classical Review* (1921), 19. Although they apply it in different ways, Frede and Patzig outline a view that bears similarities to mine in *Aristoteles "Metaphysik Z,"* vol. 1, 39, and vol. 2, 15. For a recent account far removed from mine, see Jonathan Lear, *Aristotle: The Desire to Understand* (Cambridge: Cambridge University Press, 1988), 270–273. See also Daniel Graham, *Aristotle's Two Systems*, 237.

[36]*Metaphysics* Z.1 (1028ª12). Again, I direct the reader to Michael Frede's "Categories in Aristotle" in *Essays in Ancient Philosophy*, where there is a different account of the connections between the What is it? question and the category of *ousia*. Whereas I take the question to be an alternative label for a kind that can be independently identified, he would likely deny that independent identification is possible.

[37]See, e.g., Myles Burnyeat et al., eds., *Notes on Book Zeta of Aristotle's Metaphysics*, Oxford Study Aids in Philosophy, Sub-Faculty of Philosophy, (Oxford University, 1979), 1.

and the "this something" schema applies to particulars, we raise the What is it? question about the particular *ousiai* to which the "this something" schema applies, and the expressions for which 'something' is a placeholder are precisely the lowest-level kind terms that provide the most complete and informative answers to the What is it? question. So, as labels for the category, the two expressions jointly highlight the idea that the primary realities of the *Categories* are particulars falling under substance-species.[38]

As early as the *Categories*, Aristotle claims that each primary *ousia* is "one in number" (4a10–13). This claim too has to be understood as importing talk about substance kinds. Invariably, Aristotle couples the denial that being is a genus with the denial that 'one thing' is a kind term.[39] Just as he insists that there is no such thing as just being a thing, he denies that there is anything that counts as just being one thing. He argues that, taken by themselves, 'one' and its numerical successors are incomplete expressions. They get a complete sense from the counting procedures in which they are used, and those procedures require the specification of some measure, a measure constituted by a universal that is truly predicable of all the objects in the plurality we seek to count:[40]

> The one evidently means a measure; and in every case there is some underlying thing with a distinct nature of its own. . . . And this is reasonable, for 'one' means the measure of some plurality. . . . The measure must always be some identical thing predicable of all the things it measures; e.g., if the things are horses, the measure is *horse*; if they are men, *man*. (1087b34–1088a9)

Talk of numerical unity, then, implies a reference to some universal that can serve as a principle for distinguishing and counting objects. To say that the things that are primary realities are one in number is to say that they fall under universals that provide us with measures for counting

[38]This is not to suggest that the What is it? question applies only in the case of the particulars at the bottom of the categorial tree. Obviously, we can ask what *man* and *animal* are. Nor is it to suggest that the only correct answers to the What is it? question posed of individual or particular *ousiai* make reference to their proper species. We can say what Socrates is by referring to his genus. The point is rather that the paradigmatic or primary instances of *ousia* are particulars and that their species provide the most complete and informative answers to the What is it? question.

[39]See, e.g., *De Sophistics Elenchis* 11 (172a12–14) and *Metaphysics* B.3 (998b21–26), K.1 (1059b31–34), and I.1 (1053b17–1054a19).

[40]See *Metaphysics* I.1–2, especially 1052b31–1052a6, 1053b9–23, and 1054a9–19. See also *Physics* Γ.7 (207b5–9), *Metaphysics* B.4 (1001a4ff.) and Δ.6 (1016b19–25). For a contrary interpretation, see Nicholas White, "Aristotle on Sameness and Oneness," *Philosophical Review* (1971), 177–197, especially 179.

their instances. It is clear from Aristotle's examples that the universals in question are substance kinds and, in the favored case, lowest-level substance kinds.[41] So the universal that marks out a primary *ousia* as what it is constitutes it as something that can be distinguished both from things of other kinds and from things of the same kind. In *Metaphysics* I.1, Aristotle tells us: "To be one is to be indivisible, being just what a 'this' is, and being capable of being separated in place or form or thought" (1052[b] 16–17). Later in the same chapter, he implies that in any given case it is the measure defining 'one thing' that effects the relevant separation. And a recurrent theme in the later works is the idea that, where $K$ is a kind term, expressions of the form 'one $K$' and '(a) $K$' are semantically indistinguishable.[42] Applied to the case of *ousia*, the idea implies that the concept of something instantiating a substance-kind just is the concept of something countably distinct from other things instantiating that kind. And although the Aristotle of the *Categories* is nowhere so explicit on these points, the fact that he formulates the claim that each primary *ousia* is one in number as a kind of gloss on the claim that primary *ousiai* are one and all subject to the "this something" schema suggests that, if he did distinguish the two claims, he took them to be intimately related.[43]

We count objects not just at a time but over time as well; at the end of *Categories* 5, we find Aristotle relating the claim that primary *ousiai* are one in number to the transtemporal case: "It is distinctive of *ousia* that, being the same and one in number, it can admit contraries as a result of a change in itself" (4[b] 17–19). In illustration of the point, he tells us: "The individual man, being one and the same, is at one time light and at another time dark, and [at one time] warm and [at another] cold, and [at one time] good and [at another] bad" (4[a] 19–21). Substance kinds, then, do not merely mark out a member as countably distinct from contemporary comembers of the species. A universal like *man* provides a principle for identifying and counting its members through time. Last winter's sallow office clerk and today's well-tanned beachcomber are *one man*. And what makes these universals measures for counting over time is the fact that in virtue of belonging to a substance kind a primary *ousia* is

---

[41] Aristotle seems to have construed lowest-level kinds as foundational in the counting of *ousiai*. At 1088[a]9ff. he suggests that the use of a genus as measure presupposes that we have already individuated the items to be counted under their species.

[42] See, *Metaphysics* Γ.2 (1003[b]26) and I.2 (1054[a]16–19), where Aristotle adds that "to be one is to be a particular thing."

[43] 3[a]10–13. See also *Metaphysics* Z.12 (1037[b]27), where Aristotle tells us that " 'ousia' signifies 'one something' (hen ti) and 'this something'." In the *Categories*, 'one in number' applies beyond the category of *ousia*; see, e.g., 1[b]6–7, where the term is used apropos of colors and pieces of knowledge as well as of particular *ousiai*.

marked out as something that has a career and can be traced throughout the course of that career. So there are two sides to the idea that a primary *ousia* is one in number. On the one hand, a primary *ousia* is a discrete instance of its substance-species, spatially separate and hence distinguishable from other instances of the species. On the other, substance-species constitute their members as things that persist through time and accordingly provide us with principles for tracking a primary *ousia* through time as one and the same member of its species.[44]

The cluster of ideas associated with the "this something" epithet, the What is it? question, and the "one in number" formula all suggest that the Aristotle of the *Categories* had a clear handle on the phenomenon we nowadays mark by talk of individuative universals, sortal predicates, count nouns, divided reference, and the like. If we couple this suggestion with his emphasis on basic subjects, it becomes tempting to portray the central thrust of the *Categories* in Strawsonian terms and to see Aristotle as simply identifying the notion of a basic subject with the notion of a particular under a sortal universal.[45] Although there is much that speaks in favor of this sort of reading, there is evidence that the early Aristotle did not achieve complete clarity here. In *Metaphysics* Δ.8, he rehearses the *Categories* criterion for *ousia*hood and includes among the things identified by the criterion what we would nowadays call stuffs:

> The simple bodies are said to be *ousia*; for example, earth, fire, and water and the others like these. And, generally, so are bodies and the things composed of them: animals, divine beings, and their parts. All these things are said to be *ousia* from the fact that they are not said of a subject but the other things are said of these. (1017$^b$10–14)

In presenting this version of the *Categories* criterion, Aristotle can be presumed to be reflecting the thinking operative in his original appeal to that criterion. So it is not unreasonable to suppose that, at the time he wrote the *Categories*, he saw the categorial tree as including not just the sortals that dominate the discussions of Chapter 5 but also notions expressed by mass terms like 'earth', 'fire', and 'water'. This suggests that the connection between the idea of a basic subject or primary *ousia*

---

[44]Again, we can reidentify individuals as one and the same plant or one and the same animal, but the favored kinds for counting *ousiai*, both over time and at a time, are substance-species.

[45]See P. F. Strawson, *Individuals: An Essay in Descriptive Metaphysics* (London: Methuen, 1959), especially chaps. 5 and 6. The idea that the Aristotle of the *Categories* has a solid hold on the notion of individuative predication is developed and defended by Furth in *Substance, Form, and Psyche*, 30–40.

and the idea of a particular under a sortal was not quite as tight as the text itself might suggest.[46]

Having registered this caveat, we can agree that the paradigmatic cases of primary *ousiai* in the *Categories* are precisely those basic subjects that are particulars under sortals. We can also agree, I think, that there is an essentialism at work in Aristotle's characterization of these paradigms. It is an essentialism quite different from contemporary views that go by that name in that modal notions do not figure in the formulation of the view.[47] It may turn out that the full articulation of the view requires an appeal to the notions of metaphysical necessity and possibility, but, as Aristotle presents the view, the central idea is a contrast between those universals that mark out a primary *ousia* as what it is and those that merely determine how it is. The former, he wants to say, provide us with object concepts for the primary realities. The universals in question include both the genera and species under which the basic subjects or primary *ousiai* fall, but, according to Aristotle, its infima species most fully identifies what a primary reality is. To repeat the key formula: to be, for a primary *ousia*, is to be a member of its lowest-level substance-kind.

---

[46]Passages 8ᵃ24 and 9ᵇ1 confirm that the Aristotle of the *Categories* does not distinguish clearly between stuff-kinds and thing-kinds. This is a point, however, about which Aristotle's thinking undergoes change. See, e.g., *Metaphysics* Z.16 (1040ᵇ5–10), where he seems to deny stuffs status as *ousiai*. *Topics* Δ.5 (135ᵃ20ff) and E.1 (139ᵃ24–35) do, however, suggest a good sense of the logic of mass terms.

As regards the more general question of the early Aristotle's clarity on kind terms as sortal or individuative predicates, a key passage is 3ᵇ10–24. Aristotle is clearly trying to show that kinds from the category of *ousia* are essentially predicative and that the terms expressing them cannot be assimilated to the class of proper names or singular terms; while showing this, he is trying desperately to distinguish them from nonsortal general terms from other categories, for which he would insist on the same anti-Platonic themes.

It is interesting that the issue of numerical unity at work in this passage arises immediately after the claim that substance-universals and their instances are synonyms. That claim might suggest that the species *man* is one more man. In denying that kinds are one in number, Aristotle may merely be denying that they are countable by the same count nouns as their members (i.e., the count nouns whose applicability their own being said of those members underwrites). If I am right here, this is a text we need to factor into our account of Aristotle's early responses to the Third Man argument, for clearly a critical premise in that argument is the assumption (stronger than what is called the self-predication assumption) that a universal *K* is itself one more *K* to be added to the collection of individual *K*'s it supports. See Chapter 6 for more on this theme.

[47]For discussions of the relations between Aristotle's views and contemporary versions of essentialism, see Nicholas White, "The Origins of Aristotle's Essentialism," *Review of Metaphysics* (1972), 57–85; S. Marc Cohen, "Essentialism in Aristotle," *Review of Metaphysics* (1979), 387–405; Michael V. Wedin, "Singular Statements and Essentialism in Aristotle," *Canadian Journal of Philosophy* (1984), sup. vol. 10, 67–88; and Charlotte Witt, *Substance and Essence in Aristotle*, especially chap. 6. See also Chapter 3, where I discuss these issues in greater detail.

V

We get to the heart of Aristotle's conception of *ousia* in the *Categories* if we focus on the interface of the themes we have been discussing, in particular, the basic-subject criterion for *ousia*hood and the essentialist interpretation of *ousiai*. Something is a primary reality, we have said, just in case it is a basic subject; a basic subject is something which, while neither said of nor present in other things, is something of which other things are said and in which other things are present. The things Aristotle takes to satisfy this criterion are one and all objects falling under substance-species; that is what they are. Brought together, these two themes yield an interesting and perhaps unexpected consequence, namely, that a primary *ousia*'s falling under its substance-species is a primitive or unanalyzable fact about that object.

To see this, we need only reflect on the two notions central to the concept of a basic subject, being said of and being present in. These are the tools, the only tools, Aristotle has at his disposal in the *Categories* for the enterprise of ontological analysis or reduction. Take something that by the lights of the *Categories* is a primary reality, a certain man. Let the man be Socrates. Socrates is supposed to be a basic subject, and *man* is the kind that Aristotle's essentialism requires he instantiate: what Socrates is is a man. Suppose, then, that Socrates' being a man were to rest on or be analyzable in terms of some prior instance of one thing's being said of or present in another. Suppose, that is, that there is some entity $x$ (distinct from Socrates) and some entity $y$ such that the proposition that Socrates is a man is true only because $y$ is said of or present in $x$. Then, this new entity $x$ would turn out to have a better claim than Socrates to the title 'primary reality', for Socrates' being what he is, the subject that he is, would rest on the fact that this new entity $x$ is a subject for the entity $y$. Socrates might still satisfy the definition I have given for the concept of a basic or ultimate subject, but pretty clearly he would do so only in a derived or dependent way. Given the intuitions motivating the account of primary *ousia* in the *Categories*, that way of satisfying the criterion is not sufficient grounds for laying claim to the title 'primary *ousia*'. After all, the very point of providing an inventory of the primary realities is to isolate a set of objects that has a certain explanatory power. And the set has to be the right set; it has to be the *smallest* set such that we can say of the members of the set, If none of these things were to exist, nothing else would either. Affording Socrates the courtesy of membership in that set turns out, however, to be overly generous, for there is a smaller set (the proper subset of that set containing all its members except Socrates) with the same explanatory power as the original set. So, if what Socrates is is a man, if his being the individual he is is his being the man he is, then, if his being a man is analyzable in terms of some prior case of one thing's being said of or present in another, Socrates cannot be a primary *ousia*.

The interaction, then, of the basic-subject criterion for *ousia*hood and the doctrine of essentialism yields the result that nothing that qualifies as a basic subject falls under its proper substance-species in the derivative way suggested by our Socrates example. The fact that a basic subject falls under its species cannot rest on or be grounded in some prior instantiation of the said-of or the present-in relation; and, as I have said, these two relations exhaust the tools Aristotle has at his disposal in the *Categories* for ontological analysis or reduction. But, then, the result of the interaction of our two themes is that a basic subject's falling under or belonging to its lowest-level substance-kind is a primitive, bedrock fact about the world, a fact not susceptible of further analysis. For want of a better name, let us call this result the *Unanalyzability Thesis*.[48]

This thesis does not carry with it the precise locus of its application. One who is committed to the thesis is only committed to the idea that at whatever level one applies the basic-subject criterion to generate an inventory of primary *ousiai*, at that level it must be the case that the objects in question are primitively or unanalyzably what they are, members of their proper substance-kinds. In our thought experiment, presumably the hypothetical object $x$ would have been something subject to what I have called the Unanalyzability Thesis. Given essentialism, $x$ must fall under some lowest-level kind and, presumably, its doing so would just be a brute fact, the kind of fact the ontologist begins with but does not seek to explain, what Aristotle often calls a principle. If, like Socrates, $x$'s being what it is were to rest on some prior instance of one thing's being said of or present in another, we would have to resort to some more basic level in our search after the primary realities. And we can be confident that Aristotle, at least, would not countenance the idea that the search after a subject that just is unanalyzably or primitively whatever it is could be frustrated by an endless series of ever more basic things whose membership in their respective kinds is always deriva-

---

[48]Montgomery Furth speaks of the opacity of the individual substance in the *Categories* (*Substance, Form, and Psyche*, 50), and Daniel Graham speaks of the simplicity or indivisibility of the individual substance (*Aristotle's Two Systems*, 34–36). Although these two claims are related to what I call the Unanalyzability Thesis, they are not the same claim. Both authors simply mean to record the fact that primary *ousiai* are not, in the *Categories*, hylomorphic composites. To get the Unanalyzability Thesis, one has to focus on the essentialist interpretation of 'to be' for primary *ousiai* and the idea that what they are is delineated by the species to which they belong. It is their so belonging that the Unanalyzability Thesis takes to be a primitive and irreducible fact.

tive.[49] At some level, we can be sure, there are suitable candidates for the title 'primary *ousia*'. Aristotle's own view is that that level is constituted by the familiar objects of common sense, the man and the horse of *Categories* 5.[50]

VI

Although the Unanalyzability thesis is a consequence of themes central to the *Categories*, we do not find anything like a statement of the thesis in that work. Aristotle does, however, endorse claims whose effect is to preclude an analysis of species-predications in more basic terms. The suggestion that a primary *ousia*'s membership in its infima species can be analyzed in terms of the notion of one thing's being present in another is certainly countered by Aristotle's firm denial that substance-kinds and substance-differentiae are present in anything.[51] That denial goes hand in hand with the claim that substance-predications relate synonyms rather than paronyms or homonyms.[52] In underlining the logical gulf between sentences expressing instances of the said-of relation and those expressing instances of the present-in relation, that claim serves as a warning against attempts to assimilate or reduce the former to the latter.

Likewise, the *Categories* account of the case of a genus being said of a particular calls into question the idea that species-predications can be analyzed in terms of some prior instance of the said-of relation. As we have seen, Aristotle wants to deny that the predication of a genus of some primary *ousia* stands on its own. It is only because one of the species subordinated to that genus is said of that same individual that the former predication holds. This priority of species-predications precludes an account of species-predications in which Socrates' member-

---

[49]For a proof that there must be basic subjects, see *Posterior Analytics* A.22; I discuss that text in the following section.

[50]A text in which Aristotle argues much as I do in this section is *Metaphysics* N.1 (1087ª28–35). See also *Physics* A.3 (186ᵇ30–34).

[51]3ª7–27. See also *Topics* D.6 (127ᵇ1–4).

[52]One might point to *Categories* 13 (15ª5–8) as well as *Topics* E.5 (141ᵇ26–34) to challenge the idea that the early Aristotle took the predication of a species to underlie that of its genus. In both passages, we are told that the genus is prior to its species, but it is important to understand the force Aristotle attaches to the claim. The priority he points to simply consists in the fact that, where S is a species and G, its genus, the proposition that x is (a) S entails, but is not entailed by, the proposition that x is (a) G. But to say that one thing is, in this sense, prior to another is merely to say that they are related as more general to less general; it is not to make a substantive claim that calls into question the view I am attributing to Aristotle here. I discuss this issue further in Chapter 5.

ship in the species *man*, for example, is to be analyzed in terms of his antecedently satisfying the universals *animal* and *biped*. And in the *Categories* we find the beginnings of a response to the more general idea that a substance-species is a derived entity, a mere construction whose existence turns on some predicative tie between its genus and differentia, when Aristotle excludes the genus from the predicative range of the differentia.[53] In the *Topics* he rounds out the response, explicitly denying both that a genus is predicated of its differentiae and that they are predicated of it.[54] And throughout the *Organon* Aristotle warns us not to be misled by the logical form of a definition: although a definition makes reference to a genus and a differentia, definition is the formula of *one* thing.[55]

None of these points represents more than indirect evidence for the claim that Aristotle endorsed the Unanalyzability Thesis. More direct evidence can be found in a series of texts from the *Posterior Analytics*. The first passage I consider is a difficult section of A.4. Aristotle is specifying the various senses of the technical term *'kath hauto'* (in its own right, or per se), and he identifies as one sense "that which is not said of some other subject." He goes on to explain:

> for example, that which is walking is something different that is walking; and, likewise, with the white thing; but in the case of *ousia* and whatever signifies "this something," it is just what it is not being something else. The things not said of a subject I call things in their own right [*kath hauta*], and those that are said of a subject I call coincidentals [*sumbebekota*]. (73ᵇ5–10)

Given the examples (walking and white), we must take Aristotle's use of 'said of' here to be more general than that in the *Categories* and to have the force of 'predicated of'.[56] We might go on to claim that in this passage Aristotle is merely rehearsing the familiar distinction between basic subjects and what they are subjects of, but that would be a mistake. Although he puts the term *'sumbebekos'* to a wide variety of uses, he never gives it a sense so broad as to cover the case where a substance-universal is predicated of a primary *ousia*. Nor can we take Aristotle to be concerned with the distinction most frequently marked by the terms

---

[53]See 3ᵇ1–2, where only the species and individuals are included in the predicative range of the differentia.

[54]*Topics* Δ.2 (122ᵇ20–24 and 123ᵃ7–8) and Z.6 (144ᵃ29–144ᵇ3).

[55]See, e.g., *De Interpretatione* 11 (20ᵇ17–19), *Posterior Analytics* B.3 (90ᵇ35–37) and B.6 (92ᵃ28–32).

[56]For a similar use of 'said of', see *De Interpretatione* 3 (16ᵇ10–11). In general, after the *Categories*, *'legein'* tends to have this more general sense.

'*kath hauto*' and '*kata sumbebekos*'—that between essential or what-predication and accidental or how-predication. He has already provided a rudimentary characterization of that distinction in the preceding lines of A.4 (73ª34–73ᵇ5). Furthermore, the notion of essential predication is not restricted to the category of *ousia*, whereas the present passage restricts what it is labeling the *kath hauto* to the case of *ousia* and "this something." Finally, our passage seems to be concerned to contrast, not the ways one thing can be predicated of another, but things that are *kath hauta* and things that are *sumbebekota*. '*Sumbebekota*' appears in the plural without '*kata*', and even '*kath hauta*' appears to be functioning as a substantive in the plural rather than as an adverbial modifier.

But, then, which contrast is Aristotle seeking to identify? It is not easy to say. It is not that we cannot, by looking to other texts, piece together what he wants to tell us. I think we can. The problem is rather one of reading the text in terms of a straightforward distinction. The points he wants to make so straddle traditional dichotomies between term and proposition, particular and universal, and use and mention that it is difficult to summarize his remarks, as he seems to want to, in terms of a single distinction between what is *kath hauto* and what is *sumbebekos*. So let us try to get clear on what Aristotle wants to say and leave the distinction itself until the end.

It is, I think, fairly clear that Aristotle intends to contrast two different cases. We seem to be given examples (the walking thing and the white thing) of one of the cases. We are told, apropos of those examples, that the walking thing and the white thing are each something different, these evidently being examples of "things said of a subject." The other case brings *ousia* and "this something" on the scene. We are told that, in this case, the thing is just what it is without being something else; this case, presumably, is marked by the phrase "not said of a subject."

What we need here are examples of this second kind of case. In later passages in *Posterior Analytics* A, in which we meet once again this strange use of locutions like "being something different" and "not being something different," the examples come by way, not of terms, but of sentences. In A.19 (81ᵇ25–27), for example, we are told that if

(1)  The man is white

is true, then it is not the case that the thing of which we truly predicate 'white' is white, "being something different." And in A.22, Aristotle tells us that, if it is true that

(2)  The log is white,

then the log is the underlying subject for white "without being something other than just what is a log or a particular log." Aristotle contrasts
(2) with

(3)  The musical thing is white,

which he insists amounts to

(3')  The man who is accidentally musical is white,

so that it is in virtue of being something different—a man—that the
musical is white. He summarizes the discussion by telling us that sentences such as (1) and (2) do, but sentences such as (3) do not, express
genuine instances of predication.

Aristotle is claiming that some of the sentences by which we express
facts of predication do a better job than others. In some cases, we pick
out that of which a universal is predicated by an expression [like 'man'
in (1) and 'log' in (2)] that succeeds in identifying the actual subject of
the predication. The resulting sentences, Aristotle wants to say, perspicuously represent the predication. In other cases, however, we identify what a universal is predicated of by an expression [like 'musical
thing' of (3) and, presumably, 'walking thing' and 'white thing' of A.4])
that fails on this score, and the resulting sentence fails to portray the
actual structure of the predication—or, as Aristotle puts it, it manages
to express the predication only by a kind of accident ($83^b14-18$).[57]

This difference apparently has its source in the fact that, whereas
something is a walking thing, a white thing, or a musical thing only
"being something different," it is a man or a log "not being something
else." We can make a start toward getting clear on all this if we recall that
expressions like 'the walking thing', 'the white thing', and 'the musical
thing' all exhibit the semantics of paronymy. They enable us to identify
a thing only in terms of other things—an action it is performing, a body
of knowledge it has acquired, or a color it possesses. And, as Aristotle
reminds us in A.22 ($83^b20-21$), these things are all accidents and so have
to be present in something else. They require independently identifiable subjects of their own, and the identificatory devices that make
reference to them do not tell us what those subjects are. So, as devices
for identifying subjects of predication, these expressions have serious
shortcomings. They are supposed to enable us to pick out the subject of

[57]$83^b14-18$. For an excellent discussion of the distinction between genuine or natural
predication and unnatural predication or predication by accident, see Jonathan Barnes,
*Aristotle's Posterior Analytics* (Oxford: Oxford University Press, 1975), 115–118.

which some universal is predicated, but instead of identifying that subject they merely point to another case of a universal being predicated of something, without actually identifying the subject for either predication. They cannot, then, be the linguistic subjects of the canonical sentences that perspicuously represent the metaphysical structure of a genuine predication. And since the objects of which these expressions are true are identified by reference to attributes that can exist only in some subject, nothing can be just a walking thing, a white thing, or a musical thing. If something is one of these things, it must be something else besides, something that can be a subject for the action, the knowledge, or the color.

Aristotle also wants to say that we can pick out that something else by the appeal to a substance-predicate, an expression that identifies a primary *ousia* in terms of a universal essentially predicated of it; both his examples and his use in A.4 of the "this something" schema suggest that it is terms expressing substance-species that are paradigmatic here. So, if something is a musical thing, it must be something else, a man who is musical; if it is a walking thing, it must be something else, a giraffe, say, who is walking; and if it is a white thing, it has to be something else, a horse, perhaps, that is white. But Aristotle wants to deny that things are men, giraffes, or horses "being something else." There is not some further independently specifiable subject implicit in these identifications. A substance-predicate picks out a thing as just what it is; what it picks out is a basic subject of predication—something of which other things are said, but which is not itself said of some other subject. Accordingly, substance terms can serve as grammatical subjects of sentences that canonically represent the actual structure of a predication.

There is more here than a delineation of the proper logical form of sentences expressing predication. Indeed, the formal mode is something I have imposed on the text to facilitate our understanding. Aristotle himself uses the material mode throughout. We can put the point in the material mode by saying that the universals in virtue of which something is musical, walking, or white require subjects in which they might be present; and the existence of those subjects turns on their membership in their respective substance-species. So the instantiation of the universals that underlie a thing's being musical, walking, or white presupposes the prior instantiation of substance-kinds; a thing is musical, walking, or white only because of a kind of "coming together" or coincidence of two universals, the appropriate attribute and the substance-species whose instantiation provides it a subject. Accordingly, Aristotle calls the walking thing and the white thing "coincidentals" in A.4; and when he tells us that coincidentals are things said of a subject, he is pointing to the fact that the universals in virtue of which a thing is musical, walking, or white require independently identifiable subjects of which they are said or predicated.

Aristotle wants to deny, however, that in the case of substance-universals we have something said of some other subject; what he means is that the instantiation of those universals does not, in the same way, presuppose the prior instantiation of some other universal. Men, giraffes, and horses do not instantiate the relevant kinds, "being something different." It is just men, giraffes, and horses that instantiate these universals. There is no prior, independently identifiable subject of which any of these kinds is predicated; a substance-kind's predication of its members does not rest on some prior case of predication, where a more basic universal is predicated of a more basic subject. Members of substance-species are the ultimate subjects of predication, and *what* they are is given by their lowest-level substance-kinds. A species and its members are synonyms: one name applies and one account of what the thing is.[58] As Aristotle puts it in the later *Metaphysics* Γ.4, predicates that signify *ousia* signify for that of which they are predicated that "to be for that thing is nothing else" (1007a26).[59] Substance-kinds provide conditions for the existence of their members, and their members are the ultimate or basic subjects of predication. So the attempt to identify a prior subject to explain the predication of a substance-species leaves us with no subjects of predication at all. Whereas things like the walking thing exist only in virtue of a coming together of distinct things, there is no parallel coincidence underlying something's being a man, a giraffe, or a horse. If Socrates is a man, then, he is a man all by himself or in his own right; but since to be for Socrates is to be a man, we can follow A.4 and just say that Socrates is in his own right.[60]

This idea that the basic subjects or primary realities are what they are in their own right, that they are *kath hauta*, comes close to what I have called the Unanalyzability Thesis. If we probe the very difficult A.22 a bit more deeply, we come to see that the two are, in fact, exactly the same claim. One of Aristotle's concerns in this chapter is to show that substance-predications do not constitute an infinite series, as he puts it,

[58]*Topics* B.2 (109b5ff.) and D.3 (123a27–29).

[59]It is likely that in this passage Aristotle is using the term *'ousia'* in the generalized sense Frede focuses on in "Categories in Aristotle" in *Essays in Ancient Philosophy*. See also Russell Dancy's discussion of this point in *Sense and Contradiction: A Study in Aristotle* (Dordrecht: Reidel, 1975), 107ff., and G. E. M. Anscombe, *Three Philosophers*, 39ff.

[60]This notion of primary *ousiai* as things in their own right is discussed at length in Dancy, *Sense and Contradiction*, especially chap. 5.

"either in an upward or a downward direction." What he has in mind is a series of predications like the following:

(a) Living being is a body.
(b) Animal is a living being
(c) Man is an animal.

Going from (c) to (a) and beyond is moving in the upward direction; moving from (a) to (c) and beyond is moving in the downward direction. If we think of the series in an upward direction, we are thinking of one thing's being subject for a more general notion, the more general notion, in turn, subject for a still more general notion, and so on; if we think of the series in the downward direction, we are thinking of a general notion as predicated of a less general notion, that less general notion, in turn, as predicated of a still less general notion, and so on (see 83$^b$6–9). Aristotle wants to show that the series of predications must have an upper limit in the form of a most general predicate that is subject for nothing else as well as a lower limit in the form of something which, while subject, is predicated of nothing else and that there is only a finite number of predications separating these limits. His own view, of course, is that those limits are provided, on the one hand, by the notion of *ousia* itself construed as a category or highest kind and, on the other, by the basic subjects or primary *ousiai* of the *Categories*.[61]

His argument to show that the series is finite invokes the idea that, although we can grasp or define *ousia*, we cannot traverse an infinite series in thought (83$^b$6–9). It has been claimed that if we accept this consideration as decisive we get only the result that an upward regress is impossible.[62] But, although Aristotle never explicitly makes the point, he may be assuming that the possibility of grasping or defining a kind presupposes our ability to identify what I have called concrete instantiations of the kind.[63] If the assumption is correct, then the possibility of definition would seem to ensure that the downward series terminates in a predication like that expressed by "Callias is a man," Aristotle's own candidate for a bedrock predication. But, for our purposes, the actual proof itself is less important than Aristotle's statement of what he believes it establishes. As I have said, his own candidate for a

---

[61]See his candidate for a terminal proposition at 83$^b$5.

[62]See Barnes, *Aristotle's Posterior Analytics*, 167.

[63]This assumption is just the epistemological counterpart to the metaphysical principle that every universal has at least one concrete instantiation. Given Aristotle's realism, it is an assumption that contemporary defenders of causal or historical theories of kind terms would endorse as well.

terminal predication in the downward direction is a proposition such as "Callias is a man," where an infima species is predicated of one of its members. He tells us by way of summary that "it is necessary that there be something of which something is predicated primitively" (83$^b$28–30). So it is a necessary truth that there is some subject, itself having no subject, of which something is predicated directly and primitively— this, of course, being the lowest-level substance-universal that the subject instantiates, that is, its infima species. There is nothing mediating this predication. That it holds is a primitive fact; it is this, I think, that Aristotle has in mind in A.4 when he tells us that the basic subjects are what they are in their own right or *kath hauta*. The things that are basic subjects just are, all by themselves, the kinds of things they are. In virtue of being a member of its infima species, however, a basic subject is fitted out to be the subject of other predications. Accidents can be present in it, hence predicated of it. And since the genus that it subordinates is directly predicated of an object's infima species, that genus can be predicated of the object; but the predication is one that is mediated. Indeed, this picture of a series of predications is precisely what motivates the formal remarks on the transitivity of the said-of relation in Chapter 2 and Chapter 5 of the *Categories*. So what Aristotle takes himself to have proved here is precisely what I have called the Unanalyzability Thesis. The fact that a basic subject falls under its infima species is a primitive fact, one not susceptible of further ontological analysis. It is because this fact holds true of them that the ordinary, familiar objects of the *Categories* are the basic subjects it says they are; Aristotle summarizes all this by saying that the basic subjects are *kath hauta*.

## VII

While conceding that the relevant texts from the *Posterior Analytics* confirm my interpretation, of *kath hauto* beings, one might be less willing to concede that the framework Aristotle develops in those texts has the philosophical implications he claims for it. The concern here comes from two directions. First, the central idea is that of a series of substance-predications linking basic subjects with their species, these species with their genera, these, in turn, with higher-level genera, and so on to the category of *ousia* itself. The problem is that a direct, unmediated relationship between subject and predicate is not unique to the initial predication in the sequence; it is reiterated at every level in the sequence. Indeed, the "just what it is" formula that we have invoked over the last few pages is one Aristotle seems willing to invoke at each level in the series. A man may be just what Socrates is, but, in the same way, (an) animal is just what (a) man is. And just as Socrates is a man without being anything different, so man is an animal without being something else. But, then, we must ask whether the idea of a thing's being just what it is, of its being whatever it is in its own right, is one that uniquely picks out Aristotle's basic subjects.

A second problem is that this picture of a series of predications is not restricted to the category of *ousia*. In dealing with the accidental categories, Aristotle focuses on the case of transcategorical or intercategorial predications, where we predicate an accident of some subject in which it is present. But the What is it? question can be raised in the case of qualities, quantities, and the like; by posing this question at successively higher levels we generate the materials for constructing a series of predications analogous to that found in the category of *ousia*. The idea of such a series seems appropriate, since there is intracategorial as well as intercategorial predication of accidents. In the language of the *Categories*, while present in substances, accidents (at least those of the appropriate level of generality) are said of the accidents falling under them. But, then, even outside the category of *ousia* we have the idea of direct, unmediated predicative ties; and since the relevant series cannot be infinite, we have once again the idea of primitive subjects of predication that serve as the starting point of a sequence that terminates in a category. Since these subjects would seem to be related to their kinds in precisely the way individual *ousiai* are related to theirs, it is unclear that Aristotle's conception of basic subjects as things that are what they are in their own right succeeds in pointing to features that uniquely pick out the objects he wants to call the primary realities.[64]

I am inclined to think that Aristotle would concede both points. He could hardly deny that, in some sense, accidents can be defined in terms of more general notions from their respective categories. He sometimes even speaks of identifying the *ousia* of qualities, quantities,

[64]On the interpretation that Michael Frede offers in *Essays in Ancient Philosophy*, this issue does not arise. As regards the machinery of *Posterior Analytics* A.4, 19, and 22, I think that it is fairly clear from the use of the "this something" epithet in A.4 and Aristotle's examples throughout that the central focus here is the category of *ousia* thought of as a classification of entities. But it is also clear that the framework developed with that category as the focus applies to the intracategorial predication of accidents. Aristotle would certainly claim, for example, that the arguments developed in A.22 show that no regress is possible in any of the categories, where a category is construed as a classification of objects. So, although Frede and I would probably understand Aristotle's use of '*ousia*' in these texts differently, we would agree on the generality of the argument against infinite regresses in demonstration. See also Barnes's discussion of A.22 in *Aristotle's Posterior Analytics*, 166–173.

and the like,[65] and, as I have already acknowledged, his use of the various mystifying formulae is not restricted to his characterization of the relationship between a substance-species and its members. Indeed, although Aristotle's examples of terms that serve to identify the basic subjects of genuine predications are terms expressing infimae species, nothing in the text precludes us from holding that genus terms like 'plant' and 'animal' can play this role, albeit in a less complete, less informative way than the terms expressing the relevant species. But to concede these points is merely to acknowledge that the formal structures operative in the *Posterior Analytics* are not by themselves sufficiently powerful to express the conception of *ousia* that has its origin in the *Categories*, and I do not believe Aristotle intended them to play this role. The technical machinery operative there must, I think, be supplemented by the principles of instantiation from the *Categories* (i–iii, see p. xx) and the *Categories* intuition that every universal presupposes what I have called a concrete instantiation. So supplemented, the framework goes a long way toward capturing the central insights Aristotle wants to defend.

Consider the case of accidents. It is true that accidents fall under kinds; and, although the A.22 picture suggests that the predicative tie between adjacent accident-kinds is direct and unmediated, the fact remains that, for Aristotle, the existence of a quality, quantity, or action (of whatever degree of generality) presupposes that some individual *ousia* possesses or instantiates that accident. But, then, the truth of propositions about an accident presupposes that there be some primary *ousia* in which the accident is present. The proposition that vermillion is a color can be true only if there is some *ousia* that is colored vermillion; the proposition that running is an action presupposes for its truth that some primary *ousia* is running; the truth of the proposition that triangularity is a shape requires that some primary *ousia* has the triangular shape. So the intracategorial predication of accidents does not stand on its own; the truth of propositions expressing the intracategorial predication of accidents hinges on the truth of propositions in which accidents are predicated transcategorically. But, then, although it is true that vermillion is a color, it is not a color all by itself or in its own right; and although it is true that running is an action, its being what it is depends on its being an action of something that, while running, is something else besides.

Likewise, the principles of instantiation at work in *Categories* 5, especially (i) and the requirement of concrete instantiation, preclude the

---

[65]See, e.g., *Posterior Analytics* B.13 (96ª34–36 and 96ᵇ6).

existence of a kind without members. Accordingly, the truth of propositions relating higher-level substance-kinds ultimately turns on the existence of individuals falling under the infimae species subordinating those kinds. But Aristotle denies that the relationship tying a basic subject to its species is, in the same way, mediated by the existence of other predicative relations. Basic subjects are primitively or unanalyzably whatever they are, so they are the only things that are what they are in their own right; and because they are what they are, other things can be what they are. So when the formalisms of *Posterior Analytics* A.22 are supplemented by the principles of instantiation Aristotle invokes in *Categories* 5, a picture emerges in which basic subjects seem to play precisely the explanatory role Aristotle accords them when he calls them the primary *ousiai*.

## VIII

My account of the *Categories* theory of *ousia* is only a very selective sketch; I have picked out certain central themes and ignored other aspects of the view, and I have tried to steer clear of important interpretative difficulties in the text to provide a background for the views Aristotle develops in Metaphysics Z–H. More significant, I have discussed Aristotle's early views on *ousia* without raising along the way difficulties that might surround those views. Still, as we conclude the account, there is a philosophical concern that is impossible to set aside. I suspect that it has been on the reader's mind since at least Section III; as it turns out, it is a problem Aristotle himself comes to have with the account in the *Categories*.

We can get at the problem if we recall that the overarching aim of the *Categories* is to identify the primary realities, the primary *ousiai*. This aim, we have said, requires the specification of criteria that serve to justify the claim that things of a certain kind, however general, are fitted out to play a certain explanatory role, that of enabling us to explain why things that are not members of that kind exist. It is Aristotle's contention that the notion of a basic subject provides the required criterion. But if the attempt to identify the primary realities is not to be a mere sham, there must be an asymmetry between the items so identified and the objects whose existence they are supposed to explain. It must be the case that the items in the favored kind provide us with the resources for explaining why things outside that kind exist, but it cannot be the case that objects outside the favored kind are required, in turn, to explain why objects belonging to the favored kind exist. Without being disingenuous, we can agree, I think, that in a wide range of cases the account of the primary *ousiai* developed in the *Categories* succeeds on this score. If we accept Aristotle's intuitions about the relationship between an attribute and what it characterizes and if we accept the intuition that an attribute's presence in a universal presupposes its presence in one or more of the particulars of which that universal is said, then we can agree that Aristotle provides an initially plausible account of the dependence of things from the various accidental categories on the things he identifies as primary *ousiai*. And, although we might have some philosophical scruples, we can probably concede that it is possible for Aristotle to tell a story about the relationship between the basic subjects and their accidental attributes which makes plausible the idea that the relationship here is asymmetrical, namely, that the basic subjects do not depend for their existence on the qualities, quantities, and other attributes present in them.[66]

Likewise, I believe, we might be able to accept Aristotle's contention that the relevant asymmetry obtains in the relationship between the basic subjects and the genera and differentiae that are said of them. Our tolerance may be becoming more strained, but, if we take as given the idea that the primary *ousiai* fall under their infimae species and are willing to endorse the incipient doctrine that higher-level universals depend for their instantiation on the instantiation of their lowest-level determinates, then, perhaps, we might agree that a case can be made for the claim that primary *ousiai* are, in the relevant sense, asymmetrically related to their genera and differentiae; we might express paren-

[66]In the interests of setting out the early theory of *ousia* as briefly and efficiently as possible, I have not gone into the details of the story required here. It is, however, worth pointing out that the story would be a complicated one. Among other things, it would have to distinguish determinables and determinates, first-order accidents and the higher-order attributes to which they give rise, and accidents contingently predicated of *ousiai* and those predicated necessarily (but not, in Aristotle's restricted sense of the term, essentially). Asymmetry is most obvious in the case of fully determinate, first-order accidents predicated only contingently of *ousiai*. According to Aristotle, there would be no such thing as the color red if there were not red objects; but he would want to say that any red *ousia* could have been some other color. Given the asymmetrical relation between *ousiai* and accidents like red, one would have to argue (as Aristotle was prepared to) that determinables (like the property of being colored) and higher-order properties depend for their existence on the determinates for which the relevant asymmetry has already been argued. The case of "necessary accidents" (like the *idea* of *Topics* A.4) presents special difficulties, since talk about the possibility of an *ousia*'s existing without an attribute does not serve to exhibit the relevant asymmetry. Here Aristotle invokes a different story, according to which accidents are dependent on their subjects by virtue of being rooted or anchored in their essences. He wants to say, that is, that a necessary accident is predicated of an *ousia* because of what the *ousia* is or because it is the kind of thing it is; and he wants to claim that the idea of "following from" or "being caused by" applies here asymmetrically.

thetically, a concern that, even with the relevant concessions, asymmetry in the case of differentiae is less clear.

If we resist such scruples and succeed in convincing ourselves of the viability of the account in these cases, we must agree that the case of the infimae species is another matter altogether. Even if we accept the view that the existence of a universal requires the existence of some concrete instantiation, the fact is that the essentialism that underlines the account of *ousia* in the *Categories* forces us to conclude that the relevant asymmetry just does not obtain in the relationship between substance-species and their members. The view is that the basic subjects are one and all members of their respective substance-species. Being members of those species is just what those basic subjects are. Their being items in the category of *ousia* at all hinges on their being members of those species. Indeed, those species give the conditions of existence for the basic subjects. But, then, surely it is the case that, were those species not to exist, the basic subjects would not exist either. So even if it is true that a condition of the existence of a species is the existence of its members, the set of related themes we have called Aristotle's essentialism forces us to conclude that the remarks of *Categories* 5 ($2^a34–2^b6$) are insufficient to establish all that is required if the case that basic subjects are the primary *ousiai* is to be made out. Indeed, given the essentialism at work there, it is difficult to see how that case could ever be made out. The required asymmetry just does not obtain. And that leads us to wonder just why we should say that substance-species or whatever it is that makes basic subjects be what they are are only derivatively or secondarily *ousiai*. Do they not have as much right to the title 'primary *ousia*' as the basic subjects themselves? Anyone who asks this question has already set out on the road that leads to the central books of the *Metaphysics*.

# CHAPTER 2

# Complications

## I

If we set aside the problems raised at the end of the previous chapter, the overall picture of the early theory of *ousia* is fairly clear. The search after *ousia* leads Aristotle to endorse what I have called the subject criterion for *ousia*hood: it is basic subjects (things which, while subjects for other things, do not themselves have subjects) that have the best claim to status as the primary *ousiai*. But these are things falling under kinds. Being members of those kinds is *what* they are, so that to be for a primary *ousia* is to be a member of its respective kind. The consequence of endorsing both this form of essentialism and the subject criterion is commitment to what I have called the Unanalyzability Thesis, the claim that what a primary reality is, its being a member of the kind to which it belongs, is a primitive, unanalyzable fact about it. I have tried to show how Aristotle expresses this thesis in terms of talk about direct and immediate predicative ties linking basic subjects with their lowest-level kinds, and I have argued that when supplemented by the principles of instantiation of *Categories* 5 this idea enables Aristotle to explain how things other than the basic subjects depend on basic subjects for being what they are and thereby vindicate his initial selection of basic subjects as the primary realities.

In *Metaphysics* Z and H, the search after *ousia* is undertaken within a quite different framework, and notoriously the middle books are among the most difficult in the corpus. They are especially difficult for one who turns to Z and H directly from the *Categories*. The difficulty is that the new framework is operative from the start, so that the questions raised and the strategies for answering them presuppose the very framework Aristotle invokes and develops in Z and H. Nonetheless, understanding what he says in the middle books presupposes an appreciation of the themes central to the *Categories*; for it is both in reaction to certain of those themes and in defense of others that he develops, from within the new framework, that new framework itself. So the themes we are familiar with are never presented in their own right, but always from within the new framework; and when we move from the *Categories* to Z and H we are like time travelers who are thrust into a later epoch, with some major scientific revolution intervening. The theoretical and practical concerns of the new epoch are shaped by this shift; and, while the framework of our own epoch has been displaced, the new framework was developed in reaction to our familiar framework, so it cannot be understood except in terms of that old framework. Both what has been rejected and what has been preserved of the old framework are, however, now expressed in terms of concepts of the new framework. Our task as visitors is to understand how things are in this new epoch; the problem is that we are thrust into the new framework in medias res. We have no access to the revolutionary period that witnessed the displacement of the old by the new. Yet, it might be argued, the analogy with the move from the *Categories* to Z and H breaks down here. We do not have to jump into the new framework in medias res. It is easy to identify the conceptual shift separating the *Categories* conception of *ousia* from that expressed and developed in Z and H. The shift is documented in the physical and biological writings, where Aristotle develops and applies the insight that the basic subjects of the earlier writings have an internal structure, that somehow they are composites of matter and form. Accordingly, readers of the *Categories* need merely work their way through the *Physics*, *De Anima*, and so on; then, the materials for understanding Z and H will be mastered.

Unfortunately, things are not quite so easy. Although we do occasionally find hints and suggestions of the perspectives of Z and H in the physical and biological writings, they are only that; as often as not, they can be understood as the hints and suggestions we want to take them to be only by being read in the light of the concerns of Z and H. The fact is that the basic theoretical concerns of the *Categories* and *Metaphysics* Z and H are not, in general, those of the physical and biological works; the formulation of the conceptual framework that makes Z and H an alien land for readers of the *Categories* is undertaken largely in isolation from those concerns.

This is not to say that it would not be profitable to go through the critical texts of the physical and biological writings and, only then, to move on to Z and H; but to approach things in this way would be to write a different book from this one—a much longer book.[1] In any case, the themes I want to highlight are such that we can make our way into Z and H without the detour through the physical and biological writings. We do, from time to time, find ourselves compelled to look at texts from the *Physics, De Anima, De Generatione et Corruptione*, and so on; but I propose that, like the time travelers, we jump into the fray that is Z and H in medias res.

A good landing place is Z.3. It is good because, in spite of the intrusion of the new doctrine that 'being' has focal meaning, (1028[a]10–20), Z.1 and Z.2 cover familiar ground. They show that Aristotle's own attempt to identify *ousia* is continuous with the efforts of his predecessors, and we are already acquainted with the idea that the search after *ousia* is the attempt to identify some thing or things that can plausibly be thought to play a certain explanatory role, an attempt that is common to the efforts of Aristotle, Plato, and Democritus. But Z.3 is a good landing place for another reason: in that chapter, Aristotle considers some of the familiar themes of the *Categories*. His treatment of those themes gives us insight into how much things have changed, and it raises a whole host of questions answering which turns out to be the central concern of Z and H.

II

Aristotle begins Z.3 (1028[b]33–36) by introducing four candidates for the role of *ousia*. The first three are introduced as things that might be thought to be the *ousia* of a thing, where the term '*ousia*' is used as an abstract expression. This new use of the term will come to dominate the discussions of Z and H and calls for further attention; but, for the present, we can be content merely to note the new use. One of the three items identified as a possible claimant for status as *ousia* in this new sense, the *ti ein einai* (the what it is to be; usually translated as 'essence'),

[1]Recent attempts at tracing the development of Aristotle's thought from the *Categories* through the *Metaphysics* by way of the physical and biological works can be found in Furth's *Substance, Form, and Psyche* and Graham's *Aristotle's Two Systems*. Furth emphasizes the biological writings as the link between the early and later works; Graham gives prominence to the *Physics*. Neither is concerned to provide the detailed analysis of Z and H that is my aim. Had they been, neither would have succeeded in writing a single-volume work.

is unfamiliar; again we set this aside for later treatment. We have already met the other two claimants, the universal and the genus. If we assume that by 'universal' Aristotle means to refer to the species, then these two claimants were, in virtue of being branches of the categorial tree, labeled secondary *ousiai* in the *Categories* (2ᵃ13–18). The fourth candidate is our old friend the subject. It is listed outside the scope of the expression 'seem to the *ousia* of each thing', so subjects presumably have a claim to the title '*ousia*' as it was used in the *Categories*; it is that claim Aristotle wants to evaluate in Z.3.

That it is the criterion of the *Categories* Aristotle wishes to examine is clear at the outset. Using the expression 'said of' in the general sense of *Posterior Analytics* A.4 (where it spans the *Categories* notions of 'said of' and 'present in' and means 'predicated'), Aristotle tells us:

> The subject is that of which the other things are said, but it is in no way said of anything else. (1028ᵇ36–37)

So the subjects of Z.3 are what we have been calling basic subjects; when Aristotle tells us that it is "the primary subject that most of all seems to be *ousia*" (1029ᵃ1–2), he is merely echoing the criterion for *ousia*hood that lies at the core of the *Categories*.

If we have been on familiar ground up to this point, Aristotle injects an alien theme when he tells us that this criterion does not unambiguously point in the direction of just one sort of thing. The assumption of the *Categories* was that the criterion uniquely selects the familiar particulars of common sense as the genuine realities; now Aristotle tells us that any gesture in their direction is, initially at least, open to three interpretations. We might mean the matter, the form, or that which is composed of these (1029ᵃ2–3). He explains by way of an example:

> By 'matter' I mean, for example, the bronze; by 'form' the figure of its shape; and that which is out of these is the statue, the composite thing. (1029ᵃ3–5)

Like many of the examples Aristotle uses in Z and H to clarify his claims about *ousia*, this example involves reference to something the reader of the *Categories* might be reluctant to construe as a genuine reality.[2] We have here an artifact rather than something falling under a natural kind, and the reader of the *Categories* might insist that any

---

[2]See, e.g., H.2 (1042ᵇ15–1043ᵃ11), where Aristotle acknowledges (at 1043ᵃ4–5) that the examples that serve to clarify the way that matter and form enter into the recipe for an object are not instances of genuine *ousiai*.

analysis of the concept of a statue requires an appeal to the notion of an accident or something present in something else.[3] But if the example suffers on this score, it more than compensates by way of its clarity. We are to imagine a statue, say, of George Washington. It was cast from a certain quantity of bronze. In the casting it was made to take on a certain shape, and in virtue of taking on that shape the bronze constitutes a statue of the first president of the United States. So we have our bronze, the shape that was imparted to it, and the resulting statue: matter, form, and composite. Readers who object that statues are not part of the intended extension of the notion of a basic subject are presumably counseled to apply the analysis to their favored cases. In virtue of his own success in the physical and biological writings in applying the analysis to a wide range of cases, Aristotle is confident that the general point will hold. As a gesture toward the preferred subjects of the *Categories*, the criterion puts us in contact with contexts that include not only the familiar particular of common sense, what Aristotle now calls the composite, but also the matter "from which it came to be and which persists" (194$^b$24) and the form that matter takes on.

Aristotle goes on to tell us that, viewed from the perspective of this new set of explanatory concepts, the criterion is inadequate, and he gives us two reasons for thinking that the criterion cannot tell the whole story about *ousia* (1029$^a$9). It is, he tells us, unclear (1029$^a$10), but he fails to elaborate on this remark. Commentators often suggest that what is unclear about the criterion is that it does not unambiguously pick out a candidate from the list of three.[4] It is, however, unlikely that this is what Aristotle has in mind here since his second objection is just that the criterion, taken in isolation, does unambiguously pick out a single candidate, the wrong candidate—matter. It may be that what is unclear about the criterion is the fact that it includes a negative condition, thereby identifying the genuine realities not in terms of what they are but of what they are not. Or it may be that Aristotle finds the appeal to the essentially relational notion of a subject problematic on the grounds that the criterion succeeds in identifying the primary *ousiai* only by reference to a role they play relative to other things. Or, perhaps, he finds the criterion unclear on both grounds.

---

[3]See, e.g., *De Interpretatione* 11 (20$^b$15–21), where Aristotle argues that, where an accident and a substance-universal coincide, the resultant complex does not represent a universal with the kind of unity associated with the relevant substance-universal.

[4]See Russell Dancy, "On Some of Aristotle's Second Thoughts about Substances: Matter," *Philosophical Review* (1978), 372–413, especially 393, and Malcolm Schofield, "Metaphysics Z.3: Some Suggestions," *Phronesis* (1972), 97–101, especially 97.

## III

In the end, it does not much matter what Aristotle finds unclear at 1029ª10, since it is the second difficulty with the subject criterion that he is concerned to press. If we employ the idea of a basic subject as our principle for selecting *ousiai*, we must conclude that it is matter rather than the familiar objects of the *Categories* that has the best claim to the title '*ousia*'. That this is an unsatisfactory result Aristotle argues at 1029ª10–30, as follows:

(1)  If this is not *ousia*, it is unclear what is.

(2)  For when the other things are stripped away, nothing [else] seems to be left;

(3)  for the other things are affections and qualities and capacities of bodies;

(4)  and length and breadth and depth are certain quantities and not *ousia*;

(5)  for the quantified is not *ousia*, but rather the primary thing to which these belong, that is, *ousia*.

(6)  But when length, breadth, and depth are stripped away, we see nothing left unless it is something that is marked out by these,

(7)  so that to those who are taking this perspective, matter seems to be the only thing that is *ousia*.

(8)  I mean by 'matter' that which is said to be neither (a) something nor quantified nor any of the other things by which being is marked out.

(9)  For there is something of which each of these is predicated for which the to be is different from that of each of the things predicated.

(10)  For the others are predicated of *ousia*,

(11)  but this is predicated of the matter,

(12)  so that the last thing is in its own right neither (a) something, nor quantified, nor anything else.

(13)  Nor is it their negations since these too will belong only by accident.

(14)  Accordingly, for those who see things in this way, it follows that matter is *ousia*.

(15)  But this is impossible;

(16)  for being separate and "this something" most of all seem to belong to *ousia*,

(17)  so that the form and what is composed of both would seem to be *ousia* more so than the matter.

The overall structure of the argument is clear. Aristotle argues for the claim [stated tentatively in (1) and (7) and then without qualification in

(14)] that the subject theorist is committed to construing matter as characterized in (12) and (13) as *ousia*. In (15), Aristotle tells us that, for the reasons stated in (16), this is an unacceptable result, and he concludes in (17) with the claim that the composite and the form have a better claim to status as *ousia*.[5]

Unfortunately, it is less clear just how we get to the conclusions of (15) and (17). The prevailing view among commentators is that Aristotle is inviting us to engage in a sort of thought experiment.[6] We are invited to take some sample object (the statue of 1029ᵃ6, commentators often tell us) and mentally to strip away the features of the object that are predicated of something else. The result of the relevant subtractions is that something else, that in the thing that is subject but never predicate and, hence, by the subject criterion, *ousia*. However colorless the terminus of this thought experiment, the talk of stripping away is colorfully picturesque; we sometimes meet with the suggestion that central to the thought experiment is the attempt to perceive or picture to ourselves[7] the result of what has been called Aristotle's "strip-tease."[8] Since the stripping removes "affections, qualities, and capacities" as well as "length and breadth and depth," the experiment seems to demand that we perceive or imagine something lacking all color, taste, odor, tactile properties, as well as spatial dimensions. A challenging thought experiment, indeed.

It is not surprising, then, that commentators who see the talk of stripping as so richly suggestive have developed revisionist readings of Z.3. William Charlton, for example, contends that the stripping represents a process Aristotle himself takes to be illegitimate but wants to attribute to some wild-eyed opponent (presumably, a subject theorist) and that steps (1–13) represent the views of this opponent, with Aris-

---

[5]This sketch of the argument would not generally be thought controversial. However, Richard Blackwell, in "Matter as a Subject of Predication in Aristotle," *Modern Schoolman* (1955), 19–30, takes the reasoning of the argument to be that, if matter is ultimate subject, then it is *ousia*. But since it is neither separable nor subject to the *tode ti* schema, it cannot be *ousia*; hence it cannot be ultimate subject of predication. This reading strikes me as a complete inversion of Aristotle's argument with little or no textual warrant. Although he would probably endorse the general account I have given of 1029ᵃ10–30, Terence Irwin understands the role of these lines in the context of Z.3 quite differently. He claims that the Aristotle of Z–H takes form to satisfy the subject criterion par excellence. Accordingly, Irwin takes the argument of 1029ᵃ10–30 to signal, not general dissatisfaction with the subject criterion, but rather the need to engage in fine-tuned analysis to show that the hylomorphic framework can avoid the conclusion that matter is the paradigmatic subject. See Irwin's *Aristotle's First Principles*, 204ff.

[6]See, again, Dancy, "Aristotle's Second Thoughts," 396.

[7]Schofield, "*Metaphysics* Z.3," 98.

[8]Dancy, "Aristotle's Second Thoughts," 396.

totle's sane response coming only in (14–17).[9] There is, however, little in the text to warrant the idea that (1–13) are within oratio obliqua. Indeed, the role in the argument of premises [like (9–11)] expressing what we will come to see as characteristic views of Z and H suggests that it could be no one but Aristotle who is developing the line of argument leading to (15) and (17).

Likewise motivated by the suggestive language in which Aristotle describes the alleged thought experiment, Malcolm Schofield takes Aristotle to be arguing that when we strip away the features listed in (3) and (4) we are at (6) left with nothing at all, so that for anyone who endorses the subject criterion the only remaining candidate as *ousia* is matter. But (6) does not say this, so we have to take its concluding clause as "irrelevant and puzzling," "an inept gloss."[10] Apart from the liberties it takes with the text, this reading strains our credulity. We are to suppose Aristotle to think away every feature in virtue of which something might be an identifiable object of thought; and then, with no explanation at all, to tell us that the only remaining candidate for status as logical subject is matter. But how did matter appear on the scene? Why should we suppose that, if the stripping process is so effective in annihilating our sample object, the matter out of which it is composed should fare any better?

The mistake here is the assumption that the metaphorical talk of stripping away presents us with a process that might be expected to terminate in anything we could picture to ourselves. The only suggestion that this is so is the use of '*horomen*' at 1029ª17. But like our 'see', that verb has nonperceptual as well as perceptual uses; if we take it in its perceptual use, it is difficult to explain why we have to await the stripping away of length, breadth, and depth to have problems with perceptual representability. Those problems would have been at our doorstep as early as (3), when the qualities of our sample object (including its perceptible qualities) were stripped away. But more generally, it is unlikely that anyone who takes the proper and common sensibles to be direct objects of perceptual consciousness could believe or attribute to anyone else the belief that their elimination might result in anything we could perceive or picture to ourselves.[11]

If there is a thought experiment here, then, it has to be something a bit more sane. One suggestion is that the thought experiment does not

[9]William Charlton, *Aristotle's Physics Books I and II* (Oxford: Oxford University Press, 1970), 136–138, and Charlton, "Prime Matter: A Rejoinder," *Phronesis* (1986), 197–211, especially 204–205.

[10]Schofield, "Metaphysics Z.3," 98–100.

[11]See, e.g., *De Anima* B.6 (418ª6–19).

seek to bring forward a new thing.[12] What we are doing is merely considering our sample object (the statue of 1029$^a$5, perhaps) from the perspective of change. Aristotle is not suggesting that if we strip away the features of our sample we will find hidden beneath them some new object; he is merely inviting us to think of that sample as something that can undergo variations in its affections, qualities, and capacities and in its length and breadth and depth. On this reading, matter is just the original object thought of as variable in this way; thought of in this way, things do not have a claim to status as *ousia*.[13]

This is an intriguing view, but it does does not seem to be the view Aristotle is developing in our passage. The connections between the concept of matter and the phenomenon of change are surely tight in Aristotle's thought, but he does not exploit those connections in the argument of Z.3. As even a quick reading of (8–13) shows, the argument hinges on facts about predication rather than about change; although the context of change may well be in the back of Aristotle's mind,[14] the argument proceeds without so much as a reference to the fact that our sample object, whatever it might be, is something that can undergo variations in its predicates. Further, however inviting an intentionalist interpretation of matter might be, in this text at least, the facts about predication Aristotle invokes surely seem to identify [in (11)] as ultimate subject something that is not just intentionally but numerically different from the sample object with which we began. And it turns out that the causal role the Aristotle of Z and H assigns to matter vis-à-vis the composite whose matter it is requires that we have a real and not merely intentional difference here.

That facts about predication should prove central in a context in

---

[12]See Hugh R. King, "Aristotle without *Prima Materia*," *Journal of the History of Ideas* (1956), 370–389, especially 387–388; Dancy, "Aristotle's Second Thoughts"; and Donald E. Stahl, "Stripped Away: Some Contemporary Obscurities Surrounding *Metaphysics* Z.3 (1029$^a$10–26)," *Phronesis* (1981), 177–180.

[13]Dancy, "Aristotle's Second Thoughts," 408–410, and Stahl, "Stripped Away," 178–179. One finds the intentionalist interpretation defended independently of Z.3 in Hartman, *Substance, Body, and Soul*, 97–103, and Sellars, "Substance and Form in Aristotle" in *Philosophical Perspectives*, 127–136. Daniel Graham denies that Aristotle endorsed an intentionalist or aspectual theory of matter but believes that had he done so he would have been able to avoid a plethora of problems that Graham contends arise for the theory of Z and H. See *Aristotle's Two Systems*, 274–276.

[14]There are important relationships (which I discuss later) between the structure of change and the structure of predication. Aristotle likes to think of change as a kind of process toward the obtaining of a predicative state of affairs, where the form is predicate and matter, subject; hence the use of 'subject' in both contexts. But it is the facts about predication proper that are central in this argument. See Burnyeat et al., eds., *Notes on Book Z*, 11–16, for an interpretation which, like Dancy's and Stahl's, takes change to be critical in Z.3.

which we are assessing a criterion for *ousia*hood formulated exclusively in terms of the notion of predicating one thing of another seems reasonable; it seems equally reasonable to assume that the attempt to identify what its proponents are committed to construing as *ousia* should proceed by some kind of stripping away of predicates. But we should be careful here, for we might take this insight as license for thinking that, since the criterion takes *ousia* to be the subject that is never predicate, the proper strategy for identifying its candidates for status as *ousia* is to think away every feature of an object in the hopes of finding the featureless substratum of which those features are predicated. This line of thought (plausibly attributed to Locke, Bergmann, and Russell)[15] has certainly been associated with our Z.3 text,[16] and it has been justly derided.[17] But any attribution of this line of thought to Aristotle must be problematic. For one thing, it commits Aristotle to the perplexing assumption that, when we mentally strip away that universal in virtue of which a thing is *P*, the result of our mental operation is something that is not *P*.[18] For another, it totally ignores the background against which Aristotle develops the argument of Z.3. The subject criterion does not come out of thin air, and the subject theorist is not an invented straw man. In Z.3, Aristotle is criticizing views he once held himself. However naive subsequent proponents of ultimate subjects may have been, the Aristotle of the *Categories* and the *Posterior Analytics* was far too sophisticated to be refuted by any argument that takes basic subjects to be unpropertied possessors of properties, and the Aristotle of Z.3 can be depended on to realize this. So we should expect to find some common ground that the early Aristotle might accept if he is to be convinced that his criterion for *ousia*hood is unacceptable. That common ground is suggested in (9), for, although the Aristotle of the *Categories* would surely reject (9) as it stands [and, hence, we need to argue for it in (10) and (11)], the idea that the to be of a subject is different from that of at least some (perhaps, most) of the things predicated of it is one that we have seen to be critical in Aristotle's early

---

[15]See Locke's *Essay*, bk. 2, chap. 23; Gustav Bergmann's *Realism* (Madison: University of Wisconsin Press, 1967), 24–25; and Bertrand Russell's "The Philosophy of Logical Atomism" in *Logic and Knowledge*, ed. R. C. Marsh (London: George Allen and Unwin, 1956), 199–204.

[16]Among others, I make this mistake in *Substance and Attribute* (Dordrecht: Reidel, 1978), 110–111.

[17]Dancy ("Aristotle's Second Thoughts," 398) calls the view an "idiocy."

[18]See Stahl, "Stripped Away," 178–179, for a discussion of this assumption. Stahl mistakenly assumes that if we reject this assumption we have to deny that the terminus of stripping is something really and not just intentionally different from our initial sample object.

theory of *ousia*. I want to suggest that this idea lies at the core of Aristotle's metaphorical talk of stripping away.

As I see it, Z.3's notion of stripping away is continuous with and no more problematic than the formulae used in *Posterior Analytics* A.4 and A.22 for identifying basic subjects. The idea there was that if we wish to specify the proper subjects of genuine predications we should look to the general terms that hold true of a thing and eliminate those that hold true of it in virtue of its "being something different."[19] Having set these expressions (those signifying mere accidents) to one side, we were assured that the remaining general terms identify the thing as that something different and, accordingly, apply to it "not being something different"; and we were told that such expressions pick out basic subjects and signify "this something" and *ousia* (73$^b$7–8). It is just this insight, I take it, that the Aristotle of Z.3 exploits in arguing against his own early attempt at identifying *ousia*. To determine what the basic-subject criterion is committed to according status as *ousia*, we take some sample object and strip away those features that belong to it in virtue of its being something else. So, in (3) we eliminate the affections, qualities, and capacities of the sample, since clearly the angry, the pale, and the physically strong are so called only in virtue of being something different. In (4) we eliminate the quantitative features (both determinate and determinable[20]) that give spatial shape, figure, and size to an object; once again, the tall, the fat, the six-footed are so called in virtue of being something different. In (5), we remind ourselves why we are stripping these off: they are accidents and require something else as their subjects. This latter, by our criterion, should be *ousia*.

But, then, what is left in (6)? We are told that it is something that is marked out by the spatial dimensions stripped away in (4), and commentators often take this something to be matter, something like the bronze making up the statue of 1029$^a$5.[21] Initially, (7) seems to confirm this reading, since it appears to state the terminus of the stripping process initiated at (2). But (7) does not follow from (2–6); nor, I think, did Aristotle take it to follow. At this point, we have set to one side only the various accidental features of our sample. The substance-predicates have not yet been stripped away. Indeed, it is only in (8), where Aristotle tells us that matter is not something essentially or in its own right, that the substance-predicates of an object enter the discussion, and it is

[19]See 73$^b$7, 81$^b$27, 83$^a$13.
[20]See Schofield, "*Metaphysics* Z.3," 98–99, for a discussion of this issue.
[21]See Dancy, "Aristotle's Second Thoughts," 395; Joan Kung, "Can Substance Be Predicated of Matter?" *Archiv fur Geschichte der Philosophie* (1978), 140–159, especially 150–153; and Irwin, *Aristotle's First Principles*, 208–209.

not until (9–11) that we are given any reasons for thinking that sub-stance-universals can, in any fashion, be stripped away; and the fact is that if the argument is to convince a proponent of the early view, reasons have to be given here.

It is not just (6) and (7) that can lead us astray on this score. If we assume that the sample Aristotle has in mind throughout this argument is the statue of 1029ᵃ5, this is a natural mistake to make. Although it serves as a handy tool for introducing the notions of matter and form without intrusive commentary, the statue is precisely the wrong kind of example to invoke in a criticism of *Categories* theorists. As we have seen, such theorists would object that statues are not things they number among the basic subjects and would contend that precisely the consid-erations underlying their refusal so to classify them make them inap-propriate samples for a stripping process grounded in the formulae of *Posterior Analytics* A.4 and A.22.[22] Statues are artifacts, so a sharp and clear distinction between what is predicated essentially and what is predicated accidentally just does not obtain here. The spatial features that determine the shape of the bronze or the marble are included in the features that we abbreviate in calling it such and such a statue. Accord-ingly, if we have this kind of example in mind, it is only natural to assume that once we have set length and breadth and depth aside all that remains is bronze, our earlier paradigm of matter. But any example that assimilates or reduces substance-universals to universals only acci-dentally predicated of a thing is one that a theorist schooled in the *Categories* and *Posterior Analytics* is bound to reject; the fact that the Aristotle of Z.3 feels compelled to give substance-universals special treatment in (9–11) shows that he appreciates this fact.

The kind of sample Aristotle has in mind throughout the argument is not a statue, then, but some such thing as an olive tree or a man. In (2–5), we set aside those features of our sample that are present in some-thing else; what we have in (6) is just what the formula of *Posterior Analytics* A.4 and A.22 promises us, that which our sample is without being something different, a man or an olive tree. But, then, (7) cannot be a statement of what has already been shown. Indeed, it is not until we reach (14) that we have the conclusion stated only tentatively in (7). Step (7) does no more here than provide a prospective statement of what follows if we supplement the stripping process as so far carried out with whatever further stripping might be justified by (8–11).[23] The

[22]For the Z–H expression of this view, see H.2 (1042ᵇ14ff., especially 1043ᵃ4–5).

[23]The repeated use of '*gar*' (at 1029ᵃ21 and 23) confirms the hypothesis that (7) is a prospective statement of what Aristotle seeks to prove rather than a statement of what has been proved.

something mentioned in (6), as I have argued, is not matter but a perfectly familiar thing like an olive tree or a man; the idea that it is marked out by length, breadth, and depth is just the idea that men and olive trees come in definite heights and sizes, that we can think of these attributes as different ways in which the instantiations of substance-kinds are made spatially determinate. Indeed, it may even be that the use of 'something' in (6) is precisely the use it has in (8) and (12), where it functions not as a topic-neutral quantifier but as a placeholder for substance-predicates.[24]

It seems, then, that more work needs to be done if we are to succeed in showing that the subject theorist is committed to the idea that it is matter as characterized in (8) that has the best claim to status as *ousia*. Although it turns out to be slightly misleading, we can put the point by saying that the stripping process must be carried one step further—and this is precisely what the theorist of the *Categories* denies is possible. This theorist insists that once we have stripped away affections, qualities, capacities, and quantitative features, what we have are such things as men and olive trees; these things represent the terminus of the stripping process. The theorist may concede that the pale, the strong, and the upright are all so called in virtue of being something different, but a man is a man without being something else. A man is just what he is, so men provide us with basic subjects, and the familiar criterion yields precisely its intended result.

What we have here is an appeal to the early essentialism. The *Categories* theorist insists that the substance-universals marking out a thing as what it is serve to constitute the basic subjects of predication and so cannot be stripped away. Although a quick reading of the text might suggest otherwise, the strategy of Z.3 is not to challenge this claim but to ignore it. Instead, Aristotle implicitly appeals to a line of argument we discussed briefly in Chapter 1, section 5. We considered there the hypothetical possibility that one of Aristotle's favored candidates for status as *ousia* might belong to its lowest-level kind only in virtue of some prior predicative tie linking a lower-level subject to something said of or present in it. We argued that, were this possibility to be realized, the subject theorist would be committed to denying that the mere fact that our original object satisfied our definition of a basic subject would constitute sufficient grounds for construing it as a pri-

---

[24]In (8) and (12) it is a placeholder for substance-predicates; but the predicates in question are probably not substance-kind terms, but substance-form terms, although it would be easy enough to reformulate my claims if we were to insist that '*ti*' is playing its more familiar role as placeholder for substance-kind terms. The relationships between the two kinds of substance terms is explored in Chapter 4.

mary *ousia*. Its status as basic subject would, in that situation, be only derivative; it would be the lower-level subject with the stronger claim to status as *ousia*. The insight underlying (9–11) is that the situation just described is no merely hypothetical possibility but the sober metaphysical truth. Even if the individual man and horse of the *Categories* belong to their kinds essentially and their so belonging cannot be stripped away, they do not thereby provide the subject theorist an appropriate terminus in the search for a basic subject.

What I claim, then, is that Aristotle's strategy is to argue that the Unanalyzability Thesis fails in the case of the subject theorist's favored candidates for status as basic subjects; his argument for this claim is found in (9–11). In (9), he makes a general claim that the *Categories* theorist is bound to resist, that "there is something of which each of these is predicated for which the to be is something different from that of each of the things predicated." The preceding step (8) makes a reference to predicates from all categories, not just accidents but substance-universals as well, so the reference in (9) cuts across universals from all categories. The claim seems to be that, for all such universals, that of which they are predicated is something which, while characterized by those universals is nonetheless something different. Since the *Categories* theorist endorses (9) only when it is restricted to the case in which what gets predicated is something present in another, Aristotle needs to make plausible the extension of (9) to cover the case of *ousia*. So, after repeating in (10) the contention of *Posterior Analytics* A.4 and A.22 that "the others" one and all require *ousia* as subject, Aristotle tells us in (11) that *ousia* is predicated of matter.

Unfortunately, it is easy to misunderstand Aristotle here.[25] The argument delineated by (1–17) operates at a fairly general level. It is meant to provide a kind of overview of the terrain, so Aristotle proceeds by way of broad strokes and fails to fill in the details. The result is that frequently the bald statements of Z.3 stand in need of elaboration and fine tuning. That turns out to be the case as regards the claim that matter as characterized in (8) is what we get when we apply the subject criterion.[26] It is also true in the case of the suggestion in (17) that both form and composite are separable and "this something."[27] More to the point,

[25]Schofield, I fear, does. If I understand him, he is suggesting that the concrete thing can be predicated of the matter. See "*Metaphysics* Z.3," 97.

[26]I am thinking here of the fact that Aristotle's characterization does not make it clear whether it is prime matter or familiar, proximate matter that he has in mind. I discuss the problem below.

[27]The question here is whether it is in a single sense that form and composite are (a) separate and (b) subject to the "this something" schema. This is a problem I deal with in later chapters.

the claim made in (11) that *ousia* is predicated of the matter in conjunction with the claim in (10) that "the others" are predicated of *ousia*
suggests that Aristotle is talking about one and the same thing in the
two cases, that the very *ousia* that is subject of accidents is the "this" he
tells us in (11) is predicated of matter. But this grotesque suggestion is
completely at odds with what we find elsewhere in Z and H.[28] Indeed,
the ensuing chapters of Z and H as well as texts from *Metaphysics* Θ
make it perfectly clear just which doctrine Aristotle means to be abbreviating in the very curt (11).[29] The *ousia* that is subject for accidents is the
composite. It is a particular, and Aristotle nowhere wants to suggest
that it is predicated of anything at all. Nor does he want to suggest that
the kinds under which an individual composite *ousia* falls are predicated
of it or of anything else accidentally. Socrates is still essentially a man;
we cannot strip away his being a man. A central doctrine of Z and H
(one we later examine in great detail) is, however, the contention that
Socrates' being a man itself hinges on a prior predication. It is because
the matter making up Socrates has predicated of it the relevant form
that Socrates is a man, so his belonging to his lowest-level kind turns
out to be analyzable in terms of some more basic predicative tie, one
relating the form (which, in anticipation of later results from Z and H,
he here calls *ousia*) and the matter. It is this predication that Aristotle has
in mind in (11), and this predication, it turns out, holds only accidentally. To use the language of *Posterior Analytics* A.22, the form applies to
the matter in virtue of the matter's being something different. Accordingly, Aristotle can deny in (8) and (12) that matter is (a) something (i.e.,
subject for *its* substance-predicate, form) in its own right, and the
predication he mentions in (11) turns out to conform to the general
characterization provided in (9). Just as in the case of an accident being
predicated of an ordinary particular, the predication of form of matter
(the very predication on which rests the ordinary particular's being the
kind of thing it is) involves a subject "for which the to be is something
different from that" of the thing predicated. The upshot is that the
*Categories* theorist, being committed to denying that things that are basic
subjects only derivatively deserve status as *ousia*, is forced to descend a

---

[28]Actually, things are even more complicated. The problem is not merely that the use of
'*ousia*' in (10) and the use of 'this' in (11) suggest (what is false) that there is one and the
same thing that is subject for accidents and predicate for matter. There is the further
difficulty that in (10) and (11) '*ousia*' is playing a role quite different from that operative
throughout the rest of Z.3. Elsewhere in the chapter, '*ousia*' has its standard sense; but in
(10) and (11) the term and its stand-in 'this' serve as tags for picking out the things that the
Aristotle of Z and H wants to construe as the realities—the composite and the form.

[29]See, e.g., H.2 (1043$^a$5–11). This doctrine is examined in detail in Chapters 4 and 5.

level in the search after the primary realities and to hold that it is matter that is *ousia*.

IV

But what is the force of the claim that matter is *ousia*? It might be thought that the characterization of matter provided by (8) and repeated and expanded in (12–13) provides an answer, but it turns out that the characterization is subject to two quite different interpretations, each entailing a different answer to our question. Step (8) tells us that matter is "that which is said to be essentially neither (a) something nor quantified nor any of the other things by which being is marked out." Step (12) abbreviates (8), and (13) expands on it by denying that what Aristotle has in mind in (8) has predicated of it essentially the complements of any of the predicates within the range of (8). The reading we are initially tempted to give takes these formulae to deny that anything that might be predicated of what Aristotle calls matter is predicated of it essentially. Matter is, then, something with no essential features whatsoever. If we look for something that satisfies this characterization (we will not ask whether it does so essentially or nonessentially!), we are led to what Aristotle elsewhere calls first, primary, or prime matter.[30]

We can get at this idea if we recall that in *Physics* B.2 Aristotle tells us that 'matter' is a *pros ti* or relative term (194b9–15).[31] A portion of bronze, for example, is not said to be matter in its own right, but only in relation to some form that it might take on (in which case, it is said to be potentially whatever that form is) or that it has taken on (in which case, it is said to be actually that).[32] So our piece of bronze can be said to be matter for the shape in virtue of which it is a statue of George Washington. Before the casting, it can take on that shape; after the casting, it actually has or is that shape and so constitutes the statue.[33] But we can also think of the piece of bronze all by itself, and then it is not being thought of as matter at all. Indeed, given Aristotle's chemical theory, we can think of it as something having a matter and form. It is something made up of portions of more elementary kinds of stuff organized,

---

[30]But Aristotle does sometimes use 'first matter' to refer to the proximate matter (which he usually calls 'last matter'). See King, "Aristotle without *Prima Materia*," 370–374, for a nice discussion of the different uses of 'first' here.

[31]See also *Metaphysics* H.4 (1044ª15–24).

[32]See *Metaphysics* Θ.6 (1048ª25–1048b8) and Θ.8 (1050ª15–17).

[33]I do not mean to suggest that the statue is the example operative in the argument expressed in (1–17). The statue just provides a handy example of the relativity of matter.

structured, or put together in some particular way. And, perhaps, each of those portions of stuff can likewise be understood to be composites of something that plays the role of matter and something that plays the role of form.[34] Aristotle's own view is that the four Empedoclean elements (what he often calls the simple bodies) represent the terminus of this kind of chemical analysis. He believes, however, that the elements are reciprocally generated from each other. Water comes to be from air; air, from fire; and so forth. Consequently, commentators tell us, there must be some matter common to the four elements.[35] Although it always exhibits one of the clusters of features (Aristotle calls them contrarieties) that characterize the elements,[36] it is potentially some other element; therefore, it has none of these clusters of features essentially. So, the story goes, we have something that fails to exhibit even the most elementary characterizations of physical stuff in its own right or essentially. Accordingly, it satisfies the characterization of (8), (12), and (13): there is no universal, regardless of category, that is predicated of it essentially.

There are a significant number of texts that confirm the hypothesis that Aristotle accepted a first matter of this sort,[37] so a common (perhaps, the most common) reading of Z.3 takes Aristotle to be referring to this notion of matter and to be arguing that it is this that the subject theorist is committed to construing as *ousia*.[38] On this reading it is easy to see how the argument goes. The notion of separation at work in (16) is subject to a variety of interpretations.[39] Since I examine this issue

[34]See, again, H.4 ($1044^a15-24$).

[35]For accounts defending the traditional view of prime matter, see Friedrich Solmsen, "Aristotle and Prime Matter," *Journal of the History of Ideas* (1958), 243–252; H. M. Robinson, "Prime Matter in Aristotle," *Phronesis* (1974), 168–188; C. J. F. Williams, *Aristotle's De Generatione et Corruptione* (Oxford: Oxford University Press, 1982), especially 211–219; and Dancy, "Aristotle's Second Thoughts."

[36]The contraries hot/cold and dry/moist pair off (hot/dry; cold/dry; hot/moist; cold/moist) to give us fire, earth, air, water.

[37]Solmsen, Robinson, and Williams (see note 35) list and discuss the relevant texts. The most revealing text is *De Generatione et Corruptione* B.1 ($329^a24-329^b5$).

[38]See Interpretation A in Burnyeat et al., eds., *Notes on Book Z*, 11–16; Robinson, "Prime Matter in Aristotle," 183–187; Joseph Owens, *The Doctrine of Being in the Aristotelian Metaphysics* (Toronto: Pontifical Institute of Medieval Studies, 1957), 200–202; Joseph Owens, "Matter and Predication in Aristotle," reprinted in J. M. E. Moravscik, *Aristotle* (New York: Doubleday, 1967), 191–214; W. D. Ross, *Aristotle's Metaphysics* (Oxford: Oxford University Press, 1924), vol. 1, xciii–xciv; and Alan Code, "Aristotle on Essence and Accident," in Richard E. Grandy and Richard Warner, eds., *Philosophical Grounds of Rationality* (Oxford: Oxford University Press, 1983), 411–444, especially 434.

[39]See, e.g., Gail Fine, "Separation," *Oxford Studies in Ancient Philosophy* (1984), 31–87; Donald Morrison, "Separation in Aristotle's *Metaphysics*," *Oxford Studies in Ancient Philosophy* (1985), 125–157; Dancy, "Aristotle's Second Thoughts," 399–408; and Kung, "Can Substance Be Predicated of Matter?" 144–148.

later, I do not here choose between these interpretations; but it should be clear that however we understand the notion (whether in terms of ontological independence, numerical distinctness and individuation, etc.), prime matter turns out to lack the requisite separability. If we leave, for the time being, the notion of separation unexplained, the appeal of (16) to the "this something" schema has, as we have seen, a ready explanation in terms of the themes we have called Aristotle's essentialism; and having no features whatsoever essentially, prime matter surely fails to conform to this schema. There is no universal such that being a particular instance of that universal is *what* prime matter is; hence (15), and hence the inadequacy of the subject criterion.

How exactly does the argument we are considering bring prime matter on the scene? Presumably, we are to understand the stripping away licensed by (11) to be reiterated for whatever matter the original appeal to (11) introduced into our analysis and to continue in this way until we reach prime matter. If our sample is an olive tree, then (11) tells us that it is an olive tree in virtue of a predicative link tying the matter composing it to the appropriate form. Suppose that matter is a portion of cortex and a portion of phloem. Since each of these can be treated as a composite, (11) tells us that the Unanalyzability Thesis fails for them as well. Accordingly, we must descend a level, identifying, for each, the matter and form in virtue of which they are the kind of stuffs they are— and so on until we reach a matter for which the Unanalyzability Thesis is not falsified.[40] It turns outs, however, that the fact that that thesis is not falsified by the relevant matter is no consolation for the subject theorist, since it is only because there is no sort of thing such that the matter is essentially that sort of thing that the thesis is not falsified. Since the matter does not submit to the "this something" schema, we have only vacuous nonfalsification. So the subject theorist, on this interpretation, cannot locate a basic subject that conforms to both essentialism and the Unanalyzability Thesis. Hence (15); hence the inadequacy of the subject criterion.

However clear this interpretation may seem, it has its problems. First, not all commentators take it to be so obvious that Aristotle actually endorses the view that there is such a thing as prime matter.[41] In part,

---

[40]*Metaphysics* α.2 (994ª1–994ᵇ6) assures us that the descent will have only a finite number of steps.

[41]See King, "Aristotle without *Prima Materia*"; Charlton, *Aristotle's Physics I and II*, 129–145; Charlton, "Prime Matter: A Rejoinder"; and Furth, *Substance, Form, and Psyche*, 221–226. See also Barrington Jones, "Aristotle's Introduction of Matter," *Philosophical Review* (1975), 474–500. Although Jones is primarily concerned with *Physics* A.7, he challenges the assumption that Aristotle endorses a doctrine of prime matter; see especially 474–476.

one suspects, their reluctance to attribute the notion to Aristotle stems from their own view that the concept is (like Locke's "something I know not what" and Bergmann's bare particulars) a source of philosophical embarrassment; still, they are able to point to texts that seem to call into question the relevant attribution.[42] But even if one has no qualms about making the attribution, there is nothing in the argument of Z.3 that dictates or even suggests the multiple reiterations of the stripping process that are required by the interpretation that reads prime matter into Z.3. Aristotle never uses the term 'prime matter', and he never relates (11) to the themes of chemical analysis, reciprocal generation of simple bodies, and the like which surround his alleged appeal to prime matter.

There is, then, reason to question the original reading of Z.3. But is it not the case that (8) and (11–12) tell against any alternative reading? Do they not require as ultimate subject something that has predicated of it essentially nothing whatsoever? Not necessarily. Although one can take (8) and (11–12) to deny that there is anything at all that is predicated essentially of the matter that is Aristotle's focus in Z.3, one can also take his denial to be contextually restricted to the predicates that the process of stripping off has so far eliminated.[43] In the case of predicates from categories other than *ousia*, the restriction would likely be vacuous,[44] but in the case of substance-predicates, it would have real force. On this reading, the denial that matter is something essentially is merely the denial that the matter we are focusing on has predicated of it essentially that form in virtue of which the individual it composes is the kind of thing it is; but the denial would extend no further. Accordingly, the matter in question might in fact be quite familiar stuff that is in its own right whatever kind of stuff it is (e.g., flesh, bone, cortex, phloem).[45] Aristotle's point would be that, relative to the substance-predicate

---

[42]King and Charlton (see note 41) list and discuss the relevant texts. See, especially, *De Caelo* Γ.6 (305ᵃ14–32).

[43]Dancy's intentionalist interpretation of matter allows him to claim that (11–12) are verified by any instance of matter (i.e., any object viewed from the perspective of changeability), so talk of level restriction is unnecessary on his account.

[44]I say "likely" here since one might want to hold that the matter making up an object has accidents that cannot be understood to be accidents of the individual it makes up. But to deny, as (10) and other texts (e.g., 1038ᵇ5–6 and 1049ᵃ26–34) suggest we should, that matter is the subject of accidents is not to deny that there is an important connection between the accidents whose subject is the composite *ousia* and the matter composing that *ousia*. *Metaphysics* E.2 (1027ᵃ13) suggests that the matter making up a composite *ousia* is somehow the source of the accidents predicated of the composite.

[45]Dancy ("Aristotle's Second Thoughts"), Schofield ("Metaphysics Z.3"), Kung ("Can Substance Be Predicated of Matter?"), and Furth (*Substance, Form, and Psyche*) all take the matter of (14) to be familiar matter. While believing Aristotle to be committed (on empirical rather than philosophical grounds) to the existence of prime matter, Dancy thinks it does not appear in Z.3.

which at that stage of the analysis we are interested in, the matter is not separate, nor does it have predicated of it essentially the corresponding form. So the point would be that, relative to the level of substance characterization under consideration, what we identify as matter fails to meet, for that level of characterization, the test of essentialism; is it not, relative to that level, something that has the separability (however interpreted) of the individual it composes. Hence (15); hence the unacceptability of the basic-subject criterion.

It might seem to be a shortcoming in Aristotle's argument as so interpreted that the subject theorist can concede the objection but overcome it by pointing to the fact that there is some lower-level substance-predicate such that the matter in question has that predicate holding of it essentially. But if the theorist invokes that strategy, then it is presumably open to Aristotle to repeat the pattern of reasoning in the case of that matter—arguing that, since for that lower-level substance characterization the Unanalyzability Thesis fails, something of a yet lower level will turn up playing the role of matter for form. And, like our original matter, it will fail to meet the standards of minimal essentialism for that level of analysis. Hence, again, (15); hence, again, the unacceptability of the basic-subject criterion.[46] Unless obtuse, the subject theorist will come to appreciate the impossibility of identifying a basic subject of predication which, *for one and the same level of analysis*, meets the requirements of essentialism and passes the unanalyzability test—the impossibility, that is, of finding a nonderivative basic subject for which there is something such that being that is just what the subject is.

There are, then, two ways of reading the claim that the subject theorist is committed to identifying matter as *ousia*. Quite frankly, I am not certain which reading is correct. As I argue later when I discuss the notion of prime matter at greater length, the textual evidence in favor of the view that Aristotle believes in prime matter is weighty; and the notion is less philosophically troublesome, I think, than philosophers

[46]Just how many levels one can descend here depends on whether one sees Aristotle as endorsing a doctrine of prime matter. Those who do not must offer an account of the elemental transformations. King and Furth, for example, understand the generation of the elements in terms of the replacement and recombination of the hot, cold, dry, and moist, taking Aristotle to hold that only one of a pair of the four principles is replaced at a time, so that the remaining contrary persists. See King, "Aristotle without *Prima Materia*," 377–385, and Furth, *Substance, Form, and Psyche,* 221–226. Charlton insists that for Aristotle the underlying subject of change need not persist through the change. It is merely that which exists prior to the process and changes into whatever it is that comes to be. Accordingly, fire can be the subject for elemental transformation by changing into, say, air without anything remaining through the change. See Charlton, *Aristotle's Physic I and II,* especially 140. See Section II of Chapter 7 for a detailed discussion of these issues.

often lead us to believe.[47] I also think that the initially more natural reading of (8) and (13) is that which gives unrestricted range to the denial that matter is something essentially. But the reading that restricts the denial is surely a possible reading, one that is confirmed by the fact that Aristotle neither refers to prime matter by name here nor suggests the reiteration of the stripping process for the descending levels of substance characterizations.

In the end, it does not much matter which reading is correct, since the argument of Z.3 seems to go through in either case.[48] Indeed, the logic of the argument is much the same on both readings. Leaving aside the issue of separation for later treatment and taking the reference to sub-stance-predicates in (8) and (11) to have unrestricted range, we can take the argument to be that, since at each successive level of substance-characterization the Unanalyzability Thesis fails, the subject theorist is led to construe as *ousia* something that has nothing whatsoever predi-cated of it essentially. On the other hand, if we take the reference to substance-predicates to have the restricted range of the second inter-pretation, then the upshot of Aristotle's argument is that at whatever level of substance characterization the subject theorist cares to apply the criterion, the failure of the Unanalyzability Thesis at that level entails that the theorist's candidate for *ousia* will, relative to that level, fail to exhibit a substance-predicate essentially. On either interpretation, then, we have the failure of the Unanalyzability Thesis precluding joint ac-ceptance of the subject criterion and essentialism.

It is not surprising that the argument turns out to be the same on both interpretations, for what drives the argument just is the overarching pattern of reasoning in which the component themes of the early work are embedded. Aristotle concedes, indeed exploits, the idea that to accept both the subject criterion and essentialism is to commit oneself to the truth of the Unanalyzability Thesis for the things one construes as the primary *ousiai*. But since he now takes the explanatory framework of matter and form to show that the Unanalyzability Thesis fails for the primary *ousiai* of the *Categories* as well as for the matter out of which they are composed, he sees the subject theorist as committed to construing

[47]A really ingenious defense of Aristotle is found in Sheldon Cohen, "Aristotle's Doc-trine of the Material Substrate," *Philosophical Review* (1984), 171–194. I find myself agreeing with most of what Cohen says; but Daniel Graham, in "The Paradox of Prime Matter," *Journal of the History of Philosophy* (1987), 475–490, does not; see especially pp. 484–488. See also G. E. M. Anscombe's "Aristotle" in Anscombe and Geach, *Three Philosophers*, 51–52, for a defense of the concept of matter.

[48]Here I agree with Carl Page, "Predicating Forms of Matter in Aristotle's *Metaphysics*," *Review of Metaphysics* (1985), 57–82. See especially 73.

as *ousia* something for "which there is no saying what" it is.[49] On the reading that assumes prime matter, there is no saying at all since there is nothing whatsoever that prime matter is essentially. On the second reading, although there may be something such that it is what the candidate for *ousia*hood is, it is always the wrong thing; and even it slips through our fingers when we press it in vindication of essentialism.


V


We have seen in the previous section that what appears to be an attack on the subject criterion of the early theory is really a formal pronouncement of Aristotle's assessment of the whole theoretical framework in which that criterion is embedded. But if it succeeds on this score, it does so only at the cost of raising a plethora of questions. The argument concludes with (17), which tells us that, in the light of the standards set by the separability condition and the "this something" schema, the composite and the form have a stronger claim to status as *ousia* than does matter. As I suggested earlier, it turns out to be no easy task to explain how both form and composite can be separate and admit the "this something" schema.

Furthermore, if we think back to the beginning of the argument, we recall that Aristotle introduces (1–17) to show that the basic-subject criterion fails to tell the whole story about *ousia*. The suggestion was that, although there may be something right in the criterion, we need more if we are to succeed in properly identifying *ousia*. But Aristotle has failed to tell us what, if anything, is right in the criterion; if there is an insight here that is worth preserving, just how does Aristotle think it needs to be supplemented when he tells us that it is not enough?

The argument raises other questions as well. As we have seen, it relies heavily on doctrines it neither explains nor justifies. Just what is involved in Aristotle's claim that the Unanalyzability Thesis is falsified in the case of the concrete particulars of the *Categories* and the matter composing them? The suggestion seems to be that some prior instance of predication (one relating matter and form) underlies their belonging to their respective kinds. But what precisely does Aristotle have in mind here? What, if anything, is the ordinary expression of the relevant predications? What is there about the matter/form analysis that would lead us to see these predications as more basic than those the *Categories*

---

[49]This useful phrase comes from Dancy, "Aristotle's Second Thoughts," 373.

and *Posterior Analytics* took to lie at the foundation of any true account of the world?

If we endorse the picture hinted at in the argument, are we forced to see ordinary objects as mere constructions out of more basic, more real things and the species terms that apply to them as analogous to terms like 'merchant' and 'bricklayer' which appear to signify some one thing but in reality do not? In short, does the picture of levels of predication that seems to underlie the argument represent a kind of reductionism, however sophisticated, that renders the plain man's conception of the world as constituted by things like dogs, oak trees, and persons like himself just a sham? We are told in (17) that both form and the composite are better claimants to the title '*ousia*' than is matter. That may reassure us, but Aristotle does call them composites (are they *mere* composites?), and our reassurance is considerably weakened when we find Aristotle adding (repeating the suggestion of 1029ª6–7) that the composite is posterior to the form.

It is clear from (1–17) that the subject criterion, taken by itself, fails to provide the core for a theory of *ousia*. But what happens to the other components of the *Categories* account? Aristotle seems unwilling to give up the view that *ousia* is something or other essentially, that it has a what. But we have already noted the apparently cavalier attitude he seems inclined to take as regards the relationship between a composite and its kind. So how does the essentialism he wants to preserve find its expression in the theory of *ousia* he wants to defend? And what becomes of the Unanalyzability Thesis? If it fails in the case of ordinary objects, does it or anything analoguous to it continue to play a role in Aristotle's account of *ousia*? And if the answer is affirmative, what is the warrant for an appeal to a thesis whose underpinnings have been so severely undermined?

Z.3 may make a pronouncement on the early views, but it raises more questions than it answers. I think it was intended to do just that. It is, after all, a kind of introduction to what follows; if it leads us to the questions and puzzles that are the focus of the middle books, it has, I think, the intended result. Armed with these questions, then, let us try to work our way through the jungle that is Z and H.

CHAPTER 3

# A Framework for Essences

I

As we have seen in Chapter 2, the opening lines of Z.3 suggest the *ti ein einai* as one candidate for status as *ousia*. At the beginning of Z.4 (1029$^b$ 12–13), Aristotle invokes the suggestion to motivate a discussion of the *ti ein einai* that carries us through Z.6. '*To ti ein einai*' is usually translated 'essence', and although I follow the custom it requires some commentary. We are accustomed to understand the distinction between the essential and the nonessential in terms of the distinction between what is de re necessary and de re contingent. To the extent that he had a firm grasp of the concept of de re modality, Aristotle did not see it as fundamental in the distinction between the essential (*kath hauto*) and the accidental (*kata sumbebekon*).[1] There are attributes (the *idia* or properties introduced at *Topics* A.4) which are de re necessary to their subjects but which Aristotle would not, in the strict sense, take to be essential to them.[2] The central contrast, we have seen, is that between universals

---

[1]For attempts to understand the relationship between Aristotelian essentialism and contemporary discussions of de re modality, see Nicholas White, "Origins of Aristotle's Essentialism"; S. Marc Cohen, "Essentialism in Aristotle"; Alan Code, "Aristotle's Response to Quine's Objections to Modal Logic," *Journal of Philosophical Logic* (1976), 159–186; Michael Wedin, "Singular Statements and Essentialism in Aristotle"; and Charlotte Witt, *Substance and Essence in Aristotle*, chap. 6.

[2]See 102$^a$17–19 together with 102$^b$4–7, 103$^b$7–11, 73$^b$16–21, 74$^b$5–6, and 75$^a$13–14. Aristotle sometimes defines *kath hauto* predication disjunctively, so that one thing belongs to another *kath hauto* just in case either the first belongs to the What is it? of the second or the

that mark their subjects out as what they are and those that do not; although Aristotle tells us that those that do are necessarily predicated of their subjects, the necessity is derivative.[3] It is because a universal $U$ marks out a subject $s$ as what $s$ is that it is not possible for $s$ to exist and fail to instantiate $U$. Even in the case of universals necessarily but not essentially predicated of their subjects, Aristotle insists that the necessity be explained in terms of features that are, in his narrower sense, essential to those subjects.[4] Finally, Aristotle would likely challenge the idea that we have a notion of existence which can be understood independently of the features that are, in his narrower sense, essential to their subjects and to which we could appeal in an analysis of the essential in terms of the impossibility of an object's existing without instantiating a particular universal. There is no such thing as just existing; to exist is to instantiate a lowest-level essential predicate. So the prejudice in favor of those universals that enable us to identify what an object is runs deep; it extends to the analysis of 'exists' itself.

The notion of what, in this narrower sense, is essentially predicated of its subjects is not, however, quite the notion of the *ti ein einai*. Although the expression does not appear in the *Categories*, we find it in the *Topics* and the *Posterior Analytics*. Aristotle typically appends a kind term in the dative case to identify just which *ti ein einai* he is interested in, producing expressions that translate as 'the what it is to be for a man', 'the what it is to be for a horse', and 'the what it is to be for an olive tree'.[5] Aristotle tells us, first, that the *ti ein einai* for any sort of thing

---

second is the first recipient/proper subject of the first and enters into its What is it. See, e.g., 73ᵃ34–73ᵇ3. What I am calling essential predication is what is characterized in the first disjunct of this definition. Aristotle himself appreciates that the definition brings together two distinct kinds of case. See, e.g., 1022ᵃ24–32 and 1029ᵇ16–19, where the two cases receive separate treatment.

[3] See, again, *Posterior Analytics* A.4, where Aristotle defines the idea of one thing's belonging to another (at 73ᵃ34–73ᵇ1) *kath hauto* without reference to modal notions and then later (at 73ᵇ16–24) argues that this notion of a *kath hauto* connection must be the notion of a necessary connection.

[4] I have in mind here the idea that among the things we seek to establish by demonstration is the connection between a subject (some kind or other) and the properties commensurately universal with it and that we do so by reference to a definition that functions as middle term in the relevant demonstration.

[5] There is much discussion in the literature on the origins of the expression '*to ti ein einai*' and its precise sense. See, e.g., Emerson Buchanan, *Aristotle's Theory of Being* (Greek, Roman, Byzantine Monographs 2) (Cambridge, Mass., 1962); G. E. M. Anscombe, in Anscombe and Geach, *Three Philosophers*, especially 43; Christopher Kirwan, *Aristotle's Metaphysics, Books Γ, Δ, and E* (Oxford, 1971), especially 100; Hermann Weidemann, "In Defense of Aristotle's Theory of Predication," *Phronesis* (1980), 76–87; and Alan Code, "On the Origins of Some Aristotelian Theses about Predication," in James Bogen and James E. McGuire, eds., *How Things Are* (Dordrecht: Reidel, 1985), 101–131, especially 111. I am going against the mainstream in my suggestion that the expression in the dative

is that which is expressed by the definition of that sort (1030ª6–7) and, second, that definition gives us a complete account of what something is.[6] But this abbreviates. In the paradigmatic case, talk of the *ti ein einai* doubly involves an appeal to the What is it? question. The idea is that by reference to universals such as *man, horse,* and *olive tree* we can correctly answer the What is it? question posed of some sample object. But, then, we can go on to pose that question in the case of the universal that our original appeal to the question brings on the scene. In this context, the appeal to the question is not a request for a more general characterization of our sample object by way of some generic universal that *man, horse,* or *olive tree* subordinates.[7] It is rather a request for a complete account of what it is for something to be a man, a horse, or an olive tree. Given the idea that to be just is to instantiate a universal like one of these, the idea that to provide the relevant account is to identify what it is for things of the relevant kind to be would seem to be natural. Hence, perhaps, the awkward piece of technical jargon.

So the *ti ein einai* for a kind is what is expressed by an account that identifies what it is to be for things of that kind, and Aristotle frequently seems to take the idea of this account as fundamental. In both *Posterior Analytics* A.4 and *Metaphysics* Δ.18, he suggests that a universal is predicated essentially of a subject just in case reference to that universal is ingredient in stating the formula expressing the *ti ein einai* of that subject.[8] As it stands, the suggestion fails to give us a general characterization of essential predication since neither the lowest-level universal enabling us to answer the What is it? question for its subject nor the whole of what is expressed by its definition turns out to be essentially predicated of a subject; but the suggestion does mark Aristotle's intuition that the notion of *to ti ein einai* is a basic or fundamental notion and not the idea of a mere construction out of antecedently given features that are essential to their subjects.[9]

---

case does not translate as predicate nominative. Here, I agree with Weidemann. I see 1031ᵇ5–9 as providing some support here; but, as Code suggests, any account of the expression is conjectural.

[6]See, e.g., *Topics* A.5 (101ᵇ37–102ª2).

[7]As it is in *Topics* A.9, where Aristotle suggests the use of the What is it? question in connection with the categories. On this point, see the discussion of Section I of Chapter 1.

[8]See 73ª34–37 and 1022ª26–28. This is, to be sure, only a suggestion on Aristotle's part, but clearly attributing this kind of holism to Aristotle would help reinforce the idea in the early theory of *ousia* that species are not constructions out of a preexisting genus and differentia. It would also help us understand what Aristotle might be up to in Z.13, where (on one plausible interpretation) he is arguing against the idea that lowest-level forms are posterior to their genera. See the discussion of Section III of Chapter 6 for more on this point.

[9]For a different interpretation, see Code, "On the Origins of Some Aristotelian Theses about Predication," 111.

The idea of the *ti ein einai*, then, is the idea of what is expressed by a complete account of what it is to be for a certain kind of thing. Occasionally (as at 1022ª25–28), we find Aristotle referring to the essence of this or that individual. Although these references call for more detailed discussion later, let us assume that they do not imply that there is something necessarily unique to an individual such that existing for that individual and that individual alone consists in just that. Aristotle tells us that there is definition and hence essence only for universals, but the definition of a kind applies to all its members. Being members of that kind is just *what* they are, so instantiating the essence expressed by the relevant definition is what to be consists in for them. In a derivative sense, then, it is *their* essence. [10]

## II

Aristotle tells us that the concept of the *ti ein einai* presents us with a plausible candidate for status as *ousia*. But why should he have thought this? Toward answering this question, one might want to point to such texts as *Posterior Analytics* A.22 (83ᵇ14–15), where Aristotle says that universals essentially predicated of a subject are "in its *ousia*," or *Posterior Analytics* B.13 (96ª34–35) and (96ᵇ6), where we meet with the idea that a complete definition isolates "the *ousia* of the thing," and to relate these texts to the *Categories* idea that infimae species (the paradigmatic objects of definition in the *Organon*) are themselves *ousiai*, albeit secondary *ousiai*. The idea would be that even in the earliest writings on *ousia* Aristotle found the idea that what a thing is deserves the title '*ousia*' attractive, so that the suggestion of Z.3 and Z.4 is merely an outgrowth and development of Aristotle's own early thinking on *ousia*.

There is no doubt that, in the light of the mature view that identifies *ousia* with one case of essence, the Aristotle of Z and H exploits the kind of formulae we meet in the *Posterior Analytics* and that they are put to the service of the doctrine of the middle books. But it would be a mistake to read too much into their role in the logical writings. The idea that a complete definition or its constituent substance-predicates signify the *ousia* of a thing does not, in those works, express the emergence of any novel metaphysical insights. [11] Indeed, in two of the three *Posterior Analytics* texts I have mentioned, it is universals and definitions outside

---

[10]For a nice discussion of the ambiguity of 'essence of', see Montgomery Furth, "Aristotle on the Unity of Form," in Mohan Matthen, ed., *Aristotle Today* (Edmonton: Academic Printing and Publishing, 1986), 77–102, especially 79–80.

[11]For a possibly opposing view, see Dancy, *Sense and Contradiction*, 109–111.

the category of *ousia* that Aristotle is discussing. Although he was certainly committed to an essentialist interpretation of *ousiai*, he was firmly in the grips of the subject criterion at the time he wrote those texts. Even in the *Categories* the suggestion that species and genera can be called *ousiai* seems to be a source of modest embarrassment for Aristotle and is justified only by the fact that substance-kinds are themselves subjects of predication, although not basic subjects.[12]

Even if these uses of '*ousia*' are not precursors of the idea that essence is *ousia*, the early view contains the seeds of that idea. At the end of Chapter 1, I suggested that if we take seriously the central themes of the early theory, the idea that an inventory of basic subjects (where these are the familiar particulars of common sense) exhaustively determines the primary *ousiai* becomes questionable. Primary *ousiai* are the things on which other things are ontologically dependent but are not themselves, in the same way, ontologically dependent on other things. However, the essentialist claim that what basic subjects are is given by their *infimae species* suggests that those species deserve a status the early Aristotle refused to accord them. Even if we concede that species require concrete instantiations and hence depend on basic subjects for their existence, those basic subjects, in turn, could not exist without being instances or members of those same species. So, despite the fact that the Aristotle of the *Categories* grants only lowest-level species secondary status as *ousiai*, the mutual dependence here suggests a more liberal approach to the whole business of identifying primary *ousiai*, one that includes in the overall inventory of ontologically basic items those universals that fully mark out basic subjects as what they are. This is not quite the idea that essence is primary *ousia*, since the claim that species actually *are* essences has not yet been made out; it is, however, close enough to make the hypothesis that essence is *ousia* one worth investigating.

This hypothesis is also suggested by the intersection of two lines of thinking, one new and one old. The novel line of thinking is presented and developed in Z.4, where Aristotle argues against a democratic treatment of essence which accords equal status to the concept of *to ti ein einai* wherever it appears and suggests instead what I call a hierarchical conception of essence. The picture he conveys is that of a framework of levels of essence whose higher levels are constituted by essences that presuppose or depend on those of the various lower levels and whose fundamental or basic level is constituted by essences which, in the relevant way, presuppose or depend on no other essences. The old line

---

[12]See, once again, *Categories* 5 (2ᵇ37–3ᵃ5).

of thought is the familiar idea that the search after the primary realities is the search after things suited to play a certain explanatory role. As we have said, to identify the primary *ousiai* is to identify things whose existence does not turn on anything else and by reference to which we can explain why all other things exist. Given Aristotle's essentialist interpretation of existence, this explanation comes to focus on what things are, and the idea of primary *ousiai* becomes the idea of things such that, first, their being what they are hinges on nothing else and so stands in need of no explanation and, second, by reference to their being what they are, it is possible to explain why other things are what they are.

If we now reflect on the idea that the hierarchical conception of essence imposes on the theorist the task of identifying those essences that are fundamental in the sense that they presuppose no prior essences but essences of all other levels ultimately presuppose or depend on them, then a striking parallel emerges between the new attempt to identify basic essences and the older attempt to identify primary realities. In both cases, there is a concern with what things are; in both cases, the assumption is that there is a system of priorities and dependencies in virtue of which things are what they are and that the task of the theorist is to identify things basic to that system. Indeed, the parallel is so striking that it is difficult to resist the hypothesis that, perhaps, we do not have two searches here at all, but that the search after the fundamental essences and the search after the primary *ousiai* are just one and the same search.

III

As we begin Z.4, the idea that essence is *ousia* is only a hypothesis to be tested.[13] It is not confirmed until Z.6 ($1032^a5$ and $1031^b33–1032^a1$), where Aristotle argues that things that are both "primary and said to be whatever they are in their own right" are necessarily one and same as

---

[13]It might be objected here that since the Aristotle of Z and H shows a tendency to use the terms '*ousia*' and 'essence' almost interchangeably it is just an assumption of Z and H that essence is *ousia*. The fact is, however, that Z.6 is given over to a proof that certain essences (what I call the basic or foundational essences) are the primary *ousiai*. Once this has been proved, it is understandable that Aristotle would refer to the primary *ousiai* as essences and to the fundamental essences as *ousiai*. But there is an abbreviation convention at work here, for it turns out that not all essences are *ousiai*. Only the fundamental essences are. But even the thesis that the fundamental essences are *ousiai* is something Aristotle feels the need to prove. It is not an assumption of the Z–H analysis. For more on this point, see Section VII of Chapter 5.

their essences. In Z.4, Aristotle's concern is the more basic one of presenting and making plausible the hierarchical conception that suggests the hypothesis. The chapter begins with what looks like the attempt to provide a general characterization of the notion of essence, but it turns out that in the first half of the chapter Aristotle reserves the term 'essence' for the case of *ousia* and provides a set of progressively more stringent conditions geared to generate the result that only within that category do we have the notion of the what it is for something to be.

We are to proceed, Aristotle tells us, by focusing on linguistic facts related to the notion of essence; the first such fact he adduces is that "the essence of each thing is what it is said to be in its own right (*kath hauto*)" (1029$^b$13–14). This fact is introduced to locate talk of essences within the general context of essential predications, cases in which the predicate marks out its subject as what it is. But since Aristotle's use of the phrase '*kath hauto* predication' spans the case of essential predication and the case of an attribute being predicated of its proper subject or first recipient, he excludes the latter case (1029$^b$16–17). But even the notion of essential predication is too broad to capture the idea of the *ti ein einai*. A genus, for example, serves to answer the What it is? question with respect to its species. But an account of the essence of a species by reference exclusively to its genus is not sufficiently restrictive, so Aristotle sharpens the account by telling us (1029$^b$17–18) that we succeed in identifying the essence of something, *x*, by reference to something, *y*, only if it is true that to be *x* is to be *y* (or, if being *x* is being *y*). But this condition is trivially satisfied if we identify the essence of a universal *U* by referring just to *U* itself (the case where the *x* and *y* of our criterion are one and same term), so Aristotle tells us that "this is the formula of the essence of each thing, that formula which expresses the thing, but in which the thing itself is not present" (1029$^b$19–20). Tightening up the characterization to eliminate the use/mention confusion,[14] we can express Aristotle's proposed restriction here by saying that a formula (*logos*) *L* gives the essence of *x* just in case *L* provides an account of what *x* is without mentioning *x* itself.

But Aristotle finds even this account too broad. Toward convincing us of its inadequacy, he asks us (at 1029$^b$27–28) to suppose that the term 'cloak' abbreviates the expression 'white man'.[15] The characterization

---

[14]This may not be a use/mention confusion, but rather a kind of abbreviation convention. See Frank Lewis, "What Is Aristotle's Theory of Essence?" *Canadian Journal of Philosophy*, supp. vol. 10 (1984), 89–131, especially n. 7.

[15]The discussion of *cloak* is intriguing. At 1029$^b$29, we meet the objection that 'cloak' fails to signify something that is a *kath hauto legomenon*. Of course, Aristotle himself is committed to endorsing the view expressed in the objection, but for dialectical purposes he

just provided gives the result that the formula 'white man' expresses the essence of cloak, and Aristotle relies on our intuition that there is no essence here at all. As he puts it,

> Essence is just what something is; and whenever one thing is said of another, we do not have just what a "this something" is. For example, white man is not just what a "this something" is if indeed "this something" belongs only to *ousiai*. (1030ª3–6)

He concludes that we must restrict the proposed characterization by specifying that the formula L be a definition (1030ª6–7). In support of this restriction, he tells us that we have definition only in the case of things that are primary (1030ª10), and the primary things, of course, are *ousiai*.

These early remarks in Z.4 can be puzzling. We have already noted that when we look to *Posterior Analytics* A.4 or *Metaphysics* Δ.18, where Aristotle explains what he means by *kath hauto* or essential predication, we seem to find him telling us that essential predication occurs when what is predicated of a subject is something mentioned in the account of its *ti ein einai*, so the appeal to essential predication in the characterization of the notion of essence might strike us as circular. Further, Aristotle's choice of examples appears bizarre. Why appeal to the Goodmanesque universal *cloak* and use our reluctance to associate with it the notion of a what it is for something to be as grounds for concluding that essence is restricted to the case of *ousia*? One might agree that there is no essence for *white man* on the grounds that we really have two essences here, the essence of *man* and the essence of *white*.[16] But if that is our reason for refusing to posit an essence in the case of *cloak*, we are likely to find Aristotle's rush to the conclusion that only *ousiai* have an essence a trifle precipitous. We will want reasons for supposing that the color white lacks an essence, reasons we are not given here. In a similar vein, we are likely to question the appeal to the familiar formulae associated with the notion of *ousia* ("this something" and "just what something is")

---

puts an interpretation on '*kath hauto*' quite different from that intended in the objection and forestalls the objection, keeping cloak's claims to status as a *ti ein einai* alive until 1030ª2.

[16]It might be claimed that Aristotle would himself suggest that cloak fails to have an essence on the grounds that to call something a cloak is not to say what it is; it is rather to say how man is, namely, white. But if that were his view, it is difficult to see how, after things have been loosened up with the introduction of focal meaning, he can say that *white man* might have an essence after all. See 1030ᵇ12–13. In any case, there has been no argument to show that there is no essence associated with accident terms when these function as names of accidents rather than as predicates of *ousiai*.

and the assumption that their introduction settles matters. And finally, we cannot resist the suspicion that Aristotle's use of the term 'definition' here involves a mere stipulation that can hardly prove decisive.[17]

The fact is, however, that the opening remarks of Z.4 are not meant to establish or prove that only *ousiai* have essences. In the end, that is not even Aristotle's view. In Z.4 and Z.5, Aristotle tries to make plausible the idea that the totality of essences form a structured hierarchy of the sort I have described, and we can expect that in any such Aristotelian hierarchy, the essences that turn out to be foundational are those associated with the category of *ousia*. But Aristotle's strategy here is not to present us with an initial picture of a hierarchical framework and argue that the essences of *ousiai* constitute its foundation. On the contrary, he begins by characterizing a restrictive use of 'essence', one that he just stipulates is appropriate exclusively in the case of *ousia*. There is no argument in favor of the restriction on the term, although Aristotle surely relies on our willingness to agree that privileged status has to be accorded the category of *ousia*. It turns out that the restrictive use just is the use of the term to identify the foundational essences. But Aristotle's strategy at the beginning of Z.4 is to delineate a conception of essence which, although ultimately basic, is just too restrictive; his initial account is formulated to prompt questions and objections on precisely this score. Addressing those objections provides him the occasion to generalize the use of the term 'essence' and to argue that the relevant generalization presupposes the kind of hierarchical picture he wants to develop.

But things are a little more complicated than this. First, Aristotle's attempt to delineate this restrictive use of the term 'essence' has already planted the seeds of the idea that we cannot treat essences democratically. That was precisely the point of the cloak example. In introducing the case, Aristotle recognizes that, although we may agree with him in deciding to withhold the term 'essence' here, it was a tough decision. After all, there is such a thing as being a white man, so there ought to be something that this consists in; there ought to be an essence here. If, in the end, we did not challenge Aristotle's stipulation that there is none, it was, as we noted, only because we concluded that what it is for a white man to be is a kind of construction out of preexisting materials, materials provided by the essence of *man* and the essence of the color white.

---

[17]In Section IX, where I discuss Z.5 and the notorious discussion of snubness, I come up with an account that might explain his reluctance to use the term 'definition' in the case of accidents. The argument of Z.5, I suggest, is that in stating the definition of an accident we can never get it just right. Either we say too little or we say too much. But, then, if we take literally the idea of "setting boundaries" that is present in the term '*horismos*', we have to agree that we cannot, in a strict and literal sense, define accidents.

But it is precisely this line of thinking that Aristotle wants to drive us to; for to say that the essence of *white man* somehow presupposes other essences is already to endorse the kind of hierarchical picture Aristotle wants to develop. In the end, Aristotle concedes that there is an essence here, but an essence that is relatively far removed from the foundational level of essences. So when Aristotle introduces this example, he is deliberately confronting us with a marginal case, one for which, if we are willing to find essence at all, it is going to be a derivative sort of essence. He is softening us up for the hierarchical picture he introduces later in the chapter.

There is a second complication: although there can be no doubt Aristotle is stipulating that we reserve the term 'essence' for the case of *ousia*, the precise effect of this stipulation is left unclear. Readers of Z.3 (1029ª23–24) may recall Aristotle gesturing toward a doctrine, one presumably to be developed later in Z and H, that a composite *ousia*'s being the kind of thing it is rests on a prior predication, that in which the form is said of matter. Further, at 1029ª5–7 and 30–32 Aristotle has suggested that form's claims to status as *ousia* might be prior to those of the composite. But, then, the restriction of essence to the category of *ousia* could be understood in at least two different ways. Aristotle might be restricting the use of the term 'essence' to the case of form or to the case of the composite. Or does it matter? It turns out to matter, and to matter immensely, but in Z.4 Aristotle leaves these complications out of the picture. Indeed, readers of the *Categories* could read Z.4 and nod with approval, for Aristotle tells us only that essence is restricted to the case where we have something

> that is said to be whatever it is not by way of one thing's being said of another,

so that

> there will not be essence for anything that is not an *eidos* of a *genos*; but of these only will there be essence; for these do not seem to be called what they are by way of participation or affection or as an accident. (1030ª10–14)

Since readers of the *Categories* will refuse to see his lowest-level kinds as resting on some predicative link tying genus and differentia, they will read Aristotle's first remark as a claim whose force is to withhold the concept of essence from the case of *cloak* since something is called a cloak only if one thing (*white*) is said of another (*man*); and they will understand the second remark as restricting the notion of essence to the case of lowest-level substance-kinds. But '*eidos*' is typically used in Z and H to pick out form; and, since the notion of a form is subject to generalization by way of higher-level kinds,[18] the second remark could just as well represent the stipulation that only lowest-level substance-forms have an essence. It is not surprising that commentators disagree on just what Aristotle has in mind when he speaks here of things that are *eide genous*.[19]

What is clear is that, in the end, Aristotle insists that the infimae species of the *Categories* apply only in virtue of one thing's being said of another and concludes that the essences of forms rather than those of species constitute the fundamental level in the hierarchy he proposes. It would, however, be a mistake to appeal to these facts to support the claim that the use of '*eide*' here involves a direct reference to form. The business of stipulating a restrictive use of 'essence' is supposed to lead us to a picture of a hierarchical framework; the main point of Z.4 is to make this picture plausible. The business of filling out the details of the framework, including the precise identification of the essences that are to occupy the various levels in the hierarchy, must await the actual development of a theory of *ousia* in the ensuing chapters of Z and H. So it is in Aristotle's interest to leave as many issues unresolved as is consistent with the aim of making his conception of essence plausible. He wants to make all the friends he can, and insisting at this early stage on an excessively restrictive use of 'essence' would hardly have that effect. I am inclined to think, then, that the use of the expression '*eidos*' might be deliberately ambiguous. Looking back to Z.4 from the perspective of Z.17, say, or H.2, we will certainly want to claim that only in the case of form do we have fundamental essences; but at this stage of the analysis, Aristotle would likely be reluctant to disambiguate.

IV

As we have suggested, there is little in Z.4's initial delineation of the notion of essence to motivate the idea that accidents lack essences.

---

[18]This idea plays a key role in Z.10 and Z.12, but it can be found already in *Physics* B.3 (194$^b$26–28).

[19]See Ross, *Aristotle's Metaphysics*, vol. 2, 167, for the species interpretation, and Frank Lewis, "Form and Predication in Aristotle's *Metaphysics*," in James Bogen and James E. McGuire, eds., *How Things Are* (Reidel, 1985), 59–83, especially 74–75, for the form interpretation. I agree with Lewis that we cannot rush to judgment here and read this as 'species of a genus', but I suggest that Aristotle caught the ambiguity and saw in it a useful tool in Z.4 for making plausible the idea that only in the case of *ousia* do we have essence and definition. If I am right, then we should not insist on the translation 'form under a genus'. Unfortunately, we do not have ready at hand in English an expression with the

Aristotle points out that we cannot identify the essence of an *ousia* by reference to its accidents (1029[b]14–16), and he insists that there is no essence for "complexes" like *cloak*.[20] He does not in the initial discussion explicitly address the issue of essences for accidents themselves. So the most natural response to his restrictive account is to object that there are such things as the color *white* and the property of being musical and that there is such a thing as explaining what they are. Saying what these things are is not, as Aristotle seems to want to claim (see 1030[a]7–9, 14–16), just a matter of saying what certain words mean. The case of explaining what being musical or the color white is is not like the case of explaining how expressions like 'or', 'every', and 'for the sake of' function in English; it is, we want to say, a real case of explaining what it is for something to be.

Aristotle recognizes that his account prompts this objection; as soon as he has set out the restrictive account that limits the notion of essence to the case of *ousia*, he concedes that we can talk about the what it is of things other than *ousiai*. This concession leads him into a discussion of the semantics of the expressions 'what it is' and 'what it is to be'. He claims that, as they apply to qualities, quantities, and the like, these expressions have senses other than that operative in the case he has delineated. After considering a number of models for understanding the fact that these terms "are said in several ways," he fastens on the model provided by focal meaning, or the *pros hen*.[21]

The suggestion that there are distinct senses of the term 'essence' corresponding to the various categories might initially strike us as gratuitous, and the claim that the *pros hen* analysis provides us with the proper model for understanding the fact that 'essence' is said in several ways a somewhat feeble and rather artificial attempt to preserve, in the face of recalcitrant facts of usage, something of the restrictive account already outlined for us (for, of course, it turns out that it is the restrictive use that identifies for us the core meaning of the term 'essence'). But in fact Aristotle is antecedently committed to something like a *pros hen*

---

ambiguity that '*eidos*' has in Greek. Perhaps the best we can do to get the flavor of '*eidos*' here is the rather feeble 'species/forms under a genus'.

[20]Aristotle uses several different expressions for *ousia*/accident hybrids like *white man*. In Z.4 (1029[b]23) he speaks of *suntheta kata allas kategorias* and in Z.5 (1030[b]16) of *sundeduasmena*. Although the use of the term 'complex' can cause confusion (since *ousiai* themselves can be called matter/form complexes), I use the term to pick out *ousia*/accident hybrids and typically translate the terms Aristotle uses for matter/form compounds ('*sunolon*', '*suntheton*', and '*suneclermmenon*') as 'composite'. To guard against confusion, I use scare quotes to mark this special use of 'complex'.

[21]See 1030[a]17–20 and 1030[a]32–1030[b]3. For a slightly different approach to this section of Z.4, see Witt, *Substance and Essence in Aristotle*, 108–111.

·analysis of the term 'essence'. He holds that 'to be' exhibits focal meaning, and since his term for essence, 'what it is to be', is constructed out of that verb, it seems inevitable that it would inherit the semantical peculiarities of 'to be'.

Aristotle's inquiry into *ousia* opens in Z.1 (1028ª1–20) with a statement of the doctrine that 'to be' is a *pros hen* expression,[22] that it has focal meaning, so the doctrine can be assumed to be as fundamental as any to his mature thinking about *ousia*. The central idea here is that, although things from different categories are not said to be or to be beings synonymously (as Plato would likely have claimed), the term is not applied to them homonymously (as the early Aristotle would likely have insisted) either. The various senses of 'to be' are related: one is the core or basic sense, with the other senses to be explained, in different ways, by reference to it. It is *ousiai* that are said to be in the core or fundamental sense; other things are said to be in virtue of entering into various specifiable relations to *ousiai*. In some cases, the requisite explanation is straightforward. Walking, for example, is said to be because it is an action performed by things (animals) that exist in the core sense; colors are said to be by virtue of being features of surfaces; these, in turn, are said to be because they belong to things (bodies) that are beings in the core sense. But Aristotle's conception of the semantics of 'to be' is considerably more complex than reflection on these kinds of example might suggest. For one thing, there is not just one very general sense of 'to be' associated with the category of *ousia*, or with any category for that matter. As we have seen, Aristotle holds that talk about existence or being is ultimately to be parsed in terms of talk about what things are. Accordingly, although he would agree that there is a very general sense of 'to be' in which we can truly say that all the things that are *ousiai* are beings (a sense given by the term '*ousia*' itself), he claims that this is restricted by a series of more and more specific families of senses. Thus we find him saying that there is a sense of 'to be' appropriate to human beings, a distinct sense appropriate to dogs, and a sense that applies exclusively to olive trees,[23] and there is no reason to suppose that he would not have given a parallel account of 'to be' in its use in the case of each of the other categories. For another, we should not suppose that our attempts to identify these derivative senses of 'to be' will be as straightforward as those provided for the case of walking and color. The stories we have to tell here will often contain complicated plots and subplots, so that the overall picture of the seman-

---

[22]For a useful discussion of Z.1, see Witt, *Substance and Essence in Aristotle*, chap. 2.
[23]See H.2, especially 1042ª25–26.

tics underlying our use of 'to be' is one of a complex and multilayered system of priorities and dependencies.

The expression 'what it is to be' is built out of 'to be', and the occurrence of the infinitive there is a genuine or essential occurrence. Aristotle's conception of essence is the idea of the determinate content corresponding to a raw attribution of existence. To identify the essence of a thing is to provide a complete account of what to be consists in for that thing; it is, just as the name suggests, to specify what it is for that thing to be. But, then, we can expect the term 'essence' to share the complex semantical structure of 'to be'. At the most general level, the upshot is that there is a core sense of 'essence', appropriate exclusively within the category of *ousia*; that sense, we can assume, is precisely what Aristotle's initial restrictive characterization of essence has identified for us. And just as things other than *ousiai* are said to be by virtue of various relations of dependence tying them to the things that are in the core sense of 'are', we can assume that to speak of the essence of a quality or quantity always involves a reference to the core case. These things are called essences only because they bear some relation of dependence to things that are said to be essences in the fundamental or basic sense of that term.

If this account is fully to escape our initial charge of artificiality, it must be supplemented by a story that gives independent reasons for thinking, first, that the relevant dependencies actually obtain and, second, that those dependencies must play a central role in any account we might give of the essences of things outside the category of *ousia*. Unfortunately, Z.4 is not helpful here. It fails to identify the kinds of patterns of dependence that must be operative in the case of 'essence' if the *pros hen* analysis is to succeed. Indeed, Z.4 does not so much as make the point that a system of dependencies and priorities is required here. Although we can find themes in Z.5 that would be relevant to an attempt to support a *pros hen* analysis, Z.4 seems content to tell us, without much elaboration, that the extension of the term 'essence' beyond the category of *ousia* is an instance of focal meaning.

There is, I think, a ready explanation for this gap in Z.4. Aristotle has just a few pages earlier provided a nice statement of the *pros hen* analysis of 'being', and we can suppose him to believe that the account presented there is both sufficiently extensive and sufficiently fresh in the reader's mind to make it unnecessary for him to go through the tedious business of filling in the details surrounding the application of the parallel analysis to the case of 'essence'. In fact in supporting the idea that *ousia* provides the shared focus for the various derivative uses of 'to be', Aristotle provides the material we need if we are to give the requisite content to the claim that applications of the term 'essence' outside the category of *ousia* all involve a reference to the core case.

Z.1 pretty clearly relies on the kinds of patterns of dependence that Aristotle had in mind already in the *Categories* when he told us that in the case of things present in another "it is impossible for them to exist apart from that in which they are" (1ª23). Part of the force of invoking the *pros hen* doctrine in Z.1 is to insist that the relevant patterns are built into the meaning of 'to be' as it applies to qualities, quantities, actions, and the like. And, as we have noted, if those patterns enter into the meaning of 'to be', they can be expected to show up in any correct analysis of derivative uses of the expression 'what it is to be'. But, although a start in the right direction, this relatively general line of argument does not quite give us what we want. To make sense of a *pros hen* analysis of 'essence', we need to see those patterns of dependence expressed in an account of just how our use of the term 'essence' outside the category of *ousia* always involves a reference, however circuitous, to essences within that category.

Toward the end of Z.1, Aristotle provides the missing piece to our puzzle. He is attempting to provide support for the view that *ousia* represents the focus for our use of 'to be', and he tells us that *ousia* is prior in formula (*logos*) to entities from other categories. He explains what this priority comes to: "It is necessary that in the formula of each [of these things] there be the *logos* of (an) *ousia*" (1028ª35–36). The explanation is curt, but what Aristotle means to say is fairly clear. He is telling us that it is impossible to provide a formula or definition of an accident without reference to the formula of an *ousia*, the *ousia*, presumably, on whose existence the existence of the accident we seek to define ultimately depends or turns.[24] Since Aristotle holds that to define something is to provide a complete account of its essence, he is telling us that it is impossible to identify fully the essence of an accident without identifying, in turn, the essence of the *ousia* on which it depends. But, then, we are justified in calling an account of something outside the category of *ousia* an account of a thing's essence only in virtue of its including an account of the essence of some *ousia*. And that is just to say that things outside the category of *ousia* are called essences only because they stand in some relation to what, in the core or basic sense, is said to be an essence; it is to say that the *pros hen* analysis genuinely applies.

---

[24] In Z.5 (1030ᵇ23–24) Aristotle puts it a little differently, suggesting that either the formula or the name of the subject appear in the formula of the attribute; but since the name of an accident and its definiens signify the same thing and are intersubstitutable, this suggestion does not change matters. For a discussion of the use of '*logos*' in the Z.1 passage, see Burnyeat et al., eds., *Notes on Book Zeta of Aristotle's Metaphysics*, 5–6.

This vindication of Aristotle's application of the *pros hen* analysis to the terms 'essence' and 'definition' is not, by itself, all that interesting. It makes it clear that it is possible to do what Aristotle claims (but never actually shows) we can do, namely, extend, point for point, the kind of analysis he applies to expressions like 'medical', 'healthy', and 'being' to the case of 'essence'. But since it is not clear that anything of genuine philosophical significance hangs on the semantical features of such technical terms as 'essence' and 'definition', the relevant vindication can strike us as a rather pedestrian exercise in the subtleties of Aristotle's philosophical jargon. And it is true that not much hangs on the semantics of 'essence' and 'definition'. Aristotle concedes as much when he tells us (1030$^b$3–4) that, in the end, it makes little difference how we describe our use of 'essence', and he himself might be accused of violating the strictures implied by his own analysis when at the beginning of Z.6 (1031$^a$15–16), for example, he uses the term 'essence', in one and the same sense, to refer to all essences.

Significant here is the idea of priority and dependence that underlies the appeal to the *pros hen* account. The idea is that certain essences suffer from what we might call identifiability dependence. The language is borrowed from Strawson,[25] but I mean to disassociate the term from its Strawsonian implications. When Strawson speaks of identification, he uses the term broadly to include all cases in which we referringly introduce an object into discourse. In this sense, there are all sorts of ways of identifying essences; we can use a nonrigid designator like 'the thing Plantinga described on line 15, page 227, of *The Nature of Necessity*' as well as a more standard referring device like '*man*'. As I use the term, the identification of an essence is not a mere reference to it but involves the complete articulation of the essence, the full specification of its structure and content. The identification of an essence in my sense is possible only by way of what Aristotle calls a definition.[26] Z.1 tells us that, when we identify, in this sense, what it is for a given accident to be, we must make reference to what it is to be for the *ousia* or kind of *ousia* on which that accident ultimately depends. And at the end of Z.4 (1030$^b$12–13) Aristotle implies that the relevant identifiability dependence is not restricted to the case of accidents. Conceding that it makes sense to speak of what it is for a white man to be, Aristotle extends the

[25]See P. F. Strawson, *Individuals*, chap. 1.

[26]Aristotle speaks of priority in definition. See *Metaphysics* Δ.11 (1018$^b$30ff.) I run the risk of misleading the reader by putting this Strawsonian term to this special use, but it is a handy term that brings out nicely the Aristotelian idea that there is a canonical way of expressing essences and that the project of providing full articulation of essences gives rise to the kind of hierarchy characterized in Z.4.

idea of derivative senses of 'essence' beyond the case of accidents and
tells us that talk about the essence of a "complex" like *white man* involves
a sense of 'essence' distinct from any we have so far met in Z.4. A
remark in *Metaphysics* Δ.11 makes it clear just what it is going on here:[27]

> The accident is prior to the whole according to formula. For example, the
> musical [is prior] to the musical man; for it will not be possible to specify
> the whole formula without the formula of the part, even though it is not
> possible for the musical to be unless there is something that is not musi-
> cal. (1018$^b$34–36)

Aristotle is saying that, despite the fact that *musical* presupposes as its
subject something that is not musical (here, the *man* in *musical man*),
*musical* is prior in formula to the "complex" *musical man*. So precisely the
kind of identifiability dependence that ties the essences of accidents to
the essences of *ousiai* binds the essences of what Aristotle often calls
"complexes" (e.g., 1029$^b$23, 1030$^b$16) to the essences of those accidents
out of which they are constructed. In Z.4 Aristotle expresses this fact in
terms of even more derivative senses of 'essence'.

But, then, this talk of primary and secondary and even more derivative senses of such terms as 'definition' and 'essence' is Aristotle's
vehicle for conveying the picture of a structured framework or hierarchy
of essence. The basic idea is that of various levels or strata of essences,
where the level an essence occupies in the scheme is a kind of function
of the relations of dependence it bears to other essences, so that an
essence occupies that lowest level in the hierarchy such that there is no
essence at that level or any higher level on which the essence in question is, in my special sense, identifiability-dependent. The hierarchy as
a whole rests on a foundational or basic level of essences. These are, of
course, the essences Aristotle tries to isolate in his initial, restrictive
characterization of the concept; they are the essences which, when he
finally invokes the less restrictive, more tolerant account provided by
the *pros hen* analysis, he tells us constitute the core cases in terms of
which the other senses of the term are to be explained.

In Z.4, we have seen, he characterizes these as the essences of things
that "are not said to be whatever they are because one thing is said of
another" (1030$^a$10–11). In Z.6, he generalizes by telling us that the
fundamental essences belong to things that "are not called what they
are in virtue of something else" (1031$^b$13). He also invokes the familiar
language of the *Posterior Analytics*, telling us that these things are "called
what they are in their own right" (1031$^b$13–14). So the things whose

[27]See also *Metaphysics* M.2 (1077$^b$1–7).

essences occupy the lowest level in the framework are, to use the language of Z.1, posterior in formula to nothing else. Aristotle can say, as he does at the end of Z.4, that their essences are primary.[28] While all other essences are, in the end, identifiability-dependent on them, the fundamental essences are identifiability-independent.

This talk of dependence in identification can be misleading to a contemporary reader, since it might suggest that what is really fundamental here is the epistemological idea of definitional priority and that to talk about an ordering of essences is just to make a disguised claim about the way we go about the business of defining. For Aristotle, however, the kinds of gap we like to find between the metaphysical and the epistemological tend not to exist; they most certainly do not exist in the case of definition and essence. Just as he would deny that what counts as the correct answer to a What is it? question is a matter of convention, he would reject an antirealist account of definition that interprets success here as a mere function of the variable interests and goals of an inquiring community. Although he would surely understand the search after definitions as a procedure rational beings engage in, he insists on the anticonventionalist or realist line that "definition is the formula of the what it is to be" ($101^b38$). Accordingly, if it is impossible for things of a certain sort to be defined without reference to the definition of things of another sort, it is because the essences expressed by those definitions are related in significant ways. Where an essence $E$ is identifiability-dependent on an essence $E'$, $E$ presupposes or depends on $E'$. There would not be such a thing as the what it is to be that is $E$ unless there were that what it is to be that is $E'$, but not conversely. So, although it is reflection on facts about definition that might provide us with our initial access to the idea of an ordering of essences, the idea of a hierarchical framework of essences which Aristotle proposes for us in Z.4 is not essentially, or even primarily, an epistemological notion.

If we were to go by the evidence provided by Z.4, we might suppose that Aristotle construes the framework as a three-tiered hierarchy. At the foundation are essences from the category of *ousia*; the second tier is constituted by essences from the various accidental categories; and, finally, we have essences corresponding to substance-accident hybrids. But once again we have to remember that in Z.4 Aristotle is merely trying to make the idea of this kind of hierarchy plausible. In doing this he relies on clear-cut cases where we are likely to find precisely the kinds of priority relations he takes to constitute the basic structure of the hierarchy. He is not in the business of presenting for our inspection a

[28]I take the force of the remark at $1030^b5$–6 that "*ousiai* primarily have definition and essence" to imply that their essences are primary.

fully articulated framework in which each essence has its proper place. As we have already noted, a framework of that sort must await the development of a general theory, and we are in Z.4 only beginning that task. In fact, the articulated framework we ultimately arrive at looks quite different from what the hints and suggestions of Z.4 might lead us to suppose. We have already seen that Aristotle's contention that the fundamental or primary essences fall within the category of *ousia* leaves it unclear just which essences are foundational; for all that Z.4 tells us, there might be (in fact, is) a stratum of essences above the basic level but below the level occupied by accidents. Further, reflection on the fact that some accidents (e.g., colors) have as their primary subject other accidents suggests that a fully articulated theory might well deny that a single stratum of essences is sufficient to do justice to the complexities of the priority relations operative in the case of accidents. Finally, must we suppose that the essences of what Aristotle calls "complexes" constitute just one level in the hierarchy? There are, after all, left-handed hoplites; one might argue that, since what it is for a left-handed hoplite to be is something different from what it is for a hoplite to be, we are forced to confront the idea of still higher levels of essence.[29]

V

Aristotle is no democrat about essences. As we have seen, he sometimes expresses this antiegalitarian view in bold and slightly misleading terms by saying that only *ousiai* have essences, but his considered view is that the term 'essence' has focal meaning.[30] The case of *ousia* provides the core case or focus for its application; outside that category, it applies only because the things it picks out stand in some specifiable relation to

---

[29]It turns out that this is an issue on which Aristotle's views undergo change. In *Topics* E.4 (133$^b$17–21), he suggests that an *ousia*/accident "complex" can team up with an accident to form a further "complex"; but in *Metaphysics* Γ.4 (1007$^b$1ff.), Aristotle denies that this is possible. The later work argues that "complexes" can have at most two terms on the grounds that (a) an accident requires an *ousia* as its subject, and (b) an *ousia*/accident "complex" is not an *ousia*. On this view, if we assume that 'hoplite' signifies a genuine "complex" with *man* as subject, we have to deny that the attribute of being lefthanded can combine with *hoplite* to form a further "complex." It can, of course, combine with *man* to form the "complex" signified by 'lefthanded man', but that "complex" (like that signified by 'hoplite') has an *ousia*/accident structure. If we assume that the Aristotle of Z and H holds the view expressed in Γ.4, then we have to concede that "complexes" yield at most one stratum in the hierarchy of essences. I am indebted here to Frank Lewis, who points to these two texts in his insightful discussion of what he calls accidental compounds in "Substance and Predication" (unpublished manuscript). See also Lewis's "Accidental Sameness in Aristotle," *Philosophical Studies* (1982), 1–36.

[30]See 1031$^a$1–11, where we once again get two options.

the essences of *ousia*. Underlying this semantical claim is the idea that essences from the category of *ousia* are basic or primary in that they presuppose or depend on no prior essences and accordingly are independently identifiable. Other essences, however, presuppose these primary essences and can be identified only by reference to them, and still other essences presuppose these and are identifiability-dependent on them. What emerges, then, is a hierarchical framework of essences at the foundation of which are essences from the category of *ousia*, with succeeding levels constituted by essences that presuppose essences of lower levels.

The things whose essences constitute the foundations of this hierarchical structure are precisely those which, to use the language of the early theory of *ousia*, are the primary realities. They are the things whose being what they are serves to explain why other things are what they are but themselves stand in no need of explanation. Despite the introduction of the notion of the *ti ein einai*, then, the account of Z.4 and Z.5 bears interesting resemblances to the older view; as we have noted, the reader of the *Categories* might have considerable sympathy with those chapters. This reader will, however, want to ask about the relationship between the essences that constitute the foundations and the primary realities whose essences they are; and Aristotle only adds urgency to the question when in Z.6 ($1031^b13$) he echoes the language of *Posterior Analytics* A.4 by characterizing the primary essences as essences of things that are *kath hauta legomena*, things said to be whatever they are in their own right. We recall that in that setting the idea of a thing that is a primary reality is the idea of something such that what it is is a basic or unanalyzable fact about it. As I put it in Chapter 1, the claim that primary realities are *kath hauta* (things in their own right) is the early Aristotle's way of expressing what I called the Unanalyzability Thesis; it is that thesis the reader of the *Categories* recalls when asking about the relationship between the basic essences of Z.4 and Z.5 and the primary realities whose essences they are.

In the light of Z.3's challenge to the subject criterion, this question has special point. As the *Categories* theorist saw things, commitment to the Unanalyzability Thesis followed from a joint commitment to the subject criterion and an essentialist interpretation of the primary *ousiai*. But Z.3 turns things upside down. In that chapter, Aristotle tells us that the thesis fails as an account of the objects to which the *Categories* theorist was anxious to apply it, the familiar particulars of common sense. In the light of that failure, the mature Aristotle argues that the subject criterion and essentialism come into conflict, and the Aristotle of Z.3 insists on an essentialist interpretation of the primary realities, whatever they might turn out to be. Z.4 and Z.5 show that Z.3's claims in behalf of essential-ism are not mere lip service. Although talk of kinds gives way to talk about the what it is for a thing to be, the suggestion that essence itself might be *ousia*, the temptation to think that it is only in the case of *ousia* that we confront essence, and the more temperate suggestion of a hierarchical structure in which the essence of anything at all we might want to call a being has its proper place are all expressions of a serious and deep-seated commitment to essentialism.

The *Categories* theorist wants to know what, within the context of these new expressions of essentialism, becomes of the insights underly-ing our old friend, the Unanalyzability Thesis. In Z.6, Aristotle ad-dresses this concern. The upshot of that chapter is, first, that the Un-analyzability Thesis must be replaced by a stronger principle, what I call the Z.6 Identity Thesis, and, second, that commitment to this new thesis is a presupposition of the very enterprise of providing an inven-tory of the primary *ousiai*.

Nowhere in Z.6 does Aristotle use the phrase 'primary *ousia*'. He speaks instead of things that are (a) primary and (b) said to be what they are in their own right. These two characterizations, however, express the two components in the idea of a primary *ousia*. Primary *ousiai* are things such that, by reference to what they are, we can explain why other things are what they are. They are the things that are ontologically prior to everything else or, as Aristotle puts it, "the primary things." But nothing can be a primary reality whose being what it is depends on something else, so primary *ousiai* are things that are what they are in their own right. If we concede that there is nothing that fails to enter into relations of ontological priority and dependence with something else, then we must agree that all and only primary things are things in their own right or *kath hauta legomena*; these are the primary *ousiai*. The underlying theme of Z.6 is that the attempt to identify the primary *ousiai* presupposes that the items so identified are such that, in their case, the kind of question for which they are to provide us with a final answer does not and cannot arise. And, of course, our questions were ques-tions about why things are what they are, so the relationship between a primary *ousia* and the fundamental essence corresponding to it must be tight.

But the Aristotle of Z.6 wants to claim that the earlier talk of direct and unmediated predicative ties is too weak to capture the relationship required here. Suppose a candidate for status as primary *ousia* has as its essence something distinct from it that is predicated of it. Then no matter how tight we make the predicative tie between thing and es-sence, we cannot escape the fact that what we construe as a primary *ousia* is what it is because of something else, namely, the essence predicated of it. But, then, what we are identifying as a primary reality is not a thing in its own right; its essence has a better claim than it to status as a primary *ousia*. If that essence, in turn, has as its essence something distinct from it, then, again, no matter how we characterize the relation between the two, the fact remains that our original essence fails to be what it is in its own right and so fails to qualify as a primary *ousia*. If an inventory of primary realities is to do what it claims—provide us with a final answer to questions about why things are, that is, are what they are—then its candidates for the explanatory role of primary *ousiai* must be one and the same as their essences.

Aristotle characteristically tells us that there are three different forms of unity or sameness.[31] Things can be one/the same in genus, species, or number. Those things are one/the same generically which belong to a single genus; things are specifically one/the same when the infima species of one is the infima species of the other. But neither of these forms of unity or sameness is strong enough to characterize the kind of relationship tying a primary *ousia* and its essence. Numerical unity or sameness is required here, and it cannot be a merely contingent fact that

[31]As early as the *Topics* (A.7, 103ᵃ6–39), Aristotle distinguishes these three kinds of unity or sameness. In virtually all contexts, Aristotle tells us that (individuals) $x$ and $y$ are generically the same just in case $x$ and $y$ are members of a single genus and that $x$ and $y$ are specifically the same just in case $x$ and $y$ belong to one lowest-level kind or infima species. But in different places he characterizes numerical unity/sameness in different ways. In *Topics* A.7, Aristotle tells us that '$x$ and $y$ are numerically the same' is true when '$x$' and '$y$' name one object. He goes on to contrast the case in which a single definition corresponds to $x$ and $y$ ('robe' and 'cloak') with the case in which this is not so ('the man sitting in the corner' and 'Socrates'). The former case, we are told, represents the primary and most literal use of 'numerically the same'. In *Metaphysics* Δ.6 and 9, the latter case gets separate treatment as exhibiting what Aristotle calls being one/the same *kata sumbebekos* (1015ᵇ16–34 and 1017ᵇ26–33); numerical unity/sameness gets treated as one case of what Aristotle calls being one/the same *kath hauto* (1016ᵇ32–1017ᵃ3 and 1018ᵃ4–9). In both of these contexts, Aristotle's characterization of numerical unity/sameness is restricted to the case of the composite particular; for we are told that $x$ and $y$ are numerically one/the same just in case the matter of $x$ and the matter of $y$ are (numerically) one/the same. But, although he does not label it as an account of numerical unity, Aristotle tells us in Δ.6 that "in general those things the thought of which or the thought of whose essence is indivisible and which cannot be separated either in time or place or definition are most of all one" (1016ᵇ1–3)—and that looks like a *general* characterization of numerical unity, applicable to both universals and particulars. It agrees with the *Topics* claim in making the case of numerical unity/sameness, where there is a single formula or definition, the tightest and most basic kind of unity. I call this kind of unity/sameness necessary numerical sameness or unity. It is this sort of sameness/unity that Z.6 establishes with regard to the things that are primary/*kath hauto* and their essences. I am assuming that the very strong relation of necessary numerical sameness covers the case of what we nowadays call numerical identity; hence I call the claim that primary *ousiai* and their essences exhibit this relation the Z.6 Identity Thesis.

a primary *ousia* and its essence are numerically one and the same thing. To ensure, once and for all, a stop to the kinds of questions we seek to answer, we must require that each candidate for status as a primary *ousia* bears the relationship of necessary numerical sameness or unity to the fundamental essence corresponding to it.

The response to the *Categories* theorist, then, is that the Unanalyzability Thesis must give way to what I call the Z.6 Identity Thesis. But the central contention of Z.6 is that our acceptance of this stronger principle is not a consequence of particular metaphysical claims we happen to endorse. The line of argument we have just rehearsed is perfectly general. It applies to any attempt to identify the primary *ousiai*, so the claim that a primary *ousia* and the fundamental essence in virtue of which it is what it is are necessarily one and same thing is theory-neutral. It expresses a constraint on any attempt to pick out the ontologically basic things. Commitment to the Identity Thesis, the Aristotle of Z.6 wants to claim, is a presupposition of doing anything that can genuinely be called metaphysics.

VI

Although the account in the preceding section gives clear sense to the Z.6 Identity Thesis, other commentators offer wildly different interpretations of the force, context, and implications of the thesis. G. E. L. Owen and Michael Woods, for example, see the thesis as a part of an ongoing attempt to respond to problems associated with the Third Man argument. But, whereas Owen sees it as an expression of Aristotle's mature view that it is not the familiar particulars of the *Categories* but rather their species that constitute "the primary subjects of discourse," Woods understands the thesis to apply to ordinary objects and takes Aristotle's commitment to it to entail that species-predications like 'Socrates is a man' are statements of identity.[32] Other commentators have been reluctant to attribute to Aristotle either the puzzling view that ordinary objects are not primary subjects of discourse or Woods's bizarre identity interpretation of species-predications. While some commentators (Michael Frede, Edwin Hartman, Joseph Owens, and Terence Irwin) insist that the Z.6 thesis bears on form and that a consequence of the assertion of necessary identity is the idea that for each member of a

---

[32]See G. E. L. Owen, "The Platonism of Aristotle," especially 156–163; M. J. Woods, "Substance and Essence in Aristotle," *Proceedings of the Aristotelian Society* (1975–76), 167–180.

species there is a numerically distinct form,[33] S. Marc Cohen despairs of uncovering a consistent doctrine in the thesis as stated by Aristotle and concludes that the Z.6 thesis is not to be understood literally. On his view, it is simply a slightly misleading way of making the claim about the conditions necessary for ascribing numerical identity; a less misleading way of putting Aristotle's point is to say that "to be identical with Callias is to be the *same man* as Callias."[34] The Owen–Woods view that the Z.6 thesis is a response to the Third Man Argument has likewise come under attack. Arguing that the concerns of Z.6 bear no relation at all to that argument, Alan Code insists that, if we supplement Aristotle's early views on definitions (views expressed in such texts as the *Topics* and the *Posterior Analytics*) with the claim that primary *ousia* is definable, we have all the materials we need for understanding Aristotle's commitment to the Identity Thesis.[35] Frank Lewis is slightly more sympathetic to the Owen–Woods view, but in the end he argues that the Third Man Argument is not relevant to Z.6 and claims that since the Identity Thesis is a consequence of technical notions peculiar to the middle books we cannot understand the thesis except in terms of the theoretical apparatus of Z and H.[36] And there are more mundane interpretations. W. D. Ross, for example, seems to see Z.6 as just one more occasion for Aristotle to engage in the kind of Plato-bashing we find in Z.13–16.[37]

So there is no settled view on Z.6. Indeed, the myriad interpretations to which the text has given rise bear on so many different issues and take us in so many different directions that it is unlikely that we can find in the existing debates much common ground for understanding Aristotle's aims in Z.6. We are better advised, I think, to see the Identity Thesis as a response to the kinds of concerns about essentialism and the

[33]See Michael Frede, "Individuals in Aristotle" and "Substance in Aristotle's Metaphysics," in Frede's *Essays in Ancient Philosophy*, 72–80; Edwin Hartman, "Aristotle on the Identity of Substance and Essence," *Philosophical Review* (1976), 545–560, especially 551; Joseph Owens, *The Doctrine of Being in the Aristotelian Metaphysics*, 220; and Terence Irwin, *Aristotle's First Principles*, 217ff.

[34]S. Marc Cohen, "Individual and Essence in Aristotle's Metaphysics," *Paideia* (1978), 75–85, 83.

[35]Code, "On the Origins of Some Aristotelian Theses about Predication," especially 110 (a summary of an extended analysis of the Owen interpretation of Z.6), 114–119 (a criticism of Woods' view), and 113 (a summary of his own view).

[36]Frank Lewis, "Plato's Third Man Argument and the 'Platonism' of Aristotle," in James Bogen and James E. McGuire, eds., *How Things Are*, 133–174. See 154–156 for the slightly more sympathetic reading of the Owen view, and 157–166, where Lewis deduces the Z.6 thesis from the formalized versions of a number of central themes from Z and H. I grant that Lewis' account expresses the overall view of Z–H, but I question the idea that all the formalized principles he appeals to in deriving the Z.6 thesis are already at work in Z.6.

[37]See, e.g., Ross's account of the Platonic material in Z.6 in *Aristotle's Metaphysics*, vol. 2, 177.

Unanalyzability Thesis we were exploring in the previous section and to understand the case Aristotle develops for the thesis in the light of a remark by Russell Dancy, who takes Aristotle to be "suggesting in Z.6, that any scheme whatever, any 'ontology' (the example he uses to illustrate the point in 6.1031$^b$28 and ff. is Platonism) will have to recognize a level at which there is no distinction to be drawn between the subjects of which other things are said and whatever it is that has to be true of them if they are to exist at all."[38] The context for the remark is a discussion of Aristotle's early views about *ousia*; hence the reference to "subjects of which other things are said." But, despite the prominence of the subject criterion, Dancy's remark strikes me as capturing precisely the strategy Aristotle employs in Z.6. Aristotle's argument for the Identity Thesis makes no reference to problems associated with the Third Man argument, nor does it invoke theoretical presuppositions peculiar to Z and H or Aristotle's own account of the logical features of definition. What he argues is that any attempt to identify primary *ousiai*, regardless of the theoretical and technical apparatus in which it is embedded, must hold that the things so identified are one and the same as what it is for them to be. He is telling us, that is, that the Z.6 thesis is a constraint on any metaphysical theory.

The most telling evidence in favor of this reading of Z.6 is, as Dancy points out, the fact that Aristotle's central argument for the thesis is that the identity has to hold even within the Platonic metaphysics. Although he may well have believed that Plato was not sufficiently sensitive to the constraints implicit in the Z.6 thesis,[39] Aristotle is not, pace Ross, arguing that we must scuttle Forms. On the contrary, he is telling us what is required for a theory of Forms to work. If we posit separate Forms as primary realities, he is telling us, our account has no chance of succeeding unless we concede that each Form is one and the same as what it is for that Form to be. Indeed, his line of argument allows the Platonic theory any number of controversial claims that Aristotle himself would be anxious to reject. Thus he concedes Plato a single Form, Being Itself, by virtue of participating in which things can be said to be (1031$^a$32–1031$^b$1). He argues that, if we distinguish a Form and its essence, we are committed to construing the essence of a given Form as prior to the Form itself; but, then, we must deny that the essence of a given Form exhibits any of those properties which are such that, neces-

[38]Dancy, *Sense and Contradiction*, 100.

[39]For a nice discussion of issues central to this question, see Code, "Aristotle on Essence and Accident," 411–434. It is significant, I think, that Aristotle attempts to establish the general applicability of the Z.6 thesis by showing that it has to apply in the case of a metaphysical theory that rejects his own essentialist reading of 'to be' and construes that verb as expressing a single universally exemplified nature or character.

sarily, an object exhibits those properties just in case it participates in (and hence depends on) the relevant Form.[40] The result is that, if a primary *ousia* and its essence are numerically distinct, the essence of the Form Being Itself does not exist ($1031^b8-9$), and this result carries with it the untoward consequences that nothing whatever exists.[41] The implicit premise here is that it is impossible for a thing to exist if its essence does not exist. This premise can be seen to yield the untoward consequence in either of two ways. On the one hand, the premise tells us that, since the essence of the Form Being Itself does not exist, the Form itself does not exist either; but, then, nothing else does since there is no Form in virtue of which things have being. On the other, we must be egalitarians about the essences of primary realities and agree that they all have the same ontic status. But if the essence of Being Itself does not exist, the essences of no other Forms do either; but, then, by our implicit premise, the Forms do not exist, and if they do not exist, neither does any of the things whose features they were introduced to explain.[42] Accordingly, we must suppose that even in a theory like Plato's the Z.6 thesis holds, so Aristotle can conclude that whether or not there are Forms each thing that is a primary *ousia* is numerically one and the same as its essence ($1031^b11-13$, $14-15$).

Aristotle anticipates the response that by reallocating the concept of primary reality to the case of the essences in question we can, perhaps, blunt some of the force of this critique.[43] His rejoinder is that, if we are unwilling to submit to the constraints of the Identity Thesis at this new level, we are only putting off the evil day. Indeed, unless we concede that there is some level in our burgeoning hierarchy of essences which incorporates both the explanatory role associated with the idea of a primary *ousia* and the identity of thing and essence, we will find ourselves regressing into a never-ending series of essences of essences of essences.[44] And since we will refuse to recognize any of these as fundamental or basic essences, the task of explaining why things are what they are will never be completed. His own response is that there is little

---

[40]I take it that an implicit premise in all of this is that, if *a* is prior (in essence) to *b*, then no property of *a* is to be explained by reference to *b*. This premise will cause serious problems besides those mentioned by Aristotle.

[41]I take it that this is the obvious and unstated upshot of $1031^b10$.

[42]Aristotle explicitly invokes the first (but not the second) application of the implicit premise.

[43]I take it that this response to Aristotle's argument at $1031^a28-1031^b18$ provides the backdrop for the comment of $1031^b28-1032^a6$.

[44]See $1032^a2-3$. The regress suggested here is not that associated with the Third Man Argument. One does not need, for example, any principle like the self-predication assumption to generate the ascending series of essences. All that is required to generate the series is the denial of the Z.6 Identity Thesis and the innocent assumption that everything has an essence.

point in ascending even one level in this series. We are best advised to maintain that the concept of primary reality and the identity of thing and essence hold at the very first level. As he puts it, "What is there to prevent some things from being their essences right away and straight off?" (1031ᵇ31).

In the context of his discussion of the Platonic theory, Aristotle gives (at 1031ᵇ7) a truncated version of an epistemological argument for the Z.6 thesis, an argument he takes to be sufficiently telling to be worth repeating twice more in Z.6, once explicitly (1031ᵇ20) and once implicitly (1032ᵃ1). The argument is the simple reductio that knowledge would be impossible if things and their essences were never numerically one and the same. He formulates the central premise of the argument as the claim that to know each thing is to know its essence and he leaves to the reader the routine task of constructing the regress argument generating the impossibility of knowledge. Although the argument obviously holds for the kind of epistemic state involved in definition, we are not told whether the argument is meant to apply to any less demanding epistemic states we might, in ordinary parlance, be inclined to call knowledge. It is clear, however, from the second and third appeal to the argument that it is supposed to generate necessary identity or identity in formula (*logos*).[45] The assumption is that, unless at some level a single formula or definition applies to thing and essence, it is not the case that apprehending the one is apprehending the other.[46] And, although Aristotle does not make the point explicit, the argument presupposes that it is in the case of the primary realities that the necessary identity in question holds. Here Aristotle is just assuming a theme he expresses repeatedly in other contexts, a theme that all his predecessors would have been equally confident in assuming, that the primary realities are knowable par excellence. Accordingly, the things such that apprehending them and their essences is one and same thing just are the things such that in virtue of what they are (i.e., in virtue of their having the essences they do) other things are what they are.

## VII

In any ontological theory, then, the items selected as primary *ousiai* must be necessarily the same in number as the fundamental essences

[45]See, especially, 1031ᵇ32–1032ᵃ2, where Aristotle implies that being one necessarily and being one in formula are the same thing.

[46]Code provides an interesting interpretation of the way 1031ᵇ28–1032ᵃ4 establishes that a primary *ousia* and its essence are one in formula. See his "On the Origins of Some Aristotelian Theses about Predication," 119–123.

corresponding to them. A consequence is that the hypothesis that led to the explorations of Z.4–6 is vindicated. If it is a constraint on any metaphysical theory that the items it construes as the primary realities are one and the same with their essences, then in any metaphysical theory some essences turn out to be realities or *ousiai*. Indeed, they turn out to be the primary *ousiai*. Here it is easy to misunderstand Z.6 and to suppose that Aristotle uses as a premise in the argument for the Identity Thesis the idea that the what it is to be is *ousia*, since we meet with the claim on three different occasions in the chapter.[47] But the claim is never asserted unconditionally as a premise from which we are warranted in deriving other truths. It always appears under the scope of some qualifying expression.

Aristotle first invokes the idea at the beginning of the chapter as motivation for exploring the question of the identity of object and essence. He tells us that the examination of the thesis is of value "for the study of *ousia* since each thing seems to be not other than its *ousia* and the *ti ein einai is said* to be the *ousia* of each thing" (1031ª16–18). Here again we meet with the novel use of *ousia* as an abstract term in the context '*ousia* of'. I think that we can, without distorting the themes of Z.6, postpone discussion of this new use of the term.[48] For the present, it is sufficient to note that Aristotle is not here expressing a view he feels confident to assert. Both the claim that each thing is its own *ousia* and the claim that the *ti ein einai* is the *ousia* of a thing are presented tentatively. The first is introduced as a claim that "seems" to be true. In fact Aristotle himself later repudiates the claim for all but a narrow range of cases.[49] As he see things in the end, the claim holds only for the primary *ousiai*. Nor is the second claim expressed as a thesis that is true; it is presented as a claim that "is said" (perhaps by only some people) to be true. And although the claim expresses an idea Aristotle ultimately endorses, we must be careful about just how we formulate the idea. It turns out that, in the case of ordinary objects, the thing that we would, if we were to put things very precisely, identify as their essence is not their *ousia*. Indeed, it is only in the case of primary *ousiai* that what we would, if we were to be very precise, call their essence is their *ousia*.[50] So

---

[47]See 1031ª17–18, 1031ᵇ2–3, and 1031ᵇ31–32.

[48]Here, I obviously part company with Frank Lewis, who would argue that we must understand the idea that essence is the *ousia* of a thing if we are to understand Z.6 at all. As I indicated in n. 36, I believe Lewis's account expresses correctly the doctrine of Z and H as a whole, but I do not think it accommodates Z.6 since Lewis has to import themes not yet established in Z.6 to generate the Identity Thesis. In particular, he needs the premise that essence is *ousia*; but, if I am right, that is precisely what Z.6 is meant to establish. See, once again, Lewis, "Plato's Third Man Argument and the 'Platonism' of Aristotle," 157–166.

[49]It is, I take it, only form that is its own *ousia*. I argue this point in a later chapter.

[50]The point is merely that it is the essence of the species (involving both matter and

the two claims introduced here do not represent theses Aristotle, even in the end, endorses unconditionally; they are presented merely to motivate the discussion that follows.

The claim that essence is *ousia* is found again at 1031$^{b}$2–3, but here it appears only as the protasis of a conditional and is never discharged. Aristotle has presented the theory of Forms as the view that there are certain *ousiai* to which no other *ousiai* are prior, and he points out that if the theory denies that these *ousiai* are one and the same with their essences it must countenance the idea that there are things prior to the things it has identified as the primary *ousiai*. And Aristotle tells us that the proponent of the theory who endorses the view that essence is *ousia* has to repudiate the initial characterization of the Forms as *ousiai* for which there are no prior *ousiai*. That is the extent of Aristotle's use of the hypothesis in his discussion of the Forms. It appears not as a claim Aristotle himself urges; it is merely a claim the Platonist might want to make, and Aristotle points to an embarrassing consequence that follows from both endorsing the claim and refusing to identify Form and essence.

The claim appears a third time at 1031$^{b}$31–32, again as the protasis of a conditional, a conditional that is expressed as a rhetorical question. Aristotle is here concerned with the burgeoning hierarchy of essences I mentioned a few pages back. He points out that some level in the ascending series of essence of essence of essence must instantiate jointly the notion of primary *ousia* and identity of thing and essence. Then he tells us that, if we hold that essence is *ousia*, we have all the motivation we need to construe the original essence in the series as providing us with the level in question. I have already quoted the apodosis of the conditional. The full conditional is stated as follows: "What is there to prevent some things from being their essences right away and straight off if indeed essence is *ousia*?" (1031$^{b}$31–32). The question comes late in the chapter, at a point where Aristotle would have every justification for thinking he already has provided sufficient argument to establish the identity of object and essence in the case of things that are primary and *kath hauta*. But, although Aristotle would himself certainly stop the regress into essences of essences at the first step, it is important to note that the 'if' clause is never officially discharged. We are told only that, to the extent that we endorse the

---

form) that, in the strict sense, is the essence of the individual belonging to that species, and that essence is not the *ousia* of those individuals. I discuss this issue in Chapter 5. For a clear account of Aristotle's view here, see Lewis, "What Is Aristotle's Theory of Essence?" especially 118–126.

hypothesis that essence is *ousia*, we should be prepared to hold to the identity of object and essence at the appearance of the first essence in the series. But, of course, this is only a counsel of parsimony; it is consistent with the argument Aristotle is developing that the identification of object and essence occur at some later stage in the series.[51]

So the hypothesis that essence is *ousia* does not function as an essential premise in Aristotle's arguments for the Z.6 thesis. This is not surprising. We can assume that the claim that essence is *ousia* is shorthand for the claim that certain essences (whatever turn out to be the fundamental or basic essences) are primary *ousiai*. In Z.6, however, Aristotle seeks to establish that the things that are primary *ousiai* are necessarily numerically one with their essences. Given that necessary sameness has to be symmetrical, it is difficult to see how we could succeed in making that hypothesis out to be a claim distinct from the Z.6 thesis. But if we believe we could, we must concede that the two are so intimately related that any appeal Aristotle might make to the hypothesis in establishing the Identity Thesis would prompt the charge that the whole enterprise is circular. We put a better light on what Aristotle is doing in Z.4–.6 if we take the hypothesis entertained at the beginning of each of Z.3, Z.4, and Z.6 to be either the Identity Thesis itself or an allied claim that follows trivially from it. So Z.6 is a proof that some essences (the fundamental essences) are *ousiai*.

VIII

When we couple the arguments of Z.6 with the hierarchical conception of essence that Aristotle suggests in Z.4 and Z.5, we get the conclusion that the essences constituting the fundamental level in the structure are necessarily one and the same in number as the primary *ousiai* whose essences they are. The *Categories* theorist was correct to insist on a tight relationship between a primary *ousia* and its essence, but the talk of primitive or direct and unmediated ties is not strong enough to capture the requisite intimacy. We need the stronger Identity Thesis if we are to express the relationship at work here. And our commitment to that stronger principle is not a consequence of particular metaphysical claims we happen to make in our own attempt to identify *ousiai*; it is a general constraint on any such attempt. So, unlike the earlier Unanalyzability Thesis, the Z.6 thesis is not a consequence of the particular

---

[51]Code would likely disagree with this suggestion. See "On the Origins of Some Aristotelian Theses about Predication," 121–122.

criterion for *ousia*hood we choose to endorse; its truth is something we can know in advance of any criterion we might want to propose. Indeed, it sets parameters on our selection of a criterion: given the Z.6 thesis, we can know that any criterion that identifies as primary *ousiai* things that cannot plausibly be thought to be their essences must be false.

The subject criterion, as it functions in the logical writings, is one such criterion. Let us set aside the Z.3 complications that matter brings on the scene and suppose that the criterion does indeed select as primary *ousiai* the familiar particulars of common sense. If we suppose (as Aristotle certainly does) that their essences are provided by the kinds to which they belong, then it is difficult to understand how ordinary concrete objects, the composites of Z and H, can be numerically one and the same as their essences. It is equally difficult to believe, as Woods seems to, that the Aristotle of Z.6 would have thought that they are. The essences in question are universals. Each is common to all of the members of the relevant kind, so the price of taking the Z.6 thesis to hold in the case of such things as the individual man and the individual horse of the *Categories* is commitment to the outrageous view that no kind has more than one member.[52] Indeed, the Z.6 Identity Thesis suggests that the *Categories* theorist should have followed out the ruminations of the final section of Chapter 1 and construed the infimae species to which concrete particulars belong rather than the particulars themselves as the primary *ousiai*. In their case at least, the suggestion that essence and object are one and the same is not wildly implausible.

More generally, the Z.6 Identity Thesis has the consequence that no particular whose essence is something general and hence capable of being shared with others can be a primary reality; this entails that only at the cost of ascribing gross inconsistency to Aristotle can we attribute to him the view that, first, the different members of a given species have numerically distinct forms that are one in essence and, second, these individual forms are the primary *ousiai*.[53] The Z.6 thesis entails that whatever we identify as a primary reality must be necessarily one and the same as its essence; therefore, the idea of numerically distinct

[52]Code provides a compelling critique of Woods's view. See "On the Origins of Some Aristotelian Theses about Predication," 114–119.

[53]Some remarks in Hartman's "Aristotle on the Identity of Substance and Essence" suggest that he may attribute both claims to Aristotle; see especially 551–553. See also Michael Frede, "Substance in Aristotle's *Metaphysics*," in *Essays in Ancient Philosophy*, 72–80, and Jennifer E. Whiting, "Form and Individuation in Aristotle," *History of Philosophy Quarterly* (1986), 359–377. Both Frede and Whiting interpret Aristotle as holding that there are individual forms and that the forms of members of a single species are qualitatively indistinguishable.

primary *ousiai* sharing a single essence is, by the lights of the Identity Thesis, incoherent.

So although in Z.4–6 Aristotle is not in the business of presenting an articulated framework of essences, with each kind of essence allocated its proper level in the hierarchy, his attempt to characterize the general structure of such a hierarchy and to set minimal constraints on the kinds of items that can constitute its foundations do preclude certain answers to the question, Which things are primary *ousiai*? Indeed, the Z.6 constraint on the foundational essences (that they be necessarily one and the same as the things whose essences they are) has the effect, I believe, of excluding all but two general sorts of answers to that question. One is radically nominalistic, the other seems to border on Platonism, and both have been attributed to Aristotle. The first construes primary *ousiai* as particulars each with an essence unique to it; the second takes them to be, in some sense or other, general. Since Aristotle finally insists that it is substantial form that is essence and *ousia*, the two interpretations construe him as holding, respectively, that it is individual forms, no two of which are essentially the same, that are the primary realities, and that it is form understood as something somehow common to all the members of a given species that is primary *ousia*. As my introductory remarks on essence suggest, I side with the latter interpretation, and I present Aristotle's mature theory of *ousia* in this light. When I come to a discussion of Z.13–16, I am forced to join the controversy, and my reasons for preferring this interpretation of form then become clear. For the present, I merely claim that there is nothing in Z.6 itself to suggest that the primary *ousiai* are particulars.

Defenders of the opposing interpretation would counter this claim by pointing to the concluding lines of Z.6:

> And the sophistical objections to this position and the question whether Socrates and to be for Socrates are the same are resolved in the same way; for it makes no difference either in the things out of what one would construct the question or in those from which one would get a successful solution. (1032$^a$6–10)

They claim that this passage expresses Aristotle's commitment to individual essences (such things as the to be for Socrates) and that it summarizes for us the upshot of Z.6, the identity of a particular and the individual essence associated with it.[54] But the passage provides virtually no evidence on either point. It is not completely clear which

[54]See, e.g., Hartman, "Aristotle on the Identity of Substance and Essence," 551–552, and Terence Irwin, *Aristotle's First Principles*, 217–219.

sophistical objections and which question about Socrates Aristotle has in mind. It is not even clear what holding that there is such a thing as the to be for Socrates amounts to or who it is (those raising the sophistical questions?) that wants, in the unspecified sense, to hold that there is something answering to the description 'the to be for Socrates'; nor is there anything in the text to suggest any inclination at all on Aristotle's part to construe Socrates as a primary thing or a *kath hauto legomenon*. Finally, as Code points out, the text tells us only that the relevant objections can be handled in the same way as the question about Socrates, not that the question can be handled by the strategies employed in the case of the Z.6 Identity Thesis.[55] Whatever Aristotle may have in mind here, we can be sure that, if a doctrine of individual essences as primary *ousiai* were the central point of Z.6, he would have been less oblique in telling us this and he would not have expressed such an important result as the mere afterthought this remark so obviously is.

IX

I have said that the aim of Z.6 is to specify a condition any essence must satisfy if it is to belong to the set of essences that constitute the foundation of the hierarchy Aristotle proposes for us: it must be necessarily one and same as the primary *ousia* whose essence it is. Although there can be little doubt that the central aim of Z.6 is to argue for the identity of object and essence in the case of "things that are primary and said to be whatever they are in their own right" ($1031^b13-14$), it is not totally clear whether and how far beyond the case of primary *ousiai* Aristotle wants to insist on identity of object and essence. I close my initial discussion of essence by making a few very brief and tentative remarks on this question.

Aristotle opens the chapter with the perfectly general question, "whether each thing and [its] what it is to be are the same or different" ($1031^a15-16$). After outlining arguments, none of which he finds completely satisfactory, to show that we should deny the relevant sameness in the case of "things said by coincidence" (the example is *white man*); $1031^a19-28$), Aristotle turns to a defense of the more limited claim I have called the Z.6 Identity Thesis ($1031^a28$ff.). Three times later in the chapter he formulates the claim he seeks to prove using language indicating that it is the more restrictive thesis he is concerned with ($1031^b12-13$, 19–20; $1032^a5-6$). One can, however, make a good case (as Alan Code

[55]Code, "On the Origins of Some Aristotelian Theses about Predication," 114.

does[56]) for the view that Aristotle would hold to the identity of object and essence in the case of anything that is definable or, more precisely, that for things other than the primary realities Aristotle would hold to the relevant identity to the extent that the notions of definition and essence apply to those things. Code's argument here is straightforward. The definiens and definiendum in a correct definition signify the same thing. The definiens signifies the essence of what we seek to define; the definiendum, that object whose essence it is. But that is just to say that every definable object is one and the same as its essence; and since we have sameness of formula here, we have not just numerical sameness but necessary numerical sameness. Code claims that we need only supplement this line of argument with the idea that primary *ousia* is definable to generate the Z.6 Identity Thesis.

Aristotle does not actually employ this argument in Z.6. Indeed, if my interpretation of Z.6 is correct, he could not have used this argument. Aristotle's case for the Z.6 thesis is that it is a constraint on any metaphysical theory, one that follows from the very enterprise of identifying the primary *ousiai*. But if we make it a premise of our argument for the Z.6 thesis that primary *ousia* is definable, then since only universals are definable our argument begs the question in favor of ontologies that identify universals rather than particulars as the primary *ousiai*. If we agree that Aristotle is unwilling to construe Scotistic or Leibnizian essences as the primary realities, then it is a consequence of the Z.6 thesis that primary *ousia* is definable; but this is not, as Code suggests, a premise of the argument for that thesis.

If, however, we set aside the claim that primary *ousiai* are definable, Code's contention that, since the definiens and definiendum of any correct definition necessarily signify the same thing, every definable entity is necessarily the same as its essence certainly seems to represent genuinely Aristotelian doctrine. And although it is the more restrictive thesis he argues for in Z.6, Aristotle does at one point in the chapter ($1031^b22-28$) suggest that accident terms like 'white', when they function as names of accidents rather than paronymous terms true of the particulars that are their subjects, pick out things for which the identity of object and essence holds. Code's ingenious argument provides a nice rationale for this suggestion. But without calling either Aristotle's suggestion or Code's argument into question, I think we should recognize

---

[56]See, once again, Code, "On the Origins of Some Aristotelian Theses about Predication," 110–113, especially 113. See also Code, "Aristotle on Essence and Accident," 435–436. A similar treatment of the Z.6 thesis is found in Montgomery Furth, *Substance, Form, and Psyche*, 236–238.

that there are themes in Z.5 that do not unequivocally support the idea that each accident is necessarily one and the same with its essence.

Z.5 is difficult and often misunderstood. Its aim is to provide support for Aristotle's antiegalitarian conception of essence, the support (presented in Aristotle's response to the second aporia of the chapter) coming in some reflections on one of Aristotle's favorite examples, snubness.[57] The reflections concern the identifiability dependence of the essence associated with this attribute. Aristotle argues that when we seek to identify what it is to be for snubness we find that we can never get it just right. Either we exclude from our account the proper subject for the attribute, in which case we define not snubness but a different

[57]The second aporia focuses on the semantics of such expressions as 'snub nose'. Aristotle begins (1030$^b$28–32) by suggesting that 'snub nose' cannot be semantically equivalent to 'hollow nose' since their equivalence would result in the equivalence of 'snub' and 'hollow'; given that the formula of snubness, but not that of hollowness, requires a reference to nose, these latter two cannot be equivalent. Here Aristotle is merely reminding us of the need to refer to the proper subject in the formula of snubness, lest we say too little. Then he attempts (1030$^b$32–33) to show us that the requisite reference to nose is a reference to something extrinsic to snubness, so that incorporating it in the formula results in saying too much. The basic point here is just that 'snub nose' is neither "impossible to say" (ill-formed) nor involves "the same thing said twice" (redundant). Had nose been intrinsic to snubness, we would have had one of these two results. Then there is the suggestion (1030$^b$35–36) of a looming regress. It is typically thought that the regress here is something the individual who claims that we have a genuine definition and essence of a perfectly standard sort is committed to, but it is difficult to see just how this claim takes us beyond 'hollow nose nose'. I prefer to see the reference to an infinity of noses as part of Aristotle's response to someone who wants to deny that the nonredundancy of 'snub nose' shows nose to be extrinsic to snubness. The objector here is committed to the idea (a) that 'snub' can replace 'hollow' without redundancy. But, since (b) the phrase expressing the definiens of a correct definition can replace the term naming its definiendum, the objector must agree that 'snub nose' is semantically equivalent to 'hollow nose nose'; but if we apply (a) to this we get 'snub nose nose', which by the objector's own principles should be nonredundant. There is no end of 'nose's we can generate here, and for each new appearance of 'nose' in 'snub nose nose nose . . .' . our objector is committed to the nonredundancy of the resulting phrarse. At some point, the objector must admit redundancy. But the objector's reasons for admitting redundancy at that point are reasons for admitting it precisely where our trained ear tells us there is none, namely, in the case of 'snub nose'. So we have to admit that nose is extrinsic to snubness. Hence the dilemma: in giving the formula for snubness, either we say too little or we say too much. There is no getting it just right, so in the strict sense there is neither definition nor essence. Aristotle was worried about the puzzles he confronts in Z.5 throughout his career. For his early responses to the puzzles, see *De Sophisticis Elenchis* 13 (173$^b$ff.) and 30 (181$^b$36–182$^a$6). For other quite different interpretations of Z.5, see Ross, *Aristotle's Metaphysics*, vol. 2, 172–175; J. E. Hare, "Aristotle and the Definition of Natural Things," *Phronesis* (1979), 168–179; Burnyeat, et al., eds., *Notes on Book Zeta*, 29–32; and Montgomery Furth, ed. and trans., *Aristotle: Metaphysics Books Zeta, Eta, Theta, Iota* (Indianapolis: Hackett, 1985), 110–111. See also Aristotle's account of definition by addition at 1029$^b$30–33, where it is clear that such definition goes beyond the what it is to be of the thing defined and makes reference to something extrinsic. The example given is that of defining *white* by giving the formula for *white man*.

attribute (viz., hollowness), or we include in our formula a reference to that in which snubness is found (viz., nose). But, then, it turns out that we say too much. We have what Aristotle calls a definition by addition. We incorporate in our account something extrinsic to the what it is to be for snubness. And as proof that nose is indeed extrinsic to snubness, Aristotle points out that the expression 'snub nose' is neither ill-formed nor redundant. So it is not possible to specify just what the essence of snubness is, and this is not just an epistemological problem. Since essence is what is expressed by a correct definition, the problem here lies in the essence of snubness itself. Snubness, we might say, has a defective essence. Now, Aristotle believes that the problems that arise in our attempts to identify the essence of snubness arise in the case of all accidents. If accidents are definable at all, it is only by addition, so all accidents have defective essences. Accordingly, Aristotle concludes, we are right to take *ousiai* alone to have essences in the full sense; the term 'essence' is used only in one of several secondary or derivative senses when we speak of the essences of accidents (see 1031ª1–4), which is precisely what the *pros hen* analysis of the term tells us.

We might likely encounter problems in our attempt to see how the difficulties associated with the definition of snubness can be extended to the full range of accidents.[58] Aristotle, however, apparently did not, so it is difficult to understand how, when he held that the essences we might want to associate with accidents are in this way defective, he would contend that the identity of essence and object holds here. The difficulty is one of specifying just what this contention would have us identify an accident with. In general terms, of course, it is the essence of the accident. But what is that? It cannot be that which is expressed by a formula that fails to make a reference to the proper subject or first recipient of the accident; according to Aristotle, that formula does not give us enough. Neither can it be what is expressed by the formula that expands the original formula by specifying the relevant subject; the redundancy argument tells us that that formula gives us too much.

[58]Although the participants in the monthly seminar that resulted in Burnyeat et al., eds., *Notes on Book Zeta of Aristotle's Metaphysics* interpret the argument quite differently, they see (on p. 32) that the attempt to extend what I call the "too little or too much" dilemma to the case of all accidents would seem to require for each accident a second accident related to the first as hollowness is related to snubness. But we would have an infinite regress if that condition were to be met, and the Aristotle of *Posterior Analytics* A.22 assures us that we can get from something at the bottom of *any* categorial tree to what is at the top (the category) in a finite number of steps (see 83ᵇ13–17). Leaving this difficulty to the side, the fact is that as we move beyond the idiosyncratic snubness we do not find, for each accident, the relevant second accident that enables us to invoke the "too little" limb of the dilemma.

There just does not seem to be anything determinate here that is the essence, so talk of identity seems out of place.

Code's way of putting things is actually better than Aristotle's; as we have seen, Code qualifies the general claim that every definable thing is one and the same with its essence by telling us that the identity holds to the extent that the notions of definition and essence apply. I assume that Code does not mean to suggest that identity itself is subject to degrees. What he means, I take it, is that it is our inclination to ascribe numerical sameness that is subject to degrees, and the present case might give some sense to this idea. We might be unsure whether we should speak of definition and essence in the case of accidents, but to the extent that we are willing to do so we should be prepared to speak of numerical sameness of essence and object; for if it is not fully determinate just what the essence of a given accident is, neither is it fully determinate what the accident itself is. What we have here is not one fully determinate and completely specifiable thing, the accident, whose essence unfortunately lacks the relevant determinateness and specifiability. If the essence is defective in this way, then so is the thing whose essence it is. After all, we want to say, they are not two separate things. To argue this way, I take it, is to endorse the perspective Code suggests. Unfortunately, Code is a good bit clearer on this than is Aristotle. And even if we agree that Code's way of putting things is a faithful rendition of Aristotle's intended view, we must concede that Aristotle's unqualified suggestion that we have sameness here, made as it is within the context of his formulation of the more exacting Z.6 thesis, is at the very least somewhat misleading.[59]

[59]In fairness to Aristotle, one should point out that there is evidence that he was not fully convinced of the appropriateness of speaking of the identity or sameness of an accident and its essence. See, e.g., *De Anima* Γ.4 (429$^b$10), which is most naturally read as denying identity in this case.

# CHAPTER 4

# Two Kinds of
# Substance-Predication

I

In Z.4–5 we have found the form or structure for a theory of essences; the central idea is that some essences presuppose other essences and can be identified only by reference to them. This idea unfolds into the idea of a hierarchy of essences, in which an essence occupies that lowest level in the hierarchy such that there is no essence at that level or any higher level which the first essence presupposes or is identifiability-dependent on. At the foundation of the hierarchy, then, are essences that presuppose or depend on no other essences and, accordingly, can be independently identified. These are the essences of things that are both primary and *kath hauta legomena*—the primary *ousiai*. In Z.6 we have found that the fundamental essences and the primary *ousiai* whose essences they are must be necessarily one and the same or the same in formula. In summary, then, Z.4–6 give us the form or structure of any theory of *ousia*. First, a theory of *ousia* must identify things (i.e., essences) that constitute the foundational level in this hierarchy and justify the claim that they are foundational by showing that the formal characterization of Z.4–6 holds in their case: that they can play the explanatory role associated with the notion of something primary, that they are *kath hauta legomena*, and that they are necessarily one and the same with their essences. Second, a theory of *ousia* has to exhibit the system of dependencies and priorities that tie other things to these primary *ousiai* and primary essences. This activity involves allocating the essence of anything we may want to call a being its proper place among the levels in the hierarchy. But a central point is that Z.4–6 do not do these things for us. Although the formal characterization of the proposed framework may preclude certain kinds of answers to the questions we have to ask, Z.4–6 do not give us an ontological theory. They only suggest the form or structure such a theory must take. The hard work of outlining and defending a theory remains to be done. That work is started in Z.7.

It is agreed on all sides that Z.7–9 constitute a single unit of the text of Z and H. We are frequently told, however, that the three chapters were written independently of the rest of the middle books and inserted later.[1] There is evidence to suggest that something like this may be true. Quite apart from the kinds of textual and stylistic details that are the staple of scholars' attempts to identify a given stratum of a text, there are significant chunks of Z.7–9 that just do not appear germane to the discussions that occupy us throughout the rest of Z and H. I think, for example, of Z.7's excursion into makings and Z.9's curious discussion of spontaneous coming to be.[2] But, although it is difficult to reach genuine certitude in matters related to the composition of the Aristotelian texts, I like to think that, if their composition was indeed independent of the rest of Z and H, Z.7–9 were inserted into the body of the middle books by Aristotle himself.[3] In spite of their occasional ramblings in irrelevant directions, they provide precisely what we would expect to find after Z.4–6, an introduction to the explanatory notions central to the theory which will provide content for the formal structure outlined in the chapters on essence. Here it is important to recognize that with the exception of Z.4's reference to *eidos* (a reference we have found to be ambiguous, perhaps even intentionally ambiguous) there is nothing in Z.4–6 to indicate the kind of conceptual machinery to be employed in our attempts to identify the primary *ousiai*; were we to move directly from Z.4–6 to Z.10, we would find the move disorienting.[4] In Z.10–11, Aristotle discusses the notion of essence from the perspective of the conceptual tools developed in Z.7–9. Without the detailed discussion of matter, form, and composite these latter chapters provide, we would

[1]See, e.g., Burnyeat et al., *Notes on Book Zeta*, 54; Furth, ed., *Aristotle: Metaphysics Books Zeta, Eta, Theta, Iota*, 114–115.

[2]See 1032ª25–1033ª4 and 1034ª8–29. I do not mean to suggest that one cannot make a case for the idea that these two discussions have a place within the whole of Z and H; but I think we have to agree that this would take a bit of straining.

[3]Frede and Patzig seem to agree; nonetheless, they understand Aristotle's use of Z.7–8 quite differently. See their *Aristoteles "Metaphysik Z,"* vol. 1, 24–25.

[4]For an extended discussion, the main points of which I still endorse, of the overall structure of Z and H, see my *"Ousia*: A Prolegomenon to *Metaphysics* Z and H," *History of Philosophy Quarterly* (1984), 241–266.

have nothing more than Z.3's statue example to orient us. The discussion surrounding that example is neither systematic nor theoretically satisfying; and after the rigors of Z.4–6, any insight it may provide is almost certain to be lost. So whatever their history, Z.7–9 belong where they are.

## II

Early in Z.7, (1032ª13–15), Aristotle says:

> Everything that comes to be comes to be [1] by something and [2] from something and [3] [it comes to be] something, and the something I speak of is in each category: either (a) this or how much or how qualified or where.

He goes on to identify the second item in this list with matter, and although he never explicitly labels the first and third items he seems to have in mind the agent and the form involved in a coming to be. This suggests that form is that which an object comes to be through change. The suggestion is reinforced by the opening lines of Z.8 where, after repeating the claim that things come to be "[1] by something . . . [2] from something . . . and [3] something" (1033ª23–27),[5] he goes on to talk about form. It is difficult to understand his ensuing remarks except as bearing on the third item in the list. But if Z.7 and Z.8 leave any room for doubt about Aristotle's notion of form, a remark in Λ.3 (1069ª36–1070ª2) is unambiguous:

> Everything that changes is [1] something and changes [2] by something and [3] into something. That by which it changes is the immediate mover; that which is changed, the matter; and that into which it is changed is the form.

Here he uses 'metaballein' ('to change') plus the preposition 'eis' ('into') rather than 'gignesthai' ('to come to be'), but the characterization he provides is continuous with the characterization of the third item in the lists presented in Z.7 and Z.8; further, he explicitly tells us that what we have here is a characterization of form.[6]

---

[5]The formula is repeated in *Metaphysics* Θ.8 (1049ᵇ27–29).

[6]It might be objected here that it is inappropriate to adduce texts from Λ in support of an interpretation of Z and H. My response is that the first five chapters present an account that is, in general, continuous with that of Z–H. I do, of course, have to confront 1071ª24–29, which is sometimes taken as evidence that Aristotle endorsed a doctrine of particular forms. I consider that text in my Chapter 7 discussion of Z.12–16.

Form, then, is that into which something changes or that which something comes to be through change. But that seems to imply that the canonical devices for identifying forms are expressions that can fill the blank in

$x$ comes to be (a) _____.

Thus, form words would seem to be concrete as opposed to abstract terms. In the case of the accidental categories, they would be terms like 'courageous' and 'spherical' rather than terms like 'courage' and 'sphericity'; in the case of the category of *ousia*, terms like 'man' and 'dog' rather than 'humanity' and 'caninity'.[7] Aristotle's own examples of form words tend to bear this out. In *Physics* A.7, where he introduces the notion of form, his stock example is 'musical'; in *Metaphysics* Z.7, where the concern is with forms from the category of *ousia*, Aristotle tells us that the "something (sc. which a thing comes to be) is a man or a plant or something like these" (1032ᵃ18–19). One of the examples of a form word here is the generic expression 'plant', but we can expect Aristotle to hold that nothing comes to be just a plant;[8] a thing comes to be a tulip or an aspidistra. But, then, although we can identify substance-forms generically, a more determinate label for expressing the something an object comes to be is a term like 'geranium' or 'catalpa'.

In the case of the accidental categories, the idea that form words are terms that can fill the blank in

$x$ comes to be (a) _____

might be thought to have the consequence that forms can never be the referents of expressions suited to play the role of grammatical subject; but the fact is that the Aristotle of the middle books feels quite comfortable using abstract terms to pick out accidents.[9] Indeed, he refers to the accidental categories themselves using both abstract terms like '*poiotes*' ('quality') and '*posotes*' ('quantity') and their concrete counterparts, '*poion*' ('qualified') and '*poson*' ('quantified'). (1028ᵃ12, 15, 19). As early as Z.1 (1028ᵃ20–30), however, he makes it clear that concrete terms do a

---

[7]On this particular issue, I side with William Charlton, who argues for a similar view of form in *Aristotle's Physics I and II*, especially 70–79. But on the issue of a persisting subject I am in sharp disagreement with both Charlton, who insists that that which remains and that which is subject are not the same (see, e.g., pp. 139–141), and Barrington Jones, "Aristotle's Introduction of Matter," who takes 'matter' and 'subject' to express merely the chronological antecedent in a coming to be.

[8]See *De Generatione et Corruptione* A.5 (322ᵃff.) and *Metaphysics* I.8 (1058ᵃ1–6).

[9]See, e.g., 1030ᵇ17, 19, and 31–32.

better job of expressing what accidents are than their abstract counter-parts. They identify accidents as things predicated of *ousiai*. If we as-sume that, in the case in which an expression signifying an accident fills the blank in our schema, what takes the place of *x* is always an expres-sion picking out an *ousia*, this is just what our recipe for form words implies.

On this score, the idea that accidents are forms represents a departure from the view we find in the *Categories*. It is not unreasonable to sup-pose that, at the time he wrote that treatise, Aristotle took abstract terms from the dependent categories (what he calls the names of things pres-ent in others) to be the primary vehicles for picking out accidents. He tells us that the *ousiai* of which such terms as 'courageous' and 'gram-matical' are true are paronyms of the relevant attributes; the idea that to apply these terms to an *ousia* is to say that the relevant attribute is present in that *ousia* suggests that Aristotle took such sentences as

(1)   Socrates is courageous

to be parsed or analyzed as

(1′)   Courage is present in Socrates.

But in Z and H, where accidents are what an *ousia* can come to be through change, our use of the concrete forms is construed as primary. Indeed, one can read the Aristotle of Z and H as holding that sentences incorporating abstract terms from the dependent categories can be para-phrased in terms of sentences whose only vehicles for identifying acci-dents are concrete terms,[10] so that even sentences expressing the defini-tion of an accident can be recast in terms of sentences in which we pick

---

[10]I take 1028ª20–30 to suggest the possibility of reducing contexts of the form ". . . *F-ness*. . ." to contexts of the form ". . . *F* . . ." (where '*F-ness*' and *F* are terms from the accidental categories). In "Towards an Aristotelian Theory of Abstract Entities," *Midwest Studies in Philosophy* (1986), 495–512, I use this text as the starting point for characterizing what I call the Aristotelian strategy for dealing with abstract entities. The strategy involves a set of recipes for taking us from sentences in which we appear to be referring to abstract entities to sentences whose only referring devices pick out concrete objects. One might object that I misrepresent Aristotle's remark in making it the fountainhead of strategies seeking to vindicate the nominalistic view that there are no abstract entities. The article was not, however, an exegetical piece on Aristotle, and the use I put the Z.1 text to was merely dialectical. I did not mean to suggest that Aristotle actually denied the existence of forms. Even the Z.1 text is best viewed as the attempt to characterize the ontological status of form (as something predicable) rather than the suggestion of an eliminationist strategy to support the view that there are no forms. Whatever my intentions may have been, it was unwise to use the term 'Aristotelian' to refer to the nominalistic gambit I was pursuing in that paper.

out the appropriate kind of *ousia* and apply to it suitably chosen concrete expressions.[11]

If we suppose that the Aristotle of Z and H continues to maintain that, in the case of terms from the category of *ousia*, it is one and the same expression that functions as grammatical subject and grammatical predicate, then the application of our schema to that catetgory creates no parallel difficulties. There is, however, a different problem on the horizon. Applied to the case of *ousia*, we have said, our criterion has the effect of construing words like 'man' and 'aspidistra' as terms expressing form. The difficulty is that Aristotle repeatedly tells us in Z and H that terms like these express both form and matter. In Z.8 ($1033^b25$–26), for example, he tells us that *man* and *animal* are like *bronze sphere* inasmuch as they incorporate both matter and form. The idea is reiterated in Z.10, where Aristotle claims that *man* and *horse* are composites of form and matter "taken universally"($1035^b27$–30).[12] In Z.11 ($1036^b22$–28), the point finds more dramatic expression. We are told that it is "useless labor" on the part (presumably) of the Platonist "to reduce all things to forms and to eliminate the matter." *Man*, he insists once again, can be defined only by reference to the appropriate matter. The conclusion these remarks suggest is that general terms from the category of *ousia* express both form and matter, so it would appear to be a mistake on Aristotle's part to treat such terms as 'man' and 'aspidistra' as form words; and my characterization of form words as expressions that can fill the blank in

$x$ comes to be (a) _____

would only seem to translate Aristotle's mistake into a formula.

This difficulty suggests another look at *Physics* A.7; for, although that chapter is earlier than the texts we are concerned with, it contains a number of interesting comments about the language of change. Of particular interest for our purposes is Aristotle's claim that we can identify the product of a coming to be by employing what he calls "either simple or complex expressions" ($189^b32$–$190^a5$). We can say, of

---

[11]This raises an intriguing question about the applicability of the formal theory of Being and Having (developed by Grice and Code) to the doctrines of Z and H. An account that takes the idea of one thing's Having another as a primitive notion would not, on the face of it, serve as accurate reconstruction of an account that takes sentences of the form "$x$ is $F$" to be basic and explains sentences of the form "$x$ has *F-ness*" in terms of them. See Code's "Aristotle: Essence and Accident," 414–423, for the presentation of the formal theory. A text that suggests that the Code–Grice analysis still holds is $1049^a28$–34. I suspect that the Aristotle of the middle books is ambivalent here.

[12]See also *Metaphysics* I.9 ($1058^b15$).

Socrates, for example, that he comes to be *musical* or that he comes to be a *musical man*. These two ways of characterizing the product of the change differ in that the latter, but not the former, incorporates a reference to the subject or the matter of the coming to be—the man that is Socrates. I call expressions like 'musical man' that succeed in identifying the product of the coming to be only through a reference to its subject or matter *mixed product designators*; expressions like 'musical' I call *pure product designators*. The distinction is important, since in *Physics* A.7 Aristotle insists that it is only pure product designators that function as form words.

What is suggested here is that my original characterization provides a necessary but not a sufficient condition of something's being a form word. Not all expressions that can fill the blank in

*x* comes to be (a) _____

are form words, but only those that are pure product designators. But, although the distinction between pure and mixed designators enables us to identify form words from the accidental categories, it is initially unclear how it resolves our problem with substance terms. Presumably, we are to look for a distinction corresponding to that between 'musical' and 'musical man' in the category of *ousia*. The difficulty is that an examination of substance terms reveals no parallel distinction. Our only devices for identifying the products of comings to be within the category of *ousia* are such expressions as 'man' and 'aspidistra'; and although their surface grammar might suggest that they are pure, Aristotle's treatment of these expressions seems to mark them out as mixed product designators.

In Z.10 we meet with a remark that points to a resolution of this problem. After referring to the concrete object that the sculptor fashions out of bronze as a statue, Aristotle speaks of "the statue when this is said in the sense of form" (1035ª6–9). The suggestion here is that the term 'statue' is ambiguous, that it has both a mixed product sense in which it signifies the kind of concrete object or composite that is the result of the sculptor's creative activity and a pure product sense in which it signifies only the form the sculptor imposes on the matter. Likewise, in Z.9 (1034ª23–24) Aristotle implies that the term 'house' can refer, not only to the concrete thing that comes to be, but also to its form as that is present in the housebuilder's soul; again, in H.2 (1043ª14–18) we find him making the point apropos of artifacts when he tells us that those who define house as "a receptacle that shelters goods and bodies" are using the term 'house' to refer to the form whereas those who supplement this definition by reference to "the stones and bricks and boards" out of which the relevant receptacle is made are speaking of the house that is a composite of matter and form. In H.3, however, Aristotle is more explicit:

> It is necessary to recognize that sometimes it is not clear whether the name signifies the composite or the actuality and the form. For example, in the case of 'house', whether it is a sign of the composite thing because it is a covering of bricks and stones lying there or of the actuality and the form because it is a covering; and in the case of 'line', whether it is two in length or two; and in the case of 'animal', whether it is a soul in a body or a soul. (1043ª29–35)

Aristotle's examples here do not bear immediately on terms like 'man' and 'aspidistra'. They include an artifact expression, a term from geometry, and a generic expression from the category of *ousia*. Nonetheless, the implications of the point Aristotle makes in their regard for our chosen cases should be clear. Expressions like 'man' and 'aspidistra' apply to both the form and the composite object, but they are used homonymously in the two cases. Thus substance terms like these can function as pure product designators corresponding to 'musical' from *Physics* A.7, but they can also function as mixed product designators corresponding to 'musical man'. Functioning in the latter way, they express both matter and form; functioning in the former way, they are form words.[13]

Thus the disanalogy between the case of *ousia* and the case of accident is only apparent. The appearance of disanalogy derives from the fact that a single linguistic expression does double duty as a pure and a mixed product designator. Functioning in either way, a term like 'man'

---

[13]The homonymy of substance terms is elaborated in my "Form, Species, and Predication in *Metaphysics* Z, H. and Θ," *Mind* (1979), 1–23, and "*Ousia*: A Prolegomenon to *Metaphysics* Z and H. See also John Ackrill, "Aristotle's Definitions of *Psuche*, "*Proceedings of the Aristotelian Society* (1972–73), 119–133, especially 125 ff., for an application of the homonymy doctrine to unravel a puzzle about the relation of body and soul in the person. Terence Irwin, *Aristotle's First Principles*, 243 and 567, challenges the significance Ackrill and I attribute to the distinction between what I call pure and mixed uses of substance terms. He cites 1043ª37–1043ᵇ1 as proof that Aristotle takes the distinction to be unimportant in the case of sensible *ousiai*. However, the '*tauta*' of 1043ª37 refers to the question of whether *ousia* terms are *pros hen* expressions and not to the question of homonymy. If we interpret Aristotle as Irwin does, we cannot make sense of the '*dei agnoein*' of 1043ª29, nor to the appeal to the distinction of senses of 1043ᵇ2–4. There is a straightforward reason the *pros hen* question is not an issue. Since it is so obvious that, as Aristotle puts it, "essence belongs to the form and actuality" (1043ᵇ1–2), the question of just what is primary *ousia* cannot be a matter of serious discussion. The form is the only candidate in the field, so it must be the focus for the different senses of a substance-term.

can serve as an answer to the question, What did *x* come to be? but it is only in its pure product sense that it enables us to identify the product of an *ousia*'s coming to be exclusively in terms of its form.

### III

We are not, however, likely to find clarity in this regard of any deep theoretical interest, since the idea that substance terms are homonymous is unlikely to strike us as anything more than an ad hoc device for preserving the analogy between two cases of coming to be, the case (often called qualified or accidental coming to be) of an *ousia* taking on an accident not previously predicated of it and the case (often called unqualified or substantial coming to be or generation) in which the product is an *ousia* that did not previously exist.

In fact, the doctrine that substance terms are homonymous has more significant applications in Z and H. As a first step toward getting clear on these applications, we must recognize that, with the possible (and admittedly problematic) exception of Z.4's use of the term, '*eidos*' serves in Z and H as an expression for picking out form. In Aristotle's earlier works the term serves to pick out species; this has led a large number of commentators to suppose that Aristotle simply identifies substance-forms and substance-species in his most mature writings on *ousia*.[14] I believe that this is a serious mistake. The idea of a substance-species is the idea of a lowest level kind under which particulars fall. Their species mark these particulars out as what they are and, accordingly, are said or predicated of them essentially. The familiar particulars of the *Categories* ("a certain man" and "a certain horse") are, by the lights of Z and H, composites of matter and form. And although Aristotle no longer uses the term '*eidos*' to refer to the lowest-level kinds to which those composites belong, he continues to recognize those kinds and distinguishes them sharply from the things he now wants to call *eide*. And the doctrine of the homonymy of substance terms figures prominently in these developments.

Toward showing this, I want to bring together a number of seemingly unrelated texts. The first comes from Z.10. I have already alluded to it, but it is sufficiently illuminating to quote in full:

---

[14]See, e.g., M. J. Woods, "Problems in *Metaphysics* Z, Chapter 13," in J. M. E. Moravscik, ed., *Aristotle*, 215–238, especially 215–223 (passim); G. E. L. Owen, "The Platonism of Aristotle," 160; Woods, "Substance and Essence in Aristotle," 168; Montgomery Furth, *Substance, Form, and Psyche*, 50–51; and Daniel Graham, *Aristotle's Two Systems*, 61.

> But *man* and *horse* and things like them that are said of particulars, but
> universally, are not *ousia* but a certain composite of this formula and this
> matter taken universally. ($1035^b27-30$)

Given the reference to both form (referred to as 'formula' here) and
matter, we can conclude that Aristotle is using 'man' and 'horse' in their
mixed product sense. He wants to deny that what they signify is *ousia*.
Later we will find this denial to be critical; for the present I want to focus
on the idea that in their mixed product sense terms like 'man' and
'horse' signify universals said of particulars. The very next sentence in
the text identifies the particulars Aristotle has in mind here. He tells us
that "Socrates, on the other hand, is a particular made out of the ultimate matter" ($1035^b30-31$). I suggest that the universals Aristotle is
referring to in our text are the things he called *eide* in the *Categories*. He is
talking about the lowest-level substance-kinds under which particulars
such as Socrates fall, and he is telling us that in their mixed product
senses substance terms express or signify those kinds.

First, it is significant that Aristotle uses as his examples the universals
*man* and *horse*; in the *Categories* those were his favorite examples of
infimae species. Second, the universals Aristotle has in mind are those
said or predicated of the familiar particulars of common sense. In an
Aristotelian context, it is difficult to point to universals other than
substance-kinds that could be plausibly thought to play this role. Finally, the universals in question are characterized in just the way substance-kinds should, given the doctrines of Z and H, be characterized. If
we hold, as the Aristotle of the middle books does, that the primary
*ousiai* of the *Categories* are to be construed as composites of matter and
form, then the universals that serve to provide the most complete and
informative answer to the question What is it? posed in their case have
to reflect this. They have to mark those objects out as what they are, and
universals that can be characterized as "composites of this formula and
this matter taken universally" are the only universals that fit this bill. So
Aristotle wants to hold that in their mixed product senses terms like
'man' and 'horse' are true of the familiar particulars of common sense
and express or signify the lowest-level kinds under which those particulars fall. Since we in English have different terms for species and form,
we can express the view Aristotle summarizes in this passage from Z.10
by saying that in their mixed product sense, lowest-level substance
terms express or signify the infimae species under which ordinary
objects fall.[15]

[15]John Driscoll, "*Eide* in Aristotle's Earlier and Later Theories of Substance," in Dominic
O'Meara, ed., *Studies in Aristotle* (Washington, D.C.: Catholic University of America

This passage, however, contrasts sharply with one from H.2, where Aristotle tells us that

> in the case of *ousia*, the thing predicated of the matter is the actuality itself. (1043ª5–6)

In conjunction with Aristotle's repeated claim that form is actuality, this passage entails that substance-forms are predicated of their matter. But we do not have to rely on inference here, for in Θ.7 Aristotle tells us that when the form and the this is predicated, the ultimate [subject] is matter and material *ousia*. (1049ª34–36)

A substance-form, then, is predicated of its matter; but the proper linguistic device for expressing a substance-form is the appropriate substance term in its pure product sense, so that in its pure product sense a substance word is properly applied not to individuals such as Socrates but to something else—the matter making up those individuals.[16]

Aristotle denies, then, that the contrast between the two senses of a substance term confronts us only when we are concerned to identify the product of an unqualified coming to be. Substance terms can, in both their pure and mixed senses, function predicatively. But, whereas in the former case there is a single context ('x comes to be a _____') where a substance term can be correctly employed in both its senses, there are distinct contexts for the predication of a substance expression in its pure and mixed senses. In its mixed product sense, a substance-term can appear in singular subject-predicate sentences like

(2)   George Bush is a man.

As it functions in a sentence of this sort, the substance word expresses or signifies a substance-species; the effect of applying the term is to express the fact that a species is said of one of its members. Functioning as a pure product expression, however, a substance term can serve as predicate only in sentences whose subject term picks out something other than an ordinary particular—a parcel of matter that makes up or

---

Press, 1981), 129–159; on 147–148, Driscoll points out how the use of *'epi'* in the Z.10 text matches the use of the term to identify the relation between species and members in *De Sophisticis Elenchis* 22 (179ª8–9) and convincingly argues that Aristotle withholds this term to express the relationship between a form and the individual whose form it is.

[16]See also *De Carelo* A.9 (278ª2–10 and 278ᵇ33) for confirmation of the distinction between form and species. And see *Metaphysics* Z.10 (10359ª29–30) for the homonymy thesis as applied to 'circle'. The thesis may also be implicit in *De Anima* A.1 (403ª29ff.), but I suspect that at the time Aristotle wrote *De Anima* the implications of the thesis were not fully clear to him.

constitutes such a particular. Presumably, then, we apply a substance term in its pure product sense to something like the pack of flesh and bones that makes up George Bush, the clump of cortex and phloem that makes up the oak tree in my back yard, or the parcel of stuff that makes up the geranium on the florist's shelf. In these cases, the predicated term signifies a form, and the point of applying the term is to express the fact that the form is predicated of its matter.

Sentences like (2), then, express *species-predications*. Using such sentences we pick out a concrete individual (what in the *Categories* we called a primary *ousia*) and subsume it under its lowest-level kind, thereby identifying *what* it is. Presumably, the following are examples of the kind of predication Aristotle has in mind in H.2 and Θ.7:

(3)    That pack of flesh and bones is a man.
(4)    That clump of cortex and phloem is an oak tree.

Let us say that such sentences as (3) and (4) express *form-predications*. Now, whereas sentences like (2) are used to say what a thing is, this is not the case with sentences expressing form-predications. When we say that a certain pack of flesh and bones is a man, we are not saying what that parcel of matter is; for what it is is just a pack of flesh and bones. Likewise, in the case of (4), the effect of predicating 'oak tree' is not to specify what the clump of cortex and phloem under discussion is; such a specification has already been given in the linguistic expression that functions as the subject term of (4). But the fact that the expressions that serve as grammatical subjects of (3) and (4) are definite descriptions constructed out of general terms that identify what the relevant parcel of matter is is not what is crucial here. Suppose we found it useful to employ proper names in the case of parcels of matter; suppose we called George Bush's flesh and bones Ronnie. Finally, suppose that proper names do not connote properties or attributes of their bearers, but are mere tags. Then, although

(5)    Ronnie is a man

would be true, it would be

(6)    Ronnie is a pack of flesh and bones,

and not (5), which would serve to identify what the parcel of matter is.

So, whereas a sentence like (2) expresses a relation of essential predication, (3), (4), and (5) do not. In the case in which we correctly apply a substance term in its mixed product sense, we subsume a particular under the universal that provides the most complete and informative answer to the What is it? question, the universal whose instantiation gives us the conditions for that particular's existence. Aristotle, however, has already told us in Z.3 that, where a form is predicated of its matter, "the to be of the subject is different from that" of the thing predicated (1029ª22–23). And he explicitly tells us that this is true whether the predicated form is, as he puts it, *ousia* or something from one of the accidental categories. So where a form is predicated of something other than itself, it never marks its subject out as what it is; it determines how some independently identifiable subject is. As Aristotle tells us in Z.3, the predication of a form of its matter is always an instance of accidental predication.[17]

A consequence is that whereas a sentence like (2) expresses a relationship of de re necessity, such sentences as (3), (4), and (5) do not. Since to be a man is what to be is for George Bush, it is impossible for him to exist and fail to instantiate that universal. The pack of flesh and bones that makes up George Bush could, however, exist, even if the relevant form were not predicated; it could be a corpse rather than a living human being. The same is true of the cortex and phloem that make up my oak tree.[18] The form signified by 'oak tree' in its pure product sense need not be predicated of it. That same parcel of stuff could be something other than an oak tree; it could be a desk, a table, or a pile of firewood.


IV


In discussing the predicative tie linking a form and its matter, I have taken the liberty of invoking talk about the structure and semantical interpretation of certain sentences as well as talk about the linguistic activities ingredient in the assertive utterance of those sentences. In this respect, I have gone against the mainstream of recent work on Z and H. The tendency nowadays is to draw a sharp distinction between the

---

[17]See 1029ª23–24. There are difficulties inherent in the idea that prime matter is an independently identifiable subject. These difficulties are the focus of Section II of Chapter 7. In this initial elaboration of the concept of a form-predication, I am working with the less problematic case of the analysis of a familiar object like George Bush or the oak tree in my back yard. At this level of analysis, a form is predicated of a parcel of familiar matter, and there is no problem in identifying (independently of any reference to the predicated form) the parcel of matter that is subject and saying what it is.

[18]The perceptive reader might object that if George Bush were to die we would no longer have flesh and bones but materials that are flesh and bone in name only. I would ask that reader to postpone the objection until Section V of Chapter 5.

notions of linguistic and ontological or metaphysical predication and to hold that in the middle books Aristotle is concerned exclusively with the latter. Indeed, those who have recognized the existence of what I have called form-predications have typically denied that the Aristotle of Z and H provides us any account at all of the linguistic expression of the case of a form being predicated of its matter.[19] Now, there can be little doubt that the distinction between linguistic and ontological predication is legitimate. Furthermore, we run the risk of seriously misrepresenting Aristotle's views if we construe what is intended as an account of a metaphysical relation between matter and form as a characterization of the structure of certain, selected subject-predicate sentences. Nevertheless, the text gives the lie to the view that Aristotle has no interest at all in language in the middle books. We should, in any case, be wary of the idea that the Aristotle of Z and H would have been satisfied with a theory that imputes, for a whole family of cases, an ontological relation of subject and predicate lacking any recognizable expression in ordinary discourse. As I see it, the doctrine that general terms from the category of *ousia* are homonymous just is the attempt to make plausible the idea that the ontological relation of predication tying matter and form has an expression in familiar, nontheoretical language. The suggestion is that, just as language provides us the resources for characterizing the product of a qualified coming to be in both pure and mixed terms, it affords us the machinery for drawing a parallel distinction in the case of unqualified coming to be. And, of course, the legitimacy of drawing the relevant distinction extends beyond the narrow concern with characterizing the products of coming to be, so that we can go on and identify things of which it is true to say (in the mixed product sense) that they are men or oak trees as well as things of which it is true to say this only in the pure product sense.

Still, while insisting that Aristotle provides us with an account of the linguistic expression of form-predication, I concede that it is the ontological relation between a metaphysical subject and its metaphysical predicate that is most before Aristotle's mind in his discussions of matter and form in Z, H, and Θ. Some commentators would, however,

---

[19]For the distinction between linguistic and ontological predication, see Code, "Aristotle on Essence and Accident," 422–423; Lewis, "Form and Predication in Aristotle's *Metaphysics*," 63–65; and James Bogen's introduction to Bogen and McGuire, eds., *How Things Are*. Lewis explicitly denies that Aristotle has any account of the linguistic expression of what I call form predication; see p. 64 of "Form and Predication." D. K. Modrak, "Forms and Compounds," in *How Things Are*, 85–99, especially 85, agrees. Although Daniel Graham, *Aristotle's Two Systems*, 64–65, does not distinguish form and species, he denies that the Aristotle of Z and H has any interest in the linguistic counterparts of the metaphysical relations he characterizes.

deny that the Aristotle of the middle books invokes any notion of predication, whether linguistic or ontological, in his account of matter and form,[20] and they would likely insist that when he speaks of matter as a subject he is invoking a quite different sense of the term. Matter, they would say, is a subject for change rather than for predication; matter just is what undergoes or suffers change.[21]

The claim that the matter-form relation is not that of metaphysical subject and metaphysical predicate, the denial that subjects of change are subjects of predication, and even the more cautious suggestion that we need some sort of justification for invoking the subject-predicate relation to characterize an independently identifiable relation between matter and form all strike me as serious misrepresentations of Aristotle's view. As he understands it, the matter-form relation just is one kind of subject-predicate relation—the most basic kind, it turns out. If we think back to *Physics* A.7 (189ᵇ32ff.) where the notion of matter and form are first introduced, we find Aristotle characterizing coming to be in terms of the relation of predication and then invoking the labels 'matter', 'form', and 'privation' to summarize the results of this characterization. He is, of course, concerned to show that the analytical tools he is developing grow naturally out of the familiar patterns exhibited in the language the nonphilosopher deploys in describing particular cases of coming to be, but it is the ontological structure of coming to be that he is ultimately concerned to delineate. When he calls the man who, being unmusical, comes to be musical, a subject, Aristotle is not invoking some novel and hitherto unexplained sense of 'subject'. In *Physics* A.7 he is using 'subject' in the familiar sense operative in the *Categories*. The man of A.7 is a subject in the sense that he is that of which what is expressed by the term 'musical' comes to be predicated. What drives the analysis here is the idea (which comes out so nicely in the English translation of '*gignesthai*' as 'come to be') that coming to be is a sort of movement from one instance of ontological predication to another. Since his contention is that this movement is a genuine instance of

[20]Among those who express reservations about the idea that the relation of matter and form is that of subject and predicate are Richard Blackwell, "Matter as a Subject of Predication in Aristotle," 19–30; Russell Dancy, "Aristotle's Second Thoughts, 411; Richard Rorty, "Genus as Matter: A Reading of *Metaphysics* Z–H," in E. N. Lee, A. P. D. Mourelatos, and R. M. Rorty, eds., *Exegesis and Argument: Studies in Greek Philosophy Presented to Gregory Vlastos* (Assen: Van Gorcum, 1973), 393–420, especially 400–402; V. C. Chappell, "Aristotle's Conception of Matter," *Journal of Philosophy* (1975), 679–696, especially 690–691; S. Marc Cohen, "Essentialism in Aristotle," 400ff.; and Charlotte Witt, *Substance and Essence in Aristotle*, 125–129.

[21]The suggestion that there is ambiguity here is made by Barnes, *Aristotle's Posterior Analytics*, 118; Dancy, "Matter: Aristotle and Chappell," *Journal of Philosophy* (1973), 698–699; and Blackwell, "Matter as a Subject of Predication in Aristotle," 20.

change rather than some sort of replacement of one state of affairs by a new and unrelated state of affairs, Aristotle insists that there is some one thing that remains or persists; and, pace many commentators, he insists that it persists or remains *as subject*.[22] 'Matter' is the label he places on this persisting subject, and 'form', on what it comes to be or what comes to be predicated of it. So *Physics* A.7 does not proceed by assimilating an independently intelligible pair of concepts to the model provided by a distinct pair of notions. Any understanding we had of the notions of matter and form had its origins in our prior understanding of the notions of subject and thing predicated. It is not surprising, then, that in *Physics* A.7 Aristotle introduces the technical term 'matter' quite casually, as though it were a mere variant on the term 'subject';[23] nor is it surprising that in Z.7 and Z.8 Aristotle characterizes form in terms that highlight the fact that forms are predicated entities.

The Aristotle of *Physics* A.7 is aware that reflection on cases like the man's becoming musical has only limited value in the attempt to underwrite a general characterization of coming to be. He does attempt to show that the idea of a persisting subject in the case of unqualified coming to be is not completely foreign when he defends the claim that "there is always something that serves as subject from which the thing that comes to be comes to be" ($190^{b}3–4$) by reminding us that "the plants and the animals come to be from seed" ($190^{b}4–5$). But at the end of A.7 he admits that the idea of a persisting subject of predication in the case of unqualified coming to be is something we ultimately grasp only by an analogical extension of the characterization provided for the easy cases that have been the focus of the chapter:

> The nature as subject [or, that which is nature by way of being subject] is known by analogy. Just as bronze stands to a statue, as wood (stands) to a bed, or matter and that without form before it has the form stands to any of the other things that has form, so this stands to *ousia*, to the "this something" and the "being." ($191^{a}8–12$)

[22]See, again, Charlton, *Aristotle's Physics I and II*, 74–75, 139–141; Jones, "Aristotle's Introduction of Matter," 474–500; and King, "Aristotle without *Prima Materia*," 377–385. I take $192^{a}31–32$, $194^{b}23–24$, $319^{b}13$ff., $1013^{a}4$, $1013^{a}24–25$, $1032^{b}32–1033^{a}1$, and $1069^{b}14–15$ as cumulatively providing compelling evidence that matter persists. Quite apart from Aristotle's explicit insistence (marked by his use of *'emparchein'*) that the matter that comes to be this or that is a constituent in the end product of the coming to be, there is the point (made by Dancy in "Aristotle's Second Thoughts," 386) that it is difficult to see how, if we deny that change has a persisting subject, we can avoid the result that the opposites relevant to the change act on each other, something Aristotle denies possible in, e.g., $189^{a}22–27$.

[23]Notice that the term *'hule'* is used at $190^{b}25$ (without any kind of formal introduction) as a mere variant on *'hupokeimenon'*.

Commentators sometimes take this passage to be a veiled reference to prime matter;[24] but Aristotle has nothing so specific in mind. What is operative is the more general idea that in the case of unqualified coming to be there is some persisting subject of predication and that we are to understand its relation to what Aristotle characterizes as *'ousia'*, the "this something," and the "being" by reflecting on the relationship tying what serves as persisting subject in the familiar cases he mentions to the product of the changes for which it is subject. The relation he has in mind is not that holding between the relevant subject and what it comes to be (that is, the form predicated of it);[25] the relation we are to focus on is that between the subject and the composite picked out by what I have dubbed a mixed product designator. The terms 'statue' and 'bed' are, by the lights of Z.10, homonymous expressions, signifying both composite and form; but there is no hint at all here of the homonymy doctrine of the middle books. The relationship Aristotle directs us to is explicitly characterized as that holding between subject or matter and *that which has the form*—the composite. So the analogical thinking Aristotle recommends presumably terminates in an understanding of the relation between the subject of an unqualified coming to be and the composite that is the mixed product of that coming to be; form enters the analogy since the relationship between the persisting subject (the quantity of bronze or the quantity of wood) and the statue or the bed resulting from the creative activity of the sculptor or carpenter can be identified only by reference to the form that is predicated of the subject. It is only in virtue of the fact that the relevant subject comes to have predicated of it the appropriate form that the process in question terminates in a statue or a bed. Aristotle is suggesting, then, that the composite thing (the familiar "this something" of the *Categories*) comes to be only because some persisting subject (something that exists before, during, and after the coming to be) comes to have predicated of it a form. So the analogical thinking has as its terminus only the general idea that the coming to be of the things we called primary *ousiai* in the *Categories* requires some subject of which some form comes to be predicated. This very general idea ultimately calls into question the *Categories* idea that the familiar particulars that come into being have the privileged status Aristotle accorded them in that early work, but the agnosticism of 191$^b$19–20 suggests that Aristotle has not yet sorted out in his own mind the implications of the idea. From the perspective we enjoy, however, it is easy to appreciate how radical the idea is: it implies

[24]See, e.g., Joseph Owens, "Matter and Predication in Aristotle," 209–211.
[25]As is claimed by Daniel Graham, *Aristotle's Two Systems*, 149.

that there is something with a claim to status as subject such that its standing in a predicative relation to something else is both a necessary and sufficient condition for the coming into being of things like the individual man and the individual horse of *Categories* 5.[26]

It is not surprising that Aristotle should not have fully appreciated the implications of the analogy he outlines; nor is it surprising that *Physics* A.7 gives us only the analogy without filling in the appropriate details. If we try to work our way through examples, we see that the materials required for filling in the analogy have not yet been assembled. Consider the proverbial acorn becoming an oak tree, the example suggested by Aristotle's curt remark about plants and animals coming to be out of seed. Just what is the persisting subject of predication here? The acorn, we want to say; but the acorn cannot be what we are after since, once we have the seedling ready to be transplanted, there is no longer an acorn. *It* is not the persisting subject of predication required by the analogy. Indeed, as a device for identifying what we have at the initial stage of the process, 'acorn' functions more like 'unmusical man' than 'man'. We have to see a semantic complexity underlying our use of the apparently simple term 'acorn', and that same kind of complexity has to be read into the term 'oak tree' where it is used to pick out the composite thing growing in my back yard. All of this requires the doctrine of the homonymy of substance terms, a doctrine of which we find no traces in *Physics* A.7. But more is required here; we need to engage in detailed empirical investigations into the biology of oaks if we are to identify something like the clump of cortex and phloem that serves as persisting subject of predication as well as some counterpart to *musical* that we can legitimately take to be predicated of that subject. *Physics* A.7 provides the analytical tools for constructing an account of the internal structure of the primary realities of *Categories* 5, but much work, both metaphysical and empirical, is required before the account can actually be constructed.

But the central point is that in the case of neither qualified nor unqualified coming to be is our grasp of the analytical tools Aristotle is proposing independent of our grasp of the notions of metaphysical subject and predicate. In the easy case that Aristotle begins with, the

---

[26]It is interesting how the Aristotle of the *Physics* fails to see the problems he is creating for his own account of primary *ousia*, the subject criterion, and the Unanalyzability Thesis. He rehearses the subject criterion for *ousia*hood as nonproblematic ($186^b4$, $190^a36-37$, $204^a$ 24) but at the same time insists that form is the nature of a composite *ousia* ($193^b4$ff.) and poses as a theoretical problem for future investigation the question of whether the matter or the form is *ousia* ($191^a19-20$). He obviously has a good bit of sorting out to do.

persisting subject of predication is the man and what comes to be predicated of him is *musical*; in suggesting that this easy case is one whose generalization accommodates all cases of qualified coming to be, he relies on our willingness to concede that "when a thing comes to be so much, so qualified, related to something else, or somewhere, there is some subject" (190ᵃ34–35) on the grounds that "*ousia* alone is said of nothing else as subject, but all the other things are said of *ousia*" (190ᵃ 36–190ᵇ1). The analogy that underwrites the extension of the general form of analysis to the case of unqualified coming to be does no more than point us to things, as yet uncharacterized, that play certain functional roles. If there is to come to be a certain man or a certain horse, then there must be something that is a persisting subject of predication and something else that comes to be predicated of it. 'Matter' and 'form' are simply the labels we place on the things, whatever they turn out to be, that play these functional roles.²⁷

V

The ideas of matter and form are, then, to be understood in terms of the notions of metaphysical subject and metaphysical predicate as these figure in the process of coming to be; and where the concern is the matter and form of an *ousia*, it is unqualified coming to be that is the focus. As we have seen, Z.7 and Z.8 follow the strategy of *Physics* A.7 in introducing matter and form in terms of coming to be. But the move from the idea that a composite particular comes to be only because the subject or matter comes to have predicated of it the appropriate form to the idea that the existence of the composite presupposes that same predication seems innocent enough. After all, things that come to be are, after they have come to be, whatever it is that they have come to be; it is only reasonable to assume that whatever conditions must have come to obtain if a thing is to come to be something must continue to obtain if it is to continue to be that. Innocent or not, Aristotle makes the move, and he seems to take it to require no justification whatsoever. It is, in any case, this move that brings to light the contrast between the species-predications expressed by sentences like

(1)   George Bush is a man,

²⁷The idea that the relation of matter and form is that of metaphysical subject and predicate is reiterated over and over outside the middle books. See *Physics* B.1 (192ᵇ34); *De Anima* B.1 (412ᵃ19–20); *Metaphysics* A.3 (983ᵃ30), B.1 (995ᵇ35–36), and Δ.2 (1013ᵇ21).

where a substance term is used in its mixed product sense, and the form-predications expressed by sentences like

(3)   That pack of flesh and bones is a man

and

(4)   That clump of cortex and phloem is an oak tree,

where substance terms are used in their pure product senses.

This contrast lies at the core of the theory Aristotle develops and defends in Z and H, and many of the central claims of the middle books are formulated with an eye to it. Some of these claims involve what appear to be obscure uses of demonstrative pronouns. Since these claims (we can call them the "pronomial theses") clarify the contrast between form- and species-predications and provide a natural bridge to the dominant claim that form is primary *ousia*, I want to consider them in some detail.

I begin with the claim of Z.8 that form is a "such" and not a "this." This claim is a vehicle for expressing a variety of different themes. At the most elementary level, it enables Aristotle to contrast his own understanding of form with that of Platonists who hold that "there is a sphere over and above these spheres" and a house over and above "those made out of bricks" (1033$^b$19–21). After denying that form is a "this something," Aristotle tells us that

> [form] signifies "such" [*toinde*]. A person makes or generates a "such" [*toinode*] out of a "this" [*tode*]; and when it has been generated, it is a "this such" [*tode toinde*]. (1033$^b$22–24)

The use of '*toionde*' here is reminiscent of the use of '*poion*' in *Categories* 5 (3$^b$16–20), where Aristotle denies that a term of second substance signifies an individual or a "this something." If we invoke the semantical analysis of Z and H, we can make the *Categories* point by saying that in their mixed product senses general terms from the category of *ousia* do not function in the way proper names of particulars do. Their primary role in discourse is predicative: they enable us to say something about a concrete particular. In this passage from Z.8, Aristotle makes a parallel point about substance terms in their pure product senses. Correcting for the use/mention confusion, we can say that the characteristic role of form words is that of predicate rather than of logical subject. They enable us to fill the blank in sentences of the form *x* comes to be a _____,

and after the culmination of the relevant coming to be (Aristotle here calls it a *"generation"*), they can function predicatively in such sentences as our (3) and (4). The suggestion here is that it is because he failed to appreciate this fact and treated general terms simply as names of objects that, as Aristotle likes to put it, Plato separated the forms. Aristotle, however, takes these linguistic facts about pure product expressions to reveal the nature of the forms they signify. Forms are things predicated of something else; they are *how* something else is.[28] That something else is, of course, matter. It is the "this" or metaphysical subject for form, and the predication of form (the "such" or "how") of a parcel of matter (the "this") results in what is here called a "this such."[29] Aristotle goes on to identify the resulting "this such" with the concrete composite, and he tells us that it, rather than the form, is what comes to be.

Pretty obviously, we have more in these remarks than a passing critique of Plato. Let us begin with the last claim—that it is the "this

[28]Frede and Patzig, *Aristoteles "Metaphysik Z,"* vol. 1, 32, take this discussion to show that forms are not, as Plato thought, general, but rather particular. But generality is not the issue in Z.8. It is just assumed throughout the chapter that forms are general. At issue is the interpretation we put on the generality of form. Plato took forms to be "definite objects" and "this-somethings," whereas Aristotle takes them to be "suches" or "hows." The very use of *'toionde'* implies the generality of form.

[29]Alan Code, "Aristotle on Essence and Accident," 476, agrees that matter is a metaphysical subject but denies that it is a "this." Code is operating with a technical notion of "this" whose origins in Aristotle are not completely clear to me. Nevertheless, I am not certain that our disagreement here is more than verbal. I want to distinguish the idea of being a "this" and the concept of something that admits the "this something" epithet. A "this" is just a metaphysical subject for predication. Both the composite and its matter are "thises." The "this something" schema, on the other hand, has as its core idea that of a particular instance of a substance-kind, something that for appropriate K is a "this K." Relative to the kind K to which the composite whose matter it is belongs, nothing that functions as matter is a "this K." As we see in the next section, there is a secondary sense of the "this something" epithet, according to which the form whose predication of its matter constitutes a composite as something to which the "this something" epithet in its primary use applies is a "this something." Matter also fails to admit this use of the "this something" epithet. Matter does, however, serve as metaphysical subject for form, and that is all that is required to qualify as a "this" for a "this such" predication. Like Code, Edward Regis, "Aristotle's Principle of Individuation," *Phronesis* (1976), 157–166, especially 161, denies that matter is a "this." I think that $1033^b19-1034^a7$ as well as $190^b24-25$ settle the issue. The use there of 'this' as subject of predication should not, however, be confused with a use of 'this' we meet earlier in Z.8 ($1033^b2-13$), where the term serves as a nontechnical referring device whose force is merely to point to the fact that both matter and form must enter into our account of the coming-to-be of the composite. We meet with a concern about this use of the term in Burnyeat et al., eds., *Notes on Book Zeta*, 66; the fact that the concern is only mentioned here suggests that the participants in the seminar concluded that no interesting doctrinal point (of the sort associated with the "this"/"such" contrast) is associated with this use of the term.

such," the composite, that is generated or comes to be. Aristotle is insisting that we distinguish between what a thing comes to be and what it is that comes to be. Form is that which the matter comes to be, but it is not the thing that comes to be. We can put the point by saying that, whereas it is a substance term in its pure product sense that enables us to identify what the matter comes to be through change, only a substance term in its mixed product sense enables us to identify the kind of thing that actually comes to be. In the next chapter, we explore the theoretical underpinnings of the claim that form does not come to be. For the present, I want to focus on the contrast implied by those underpinnings. The idea is that the objects we confront in the everyday world are the familiar particulars of the *Categories*, things we now know to be composites of matter and form. They are the things that come to be, pass away, and have a career in between. So composite objects have a factual or existential autonomy. As Aristotle likes to put it, they are things that exist separately. But the forms of those objects do not them-selves come to be, they do not pass away, and they do not have individ-ual careers that make up a part of the history of the everyday world. Aristotle is telling us that they lack the autonomy of the composites into whose constitution they enter precisely because (unlike Plato's Forms) they are not "definite objects" ($1033^b22$ ). They are "suches" or "hows" and accordingly exist only as things predicated of the matter making up ordinary objects.

Aristotle also wants to make a point about the particulars that exhibit the kind of autonomy form lacks. He wants to say that they have an internal predicative structure. Each is a "this such"; each is a thing whose existence just consists in the fact that a certain substantial form is predicated of the matter out of which the particular is composed. Mohan Matthen captures this idea when he tells us that, for the Aris-totle of Z and H, the familiar particulars of common sense are "predica-tive complexes."[30] An alternative way of making the point is to invoke a Bergmannian turn of phrase and to say that the internal structure of an ordinary object is that of a fact or a state of affairs, where matter is the "this" and form the "such."[31]

---

[30]Mohan Matthen, "Individual Substances as Hylomorphic Complexes," in M. Mat-then, ed., *Aristotle Today* (Edmonton: Academic Printing and Publishing, 1986) 151–176, especially 172–174. Although his notion of a "predicative complex" nicely captures the internal structural tie of form and matter in a composite entity, Matthen goes on to say that the form that enters into this structure is predicated of the composite individual. As I see it, the insights at work in the idea that the composite is a predicative complex militate against the conclusion that form is predicated of anything but the matter. See Chapter 5 for the elaboration of this point.

[31]See Bergmann, *Realism*, 3–5.

Aristotle is also anxious to insist that the structure exhibited by ordinary objects *is* predicative. He want to deny that an individual such as Socrates is constituted by a merely additive process. Socrates' coming to be is not the result of a mere conjunction or juxtaposition of things of one and the same ontological type, so that what Socrates is is "a this plus a this." There is something we can point to, a kind of a "this," and it comes to have predicated of it a categorically different kind of thing, a "such"; the thing that comes to be, Socrates, is a "this such."

This idea that the constituion of familiar particular objects is not to be understood in merely additive terms is a theme Aristotle strikes over and over in Z and H. In Z.17 ($1041^b11-13$), the idea comes out in a contrast between what Aristotle calls elements (*stoicheia*) and principles (*archai*). Although we never get anything like rigorous definitions of these terms, what Aristotle means to say is fairly clear. What he calls the elements of a thing are the analogues of the matter making up an object. They are the identifiable ingredients out of which something is made. The example he gives (at $1041^b19-21$) is the letters out of which a syllable is formed, and what he wants to deny is that the existence of the syllable is constituted merely by the existence of its elements, the letters out of which it is made. Those letters must be put together or arranged in a certain order if there is to be the relevant syllable. Their being so arranged or put together is what Aristotle calls a principle, and it is the analogue of form. He is concerned to counter the idea that what functions as principle can be construed as just one more separable element additively conjoined with those already identified. To interpret that which is supposed to serve as principle in terms appropriate to things functioning as elements commits us to the appeal to some further principle in virtue of which our original elements and this pseudo principle are arranged, ordered, or structured. If we are to explain how there can be a syllable at all, we must, at some point, posit something whose categorial characterization is radically different from that provided for the letters. A syllable, he insists, is not "a mere heap," something resulting from tossing together a bunch of things of one and the same ontological type.[32] To use the language of Z.8, a syllable is not just a pile of "thises"; it is "thises" structured or ordered such and such.

In H.3, Aristotle puts the point more explicitly than anywhere else in the middle books when he says:

---

[32]In his various discussions of unity, Aristotle repeatedly tells us that the unity of a particular composite *ousia* is not the unity found in things that are one only by contact or continuity (a pile of stones, a bundle of twigs, a plank formed by gluing together several smaller planks). See *Metaphysics* Δ.6 ($1015^b35$ff.) and I.1 ($1052^a18$ff.). The Z–H contrast between heaps and genuine unities just assumes that we accept this point.

> It is clear to those who examine the issue that the syllable is not something made out of its elements [its letters] *and* their being put together, nor is the house simply bricks *and* their being put together, nor is the mixing one of the things that are put together or mixed. (1043ᵇ4–8)

It is tempting to explain this text in terms of an analogy with cookbooks. If we think of our task as that of providing recipes for things, then Aristotle is saying that we have to distinguish between the ingredients out of which a thing is made (the things corresponding to the flour, butter, sugar, milk, and eggs listed at the beginning of a recipe) and how those ingredients are put together (what corresponds to that which is expressed by a recipe's paragraph of directions for combining and mixing the items and stuffs in the list). Just as it would be a mistake for the apprentice cook to ask the master chef where on the shelf one could find what is expressed in the paragraph of directions, so it is a mistake (one Z.8 attributes to Plato) to construe form as one more "this," or one more element, to be added to the things that we call matter. Form is how the matter, which is a kind of this, is; the matter-form composite is a "this how" or a "this such."

In these passages Aristotle is struggling to express insights for which there is no available technical terminology, and so he attempts in one stroke to develop an appropriate vocabulary and to express the relevant insight. What results is something halfway between rigorous formalism and metaphorical gesture. In reading these passages, it is difficult to resist the urge to help Aristotle by offering the aid of type theory, the notion of a function, the distinction between concept and object, or the contrast between complete or saturated and incomplete or unsaturated entities; any number of recent commentators have been unable to resist this urge.[33] They should not, however, feel too guilty about indulging themselves on this score. Despite the anachronism, the kind of point Aristotle is struggling to make is one that bears some important similarities to Fregean views.

We must, however, be careful here. Frege himself was an absolutist about the concept/object distinction. He defines concepts exclusively as the referents of predicate expressions; consequently, he is forced to deny that the referent of any expression syntactically suited to play the role of logical subject can ever be a concept. His distinction between what is complete or saturated and incomplete or unsaturated has to be

---

[33]See, e.g., Joan Kung, "Aristotle on Thises, Suches, and the Third Man Argument," *Phronesis* (1981), 207–247; Loux, "*Ousia*: A Prolegomenon to *Metaphysics* Z and H"; Lewis, "Form and Predication in Aristotle's *Metaphysics*," 60–62; and J. Lukasiewicz, "The Principle of Individuation," *Aristotelian Society Supplementary Volume* (1953), 69–82.

understood in terms of this absolutism, and his account leads to the notorious paradox that the concept expressed by the predicate term 'horse' is not a concept.[34] Aristotle avoids this kind of paradox since he allows that what we would call general terms from the category of *ousia* can show up as logical subjects; he wants to hold that abstract terms from the accidental categories signify precisely the same forms whose predication is expressed by the use of their concrete counterparts.

We can bring out the analogy with Frege and thereby sharpen our account of Aristotle's view if we note that, although Aristotle rejects Frege's absolutism about the subject-predicate distinction and concedes that a form word can appear as subject term in a sentence in which, for example, we attempt to express the definition of the form it signifies, there is a range of sentences with respect to which his own account is no more tolerant than Frege's overall account. The sentences are those that canonically express what I have called form-predications; when I speak of the canonical expressions of form-predications, I merely mean to exclude sentences in which a form-predication is expressed through the use of deviant referring devices such as definite descriptions that non-rigidly pick out their referents. Relative to this set of sentences, the "this"/"such" distinction is absolute. Certain expressions—those signifying what functions as matter—are restricted to the subject place, whereas others—those signifying form—appear only in the predicate position.

When Frege tells us that objects have a kind of completeness that concepts lack, one idea he has in mind is just an extension of these linguistic facts—that, whereas objects are the things we pick out to say something about, concepts are merely what we say about them.[35] A similar contrast is certainly operative in the application of the "this"/ "such" distinction to the set of sentences expressing form-predications. Using those sentences, we pick out a "this" or metaphysical subject and say something about it. Form is not a further "this" or metaphysical subject but merely what, relative to the sentences in question, we say about something else that is a metaphysical subject—how it is.

When Frege speaks of concepts as incomplete, however, the central theme he means to strike is the idea that concepts are functions.[36] Concepts are not the kinds of things we can pick out by anything analogous to an act of ostension but rather something like rules that

---

[34]See G. Frege, "On Concept and Object," in Peter Geach and Max Black, eds., *Translations from the Philosophical Writings of Gottlob Frege* (Oxford: Basil Blackwell, 1966), 45–46.
[35]Ibid., 54–55.
[36]See Frege, "Function and Concept," in Geach and Black, eds., *Translations from the Philosophical Writings*, 21–41.

take selected objects as arguments and generate further objects as values. Aristotle's claim that form is a principle rather than an element bears a striking resemblance to this idea.[37] As we put it, forms are not further ingredients out of which a thing is made but the characteristic way the ingredients of a thing have to be put together, combined, or organized. The analogue to the Fregean idea that, as functions, concepts are unsaturated is just the idea that in the recipe for an object form cannot appear as one more isolable item in the list of ingredients; it is the kind of thing that is expressed only in the propositional context of a set of directions.[38]

If we think of forms as functions, we can say that forms take "thises" as their arguments and yield "this suches" as their values. Substantial forms operate on "thises" like our clump of cortex and phloem and our pack of flesh and bones; their values are "this suches" like the oak tree in my back yard and our man George Bush. Aristotle invokes a familiar epithet when he calls the "this such" that is the value of a substantial form a "this something."[39] This epithet also points to a predicative tie, but the predicative ties expressed in the use of the "this such" and "this something" epithets have to be distinguished. In the "this such" epithet, 'this' serves as a placeholder for referring expressions that pick out particular parcels of matter and 'such' is a placeholder for form words,

[37]See, once again, Lewis, "Form and Predication in Aristotle's *Metaphysics*," 60–62, where this point is brought out nicely.

[38]The suggestion that forms are functions can be carried too far. It is characteristic to think of a function in set theoretical terms as a thing whose content is exhaustively given by the recipe that takes one from its arguments to its values. We import this idea into our account of form only at the cost of turning the whole theory of Z and H upside down, for Aristotle insists that substantial forms are the primary *ousiai* and fundamental essences. This demand requires that they be identifiable or definable without reference to anything else. To hold that the content of a form can be given only by the role it plays in generating composites out of appropriate metaphysical subjects would have the consequence that what is supposed to be the only thing that is independently definable can never be defined except by reference to both the matter that is its subject and the composites whose *ousia* Aristotle wants to say it is.

[39]See 103b21 and 24. David Wiggins, I think, confuses Aristotle's use of the "this such" and "this something" epithets. To bring out the idea that individuals are particular instances of sortal universals, Wiggins invokes the Aristotelian idea that particulars are all "this suches." But, although it is true that particulars are "this suches," the predication that the schema points to is not one where the particular is subject and its kind, predicate. Particulars are "predicative complexes" whose existence hinges on a form-predication; it is that predication that Aristotle refers to in the "this such" formula. The Aristotelian schema Wiggins should have invoked here is the "this something" formula. The relevant instantiation of that schema, for a given particular, picks out *that* particular and points to its memberhsip in its proper substance-species. See Wiggins, *Sameness and Substance* (Cambridge: Harvard University Press, 1980), especially 14–15 and 60. A similar confusion is found in Daniel Graham, *Aristotle's Two Systems*, 237.

so the metaphysical predication it points to is that relation of argument to function operative in a form-predication. A sentence such as (3) or (4), whose predicate term is a substance word in its pure product sense, expresses this predicative tie. But the "this something" epithet as used in Z and H has precisely the force it had in the earlier works, where 'this' is a placeholder for terms picking out predicative complexes like George Bush and my oak tree and 'something' is a placeholder for terms expressing substance-kinds.[40] The "this something" epithet, then, points to species-predications. A sentence such as (2), where a substance term in its mixed product sense serves as predicate, expresses this predicative tie. So, as it operates on its own logical subject (the particular parcel of matter that is its "this"), form yields as its value a predicative complex, a matter-form composite, which, while a "this such," is itself a "this" for a quite different predication, one whose predicated entity is not a "such"—not how its subject is, but what that subject is. We could summarize by saying that a substantial form is a function whose arguments are particular parcels of matter and whose values are particular members of substance-species.

So, when Aristotle speaks of something as a "this," he typically has in mind the idea that it is a particular or individual and hence a fit subject for metaphysical predication. Particular parcels of matter are subjects for form-predications. But the predicative complexes (the "this suches") that rest on form-predications are themselves "thises" or subjects for predications. Familiar concrete objects are members of substance-kinds and hence subjects or "thises" for species-predications; but they are also "thises" for further instances of "this such" predications, where accidental forms are functions and their values, predicative complexes such as this white man. It is doubtless these latter two kinds of predication that Aristotle has in mind when (in contexts other than those concerned with form-predication) he denies that matter is a "this" or tells us that it is merely a "this in appearance."[41] He is denying that the parcels of matter that constitute familiar particulars are themselves members of the substance-species for which those particulars are subject, and he is rejecting the view that how a familiar particular is quantified, qualified, and so on is really just a shorthand way of talking about the matter constituting that particular. Accidents, he is saying, have as their arguments precisely the familiar particulars we think of as their subjects.

[40]I am taking the liberty here of seeing an implicit predication at work in the substitution instances of the schema "this something."

[41]See 1039[a]27–30, 412[a]7, and 1070[a]10.

VI

I have read a good bit of doctrine into Aristotle's claim that form is a "such"—more, perhaps, than some would like. But I want to suggest that we can find a further theme in this claim if we contrast the discussion of Z.8 with its *Categories* counterpart. Although in the earlier work Aristotle is certainly concerned to counter the Platonic idea that general terms from the category of *ousia* function as names of separated entities with the reminder that their primary role in discourse is predicative, he is equally anxious to contrast their predicative use with that of general terms from the dependent categories. There is some fumbling around here, much of it occasioned by the elasticity of the term '*poion*'; but the bottom line is that, in their normal predicative role, terms of second substance enable us to indicate what kind of thing a primary *ousia* is (3ᵇ13–24). The Z.8 claim that form is a "such" is, however, accompanied by no parallel qualification.

One might suggest that this fact is to be explained in terms of the by now familiar idea that form-predications are how- rather than what-predications. I think the suggestion is correct, but only because there is more involved in this contrast than we have so far suggested. Although the *Categories* text denies that the "this something" and "one in number" formulae apply in the case of substance-kinds themselves, it insists that these schemata do apply to the things of which a kind is predicated (3ᵇ10–13). And, of course, they apply in virtue of the predication of the kind. To say that a primary *ousia* admits the "this something" schema is just to say that it is a particular instance of its infima species; to say that it is "one in number" is just to say that it can be individuated and counted under the substance-kind that marks it out as what it is. So, central to the contrast Aristotle wants to draw in the *Categories* is the idea that the predication of a substance-kind, unlike that of a universal from the accidental categories, provides us with principles for distinguishing and counting its members. As we noted in our discussion of the early account, this idea is continuous with contemporary insights about sortal concepts, individuative universals, expressions with divided reference, terms with an arithmetic, and the like.⁴²

But not only does the Z.8 text fail to register these insights, the contrast between the "this something" (*tode ti*) and "this such" (*tode toionde*) formulae suggests that Aristotle wants to deny that the distinctive logic of sortal universals applies in the case of form. It is not

---

⁴²For discussions of the phenomena of sortal predication and divided reference, the classic texts include P. F. Strawson, *Individuals*, chap. 5, and W. V. O. Quine, *Word and Object* (Cambridge: MIT Press, 1960), chap. 3.

altogether implausible to construe what follows the 'this' in both formulae as a placeholder. On this reading, the schemata present us with a contrast between what functions as placeholder for sortals or kind terms—the expression '*ti*'—and what functions as a placeholder for terms whose depth grammar is adjectival—the term '*toionde*'; and what Aristotle is telling us is that the latter, but not the former, applies in the case of form.[43] This suggestion becomes more attractive when we note that what instantiates a form—the matter of which it is predicated—does not, in virtue of that predication, admit the "this something" epithet; the predication of a form marks its matter out as "such." So, whereas in the case of a kind $K$ being predicated of an object $x$, $x$ qualifies as this $K$ rather than that $K$ and as one $K$ distinct from other $K$'s, in the case of a form $F$ being predicated of some parcel of matter $m$, $m$ does not qualify as one particular $F$; it is, as we might put it, only a "this" that happens to be $F$-ish.

But we need not rely on interpretation here. At the end of Z.8, Aristotle tells us that

> when we have the whole thing, the "such" that is a form in "these" flesh and bones, then we have Callias and Socrates. And they are different because of their matter (for that is different); but they are the same in their form; for the form is indivisible. (1034ª5–8)

Here the "suchness" of form is expressed in terms of the explicit denial that form is a sortal or individuative universal. Aristotle is saying here that forms lack their own built-in principle of individuation. It is only because a form is predicated of a diversity of independently indentifiable subjects (the different packs of flesh and bone) that there is a plurality of things (Callias and Socrates) with one and the same form. He is telling us, then, that the individuation of a form is parasitic on something else. On this score, a form (such as that expressed by 'man' in its pure product sense) resembles a color. It is only in conjunction with some other universal with its own principle of individuation that the color white provides us with a measure for counting. We do not count white things, but white *cows* or white *horses*. The conceptual fact is rooted in the metaphysical fact that the multiple instantiation of a color presupposes a prior diversity of subjects themselves individuated under their proper sortals. Aristotle would summarize this fact by saying

---

[43]We are, however, left with the use of '*ti*' in Z.3 (1029ª20–24), where the term seems to be functioning as a placeholder for form words. The idea that the appeal to a device such as '*ti*' might serve different (even incompatible) purposes in different contexts is, in the case of Aristotle at least, not outlandish; as I have suggested earlier, it is possible that even here the term is a placeholder for kind terms.

that *white* is a "such" or "how," and he would contrast it with a what-universal that underwrites the applicability of the "this something" and "one in number" formulae. The kind expressed by 'man' in its mixed product sense is one such universal. It provides us with the concept of countably distinct individuals. The idea of its instantiation just is the idea of something that is one individual man distinct from other men.

Aristotle is telling us that forms exhibit the logic of colors rather than of kinds. The concept of a form is not the concept of individual instances of the form.[44] The latter notion arises only when we import the notion of some other universal with its own principle of individuation. In the case of the form expressed by 'man' in its pure product sense, the appropriate universal is *pack of flesh and bones*; the diversification of that universal is what gives rise to the plurality of things with one and the same form.[45]

So the idea that forms are universals whose instantiation or predication marks out their subjects not as what they are but only as how they are unfolds into the idea that forms lack their own built-in principle of individuation. This fact about form is one that the surface grammar of language can conceal from us, for many of the grammatical structures we tend to associate with the distinctive logic of sortal universals characterize our discourse about form. In their mixed product senses, English substance terms admit pluralization and the articles; but we find the indefinite article in

(3)   That pack of flesh and bones is a man,

and it seems reasonable to suppose that the pack of flesh and bones making up George Bush and that making up Ronald Reagan are both men. But it would be a mistake to infer from these facts that in its pure product sense 'man' signifies a sortal or individuative universal. As I suggested earlier, the idea that form is a "such" is best understood as a

[44]Several commentators have misunderstood Aristotle on this point and have taken form itself to be an individuative universal. See, e.g., Wilfrid Sellers, *Philosophical Perspectives*, 80; Montgomery Furth, *Substance, Form, and Psyche*, 51; and D. K. Modrak, "Forms, Types, and Tokens in Aristotle's *Metaphysics*," *Journal of the History of Philosophy* (1979), 371–381. If we fail to recognize the metaphysical distinction between form and species and the corresponding linguistic distinction between the pure and mixed senses of substance terms, this is a natural mistake to fall into: for the central contrast between form and species is that between nonindividuative and individuative universals, and the contrast between substance terms in their pure and mixed senses is that between general terms that appear to divide their reference, but do not, and genuinely sortal predicates.

[45]This text ($1034^a5$–8) is one I discuss again in Chapter 6, where I consider the view that substance-forms are particulars. In that context, I consider alternative interpretations of the idea that cospecific individuals differ in their matter.

recommendation to interpret the depth grammar of pure product designators from the category of *ousia* in adjectival terms, so that (3) is parsed as

(3')   That pack of flesh and bones is man-ish

and (4) as

(4')   That clump of cortext and phloem is oak-ish.

We have already noted that in the *Categories* Aristotle was on his way toward recognizing the distinctive features of sortal or individuative universals, and there is good reason for thinking that by the time he wrote Z and H his appreciation of their unique logic was even firmer than it had been in the early works.[46] The idea that Aristotle grasped this logic has frequently guided commentary on his characterization of substance-kinds. Commentators have failed, however, to appreciate the fact that in calling form a "such" Aristotle is denying that the logic of sortals applies to form. Indeed, we even find some commentators insisting that it is form that individuates![47] Some remarks by G. E. L. Owen suggest that he may have glimpsed the actual force of the doctrine that form is a "such."[48] Unfortunately, even he fails to appreciate the full implications of the doctrine. Owen suggests that Aristotle's use of *'toionde'* in conjunction with form can be understood in terms of the noneliminable generality of form words in the context

x is coming to be a _____.

He points out that, if it is true that some parcel of matter *m* is coming to be an *F* (where *F* is a form word), then there is no particular *F* such that *m* is coming to be that *F*. So, if I am in the process of fashioning a chunk of bronze into a statue, there is no particular statue such that the bronze is coming to be *that* statue. Owen insists that the impossibility of existential generalization here is not a fact about the temporal dimension of the process of coming to be, but one rooted in the nature of form itself. It

---

[46]See, e.g., *Metaphysics* Z.16 ($1040^b5-10$), which denies stuffs status as *ousiai*; the contrast here is between stuffs and things. Compare this text with $\Delta.8$ ($1017^b10-14$), where the stuff/thing contrast is ignored.

[47]See, e.g., Jennifer Whiting, "Form and Individuation in Aristotle," 359–377.

[48]See G. E. L. Owen, "Particular and General," *Proceedings of the Aristotelian Society* (1978–79), 279–294, as well as Owen's remarks in Burnyeat et al., eds., *Notes on Book Zeta*, 43–53.

is this fact about form, Owen claims, that Aristotle was attempting to capture when he said that form is a "such."

Owen is certainly right that when the term 'statue' functions as a form word (i.e., when it has its pure product sense), the sentence

(7)   That chunk of bronze is coming to be a statue

does not entail

(8)   There is some statue such that the bronze is coming to be that statue.

Furthermore, Owen is right that this fact is traceable to the "suchness" of form. But a clue that Owen fails to appreciate the full implications of this doctrine is his suggestion that, once the bronze has come to be a statue (where this term has, once again, its pure product sense), there is some particular statue such that the bronze is *that* statue. The fact is that, if 'statue' is being used as a form word throughout, this suggestion is false. The force of Aristotle's claim that form is a "such" is just that in its pure product sense a term like 'statue' does not divide its reference. Its depth grammar is that of an adjective rather than a count noun, so that, in this sense of 'statue', talk of particular statues is always logically grotesque. Once I have successfully completed the artistic endeavor, the following sentence can be used to express a true proposition:

(9)   There is some particular statue such that the original chunk of bronze is that statue;

But this sentence manages to express a truth only if the term 'statue' has its mixed product sense and the second 'is' is, not the 'is' of predication, but what is sometimes called the 'is' of material composition or constitution and has the sense 'makes up', 'constitutes', or 'composes'.

VII

If we can make sense of the doctrines underlying Aristotle's cryptic remarks about "suches," "thises," "this suches," and "this some-things," we still must confront the discomforting fact that there are texts in which, according to some commentators, Aristotle seems to construe matter itself as a kind of metaphysical predicate as well as passages where he speaks of form as a "this something." Let us consider first the suggestion that matter might be predicative. The relevant text here comes at the end of Z.7. Aristotle tells us:

> In the case of that out of which things come to be in the sense of matter, some are said, once they have come to be, to be not "that" but "thaten." For example, the statue is not said to be stone, but stonen. (1033ª5–7)

A few lines later (1033ª13–19) he gives further examples of what he is trying to convey with this new pronomial obscurity: a statue made out of a block of wood is not wood but wooden; the statue made out of bronze is not bronze but brazen; a house made out of bricks is not bricks but bricken. As attempts to clarify the mysterious use of 'thaten', the appeals to 'stonen', 'bricken', and 'brazen' are only marginally helpful. The contrast Aristotle is interested in does, however, carry over into English in the case of 'wood' and 'wooden', and it is easy enough to generalize the point for the other cases. The point seems to be that matter is not best understood as a "this" or a metaphysical subject but rather as a "such" or a metaphysical predicate; or at least that is what some commentators tell us. As Dancy puts it, Aristotle "is suggesting that the picture according to which the matter of a thing appears as subject for its predicate is back-to-front: the material constitution of a thing ought more properly to appear in predicate position."[49] But if this is what Aristotle is suggesting, how are we to square this suggestion with Z.8, where, as we have seen, matter turns up pretty explicitly as a "this" or metaphysical subject? Although one might (and Dancy, perhaps, does) want to construe Z.7 as evidence that Aristotle did not mean to claim that form is predicated of its matter, the Z.8 idea that matter is a subject for form is such a recurrent theme in the middle books that a more plausible response here seems to be a general skepticism about any attempt to derive serious metaphysical doctrine from the obscure pronomial dicta of Z and H.

Such a skepticism is, however, unwarranted since Aristotle provides us with a clear explanation for our use of the adjectival forms for which the 'thaten' of Z.7 is a placeholder.[50] He tells us that although we

---

[49]Dancy, "Aristotle's Second Thoughts." Blackwell, "Matter as a Subject of Predication in Aristotle," 27–30, agrees that 1033ª5–7 show that matter is never a genuine subject of predication. See also Furth, *Substance, Form, and Psyche*, 219–220, and *Aristotle: Metaphysics Books Zeta, Eta, Theta, Iota*, 116–117 and 136, who offers an interpretation of the Z.7 passage that is a bit different from my own.

[50]My account of Aristotle's explanation of the "thaten" locution is inspired by Code's insightful discussion of the passage in "The Persistence of Aristotelian Matter," *Philosophical Studies* (1976), 357–367. I suspect that I make a bit more than Code of Aristotle's contention that if we examined things closely we would not say that the statue, for example, came to be from the bronze; I know that I put more emphasis on 1049ª36ff. than he does.

typically characterize a coming to be by a sentence of the form

_____ comes to be _____,

where the first blank is filled by an expression signifying the subject and the second, by an expression signifying the form, we can also speak of something's coming to be this or that "out of" or "from" something else. Thus we can say that Socrates comes to be healthy from being sick or that from being unmusical he comes to be musical. Aristotle contends that our characterization of that from which or that out of which a thing comes to be typically involves a reference to the privation that stands in opposition to whatever it is that the thing in question comes to be. Consequently, he denies that the characterization by which we identify that out of which or from which a thing comes to be holds true of the subject after it has come to whatever it is that it does come to be. So, after he has come to be healthy, Socrates is no longer said to be sick; after he has come to be musical, he is no longer said to be unmusical. But Aristotle tells us that

> in the case of things for which the privation is obscure or without a name (e.g., in the case of bronze, the privation of whatever shape, or in the case of bricks and boards, the privation of a house), and out of these (i.e., the bronze or the bricks and boards) things seem to come to be just as in the case of the sick one. (1033ª13–16)

So when we do not have a ready linguistic expression for the privation in question, we speak of things coming to be out of their matter, so that a statue is said to come to be out of bronze or a house out of bricks and boards. According to Aristotle, language tries to keep up appearances in these cases and to preserve the general linguistic pattern operative in the core case of speaking of something's coming to be out of or from its privation (1033ª5–12). Accordingly, once the statue has come to be, it is no longer said to be that out of which it has come to be, bronze; it is said instead to be brazen. Likewise, the house is not said to be brick but bricken. But, then, the use of the adjectival form does not point to or express genuine predication; it represents rather the attempt on the part of language to preserve an analogy between the extended use of the 'out of' or 'from' characterization and its core use. Aristotle goes on (at 1033ª19–22) to suggest that if we were being very precise we would not employ this extended use of the 'out of' or 'from' idiom. Presumably, he means to suggest that if we were pressing for precision we would enrich our vocabulary by coining terms to express the relevant privations.

In any case, it is a mistake to take Aristotle's remarks about the adjectival form of matter expressions to show that matter functions as a "such," a predicate, rather than a "this," a subject. Indeed, as Alan Code points out, the diagnosis Aristotle provides here is geared precisely to show that, despite linguistic appearances to the contrary, matter does not serve as a predicate.[51] Nonetheless, there are signs that Aristotle finds this piece of usage a kind of "felix culpa". In Θ.7 (1049ª 36–1049ᵇ1) for example, he points approvingly to the usage that converts substantival expressions for matter into adjectival forms modifying the terms signifying the composite. What makes this piece of usage a happy accident, I think, is that it serves as a reminder that, although matter may be a "this" for form, it functions as subject at a level of analysis one step below that at which the composite functions as a subject for its species and its accidents; that is, Aristotle finds the use of the idiom he identifies by way of the 'thaten' locution attractive because it brings out the idea that it is no consequence of his theory that matter and the composite of which it is a constituent are competitors for status as metaphysical subject of predication. They are subjects at different levels of ontological analysis. When we say that matter is a subject of predication for its form, we are operating at a level of analysis one step below that at which it is appropriate to speak of the composite or subject. At that level, the notion of a composite is not yet on the scene. Indeed, it is because matter is a "this" for its form that the level of ontological complexity characterized by the predicative complexes that are our familiar particulars emerge. And the fact that at this level language (admittedly, for totally unrelated reasons) has a tendency to express matter in terms that might suggest that it is something adjectival to the familiar composite has the happy consequence that we are precluded from slipping into a host of category mistakes that might otherwise stem from the insight that matter is a "this," mistakes of the sort underlying questions like, What precisely is it that is five feet six, Socrates or his body? What is it that is in full bloom now, the geranium or the clump of cortex and phloem? What exactly is it that falls under the species *white oak*, the tree or the stuff it is made of?

In spite of his own exploitation of the linguistic pattern that converts expressions for matter into adjectival forms *linguistically* predicated of the composite, Aristotle is pretty explicit in his denial that the pattern in question has the force of showing matter to be a *metaphysical* predicate. In the same way, I think, Aristotle's use of the "this something" epithet in conjunction with substantial form is no indication that he takes form to be a "this" rather than a "such," a metaphysical subject rather than a

[51]Code, "The Persistence of Matter," especially 363.

predicate.[52] Some commentators have, of course, thought otherwise,[53] and this use of the epithet does make some kind of distinction between form as particular and form as universal initially tempting. The fact that Aristotle occasionally flirts with the idea that proper names from the category of *ousia* are homonymous in just the way general terms are (e.g., 1037$^a$5–7) only reinforces this temptation. The idea that a name like 'Socrates' might signify, in different contexts, either the form or the composite suggests a kind of substance-predication distinct from both form- and species-predication. Sentences exhibiting this type of predication would be perfectly familiar, but it would not be in their familiar senses that they would exhibit it. Thus

(2)   George Bush is a man

would be a vehicle for the sort of predication in question, but only when 'George Bush' is taken to signify Bush's soul and 'man' has its pure rather than mixed product sense. Predications of this sort would provide contexts in which the predication of form is classificatory, and they would point to a relation of essential predication. Their structure would certainly justify the claim that form taken individually is a "this" or ultimate metaphysical subject.

This is not the place for a detailed discussion of the notion of particular forms. For the present, it is sufficient to point out that Aristotle never actually commits himself to the legitimacy of predications of the form just described;[54] if he had meant to reserve the epithet "this something" for forms taken individually, we would expect Aristotle to apply the epithet in contexts concerned only with particulars. The fact is, however, that the epithet appears in contexts in which form taken universally must be the focus of his concern. In Θ.7 (1049$^a$35), for example, the form that is predicable of matter is said to be a "this something," and it

[52]A sample of texts in which form is said to be "this something" includes *Metaphysics* Δ.8 (1017$^b$25), Z.3 (1029$^a$27–30), H.1 (1042$^a$29), Θ.7 (1049$^a$35), and Λ.3 (1070$^a$13). In Chapter 6, I consider the sense, if any, in which Aristotle wants to speak of form as a subject. In that connection I discuss 1029$^a$1–7 and 1042$^a$26–32.

[53]See, e.g., Michael Frede, "Individuals in Aristotle" and "Substance in Aristotle's Metaphysics," 77, in *Essays in Ancient Philosophy*; Wilfred Sellars, *Philosophical Perspectives*, 111–118; Edwin Hartman, *Substance, Body, and Soul*, 57–61; Jennifer Whiting, "Form and Individuation in Aristotle," 373; William Charlton, "Aristotle and the Principle of Individuation," *Phronesis* (1972), 239–249; Terence Irwin, *Aristotle's First Principles*, 248 and 255ff.; Charlotte Witt, *Substance and Essence in Aristotle*, 161–162; and Michael Frede and Gunther Patzig, *Aristoteles "Metaphysik Z,"* vol. 1, 39 and 52, and vol. 2, 256–257.

[54]Indeed, I am inclined to think that the idea that proper names of persons are homonymous is a Platonic view that Aristotle, given his rejection of Plato's dualism, is strongly inclined to reject. Michael V. Wedin, "Singular Statements and Essentialism," 67, disagrees. See the last section of Chapter 6 for more on this theme.

can only be form understood as a universal that Aristotle has in mind here.[55]

But if it is form taken universally that is characterized as a "this something," it is extremely unlikely that the characterization invokes the sense of "this something" we have been dealing with, the idea of a particular or subject for predication; and the fact that there are places where Aristotle explicitly denies that form is a "this something" only confirms the idea that he does not associate a single sense with this epithet.[56] If the "this something" epithet has the force we have associated with it, then forms do not admit the epithet, for whether forms are particular or general they are not themselves particular members of the associated species. The form is not something for which any substitution instance of the schema 'this $K$' (where $K$ picks out a lowest-level substance-species) is true.

Fortunately, *De Anima* B.2 ($412^a8-9$) suggests a way out of our difficulties. In that context, Aristotle tells us that form is that in virtue of which something is a "this something." Earlier in the same chapter he has denied that matter is a "this something" ($412^a7$). So he is presumably thinking of the concrete particular as subject to the "this something" schema, and he is saying that it is in virtue of its form that a familiar particular is a particular member of its substance-species and hence something for which there is a true "this something" predication.[57] This remark from *De Anima* suggests that when Aristotle refers to form as a "this something" he is invoking a derivative sense according to which something can be called a "this something" if it is that in virtue of which something else is a "this something" in the basic or primary sense. And it is precisely because form is predicated of the matter constituting the relevant individual that the individual is the particular member of the substance-species (the "this something") that it is. Aristotle's use of the "this something" epithet in conjunction with form is, then, the kind of use we might make of that epithet if we were to think

[55]Frede and Patzig take this passage to be inconclusive. While conceding that the predicability of form suggests its generality, they point to the use of the *tode ti* schema as evidence of its particularity. See *Aristoteles "Metaphysik Z,"* vol. 1, 57. But this argument just assumes the univocality of the expression '*tode ti*' and, in any case, fails to explain away the implicit claim that form is general; and the idea that forms are predicated of other things is hardly novel in Θ.7.

[56]See $1033^a29-34$ and $1043^b15-23$ (taken together), and $1037^a1-2$.

[57]This is not to say that form is an individuative universal; it is a nonindividuative universal (a how- rather than a what-universal) that is predicated of its matter. Because of that predication, the resulting composite is a particular instance of what is an individuative universal, its proper substance-species. Because of its role in underwriting (by its predication of matter) the applicability of the individuative universal that is the species, form is labeled a "this something."

of forms in Fregean terms as functions. We would speak of substantial form as a *tode ti*–forming function (i.e., a function whose value for appropriate argument is a thing for which the relevant substitution instance of the "this something" formula holds true), and it would be perfectly natural for us to abbreviate this talk of *tode ti*–forming functions by speaking elliptically of a substantial form as a *tode ti*.[58]

[58]In "Substance and Predication" (unpublished manuscript, chap. 13 section 5), Frank Lewis criticizes this strategy for unraveling the knots surrounding Aristotle's use of the "this something" epithet. He finds it puzzling to suggest that the thing responsible for the concrete composite's being subject to the "this something" epithet should itself turn out to be a "this something" only in a derivative sense. Presumably Lewis thinks that what grounds the fact that something admits the epithet should be the primary bearer of the epithet. But the criticism just assumes that there is a single sense attached to the epithet, and Aristotle's occasional denials that form is a "this something" suggest that this is not the case. As I see it, the use in Z and H of '*tode ti*' as applied to the concrete particular has precisely the force it had in the *Categories*; and the epithet as used there just does not apply to form. There is nothing problematic in the idea that form admits only a derivative use of the "this something" epithet, for, given the sense of the epithet as it applies to form, to say this just is to highlight the causal role form plays in the constitution of things that satisfy, for appropriate *K*, the schema 'this *K*'.

# CHAPTER 5

# Form as *Ousia*

I

Aristotle claims that there are two kinds of substance-predications, what I have called form-predications and species-predications. In the former, a form is predicated of its matter; in the latter, a substance-species is predicated of one of its members. Form-predications have a "this such" structure: a particular parcel of matter functions as subject or "this," the predicated form is *how* that matter is, and the predication holds only accidentally. Species-predications, on the other hand, exhibit their subjects as "this somethings": the predicated species is *what* the subject is, so that we have an instance of essential predication. Form- and species-predications come in pairs. For any species-predication, there is some form-predication in virtue of which the individual in question is the "this something" it is. When form- and species-predications are related in this way, their linguistic expression is by way of sentences in which a single term functions as predicate. In the relevant sentences, however, that term has distinct senses. In the sentence expressing the form-predication, it has its pure product sense and signifies a form; in the sentence expressing the species-predication, it appears in its mixed product sense and signifies an infima species. In the latter case, the term has divided reference: each of the things of which a substance-term $K$ in its mixed sense is true is one particular $K$ distinct from other $K$s. In the former case, the term fails to exhibit the logic of sortal predicates and has a depth grammar that is adjectival.

Since the state of affairs expressed by the sentence with the mixed product predicate obtains only because that expressed by the sentence with the pure product predicate obtains, Aristotle invokes a derivative sense of his favorite epithet and calls form a "this something"; because a form is predicated of the relevant parcel of matter, the resulting individual is the "this something" (the particular member of the corresponding substance-kind) it is.

Central to the claim that form is, in this sense, a "this something" is the idea that a form-predication is more basic or fundamental than the species-predication with which it is paired. It is in virtue of the fact that the form-predication obtains that the species-predication obtains. It is *because* a substantial form is predicated of a parcel of matter that the individual composed of that matter is a particular instance of its substance-species, so it is because a substance-predication at one level holds that a substance-predication at another level holds. This idea of levels of substance-predication is the most central insight of Z and H; it receives its formulation in a thesis that dominates all other theses of the middle books, the thesis that form is *ousia*. We have already seen this thesis at work in Z.3. It is explicitly formulated in Z.7 when Aristotle tells us at 1032$^b$2 that form is the primary *ousia* and then reiterated later in the same chapter (1032$^b$14). The thesis is alluded to in Z.8 (1033$^b$17) and Z.9 (1034$^a$30–32) and applied explicitly to the case of the soul, once in Z.10 (1035$^b$14–16) and twice in Z.11 (1037$^a$5 and 1037$^a$29). We meet the thesis again in Z.12 (1038$^a$26), then we find it the centerpiece of the string of chapters beginning with Z.17 and carrying us into H.3.

The thesis employs the expression '*ousia*' as an abstract term whose primary occurrence is in the context 'the *ousia* of _____'. It is the use of the term whose analysis I have systematically postponed over the past few chapters. Obviously we can put it off no longer. To get clear on this new use of the term, we should look to Δ.8, where after characterizing *ousia* as that which is "not predicated of a subject but of which everything else is predicated" Aristotle tells us that we can also apply the term '*ousia*' to "that which, being in such things as are not predicated of a subject, is the cause of their being."[1] The Z.3 complications that matter brings on the scene are not operative here, and the familiar formula identifying the first use of '*ousia*' has precisely the force it does in the logical works. It isolates the things the *Categories* identifies as primary realities, ordinary particulars like "a certain man" and "a certain horse." Then we are told that we can also use the term '*ousia*' to pick out

[1]1017$^b$10–16. See also 1041$^b$27–28 and 1043$^a$2–4, and 13–14 where the Δ.8 definition of '*ousia* of _____' is repeated.

something else, that constituent in a thing said to be an '*ousia*' in the first sense that is the cause of its being.

It turns out that this is not a general characterization of the expression '*ousia* of_____', since things other than the familiar particulars of the *Categories* have what Aristotle here calls an *ousia*. In Z.7 (1032ª4–5) he invokes a clearly extended use of the locution 'the *ousia* of _____' when he tells us that, in a sense, health is the *ousia* of its privative opposite, sickness, on the grounds that what sickness is is the absence of health; in Z.16 (1040ᵇ24) he even speaks of the *ousia* of the thing that Δ.8 identifies as the *ousia* of ordinary concrete objects. But, although he concedes that the idea of something's being the cause of the being of a thing has applications beyond the case specified in Δ.8, Aristotle clearly wants to claim that the expression 'the *ousia* of_____' has its primary or core use when what fills the blank is some expression picking out one of the familiar particulars of the *Categories*. Indeed, this use of the formula identifies what the Aristotle of Z and H calls primary *ousia*.

So we have the concrete objects of the *Categories*, and we are to identify that constituent of them which is responsible for their being or existence. But what exactly does this involve? Given Aristotle's skepticism about the idea that there is some one thing that just being or just existing consists in (a skepticism that significantly is reiterated in Z.16 (see 1040ᵇ16–28), the chapter immediately preceding the detailed defense and elaboration of the doctrine that form is primary *ousia*), we are ill advised to suppose that the characterization of the *ousia* of a thing provided in Δ.8 can be taken at face value. Aristotle's essentialist reading of the notion of existence, according to which to be just is to be something of a certain kind, suggests that the talk of being in the definition has to be parsed in the familiar way in terms of the appropriate kind-predication. But, then, to identify the *ousia* of a familiar concrete particular would seem to involve specifying that constituent in the particular in virtue of which the particular is the kind of thing it is, that constituent in virtue of which the thing is a member of the infima species to which it belongs.

Z.17, where Aristotle poses the general question of "what kind of thing should be said to be *ousia*" (1041ª6), bears much of this out. He insists (1041ª9–10) that the question is, as the Δ.8 passage implies, a causal question, a question whose answer is an explanation of some phenomenon;[2] but he explicitly denies (1041ᵇ4–5) that what we seek in

---

[2]As commentators have repeatedly told us, we cannot take Aristotle's use of '*aition*' to have the force of our 'cause'; in the present context, 'explanatory factor' gives the force of '*aition*'.

our attempt to identify *ousia* is an explanation of the truth of a bald existential proposition. Nor are we concerned with mere assertions of identity. Particular questions about the grounds of the self-identity of this or that thing all have a single, not very illuminating answer: each thing just is itself, and there is nothing more to say on this topic (1041ᵃ15–20). The search after *ousia* must be something else; it must be the attempt to identify something that serves to explain "why one thing is predicated of another" (1041ᵃ23–24). So far so good, and things look all the more promising when Aristotle tells us (1041ᵃ28) that what we seek must be essence. This, after all, is just what Z.6 requires. Whatever it is that plays the explanatory role associated with the notion of *ousia* must be essence. Indeed, it must be necessarily one and the same as its essence.

But if Z.17 confirms our expectations on these fronts, its examples of the kinds of predication the search after *ousia* is meant to explain do not seem to conform very precisely to the pattern we have outlined. We are reminded over and again that the explanandum must involve one thing's belonging to, being said of, or being predicated of another. Unfortunately, in Z.17 Aristotle really only gives two examples of the kinds of predication he has in mind here, and those examples are subject to two quite different interpretations. He says:

> For example, why are these things a house? Because the what it is to be a house belongs to them. And why is this a man, or why is this body being thus a man? (1041ᵇ5–7)

We have already met the first question earlier in the chapter (1041ᵃ26–27), and it is clear from that text that the use of "these things" here is meant as a reference to the materials out of which the house is made, its bricks and stones. The implication seems to be, first, that the explanandum involves the predication expressed by the sentence

(1)    These bricks and stones are a house

and, second, that the explanans resulting from the identification of the *ousia* is expressed by a sentence like

(2)    The what it is to be a house belongs to these bricks and stones.

So the suggestion seems to be that our explanandum consists in the fact that the matter, the relevant bricks and stones, is a house; and the explanans consists in the fact that the essence of house belongs to that matter.

The second example, however, suggests two quite different explananda that might be relevant to the identification of the *ousia* of a thing. It might be that we are to explain (a) why this thing (that is, this individual—Socrates, Coriscus, Callias, or whoever) is a man, or (b) why the body of such an individual is a man. This second example is not supplemented with a sample explanation, so we seem to be left without a clear sense of just what it is we are supposed to be explaining when we seek to identify the *ousia* of a thing.

One might argue that things are more straightforward than I have suggested. After all, the first sample explanandum pretty clearly involves matter's being such and such, and Aristotle uses these two cases as examples of the general form our explananda should take. He explicitly tells us (1041$^b$5) that the search after *ousia* is an attempt to answer the question, Why is the matter (a) something? So we have no option but to interpret the second example in the way delineated by (b); if the interpretation outlined by (a) is suggested by the text, we should take this to be a slip on Aristotle's part or, better, a tentative and loose formulation glossed by the concluding clause that gives rise to (b). Accordingly, the argument would go, we have to understand Aristotle as saying that the predication that functions as explanandum in any particular attempt to identify *ousia* must have matter as its subject. If we had initially supposed that the predications in question would turn out to be something different, so much the worse for our record as prognosticators.

But the issue is actually more complicated than this line of argument would have us believe. The examples of Z.17 represent only Aristotle's initial and very tentative attempt to specify just what it is we are out to explain when we attempt to identify the cause of the being of a thing. It is not until H.2 that we are given a detailed account of the explanatory patterns operative in the identification of the *ousia* of a thing. That latter chapter opens with a flurry of examples of the kinds of thing that serve as the explanans in this enterprise (1042$^b$15–36). Quite predictably, the majority involve explanations of the being of artifacts (books, boxes, lintels, thresholds, and honeywater); although the explanations are very brief and we are never told just which predications function as explananda, those explanations do not very naturally point to predications whose subjects are matter as the relevant explananda.

Then, after he has bombarded us with these examples, Aristotle reminds us (1043$^a$4) that none of them represents a genuine *ousia*-explanation. He insists that the sample explanations (he now calls them definitions) all exhibit a pattern that is, point for point, analogous to that involved in genuine accounts of the *ousia* of a thing, and he gives his summary of that pattern:

For example, if it is threshold that is to be defined, then we should say, "Wood and stones lying in this way"; and if it is house, we should say, "Bricks and boards lying in this way"; and if it is ice, "Water frozen or solidified in this way"; and a tune is this kind of mixture of high and low. (1043ª7–11)

This text is pretty clearly meant as the definitive account of the identification of the *ousia* of a thing. It is the final statement that the tentative and exploratory formulations of Z.17 and the first half of H.2 are supposed to lead us to. It is clear that the explananda relevant to the enterprise of identifying *ousia* bear on those things from the category of *ousia* that are analogues of things like thresholds, houses, chunks of ice, and tunes. Since he approaches the issue from the perspective of definition, Aristotle does not explicitly identify the individual predications that we are out to explain here, but it is clear that they are not predications whose subjects are matter. In each of the cases Aristotle outlines, what counts as matter (wood and stones for thresholds, bricks and boards for houses, water for ice, and notes for tunes) appears not in the explanandum but as subject of the relevant explanans. Indeed, if we follow the directive of Z.17 that the explanandum be expressed in terms of one thing's being predicated of another, then this passage allows only one way of identifying the relevant predications. We have to suppose that what we want to explain is why this thing is a threshold, why this is a house, why this is a chunk of ice, and why this is some particular tune or other. So it is the fact that this or that particular is the kind of thing it is that needs to be explained, and the explanation proceeds by stating that the matter out of which that particular is composed is in such and such a state or condition. The reference to that state or condition, Aristotle tells us, is analogous to the appeal to form in genuine *ousia* explanations. As he puts it, "In the case of *ousia*, the thing predicated of the matter is the actuality itself" (1043ª5–6).

Since Aristotle consistently characterizes form as actuality, the upshot is precisely what Δ.8 leads us to expect. The predication we want to explain when we seek to identify the *ousia* of a thing is a particular species-predication, and our explanation involves an appeal to the corresponding form-predication. So it is because the matter out of which some particular concrete object is composed has predicated of it the appropriate form that the particular in question is a member of the corresponding infima species.

This outcome was inevitable. The initial formulations of Z.17, when interpreted to suggest that matter functions as subject of our explananda, cannot summarize the pattern of explanation that constitutes the identification of the *ousia* of a thing. If we take the Aristotle of Z.17 at his word and suppose that what we want to explain are the metaphysical predications expressed by

(1)   These bricks and stones are a house

and

(3)   This body is a man,

we have to ask just which predications those sentences are intended to express. Given the homonymy of substance words, we can answer the question only if we disambiguate the linguistic predicates of (1) and (3). Clearly, those sentences cannot be used to express truths if 'house' and 'man' have their mixed product senses. Used in those senses, the terms signify substance-kinds (or, in the case of 'house', what is analogous to a substance-kind). Those kinds are not predicated of the matter picked out by the subject terms of (1) and (3); they are predicated of the particular concrete objects whose matter those subject terms pick out. If (1) and (3) are to express truths, their predicates must have their pure product senses; they must signify the relevant forms. Unfortunately, the truths (1) and (3) express under this interpretation are the wrong truths. What they are supposed to express are the predications we seek to explain; what they actually express, under the only interpretation where they come out true, are the very form-predications that function, in each case, as our explanans. So, if we took Aristotle at his word, one and the same thing would serve as explanandum and explanans.

But, then, what are we to make of Z.17? Aristotle's treatment of the second sample explanandum, I think, gives us a clue. Recall that Aristotle poses the question that gives rise to an *ousia* explanation as follows: "And why is this a man, or why is this body being thus a man?" (1041$^b$6–7). He gives us two different formulations of the question. The first conforms to the pattern that ultimately emerges from his exploratory attempts at delineating the structure of *ousia* explanations, but the second is subject to the difficulties outlined in the previous paragraph. Aristotle, however, seems to want to take them as alternative readings of the same explanandum. S. Marc Cohen gives us a nice account of how Aristotle might have come to this conclusion.[3] Earlier in Z.17 (1041$^a$17–18), when Aristotle is denying that the attempt to specify the *ousia* of a thing is the attempt to identify the grounds for an assertion of

[3]Cohen, "Essentialism in Aristotle," 402–405.

identity, he tells us that we are not interested in explaining the trivial state of affairs expressed by the sentence

(4)    A man is a man.

As H.2 indicates (and the tentative 1041$^b$6–7 suggests), we are interested in why this or that individual is a man. But Aristotle is worried that his formulation of this explanandum might be challenged on the grounds that it merely expresses the triviality expressed by (3). After all, someone might argue, what the individual is, on Aristotle's own account, is a man, so asking why it is a man just is asking for an explanation of the triviality expressed by (3). Aristotle's anxiety about this kind of challenge suggests that he would not endorse a direct theory of reference for proper names and demonstratives and, as Cohen notes, that he fails to appreciate scope distinctions (fails to appreciate, that is, the difference between asking why the proposition that a man is a man is true and asking, of something $x$ that is a man, why $x$ is a man).[4] In any event, to ward off this challenge, Aristotle seeks an alternative formulation of the explanandum in which the individual in question is identified in a way that is "logically independent"[5] of his/her being a human being; the device he settles on is identification by way of the matter making up the individual. That is what the second formulation of 1041$^b$6–7 is intended to be. Unfortunately, Aristotle does not express himself altogether felicitously here, suggesting that our why-question is a question about the matter itself.[6] But, since the second formulation is

---

[4]Ibid., 403. Montgomery Furth rejects Cohen's reading of Z.17 and takes the subjects of the Z.17 examples to actually be the relevant parcels of matter. See *Substance, Form, and Psyche*, 64–65. If we follow Furth here, we have a difficulty making out the kind of distinction between explanans and explanandum that Aristotle's theory requires. Like Furth, Charlotte Witt assumes that the material out of which a thing is made serves as subject for the sample explananda of Z.17. But unlike Furth, she denies that identifying the *ousia* of a composite involves specifying the principle in virtue of which the composite falls under its proper species. She insists that the *ousia* of a thing is that which explains both why the thing exists and why it is one thing, and she distinguishes these two facts from that consisting in the thing's species membership. See her *Substance and Essence in Aristotle*, 3, 103–104, 112–121. The difficulty with her interpretation is that the existence, unity, and species-membership of a composite are not three distinct and separable facts about it. We should remember once again that, for Aristotle, there is no such thing as just existing or just being one thing. For composites, to exist is to be a thing of a certain kind; to be one is to be one member of that kind distinct from others. Accordingly, for a particular composite $x$ and its proper substance-species $K$, to explain why $x$ is a $K$ just is to explain why $x$ exists and is one thing. Aristotle himself exploits these equivalences ('existing thing', 'a $K$', and 'one $K$') in H.6, his final word on the problem of the unity of the composite. See Chapter 7 for more on this theme.

[5]Cohen, "Essentialism in Aristotle," 404.

[6]Even in Aristotle's account of the explanandum there is a failure to mark scope

presented as a gloss on the first ('This is a man'), it must be understood to express the metaphysical predication intended by the first formulation, differing from it only in that it identifies the subject of that predication in descriptive terms that are supposed to be kind-neutral. The intended force of the gloss is something like "The thing (whatever it is) that is made up of this matter in this state is a man." Thus the why-question is a question about the relevant composite particular, not about his/her body. In the sentence expressing that question, the term 'man' has its mixed product sense, and the question constitutes a request for an explanation of a species-predication. Since we can assume that Aristotle would want to treat the first sample explanandum (that of the house made out of bricks and stones) in the same way, we can conclude that, despite appearances to the contrary, even Aristotle's initial attempts in Z.17 at delineating the overall pattern and context of *ousia* explanations identify species-predications as the appropriate explananda.[7]

II

An *ousia*-explanation, we have seen, takes as its explanandum some particular species-predication, and its explanans is the corresponding form-predication. It is because the matter making up an individual has predicated of it the appropriate form that the individual belongs to the associated substance-species. But delineating this pattern does not quite give us what we were looking for. We began this chapter attempting to isolate what, according to Aristotle, is *the ousia* of familiar concrete objects. Instead of an unequivocal identification of some entity, however, we are presented with a propositional content, one that serves to answer a certain why-question. And when we try to extract from that content something that might plausibly be construed as *the ousia* of an ordinary particular, we come up with not one but two different candi-

---

distinctions. Aristotle, I think, fails to see the distinction between asking why the proposition that this thing made out of these flesh and bones is a man and asking, regarding this thing made out of these flesh and bones, why it is a man. It is obviously the second question that he is interested in, but the second formulation in 1041$^b$6–7 suggests the first. For a slightly different use of Cohen's account of Z.17 to justify the idea that species-predications constitute the explananda, see Frank Lewis, "Form and Predication in Aristotle's *Metaphysics*," especially 69–71.

[7] I hope that the argument of this section answers some of the challenges D. K. Modrak raises for my earliest attempts at getting clear on these issues in "Form, Species, and Predication in *Metaphysics* Z, H, and Θ." See her "Forms and Compounds," especially 98–99.

dates. The form-predication that explains the being of an ordinary particular (i.e., its being the kind of thing it is) involves both the form and the matter of that particular, so it is only plausible to suppose that both play the causal role in terms of which Aristotle defines the notion of the *ousia* of a thing. And in fact Aristotle concedes as much. Although the thesis that form is the *ousia* of ordinary objects is the centerpiece of Z and H, Aristotle counts matter as *ousia* in any number of places.[8] Most significant, he does so in both H.1 and H.2, chapters where the explicit concern is to identify "the cause of the being" of ordinary objects.

But, then, why the special prominence accorded the thesis that its form constitutes the *ousia* of a thing? Aristotle suggests an answer when he tells us (1042b9–10) that the causal role of matter is easily grasped and generally recognized, so presumably not in need of further elaboration. But this is only part of the answer and certainly not the crucial part. When Z and H direct us to identify the *ousia* of things, the proposed enterprise is not something different from the project way back in the *Categories* of identifying the primary realities. Indeed, Aristotle just assumes that whatever it is that functions as the *ousia* or the reality of ordinary objects is a worthy claimant to the old title 'primary *ousia*'. And to identify the primary realities, we recall, is to identify that smallest set of objects such that, first, by reference to them we can explain why all other things exist or are and, second, their existence or being does not require an explanation. Given Aristotle's essentialist reading of 'to exist' or 'to be', the project must be understood in terms of explanations of what things are, of their being the kinds of things they are.

We have found the Aristotle of Z and H expressing these two requirements on the concept of primary *ousia* by speaking of things that are (a) primary and (b) *kath hauta legomena*. The former are things that are ontologically prior to everything else; everything that is any kind of thing at all either is primary or is what it is only because some primary thing is what it is. The latter are things that just are what they are; their being what they are does not depend on anything else. We agreed that nothing is primary that is not also a *kath hauto legomenon*, and we said that, if there is nothing that fails to enter into ontological relations of priority and dependence with something else, then every *kath kauto legomenon* is a primary thing.

We never find Aristotle explicitly saying these things. He seems to think that the two expressions carry their meaning on their sleeves. We do, however, find him identifying the kinds of categorial features of objects which would preclude their satisfying the requirements associ-

---

[8]See, e.g., 1035a1, 1042a27, 1042b9–10, and 1049a35–36.

ated with the concept of a primary *ousia*, and it is failure to meet the second condition (that associated with the notion of a *kath hauto legomenon*) that most interests him. He says or implies that nothing can be a *kath hauto legomenon*[9] which is

(a)  "said to be what it is by virtue of one thing's being said of something else" (1030$^a$10–11);

(b)  "said to be what it is by participation, affection, or accident" (1030$^a$13–14);

(c)  such that its "formula signifies that this belongs to that" (1030$^a$15–16);

(d)  "said to be what it is in virtue of the fact that this is in this" (1030$^b$18);

(e)  "said to be what it is in virtue of something else" (1031$^b$13);

(f)  a "this in a this" (1036$^b$23);

(g)  "these things being in this condition (or, standing thus)" (1036$^b$24);

(h)  "said to be what it is in virtue of the fact that one thing is in something else that functions as its subject and matter" (1037$^b$3–4);

(i)  such that its "definitory formula signifies one thing (said) of another, where the one is matter and the other, form" (1037$^b$3–4).

The conditions specified in (a–i) tend to cluster around a single theme, that of a thing's being what it is because of a prior predicative relation between other more basic things. Anything whose being what it is is reducible to or analyzable in terms of some prior predicative connection fails to be a *kath hauto legomenon*. With this principle in hand,

[9]Most of these texts refer to cases where Aristotle explicitly tells us that we have a failure to meet the condition set by the notion of a *kath hauto legomenon*. Some couple the term '*kath hauto legomenon*' with the term 'primary', and some speak of things that are not primary. Aristotle's use of the two terms is not quite as rigorous as my definitions might suggest. I do, however, believe that he associated with each the respective senses I delineate. That he should not have been too scrupulous in his use of the terms is hardly surprising since (as my account suggests) he took it to be a necessary truth that all and only primary things are *kath hauta legomena*.

it is easy enough to see why Aristotle would give the prominence he does to the claim that form is *ousia*; with respect to their being what they are, there is a crucial difference between the items which, within the context of any particular *ousia* explanation, play the respective roles of matter and form.

It is what Aristotle calls proximate matter , something like our clump of cortex and phloem or our pack of flesh and bones, that enters into an *ousia* explanation.[10] But, although no complete account of why things are oak trees or human beings can fail to make reference to the kind of stuff out of which they are composed, what functions as matter in an account of this sort is itself a thing for which it is possible to provide something analogous to the *ousia* explanation into which it enters.[11] As we saw in Chapter 2, the proximate matter for an oak tree is the kind of thing or stuff it is—cortex and phloem—because some more basic matter has predicated of it its own form. But, then, the proximate matter that enters into our *ousia* explanation for the oak tree is something properly characterized by the various formulae we meet in (a–i). It is something "said to be whatever it is in virtue of something else" (1031ᵇ13), something "said to be what it is by virtue of one thing 's being said of another" (1030ᵃ10–11), something said to be what it is because "this is in this" (1036ᵇ23). It may enter into an explanation of the being of something else, but it is itself a thing whose being has an explanation, so it cannot be a *kath hauto legomenon*.

The same holds true of whatever more elementary stuff constitutes its matter. It is the kind of stuff it is because some still more basic matter is informed in some way, so it too fails to qualify as a *kath hauto legomenon*. If we attribute to Aristotle a doctrine of prime matter, then we will insist that this same pattern of analysis be reiterated until we reach a matter that is essentially no kind of thing at all, the matter for the four elements or prime matter. Since prime matter has no essence, it is not a *legomenon* at all. There is nothing that counts as what it is, so it likewise fails to be a *kath hauto legomenon*. But, then, none of the things which, within the context of *ousia* explanations, play the role of subject or matter can be characterized as *kath hauta legomena*.

Aristotle denies however, that the substantial forms whose predication is expressed in *ousia* explanations are "said to be whatever they are

---

[10]See H.4, especially 1044ᵃ15–31.

[11]It is not to be expected, however, that as we descend in our analyis of matter all of the features distinctive of our original species- and form-predications will characterize the analogues of those predications. Pretty clearly, Aristotle sees this descent as ultimately confronting "stuffs" rather than "things". Accordingly, the sortal features of our original species-predications will not be associated with the stuff-kind-predications we will confront.

in virtue of something else". There is nothing distinct from a form that functions as the cause of its being. Indeed, Aristotle tells us (1040ᵇ23–24) that each substantial form is its own *ousia*, and he means merely that the explanation for a form's being what it is is found in the form itself. So substantial forms qualify as *kath hauta legomena* and thereby meet the second condition ingredient in the concept of a primary *ousia*. And Aristotle wants to claim that they meet the first condition as well. According to Z.17–H.2, it is in virtue of the fact that some substantial form is predicated of its matter that all the other things in the category of *ousia* (not only our original concrete particulars, but also the things or stuffs that play, in the various levels of analysis, the role of matter[12]) are what they are; if we concede that the case that things outside the category of *ousia* are what they are only because they stand in some relation to something within the category of *ousia* has already been made out, we must agree that everything that is any kind of thing at all either has a form for its *ousia* or is something whose being what it is ultimately depends on the fact that form is the *ousia* of something else.

It is, then, because form is the only thing that is both the *ousia* of other things and its own *ousia* that the thesis that form is *ousia* is the dominating claim of the middle books. It was, however, a conclusion of Z.6 that whatever meets the two conditions implicit in the concept of a primary *ousia* is necessarily one and the same as its essence. As soon as he has completed his case for the *ousia*hood of form, Aristotle applies the Z.6 thesis to the case of substantial form.[13] The appeal to the Identity Thesis in this context is no mere coincidence. Were it not a necessary fact about a thing that what it is to be that thing and the thing itself are one and the same, it could not play the kind of explanatory role that the Aristotle of Z and H wants to reserve for form. Form is to provide us with a final answer to the question why things are what they are, and only if a thing is necessarily the same with what it is to be that thing do we have the requisite guarantee that there is no explanation in terms of something else for that thing's being what it is, for its being the kind of thing it is. Only if a thing is its own essence can it be its own *ousia*.[14] For a thing of this sort, the question, Why is it that kind of thing? has a ready answer that precludes the possibility of any further questions. It is the kind of

---

[12]The perceptive reader will see a cloud on the horizon, one connected with the notion of prime matter. I beg her/his indulgence on this score. I deal with the problem in Chapter 7.

[13]See H.3 (1043ᵇ1–4).

[14]Identity of a thing and its essence is a necessary but not a sufficient condition of that thing's being its own *ousia*. If Code is right, all definables are identical with their essences, but substance-species and accidents are neither of them their own *ousia* since there is an explanation in terms of other things for their being what they are.

thing it is because it is one and the same as being that kind of thing; and it could not be otherwise.

With these materials in hand, we are in a better position to appreciate the relationship between the Z.6 Identity Thesis and the earlier Unanalyzability Thesis. We have already noted that the role of the Identity Thesis in Z and H is analogous to that of the Unanalyzability Thesis in the earlier works. In both contexts, the project of identifying the primary realities presupposes that, in the case of the things that serve to explain why others things are what they are, the relationship between a thing and what it is must be intimate.[15] It cannot be a relationship that is susceptible of the kind of analysis we invoke to explain why other things are what they are. Were it so susceptible, something else would turn out to have a better claim to status as primary *ousia*. In the *Categories*, the claim was that it is because they are subjects for other things that familiar particulars are the primary realities. Accordingly, we had to deny that what those particulars are, the kinds of thing they are, rests on some prior instance of one thing's being predicated of (either said of or present in) something else; and so we spoke of direct and unmediated predicative ties linking the lowest-level substance-kinds with their members, thereby ensuring that no prior subjects of predication could emerge.

Now, however, because we want to accommodate the fact that the familiar particulars of the *Categories* can come to be and pass away, we construe them as composites of matter and form. Since the relationship of form to matter is that of metaphysical predicate to metaphysical subject, we have to concede that the predications in virtue of which those familiar particulars are what they are (the relevant species-predications) do, in fact, rest on prior predications, what we have called form-predications. Those predications, however, hold only accidentally. A form is not what its matter is but how it is; the matter could exist without the form's being predicated of it. If we fasten on what the thing that plays the role of matter here is in its own right, we find that, like our original species-predication, the predication tying it to its proper thing-

---

[15]In both the early works and the later works, Aristotle uses the term '*kath hauto*' ('*kath hauto legomenon*' in Z and H) to mark those things whose being what they are does not give rise to the sort of analysis to which things that are not primary are susceptible. A critical difference in the two accounts is that in the earlier view a thing can be *kath hauto* if its being what it is involves the predication of some universal distinct from the thing that is *kath hauto*. Thus, the primary realities of the *Categories*, particulars, are *kath hauta*, but their being what they are depends on the fact that their species are said of them. It is sufficient for a thing's status as a *kath hauto* being that this predication not be analyzable or that it be direct, primitive, or unmediated. In the later works, nothing can be a *kath hauto legomenon* if its being what it is involves a predicative link, however tight, with something else. This is just another way of stating the Z.6 Identity Thesis.

kind or stuff-kind is analyzable in terms of a prior predication that holds only accidentally. The point here is a general one: none of the things that serve as metaphysical subjects for other things are such that the predications marking them out as what they are pass the unanalyzability test. All such predications are analyzable in terms of prior predications that hold only accidentally. There are no predications tying metaphysical subjects to what they are that hold primitively, directly, and without mediation.

As early as Z.3, Aristotle tells us as much when he says that, where one thing is predicated of another, the subject is always "something for which the to be is different from that of each of the things predicated. For the others are predicated of *ousia*, but this is predicated of the matter" (1029ᵃ22–24). He is talking here about basic or noneliminable predicative ties. He insists that there are only two kinds of such ties, those linking accidents with concrete particulars and those linking substantial forms with what functions as their matter, and that both ties hold only accidentally or *kata sumbebekos*.[16] He is more explicit in other places. At the beginning of Z.13, there are only two ways something can be a metaphysical subject for something else:

> either [a] being a "this something" as the animal is to its affections or [b] as the matter for the actuality. (1038ᵇ5–6)

And in Θ.7,

> what functions as the subject or thing of which [something is predicated] is to be distinguished in this: either it is a "this something" or it is not. For example, the man (the body and soul) is the subject of its affections. . . . whenever things are thus, the last (subject) is (an) *ousia*; but when they are not thus and the thing predicated is some form and "this something," then the last [subject] is matter and material *ousia*. (1049ᵃ27–36)

So every case of one thing being irreducibly, noneliminably, or unanalyzably predicated of something else involves a relationship that holds only *kata sumbebekos*. There just are no cases of one thing being essentially and unanalyzably predicated of something else. But the connection between a primary *ousia* and what it is must be preserved. As the early theory recognized, the whole project of identifying the primary *ousia* presupposes that that connection be primitive and un-

---

[16]Whereas in *Physics* A.7 Aristotle uses the term 'matter' to refer to the persisting subject of predication in both qualified and unqualified change, in Z and H he tends to restrict the term 'matter' to what is subject for the latter case. See, e.g., H.4 (1044ᵇ8–11), which might be insisting on this alteration in terminology.

analyzable; if that result cannot be secured on the assumption that the essence is one thing that stands in some relationship to the primary *ousia* whose essence it is, the only option is to deny that we have different things here. To deny this is to embrace the Z.6 Identity Thesis. It is substantial forms that are the primary realities. So substantial forms do not have essences; they are their essences. Indeed, they are the fundamental essences.

<h2 style="text-align:center">III</h2>

So substantial forms are the fundamental essences and primary *ousiai*; because they are metaphysically predicated of their matter, the familiar objects of the *Categories* are the kinds of thing they are. This idea of levels of substance-predications is so basic to Aristotle's later metaphysics that we would expect to find it expressed in his account of the semantics of the substance terms that are the vehicles for the linguistic expression of the form-predications and species-predications that constitute the core of his account—and we do. Aristotle suggests that the homonymy of substance words is an instance of his favorite logical tool, the *pros hen* or focal meaning. In H.3, he tells us:

> 'Animal' might be applied to both [i.e., the form and the concrete object], not as something said by way of one formula but as related to one thing [*pros hen*]. (1043ª36–37)

The conjecture here is that the homonymy of *ousia* words is not merely accidental, but that the mixed and pure product senses of a substance term are so related that one is the core in terms of which the other is to explicated or defined. But which sense did Aristotle take to be basic? In Z.8, he tells us that the composite takes its name from the form,[17] and this seems to mean that the use of substance words in their pure product sense is primary.

The remark in Z.3 should not be interpreted as an empirical claim. It implies no particular story about the historical development of the substance vocabulary of an individual or a broader language-using community. Nor is it intended to summarize the nonphilosopher's intuitions about what constitute the paradigmatic cases for the application of substance terms. It represents rather a kind of summary of the metaphysician's reconstruction of our ordinary substance talk. From the perspective of Z and H, an ordinary object's belonging to its proper

---

[17]See 1033ᵇ16–18. See also Z.11 (1037ª29–30), where the same point is made.

substance-kind is not a brute fact. It is something that is to be explained in terms of the corresponding form-predication, and the appeal to the *pros hen* analysis is merely the attempt to convert these insights about metaphysical predication into a philosophical account of the corresponding linguistic predications. From the metaphysician's perspective, the use of a substance term to express the fact that a form is predicated of its matter provides the grounds for the use of that same term to express the fact that an individual belongs to its proper species; it is because the term can in its pure product sense be linguistically predicated of matter that it can in its mixed product sense be linguistically predicated of the concrete individual composed of that matter.

The H.3 passage is interesting in its suggestion that the *pros hen* doctrine applies to substance terms of any level of generality. It is not just in the cases we have been concerned with, cases of the lowest-level substance terms, that we find the kind of focal meaning we have been discussing. The same pattern of analysis can be invoked in the case of terms (like 'animal') that apply only generically. These terms have both pure and mixed senses, and these are related in just the way the corresponding senses of lowest-level substance terms are. This idea enables us to approach the dominant thesis of the middle books from a slightly different angle. In the case of lowest-level substance terms, the use of the *pros hen* analysis tells us that the core use of a term such as 'man' is the use of the term in its pure product sense to signify a certain form (here, the human soul); in virtue of signifying that form, the term can in a derivative sense—its mixed product sense—be applied to all those individuals whose matter has predicated of it the relevant form. If the analysis can be extended to terms of any level of generality, we get the result that the most general substance term in our vocabulary, the term '*ousia*' itself, has both a pure and a mixed sense. In its basic sense, the pure sense, the term signifies the various substantial forms; but in virtue of that primary application, the term can be applied derivatively (in its mixed product sense) to all those individuals whose matter has predicated of it something that is, in the pure product sense, *ousia*. So forms and ordinary objects are said to be *ousiai* in different senses of this term. Substantial form is *ousia* in the basic or primary sense; ordinary objects, the composites of Z and H, are *ousiai* in a derivative sense, the appropriateness of the derivative use of the title in their case resting on the appropriateness of the title in its primary or core sense.[18]

[18]Terence Irwin denies that there is multivocity in the Z–H use of '*ousia*' to apply to form and composite particular. See *Aristotle's First Principles*, 206ff. In part, I suspect, his unwillingness to find homonymy here stems from Irwin's view that what he calls the particular materiate form and the formal compound are one and the same thing (see note

On this score, the account of Z and H represents an inversion of the account found in the *Categories*. There, familiar particulars were the primary *ousiai*; their species were only secondary *ousiai*. Although Aristotle did not speak of essences in that early work, throughout the logical writings he held to the view that substance-species are the paradigmatic objects of definition. So the things that were the essences par excellence were accorded secondary status as *ousiai*. In Z and H, however, it is composite particulars that are said to be *ousiai* in the derivative or secondary sense, whereas what now count as the fundamental essences—substantial forms—are called *ousia* in the basic or primary sense. They are now the primary *ousiai*.

## IV

As we have seen, there are two components to the claim that form is primary *ousia*: first, the idea that everything that is any kind of thing at all is a substantial form, has a substantial form for its *ousia*, or is what it is because a substantial form is the *ousia* of something else; second, the idea that no substantial form has something distinct from itself for its *ousia*, that each substantial form is its own *ousia*. To assess the first component in the claim, we can look to Aristotle's story about the various patterns of ontological priority and dependence, to his theory of form and species-predications, to his views about the dependence of accidents on their subjects, and to his views about the reducibility of what I have been calling complexes (like the sunburned man) to their constituents. It is, however, more difficult to assess the second component. That claim is that nothing can turn up that plays, with respect to form, the causal role form plays with respect to other things; and it is difficult to see how we would go about proving that. But short of a general proof that we can ward off all possible threats to the *ousia*hood of form on this score, we would like some kind of assurance that the claim that form is a *kath hauto legomenon* does not meet the fate of the corresponding claim of the early theory on behalf of its candidates for status as primary *ousia*.

Aristotle tries to provide these assurances when he argues (1033ª28–1033ᵇ18) that form is neither generated nor corrupted. We have already

---

25). Apart from my doubts about attributing this identification to Aristotle, I find Irwin's denial here surprising. First, we have Aristotle's own explicit testimony on the homonymy of substance terms at the generic level. Second, the contrast between the use of '*ousia*' as a concrete general term and as an abstract singular term cries out for the applicability of the homonymy thesis in its case.

met the claim that forms do not come to be or pass away in our treatment of the idea that form is a "such" rather than a "this." In that context, our concern was with the contrast implied by the claim, the contrast between the concrete composite that does come to be and pass away and so has the factual autonomy of things that exist separately and the form that exists only as something predicated of something else. But in arguing for the claim that form is ungenerated and uncorrupted, Aristotle is not merely attempting to underwrite this contrast. His argument for this claim is also intended to shore up the claim that form is a *kath hauto legomenon*, a thing that is its own *ousia*. As we have seen, it was the facts of coming to be and passing away that led to the breakdown of the Unanalyzability Thesis, a thesis whose force was to claim that the primary *ousiai* of the *Categories* are what the *Posterior Analytics* calls *kath hauto* beings. In the *Categories*, Aristotle's attention to change is limited to the case of what he subsequently calls qualified coming to be and passing away. But in later works, he has to confront the fact that the primary realities of the early theory can undergo a more radical kind of change; they can come into and pass out of existence, so that there are changes that eventuate, not in such things as a white man or a musical man, but in such things as a man or a corpse. It was changes of this sort that led Aristotle to the insight that ordinary objects have an internal structure, that they are predicative complexes of matter and form; that insight, in turn, led to the breakdown of the Unanalyzability Thesis. The things we initially took to be *kath hauto* beings (things that are what they are in their own right) turned out to be the kinds of thing they are only because some substantial form is predicated of some parcel of matter. But, if it is plausible to assume that our new candidates for the role of primary *ousia* are not subject to this sort of change (unqualified change), then we can be assured that, on this score at least, there can be no threat to the claim that form is a *kath hauto legomenon*, a thing that is its own *ousia*. One reason (initially the most plausible reason) for thinking that form has an internal structure, one component of which plays with respect to form the causal role it plays with respect to the composite whose form it is, is thus countered.

Aristotle's argument here is fairly predictable. It involves the idea that coming to be (as well as passing away) presupposes a subject-predicate structure. A necessary condition of a change is the existence of some persisting subject that comes to have predicated of it some entity not previously predicated of it. The persisting subject is what we call the matter for the change; the predicated entity is its form, what the matter or subject comes to be. The analysis is perfectly general in applying to both qualified and unqualified coming to be. As we have seen, Aristotle's contends here that what comes to be is the composite; that which the subject comes to be, the form, does not itself come to be. He argues that, if we suppose that the form comes to be, we must construe it as having the relevant subject-predicate structure; but, then, the question arises whether what, in this new structure, functions as predicate or form comes to be. If the answer is affirmative, a further such structure is required and a familiar kind of regress is on the horizon. In Z.8, Aristotle makes the point apropos of the work of an artisan:

> For example, he makes a brazen sphere. This happens as follows: out of this which is bronze he makes this which is a sphere. But if he makes this, it is clear that he will make it in the same way; and the comings into being will go to infinity. Therefore it is clear that the form or whatever we should call the shape in the perceptible thing does not come to be nor does it have a coming into being; and the same holds for the what it is to be; for this is what comes to be in something else either by art or by nature or by a power. ($1033^b1$–8)

If we are, then, to provide an account of how things come to be (and pass away), we have to concede that at some level that which plays the role of predicate or form in a coming-to-be does not itself come to be. At whatever level we posit such a thing, we must concede both that it plays the causal role associated with the notion of a primary reality and that, lacking the relevant internal structure, it has a legitimate claim to be its own *ousia*. So, even if on grounds of general obstinacy we deny that the forms predicated of the matter making up familiar particulars are the relevant predicates, we must concede that something meets both conditions. For his part, Aristotle is satisfied that the forms of ordinary particulars do this.

One might experience here that general sense of unease that is all too frequently occasioned by Aristotle's contention that this or that looming regress is philosophically decisive. But I am less concerned with the acceptability of Aristotle's argument than with the fact that he sees the need to provide reasons for thinking that forms lack the kind of internal structure that might undermine his claim that each form is its own *ousia*. Despite the fact that he restates the claim that forms do not come to be in Z.9, Z.15, H.3, and H.5,[19] however, some commentators take Aristotle to be ambivalent on this point and construe the alleged ambivalence as grounds for supposing that Aristotle endorsed a doctrine of particular

---

[19]And outside the middle books, the claim is implicit in *Metaphysics* B.4 ($999^b5$–16) and explicit in E.3 ($1027^a29$) and Λ.3 ($1069^b35$–36).

or individual forms.[20] The supposed evidence for the charge of ambivalence is the claim (made on a number of occasions in Z and H) that,
although they do not come to be or pass away, forms "are and are not."[21]
The idea presumably is that Aristotle means that, for a given form F, at
one time it is true to say that F exists and, at some later time, true to say
that F does not exist. But given his views about the eternality of definable beings ($1039^b20-1040^a7$), the intended F cannot be the form taken
universally. Apart from the issue of the eternality of definables, there is
no plausibility to the idea that Socrates' death has the result that there is
no such thing as *man* (where 'man' is used in its pure product sense).
Accordingly, Aristotle must have forms taken individually in mind
when he says that they are and are not, so that when some composite
particular exists it is true to say that the form unique to it exists; but,
then, once it has passed away, the individual form is no more.

We consider the issue of individual forms in the next chapter, but
several things should be said about this interpretation of the claim that
forms are and are not. As Furth points out, it is difficult to see how, if
this interpretation is correct, Aristotle can escape the conclusion that
forms come to be and pass away; we cannot make sense of the claim that
the proposition that a particular form exists comes to be true, stays true
for a time, and then comes to be false without supposing that the form
in question comes to be and, after existing awhile, passes away.[22] And
the comment that forms are and are not is always made with an eye
toward the denial that form comes to be and passes away. Even if we
hold that his views on this point are ultimately inconsistent, it is implausible to suggest that, in one and the same context, we find him
making blatantly incompatible claims. If it is conceded that the comment as so interpreted requires that form is generated and corrupted, it
will not do to invoke the distinction between form taken individually or
particularly and form taken universally and to attribute to Aristotle the
view that the former, but not the latter, is subject to generation and
corruption;[23] for we have to agree that it is the form whose predication

---

[20]See, e.g., A. C. Lloyd's *Form and Universal in Aristotle* (Liverpool: Francis Cairns, 1981),
25–27; Henry Telloh, "The Universal in Aristotle," *Apeiron* (1980), 70–78, especially 72;
Wilfrid Sellars, *Philosophical Perspectives*, 111–118; Terence Irwin, *Aristotle's First Principles*,
251; and Michael Frede and Gunther Patzig, *Aristoteles "Metaphysik Z,"* vol. 1, 32, 52–53,
and vol. 2, 281–282.

[21]See $1039^b26$ and $1044^b21-22$.

[22]Furth, *Substance, Form, and Psyche*, 194–195.

[23]One might think that $1043^b14$ and $1060^a22$ confirm that attribution, but the latter text is
merely canvassing general opinions and not expressing Aristotle's own view. I take the
former text to be part of a reductio in which Aristotle is saying that the only way we can
make the claim that form comes to be is by holding that it comes to without ever actually

accounts for the coming into being and continued existence of a composite that we cannot, on pain of initiating the regress Aristotle takes to be vicious, construe as generated or corrupted. Even on this interpretation, however, this can only be form taken universally; but, then, since all the work that form is supposed to do is done by form understood in this way, just how did form taken particularly come on the scene and what work, other than accommodating the supposedly recalcitrant comment, does it do once there?

Rather than attribute to Aristotle an inconsistent view or one that introduces quite gratuitously a notion of form that plays no explanatory role whatsoever in his theory, we would do better to place a more innocent interpretation on his comment that forms are and are not. And this is fairly easy to do. Nothing compels us to take Aristotle's use of 'are' and 'are not' as expressing existence and nonexistence. It is more plausible to think that his use of these expressions simply points to the fact that substantial forms, things that are universals, each have a history as a metaphysical predicate. A given form takes now this parcel of matter for its metaphysical subject and now that. Once a composite *ousia* has come to be, the appropriate form is predicated of the matter making up that particular; but, then, when the composite passes away, the form is no longer so predicated. So forms are and are not; that is, at any point in time they *are* predicated of parcels of matter that at a later time they *are not* predicated of.[24]

V

When Aristotle denies that form is generated or corrupted, his central concern is to combat the idea that form is analyzable into constituents related as subject to predicate or matter to form; what makes this idea unacceptable is the requirement that what plays the role of primary *ousia* must be something that is its own *ousia*, something that is a *kath hauto legomenon*. This requirement on the concept of a primary *ousia* can be expected to show up in the definition of a form. Form is both its own *ousia* and its own essence. Indeed, to identify the *ousia* of a form just is to identify the essence that it is, and the paradigmatic way of identifying that essence is by formulating the definition of the form. So it ought to be possible to define a form without reference to any constituent intrin-

---

undergoing a coming to be. But to hold this is contradictory. What is implicit is that one cannot coherently maintain that form comes to be.

[24]For an alternative account of "are and are not," see Furth, *Substance, Form, and Psyche,* 194–195.

sic to the form that plays the role of matter or subject for something else. But the definition of a form has to be matter-free identification in a stronger sense. Substantial forms are to constitute the fundamental or basic level in the hierarchy of essences Aristotle proposes in Z.4–6, and fundamental essences are those that can be identified independently of anything else. Accordingly, it is not just the possibility that the definition of a form incorporates a reference to something intrinsic to it playing the role of matter as subject for something else that must be excluded. It also must be possible to define a form without reference to anything extrinsic to the form, in particular, without reference to the matter that is its metaphysical subject. As Aristotle puts it in H.2, form has to be "separable in formula" (1042$^a$29).

Although these ideas are presented in several places in the middle books, they receive their most detailed expression in Z.10.[25] It is significant that Aristotle formulates these themes in terms of both talk about priority (what I have called presupposition) and talk about definition (what I have called identification). Indeed, the chapter consists of successive attempts to formulate two theses which, given Aristotle's views about the relationship between definition and essence, are almost mirror images of each other. The first is the thesis that the formula or definition of a form requires reference to nothing that plays the role of matter (1035$^a$22–23). The second is the thesis that there is nothing extrinsic to the form that is prior to it, nothing presupposed by form in

---

[25]It is revealing that, in the Z.11 summary of the results of Z.10–11, Aristotle tells us that he has shown how the essence is something that is *auto kath hauto* (1037$^a$21–22), the implication being that to show that one can define form without reference to anything extrinsic is to show it to be *kath hauto*. A very different reading of Z.10 and 11 is found in Terence Irwin's *Aristotle's First Principles*, 241ff. He sees Aristotle as concerned to argue that it is what Irwin calls the particular materiate form that is primary *ousia*. The particular materiate form is a formal compound (the specific form taken with a bit of proximate matter); it is to be distinguished from what Irwin calls a materiate compound (e.g., a bronze ball). According to Irwin, Aristotle construes Socrates and Callias themselves as formal compounds. As Irwin reads them, Z.10 and 11 are chapters in which Aristotle draws these distinctions. I have difficulty finding the distinctions Irwin insists on in these chapters. But, more generally, I find the suggestion that Aristotle takes Irwin's particular materiate forms to be primary *ousia* to be problematic. First, 1033$^b$24–25 tell decisively against the idea that Socrates and Callias are formal compounds. Second, primary *ousiai* have to be *kath hauta legomena*; but if particular materiate forms or formal compounds are the general form taken with a bit of the proximate matter, then they are things said to be what they are in virtue of some predicative relation between prior and more fundamental things. Third, Z.17 tells us that primary *ousiai* are the ultimate unifying principles in virtue of which compounds constitute some one thing; but, despite Irwin's apparent protestations to the contrary (*Aristotle's First Principles*, 255–257), I cannot see how what he calls formal compounds fail to present the kinds of problems posed by the case of materiate compounds. A quite different reading of Z.10 and 11 is found in Frede and Patzig, *Aristotles "Metaphysik Z,"* vol. 2, 189–192 and 209–213. I discuss their reading in Section VII of this chapter.

the sense that, if it were not what it is, form could not be what it is (1036ᵃ19–23).

It is not surprising that the Z.10 discussion of these theses (like similar discussions elsewhere in Z and H) appeals to the arguments of Z.8 about the ingenerability and incorruptibility of form (e.g., 1035ᵃ23–29); nor is it surprising that Aristotle's formulation of both theses explicitly appeals to the distinctions central to his claims about the homonymy of substance terms (1035ᵃ6–8, 1036ᵃ16–25). If we are asked whether a notion such as *man* can be defined without reference to matter or whether it is prior to features that are broadly speaking material, we are advised to distinguish the claims that result from using the term in its mixed and pure senses. Thus, what is signified by the term 'man' in its mixed product sense can be defined only by reference to both matter and form and is posterior to both; the definition of what is signified by that term in its pure product sense requires no reference to anything material and is prior to everything but what is mentioned in its definition. Aristotle claims that these facts about form are born out by the examination of what Code usefully calls the fully expanded version of the definition of a form,[26] where this is reached by substituting for each item mentioned in the definiens of a form its definiens and then successively reiterating the procedure for the results of each such substitution until we arrive at indefinable notions.

Z. 10 is, however, problematic on two scores. First, although there can be little doubt that Aristotle here argues for the related theses that (a) it is possible to identify the essence of a form (or better, the essence that is a form) without reference to anything, whether intrinsic or extrinsic to form, that functions as matter, and that (b) form presupposes or is posterior to no other essence, the precise way Aristotle expresses these theses is disturbing. Throughout the chapter, he contrasts the case of form and composite in terms of talk about the parts of a form, telling us that the parts of form, none of which are material, are the only items mentioned in its definition and that those parts are the only things that have any claim to priority over form. The unfortunate suggestion is that form is a mere assemblage of its parts. Although we may find the idea that none of the parts of a form are related as subject and predicate reassuring, we are hard pressed to see how we are to square the talk of parts here with other ideas of Z and H, for example, that forms provide us with our terminus in the search after the primary *ousiai*, that they are to function as organizing and unifying principles for

26 Alan Code, "On the Origins of Some Aristotelian Theses about Predication," 122 and 131 (n. 77).

material elements that themselves require no further such principles, and that forms have no essences prior to them.

Second, Z.10 is paired with Z.11, in which Aristotle discusses similar themes. But Z.11 has been taken to establish precisely the opposite conclusion of Z.10;[27] it is sometimes claimed that Z.11 seeks to establish that it is, in fact, impossible to provide a definition of the substantial form of a composite entity without making reference to the matter that is its subject. That suggestion leads us to wonder whether Z.10 is indeed a final statement of Aristotle's view or just the dialectical exploration of claims he ultimately means to reject. Let us consider these two difficulties in order.

The first difficulty is one Aristotle himself appreciates. At the end of Z.11, we find him reflecting on the discussions of Z.10 and 11; he concedes ($1037^{a}12-20$) that, since form is one thing, the talk of the parts of a form which dominates those discussions requires further attention. The notion of 'part' operative in Z.10 is pretty clearly that delineated in $\Delta.25$ ($1023^{b}23-24$), where "the items in the definition that explains what a thing is" are said to be parts of that thing. The opening lines of Z.10 ($1034^{b}20-22$), which identify the parts of a thing with the items signified by the expressions making up the formula for the thing, corroborate this reading. And although a later passage in the chapter ($1035^{a}2-3$), where Aristotle explicitly tells us that only the items "out of which the formula of the form is made up" are its parts, is less sensitive to the use/mention distinction, it pretty well settles the issue of what he means when he speaks of parts of the form.

So we are not to suppose that form is some sort of complex that can be analyzed into constituents. The idea is the more innocent one that form is definable by reference to genus and differentia, that the formula expressing the definition of a form is always linguistically complex.

---

[27]See, e.g., Sheilah O'Flynn Brennan, "Substance and Definition, Reality and Logos: *Metaphysics Z–H*," *New Scholasticism* (1985), 21–59, especially 40ff.; Edwin Hartman, *Substance, Body, and Soul*, 69; and Terence Irwin, *Aristotle's First Principles*, 240ff. Frede and Patzig might be accused of making a similar mistake, but I believe that the criticism would be misguided. See *Aristotles "Metaphysik Z,"* vol. 2, 209–213, for their account and Section VII of this chapter for my reactions to it. The more general issue of the relationship between Z.10 and Z.11 is an item on which there is genuine controversy. In both Burnyeat et al., eds., *Notes on Book Zeta*, and Montgomery Furth, *Aristotle: Metaphysics Zeta, Eta, Theta, & Iota*, we find the suggestion that the chapters represent two different attempts to deal with the same set of problems. The participants in the Oxford seminar take Z.10 to be the more insightful of the two attempts (p. 93), whereas Furth sees Z.11 as the more subtle treatment (p. 120). My own view is that the two chapters have different aims. Chapter Z.10 tries to show the matter independence of form, whereas Z.11 (up to $1036^{b}32$) tries to show that the species can be defined only with reference to both matter and form. From $1036^{b}32$ onward, Z.11 attempts to summarize the subtle reasoning of the two chapters.

And, as Aristotle sees it, the idea *is* innocent. He does not construe the fact that we define a thing in terms of its genus and differentia by itself a threat to the unity or simplicity of the thing so defined. On this score, he agrees with the Aristotle of the logical works who could, in one and the same breath, point to the fact that the definition of an infima species incorporates both its genus and differentia and insist that an expression such as 'two-footed animal' picks out just one thing. Indeed, the later Aristotle calls substantial forms *asuntheta*, things that lack any kind of complexity or things that are "simples," and in $\Theta$.10 ($1051^{b}18$–$33$) he does not hesitate to apply the term to forms or actualities in the very context in which he is concerned with their definition. So, despite the fact that definition involves both genus and differentia and its linguistic expression is a complex phrase, there is not a general problem in Z and H about the unity of definition.

In Z.12 ($1037^{b}8$–$14$) Aristotle discusses the issue of the definition of form. After reminding us of our earlier discussions of definition in the *Posterior Analytics*, he invokes language reminiscent of those discussions and asks why the definition of *man* as two-footed animal results in a formula of "one thing and not many, two-footed and animal."[28] Given the homonymy of substance terms, it might seem unclear just which question Aristotle is posing here. Is he concerned with definition of a substance-species or with the definition of the corresponding form? The context in which we find the discussion (following immediately on the discussions of Z.10 and Z.11) suggests that the concern is with form. The facts, first, that the appropriate pattern for defining substance-species is not definitvely delineated until much later (in H.2), and, second, that the pattern Aristotle ultimatly settles on involves problems that are not addressed at all in Z.12 and provide the focus for the concluding chapters of H is evidence, I think, that Z.12 is concerned with the definition of form.[29] The upshot of the chapter is just that there

---

[28]Frede and Patzig claim that Z.12 is a later interpolation. See *Aristoteles "Metaphysik Z,"* vol. 1, 25–26. I find their exegetical arguments for the claim plausible; but I would insist that if Aristotle did in fact insert Z.12 into the text of Z he had good reasons. With their talk of parts, Z.10–11 create the impression that a substantial form is a kind of composite; Z.12 counters this impression by arguing that despite its linguistic complexity the definition of a form is a formula of something that is paradigmatically a unity. Furthermore, the strategy Aristotle invokes to show this leads naturally into the themes of Z.13; he argues that if we assume that genera are mere determinables we can identify a form with the last differentia mentioned in its definition. On one plausible interpretation, Z.13 seeks to justify that assumption by showing that we cannot construe genera as universals with a complete conceptual content in their own right. See Section III of Chapter 6 for more on this theme.

[29]Even if we conclude that Z.12 bears on the definition of species, there can be no doubt that it bears on the definition of forms as well.

cannot be a problem of unity here. Toward showing this, Aristotle invokes the familiar theme that genera are not full-fledged entities in their own right; they are mere determinables that get their reality from their realization or expression in the determinate forms falling under them.[30] Aristotle uses this theme as license for identifying a definition with its last differentia.[31] That differentia, he tells us, just "is the *ousia* and the form" (1038ª25–26).

The case of form contrasts sharply with that of its associated species, where the appeal in definition to a genus and a differentia is not nearly so benign. As we have seen, in H.2 the analysis of a substance-species always involves a reference to a predicative link between matter and form that holds only accidentally. We have a genuine instance of one thing's being predicated of a different thing, something for which the "to be is different from that of the thing predicated" (1029ª22–23). Thus, although definition by genus and difference by itself does not constitute a threat to ontological simplicity, the ontological complexity which, on independent grounds, we have to read into substance-species forces us to place a quite different interpretation from any found in the logical writings on the genus–differentia structure of their definition. This contrast between the definition of a form and its corresponding species leads Aristotle to take seriously the suggestion that form does not have a definition. He settles on the claim that, if we restrict the term 'definition' to be the case in which "the definitional formula signifies one thing said of another and one thing has to function as matter and other as form" (1043ᵇ30–32), then there is no definition of form. He then concludes H.3 with a theme he returns to in H.6, that there is no explaining the unity of form. Despite the linguistic complexity of the formula expressing its definition, a substantial form is one thing just in virtue of being "an actuality and certain nature" (1044ª9). As he puts it in H.6 (1045ᵇ4–5), "there is not something else that is the cause of its being one thing." On the contrary, "each [form] is straightaway something that is a being and something that is one" (1045ᵇ3–4).

---

[30]1038ª5–8. See also *Metaphysics* I.8 (1058ª1–8) and *De Anima* B.3 (414ᵇ28).

[31]1038ª19–20. Although I agree with Edward Halper that Z.12 focuses on the definition of form and H.6 on the definition of the composite, I am not completely convinced that the claim that genera are determinables does not by itself generate the conclusion that the form is the last differentia. Halper is certainly correct that, if we interpret Z.12 as I have, Aristotle's painstaking attention to differentiation by proper differentiae is gratuitous. It does not, however, make any difference to my overall contention about Z.12 if Halper is right about the structure of Aristotle's argument in the chapter, since we agree about what the conclusion is supposed to be, namely, that the last differentia in the definition of the form just is the form. See Edward Halper, "*Metaphysics* Z.12 and H.6: The Unity of Form and Composite," *Ancient Philosophy* (1984), 146–159.

This is precisely what Aristotle should say about that which is supposed to function as primary reality, organizing and unifying principle, and fundamental essence. But, then, what does he mean when he tells us that the items in the definition of "form are prior to the form itself"? Nothing, we want to say, can be prior to the primary reality. In fact, Z.10 is elastic in its use of the term 'prior'.[32] In one and the same context, the term can shift its sense from a serious notion of priority that might prove critical to the task of distinguishing the ontologically independent and dependent to a less interesting notion that is less likely to be critical to the metaphysician's analysis. The kind of priority operative in the claim that form is posterior to the items in its definition is one instance of a less interesting notion. Here, it is useful to consider an analogous claim in *Categories* 13:

> But genera are prior to species, for the sequence of their being cannot be reversed. If there is the species *water animal*, there will be the genus *animal*, but granted the being of the genus *animal*, it does not follow necessarily that there will be the species *water animal*. (15ª5–8)

The point here is that whereas

(5)   Something is a water animal

entails

(6)   Something is an animal,

(6) does not entail (5). In that sense, then, *animal* is prior to *water animal*.[33] But to say that one universal *U* is in this sense prior to another universal *U'* is not to say much more than that *U'* is logically subordinate to *U*, that *U'* and *U* are related as less and more general. It hardly comes as a shock to us to be told that genera are, in this sense, prior to their species; nor, I think, does Aristotle believe he is expressing any profoundly revealing metaphysical facts about species and genera when he makes species, in this sense, posterior to genera. Recall that in *Categories* 5 we are told that species have a better claim to the title '*ousia*' than their genera and that in *Categories* 2 we can find the first seeds of the view that any reality genera have derives from the species that are their complete and determinate expressions.

---

[32]Notice how Aristotle gives us two answers to the question whether the integral parts of a concrete particular are prior to it. See 1035ᵇ23–25 and 1036ª18–22.

[33]See also *Topics* Z.4 (141ᵇ26ff.).

So this notion of priority is one Aristotle feels comfortable in ascribing in cases in which the prior thing has a weaker claim to status as a genuine reality; it is precisely this notion of priority that is operative in the Z.10 thesis that the items included in the definition of a form are prior to the form. Aristotle is thinking of the definition of a form, as he does in Z.12, as given by a formula that identifies a very remote genus and supplements this identification with a series of ever more specific differentiating characteristics. All but the last item in this list are, in the sense delineated in *Categories* 13, prior to the form. The last differentia listed is not, of course, prior to the form in this sense. It is presumably coextensive with the form and so the asymmetry required in the *Categories* 13 analysis does not obtain here. But Z.12 tells that it should not be expected to obtain and why not: that last differentia is not just another item in the definition, just another "part" of the form; it is the form itself.

The second difficulty stems from the first half of Z.11, where some have suggested that Aristotle takes back the conclusions of Z.10 and claims that the forms of natural objects can be defined only by reference to their matter. The critical passage here is 1036$^b$21–29, in which Aristotle says:

> It has been stated, then, that there is a certain aporia about definition and what the reason for this is. And so to reduce everything in this way and to eliminate the matter is a useless piece of work; for some things surely are this in this or these things in this kind of condition. And the comparison that the younger Socrates used to make in the case of *animal* is not on target; for it leads away from the truth and makes us suppose that it is possible for a man to exist without his parts in the way the circle can exist without the bronze. But it is not similar. For an animal is something perceptible and cannot be defined without reference to movement and, accordingly, without reference to the parts being in some sort of condition.

The text is explicit in its insistence that things like *animal* can be defined only by reference to their material parts; the argument is that, since the immediately preceding lines focus on form, Aristotle must be interpreted as talking about form here rather than about the substance-kinds under which composite objects fall.

It is important to see that, if the passage does bear on substantial forms and Aristotle is referring to the animal soul rather than the relevant substance-genus, then his overall account is in serious trouble. If forms could be defined only by reference to the matter that is their subject, then no form would seem to be something said to be what it is in its own right. And if we deny that forms are *kath hauta legomena*, we have to concede that the whole later theory of *ousia* breaks down. Forms could not be their own *ousia* if they were "said to be what they are in virtue of something else"; but, then, they could not be either the primary *ousiai* or the fundamental essences. Indeed, it would be difficult to see how Aristotle could avoid denying that matter is prior to the form that is its predicate and that a potentiality is prior to what is supposed to be its actualization.

Furthermore, the essences of forms would all turn out to be defective in just the way, according to Z.5, any essence we might want to attribute to an accident is defective; for if the matter that is its subject enters into the definition of a form, the relationship between a form and its matter is precisely that between snubness and nose. Although a reference to the kind of matter that is its subject would be required in the formulation of the definition of a form, the predication in which the form is said of some parcel of matter of that kind would still hold only accidentally.[34] And since the use of a substance term in its mixed product sense does not result in redundancy, we could simply apply the argument we used in Z.5 to show that we can never get it just right in our attempt to identify the essence of a form. Either we would say too little, making no reference in our account to the matter Aristotle is allegedly telling us has to enter into the account, or we would say too much by making the relevant reference. So we would have the conclusion that there is nothing stable or determinate that can be identified as the essence of a substantial form.[35]

---

[34]The sense of '*kath hauto* predication' appropriate to the case in which an attribute is predicated of its first recipient would apply. The contrast I have in mind is that between essential (i.e., what-) predication and accidental (i.e., how-) predication. The *kath hauto* or essential predication opposed to what I here call accidental is that identified in the first disjunct of the *Posterior Analytics* A.4 definition ($73^a34$–$73^b5$).

[35]It has been suggested to me that those who construe Z and H as propaedeutic to $\Lambda$ might not find the idea that substantial forms of natural objects are defective in this way problematic. They might take the alleged defectiveness to establish the need for totally immaterial essences to which the forms of natural objects are posterior in *ousia*. The response, I take it, is that the sort of defectiveness I characterize here establishes no link at all between the forms of natural objects and the mover/s of $\Lambda$; for this defectiveness would involve a dependence on what functions as matter for natural substantial forms and nothing else. In any case, there is nothing to suggest that the Aristotle of $\Lambda$ believes that mere conceptual analysis of a natural form is sufficient to establish the existence of an essence whose instantiation is totally independent of matter. The reasoning found in $\Lambda$ is an ancestor, however remote, of cosmological, rather than ontological, arguments. Furthermore, since the Aristotle of Z–H holds that (a) natural forms are primary *ousiai* and (b) nothing is a primary *ousia* that is not a *kath hauto legomenon*, he is committed to denying this alleged defectiveness of natural forms, so the proposal linking Z–H to $\Lambda$ by way of this defectiveness would make Z–H propaedeutic to $\Lambda$ only at the cost of undermining the theoretical base of Z–H. But to say this is not to deny that the author of Z and H may have

These are disastrous consequences, so we should be wary of attributing the view in question to Aristotle. The fact is that the second half of Z.11 gives no hint at all that Aristotle questions the conclusions of Z.10. We are told at 1037ª1–2 that "there is some matter in everything that is a 'this something' rather than an essence and a form itself taken by itself," the implication being that form can be grasped or identified without reference to its matter. At 1037ª5–7, we see that "it is clear that the soul is the primary reality; the body, matter; and *man* and *animal* things made out of the two taken universally." Everything seems to be in order there, and in 1037ª24–25, which is part of a passage summarizing the results of the preceding discussions, Aristotle explicitly says that "the parts in the sense of matter are not present in the formula of the *ousia*." That, of course, is precisely what Z.10 has as its first thesis.

Second, the passage in which Aristotle allegedly contradicts that thesis need not be read as a claim about form. The reference to the younger Socrates might seem to require this interpretation. It might seem that the mistake Aristotle attributes to Socrates is that of holding a view that entails the mistaken idea that the form *man* is such that it is possible for it to be predicated of things other than the familiar packs of flesh and bones. But just how is that mistake different from that of supposing that there might be individual men that are not composed or made up of flesh and bones? There are not two mistakes here, just one. Aristotle certainly realized that the homonymy of substance terms was his own discovery, and it is implausible to suppose that he would have put an interpretation on Socrates' words that makes clarity with respect to the form/composite distinction a necessary condition of understanding what Socrates meant to say.

Further, it is not just that we need not take Aristotle to be talking about the definition of substantial forms here. The passage itself does not allow this interpretation. If we should not expect clarity from Socrates on the complex semantics of substance terms, we have to expect it of Aristotle. So when, in response to Socrates, Aristotle gives his own view about the definition of *animal*, we can be confident that his claim is sensitive to the distinction between the pure and mixed senses of the term 'animal'. The sense of the term he means to invoke here is pretty clearly identified in the remark that summarizes the view he wants to

---

taken the conclusions of the middle books to require supplementation by the account of the later chapters of Λ. Even if the doctrine of Z and H requires that form be a *kath hauto legomenon*, nothing in the middle books precludes the idea that the total framework of generable beings presupposes the existence of the first mover of Λ. It may be that passages such as 1029ᵇ4ff. from Z.3 just are indications that the author of Z–H endorsed this idea.

defend. He says that "some things surely are this in this or this thing in this kind of condition," just the kinds of characteristic formulae by which Aristotle points to the fact that composite particulars are predicative complexes, that their being what they are is analyzable by way of form-predications. So Aristotle's remarks about *animal* should be understood as invoking the mixed product sense of the term; he is telling us that to define any substance-kind we have to refer to both matter and form. This is precisely the view that he defends and develops in later chapters, in particular Z.17–H.2.

The aporia to which Aristotle responds in this passage is stated in the opening lines of Z.11, where he directs us to the question of just "which sorts of parts are of the form and which sorts are not of the form but of the composite" ($1036^a26-27$). What motivates his concern with this aporia is the attempt on the part of some philosophers (the Pythagoreans, Plato, and Speusippus) to "mathematicize" the definitions of natural objects. These philosophers note that geometrical figures can be defined without reference to the materials in which they happen to be realized, and they attempt to extend this pattern of definition beyond the mathematical case, claiming that it is only a contingent fact that such natural objects as human beings are composed of the matter we are accustomed to associate with them. The subsequent reference to the comparison of the younger Socrates must be a reference to an instance of this kind of thinking. Aristotle invokes what the Oxford *Notes on Book Zeta* aptly calls the slippery slope argument.[36] The idea is that the drive to purify our definitions of anything that might be construed as matter inevitably leads to a radical reductionism "which results in there being one form for many things whose form is clearly different"; what we end up with is a view where "all things will be one" ($1036^b19-20$).

Although one can read some of the remarks in the opening section of Z.11 as bearing on form, the initial formulation of the aporia identifies a problem concerned not just with the definition of form but with the definition of the composite as well. Aristotle is talking about the theory of definition developed by his predecessors, who did not themselves distinguish kinds from forms. As in the case of Socrates the younger, it is implausible to suppose that, in characterizing their views, Aristotle would make anything significant hang on this distinction, and the fact that he states the absurd consequence of their view by telling us that there is a single *eidos* for radically different kinds of thing is no evidence that the concern in the slippery slope argument is with the definition of form rather than kind. That distinction is too subtle for Aristotle's

---

[36]See Burnyeat et al., eds., *Notes on Book Zeta*, 88–91.

predecessors and is not operative at this stage of the discussion. In retrospect, we can say that the initial mistake these philosophers made in extending the mathematical model of definition to cases like *man* just was the mistake of confusing the definition of a species with that of the corresponding form; that, I take it, is precisely what Aristotle is saying in his concluding remarks on the definition of *animal* in the succeeding passage.

I do not, however, mean to suggest that it is a merely contingent fact about a substantial form that it takes as its proximate matter this or that kind of stuff or thing. Aristotle makes it clear in this text that the form *man* cannot be realized except in the appropriate kind of flesh and bones; more generally, he is firm in his insistence that, for each substantial form, there are limits on just what can serve as its proximate subject.[37] It must be the kind of thing that is in potentiality for the actuality that is that form. If we like, we can say that this fact constitutes a de re necessity about the form. But if we say this, we must realize that the necessity here is not one of essence, at least not as Aristotle understands the notion of essence. Although it is a definitional fact about the species *man* that its members are composed of the appropriate kind of materials, it is not (and cannot) be a part of the definition of the form *man* that materials of the relevant kind serve as its proximate subject or matter. The form *man* is a fundamental essence, so its definition can make no reference to anything distinct from it.

Nor does a substantial form enter into the definition of the kind of thing that serves as its proximate matter. Since Aristotle tells us that a form is predicated only accidentally of its subjects, there seems to be little temptation to suggest otherwise. But a couple of things might seem to entail that a substantial form does enter into the definition of the kind of thing that functions as its matter or metaphysical subject. One is the doctrine that matter and form are related as potentiality and actuality. Aristotle refuses to define for us the notions of potentiality and actuality. He seems to think that they are so basic or fundamental as to defy a definition in more elementary terms ($1048^{a}35$–37). In $\Theta.6$, he illustrates the distinction by way of examples and summarizes the examples by telling us that "in some of the examples the actuality is as motion in relation to potentiality, whereas in others it is as *ousia* to matter" ($1048^{b}8$–9), so we are left without an independent account of the force of applying the distinction to the case of form and matter. But if we are content to forego a strict definition, the idea is tolerably clear: prior to a coming to be, what functions as the proximate matter can be or

[37]See, once again, H.4 ($1044^{a}15$–31). See also H.2 ($1043^{a}12$–13).

potentially is something; after the coming to be, it actually is that. So the matter potentially constitutes something. Once the appropriate form comes to be its metaphysical predicate, it actually constitutes that.

Now, Aristotle takes it that an actuality is prior both in formula and *ousia* to its corresponding potentiality.[38] To identify a given potentiality, we must say what it is a potentiality for, and that requires a reference to the form that can be predicated of it. As Aristotle sees it, the identifiability dependence of dispositions on their actualities stems from the ontological features of potentialities; they are potentialities *for* their corresponding actualities. Given the claim that the matter-form relation is an instance of the relationship of a potentiality to its corresponding actuality, these facts of priority might seem to have the consequence that a substantial form is a component in the definition of the kind to which its proximate matter belongs.

The argument, however, requires an additional premise. We have to assume that the various potentialities of a thing themselves are parts of its definition or essence. That assumption, however, is one Aristotle rejects. He holds that the essence of the kind of thing that functions as matter for a given substantial form and the potentiality for that form are logically independent notions.[39] Here again our distinction between what is de re necessary and what is essential may come into play. It may indeed be a de re necessity about cortex and phloem that they are the kinds of stuff out of which plants can be composed, but this de re necessity is not written into the what it is to be for cortex or for phloem. We can provide a complete identification of their essences by reference exclusively to what these stuffs actually are; presumably that will involve a complex chemical story about their own material and structural features and not that of whatever it is that they potentially constitute.

Another line of argument that might lead us to think that a substantial form is written into the definition of the kind of thing that serves as its

---

[38]See Θ.6 (1049[b]13–17 and 1050[a]2–1050[b]6).

[39]See *Physics* Γ.1 (201[a]31–34) and *Metaphysics* K.9 (1065[b]25–28). One might object here that Aristotle tells us in these texts only that to be bronze and to be a certain potentiality cannot be identical and that this claim is consistent with the claim that the potentiality constitutes a part (but not the whole) of the essence associated with *bronze*. But the use to which he puts the claim shows that Aristotle holds to the stronger claim I attribute to him. He tells us that if the two were the same in definition, the actuality of bronze as bronze would be an instance of *kinesis* or motion, which it obviously is not. But this same false conclusion follows from the idea that the potentiality is just a part of the definition of *bronze*.

Aristotle's unwillingness to write its potentiality for actualization by a given substantial form into the essence of what serves as matter for that form is something that Charlotte Witt, who believes Aristotle solves the problem of the unity of a composite by reference to the act/potency distinction, overlooks. See *Substance and Essence in Aristotle*, 126–142.

matter takes as its starting point the idea of what we might call the homonymous part. As we have seen, Aristotle takes individual living beings as the paradigmatic (and perhaps the only) instances of matter-form composites that deserve the title '*ousia*' (e.g., 1043ᵇ21–23). He wants to deny that the various organic parts of these composites themselves deserve the title '*ousia*'. A living being is not an aggregate of its parts but something with an overriding unity that derives from its form.[40] In support of this idea, Aristotle frequently points to the fact that something like a hand or an eye cannot exist apart from the living being whose part it is. As he likes to put it, the amputated hand or the hand on the corpse is a hand in name only. It is only homonymously called a hand.[41]

By itself, the idea of the homonymous part provides no support at all for the idea that a form enters into the definition of its matter. Talk of hands and eyes is discourse at the level of the composite *ousia*, and the idea that a reference to substantial form or soul is implicit in this kind of discourse is precisely what Aristotle's theory of substance discourse leads us to expect. The theory does require that, at some level, we can identify something in the living being that can function as subject or matter for the predication of the form; since the predication has to be a case of *kata sumbebekos* or accidental predication, what is so identified has to be something such that what it is does not involve the form that is its predicate. But Aristotle typically tells us that the relevant subject is something like flesh and bones (things that he classifies as homogeneous parts) rather than things like hands and eyes (the heterogeneous parts that function as organs of the composite living being).[42]

There are places (e.g., 1035ᵃ17–21, 33) where Aristotle states explicitly that homogeneous parts such as flesh and bones have an essence that is independent of the form predicated of them. Unfortunately, there are also texts (e.g., *De Generatione Animalium* B.1 [734ᵇ24–26]) where he seems to suggest that, apart from the living organism, homogeneous parts such as flesh and bones are only homonymously so called; these texts might lead one to suppose that a substantial form does enter into the essence of the proximate matter of which it is predicated.[43] This line of argument raises a host of problems about

---

[40]See Z.16 (1040ᵇ5–15) and Z.17 (1041ᵇ12ff.).

[41]See, e.g., *Metaphysics* Z.10 (1035ᵇ23–25) and Z.11 (1036ᵇ30–31); *De Anima* B.1 (412ᵇ21–23); and *De Partibus Animalium* A.1 (641ᵃ3–4).

[42]For this distinction, see *De Partibus Animalium* B.1 (646ᵃ13ff.).

[43]For a more general and detailed discussion of the problem of the form independence of matter, see J. L. Ackrill, "Aristotle's Definitions of *Psuche*," 119–113. Ackrill agrees that Aristotle's account requires that the matter for a form have an essential identity independent of the form, but he insists that Aristotle's application of the dichotomy to the case of

Aristotle's methodology in the biological works and about the relationship between that methodology and the metaphysical framework of the middle books.[44] Although those issues are obviously important, they require a detailed treatment of the sort we cannot give them and are, in any case, tangential to our main concerns. But a couple of comments are in order. If Aristotle is genuinely ambivalent about the possiblity of fixing the essence of such things as flesh and bones independently of the soul of the living being whose flesh and bones they are, it does not follow that he takes a substantial form to enter into the definition of what functions as its proximate matter. The fact that his own theory of predication requires definitional independence suggests that what appears to be ambivalence about definitional independence might better be construed as ambivalence about just what it is in a living being that serves as the metaphysical subject for its soul. It may also be that the ambivalence we seem to find here reflects an intermediary stage in Aristotle's thinking about these issues. It may be, that is, that the Aristotle who expresses this ambivalence is an Aristotle who has not yet come to appreciate the full implications of the hylomorphic theory. Perhaps the Aristotle of Z and H does not share the ambivalence.[45] Finally, it may just be that Aristotle takes such terms as 'flesh' and 'bones' to exhibit an even more complex semantical structure than that delineated in the text of Z and H. It may, for example, be that in their case there is not a single sense associated with what I have called the mixed product use of a substance term but two quite different senses. It may be that we have to distinguish between a form-independent notion of such things as flesh and bones and one that is not form-independent but itself belongs to the form-dependent level of discourse that is proper

---

living beings runs into serious difficulties since what is supposed to be matter—the organic body—is what it is only because it is informed by the soul. Although I do not have the space or the expertise to establish the point, I would hope that the required form independence can, even in the case of living beings, be secured for the soul's metaphysical subject. For a useful discussion of the texts associated with the problem of the homonymous part, see section III of Sheldon Cohen's "Aristotle's Doctrine of the Material Substrate," 188–194.

[44]For discussions of these more general methodological issues, the reader should consult Martha Nussbaum, *Aristotle's De Motu Animalium* (Princeton: Princeton University Press, 1978); Richard Sorabji, *Necessity, Chance, and Blame* (Ithaca: Cornell University Press, 1984), especially chaps. 8 and 9; Allan Gotthelf, "Aristotle's Conception of Final Causality," *Review of Metaphysics* (1976), 226–254; John Cooper, "Aristotle on Natural Teleology," in Malcolm Schofield and Martha Nussbaum, eds., *Language and Logos: Studies in Greek Philosophy Presented to G. E. L. Owen* (Cambridge: Cambridge University Press, 1982), 197–222; and the essays in Allan Gotthelf and James Lennox, eds., *Philosophical Issues in Aristotle's Biology* (Cambridge: Cambridge University Press, 1987).

[45]One does not find the Aristotle of Z and H suggesting that the flesh and bones that survive the death of the composite living being are flesh and bones in name only.

to the composite. If we suppose that this kind of distinction is implicit in Aristotle's theory, then we can say that when he speaks of flesh and bones as the metaphysical subject for the soul he is using the relevant terms in their form-independent senses, and that when he denies that flesh and bones retain their essential identity apart from the living being he is invoking the form-dependent senses of the terms.[46]

VI

However we decide the issue of the homonomous part, we have to agree that, since it construes substantial form as primary *ousia* and takes the relationship between a form and its matter to be one of *kata sumbebekos* predication, the theory of *Metaphysics* Z and H commits Aristotle to two theses: first, that the essence of a substantial form involves nothing, whether intrinsic or extrinsic to the form, that functions as matter; second, that although the matter for a given form can be defined only by reference to the matter and form whose predicative relation enables us to explain why it is the kind of thing it is, what functions as proximate matter or subject for a substantial form can always be defined independently of that form. But how, in turn, are a form and its matter related to the composite particular into whose analysis they enter? Well, they are its *ousiai*. Both the particular parcel of matter and the substantial form predicated of it are causes of the being of the particular made out of that matter; in H.2 ($1042^b25$–$1043^a11$), Aristotle tells us that the sense of 'to be' unique to things of a given substance-species is fixed by the form-predications associated with that species. The idea is the familiar one that what we mean when we say that a particular is or exists is that it is a thing of a certain kind. Belonging to that kind, however, consists in the fact that a certain form is predicated of a certain parcel of matter; and, although for each member of a given substance-species there is a distinct form-predication, each has a single substantial form as predicate and a parcel of matter of a single kind as subject. So it is because they are composed of a certain kind of matter that has predicated of it a single substantial form that particulars are, that is, are members of their substance-kind; to say that they are just is shorthand for saying that the relevant kind of form-predication obtains. This is what is involved in saying that matter and form are the *ousia* of a composite particular.

---

[46]An ingenious attempt to read a distinction of this sort into Aristotle is found in Frank Lewis, "Substance and Predication" (unpublished manuscript), chap 11.

Since form is its own *ousia*, the claim that form is the *ousia* of a particular holds pride of place in Z and H; sometimes Aristotle puts the point (e.g., 1032ᵇ2) by saying, not just that substantial forms are the primary realities, but that a substantial form is the primary *ousia* of the relevant particulars. Form is also essence; but we should be careful here because, although form is essence (its own essence), it is not, in the basic sense anyway, the essence of the particulars whose *ousia* it is. Indeed, in one sense, particulars have no essence at all. In the strictest sense of 'essence of', the essence of a thing is what is expressed by the definiens of that thing's definition; as we have seen, Aristotle repeatedly tells us that only universals have a definition. But if, in this strict sense, particulars have no essence, their species do; and like the species themselves, what is expressed by the definiens of the species' definition is predicated essentially of each of the individuals belonging to the species. So, as we have already said, there is a derived sense in which we can speak of the essence of a particular composite; that essence is the essence of the appropriate species.

We have found Aristotle insisting that the species (now called "the composite taken generally") can be defined by reference to both the matter and the form. But when we attempt to specify just how they are related to the species and its members, we run up against one of the central doctrinal differences between the early and later theories of *ousia*. In the early theory (e.g., 3ᵃ6–3ᵇ6), the definition of a species made reference to both its genus and its proper differentia; both were, in the technical sense at work in the *Categories*, said of the species and each of its members. In Z and H, however, neither the matter nor the form that are components of the what it is to be of the species can be predicated of either the species or any of its members. We can appreciate this difference if we recall that, in the early works, Aristotle denies that the definiens for a species expresses any kind of predicative tie between genus and differentia. Neither is said of or present in the other. The central doctrine of the middle books, however, is that the individuals of a given species are all constituted by a predicative relation. In the previous chapter, we expressed this point by borrowing Matthen's useful expression and calling composite particulars predicative complexes. We also used Bergmannian language to say that the internal structure of a familiar particular is that of a predicative fact or state of affairs. Whatever terminology one invokes to express the predicative relation, the overarching fact is that the predicative tie binding a form and its matter is noneliminable.

To define a substance-species, it is not enough merely to identify the kind of stuff its members are composed of and the appropriate substantial form. To identify correctly the essence for that species, we must express the predicative link tying the matter and the form. Accordingly, the definiens must have an internal propositional structure that ex-presses the subject-predicate relation between the matter and the form. To be a human being is not to be composed of a certain kind of matter and to have a certain substantial form. It is to be something such that its existence is constituted by the fact that the appropriate form *is predicated of* a particular matter of the appropriate kind. So the definition does not provide us with a substantival expression like the handy 'biped animal' of the logical works which we can substitute for the term signifying the species and which like the species-term can be linguistically predicated of the various individuals belonging to the species. The best we can do here toward finding an intersubstitutable expression is an unwieldly phrase like 'a thing such that it is composed of a pack of flesh and bones such that it is a man', where 'man' has its pure product sense and signifies the human soul. And even this attempt is a mere abbreviation, since we have done nothing to identify the kind of flesh and bones required nor what it is to be a human soul. But even in this phrase, substantival though it is, we cannot extract the form from its predicative link with its subject. That is what it is predicated of, so the fact that it does enter the definition of the species provides no license for constru-ing it as a predicate of the species or any of its members.

The idea that form is not predicated of the individual members of the corresponding species is analogous to an idea we confronted in the previous chapter, that the parcel of matter out of which it is composed does not compete with the individual composite for status as subject or "this."[47] In that context, we were concerned with linguistic facts that

---

[47]For my earliest attempts at defending the idea that, where it is not reflexive, the *ousia*-of relation is not one of predication, see "Form, Species, and Predication in *Metaphysics* Z, H, and Θ." Although she denies that substantial forms are general, Charlotte Witt agrees that we cannot construe a form as a predicate of the composite whose form it is. And, although she frames her argument in different terms, I do not think that she would disagree with my claim that the problem here ultimately derives from the distinct explana-tory levels to which form and composite belong. But, although she denies that form is predicated of the composite, she insists that a substantial form is the essence of the composite whose form it is. Accordingly, she would not agree with my claim that, where the *ousia*-of relation is not reflexive, the *ousia* and essence of a given object belong to distinct explanatory levels. See her *Substance and Essence in Aristotle*, 5, 104, 120–126. Another account that might seem similar to my own is found in Frank Lewis, "Form and Predication in Aristotle's *Metaphysics*," but Lewis seems to take the idea that form is not predicated of the individual whose *ousia* it is to be a matter of parsimony rather than a cornerstone of the later theory. According to Lewis, it is merely in the interests of keeping his noneliminable predicative ties to a minimum that Aristotle denies that form is predi-cated of the composite. So, presumably, Lewis finds nothing theoretically problematic in the idea that a substantial form is predicated of an individual. Obviously, I disagree. I take

suggest that matter is predicated of the composite. As Aristotle in his inimitable way put it, the composite is "not said to be 'that', but 'thaten' " (1033ª6–7). Although Aristotle was resolute in denying that matter is a metaphysical predicate of anything and developed an elaborate story about the poverty of our linguistic resources for identifying privations to explain the linguistic illusion that matter functions predicatively, he felt no qualms about exploiting the illusion to highlight the fact that, at the level of ontological analysis where the ordinary particular is a metaphysical subject or "this," matter is not. In a similar way, the idea that form is not predicated of the particulars whose *ousia* it is draws attention to the fact that substantial form is introduced at a level of ontological discourse at one remove from that whose focus is a world of particulars falling under their substance-kinds. Form belongs to a framework of explanatory concepts that operate at a more fundamental or basic level than the framework of concepts appropriate to the individual man and horse of the *Categories*. Substantial form is a predicate, a "such," an *arche* or principle for its subjects, its "thises," its elements. But to construe form as something that plays any of these roles within the framework that it supports or underwrites is to run a serious risk of category mistake. Form is the *ousia* of ordinary particulars, but, except when the *ousia*-of relation is reflexive, to speak of the *ousia* of this or that just is to point to something that belongs to a different ontological level from the thing whose *ousia* it is.[48]

---

it to be crucial to Aristotle's whole conception of levels of substance-predication that form is predicated only of what (its matter) occupies the same explanatory level. One also finds the idea that form is not predicated of the individual in Alan Code, "Aristotle on Essence and Accident," 437. But most of the commentators who hold that form is something predicated of other things take form to be predicated of the individual composites whose *ousia* it is. See Montgomery Furth, "Aristotle on the Unity of Form," 81, and *Substance, Form, and Psyche*, 189; Mohan Matthen, "Individual Substances as Hylomorphic Complexes;" Daniel Graham, *Aristotle's Two Systems*, 239–244; Michael Frede and Gunther Patzig, *Aristoteles "Metaphysik Z,"* vol. 1, 40 and 51, which I single out for treatment in the next section; and D. K. Modrak, "Forms, Types, and Tokens in Aristotle's *Metaphysics Z*," and "Forms and Compounds," especially 89. Modrak denies that a form is metaphysically predicated of particular composites, but she takes the form-individual relation to be that of type to token, with types predicated of their tokens. I take it that she wants to deny that the predication of a form of composites represents one of the two cases of basic or noneliminable predication identified in Z.3, Z.13, and Θ.7. I agree, but I make the stronger claim that the relationship between form and composite differs from that of species and member. In the latter case, we have a predicative link, although it is reducible to or analyzable in terms of the relevant form-predication. In the former, I want to claim, there is no predicative link, whether basic or analyzable.

[48]In a derivative sense (that does not presuppose that what is the essence of a thing is predicable of it) form can be said to be the essence of a particular, since it enters into what in the primary sense is the essence of the particular. It may be that such a derivative sense

VII

As I read the middle books, then, a lowest-level substance-kind is the essence of its members. But because it belongs to the same explanatory level as its members, it cannot constitute their *ousia*. The substantial form associated with the species is what constitutes the *ousia* of the relevant particulars. The form is not, however, predicated of those particulars. It is predicated of the parcels of matter making up the particulars, and the predication at work here is accidental rather than essential.

Many commentators see things differently. A common theme in work on the middle books is that one and the same thing functions as both the *ousia* and the essence of a concrete particular. All too often, the idea is assumed rather than defended, but in the recently published Frede–Patzig commentary on Z the idea is carefully articulated and argued for in great detail. Frede and Patzig claim that a form is what an individual "ultimately and essentially is,"[49] so it is the form rather than the associated species that constitutes the essence of a concrete object. Frede and Patzig deny that the Aristotle of the middle books associates essences with the kinds of the *Categories*, and they even question the idea that he recognizes the "real existence" of substance-kinds.[50]

Their reading of the middle books is sufficiently divergent from mine and the issues relevant to the divergence sufficiently important that it is worth exploring their account. There are, as well, points of disagreement beyond those I have delineated. Most significant, Frede and Patzig deny that there is numerically one form for all the members of a given kind.[51] As they read him, Aristotle construes substantial forms as particulars rather than as universals. However, since the issue of general versus particular forms will occupy us in the next chapter, we can set that topic to the side and focus instead on the Frede–Patzig claim that concrete particulars have one and the same item as their essence and their *ousia*.

Since they take the form to be the essence of the composite, Frede and Patzig are committed to the idea that the form is predicated of the

---

is operative in 1032b1–2, where the genitive '*hechastou*' seems to be identifying which thing form is the essence of. It may, however, be that '*hechastou*' has the force of 'in each thing', so that the claim has the sense, "I call form the essence (which is found in each thing), and is its primary *ousia*." For more on the idea that form is, in a derivative sense, the essence of a particular, see Lewis's helpful "What Is Aristotle's Theory of Essence?"

[49]Frede and Patzig, *Aristoteles "Metaphysik Z,"* vol. 1, 40.

[50]Ibid., vol. 2, 190, 246.

[51]Ibid., vol. 1, 48–57, and vol. 2, 241–263.

composite. In Z.4 (1029$^b$13ff.), we see that a necessary condition of one thing's being the essence of another is that the first be predicated of the second. As Frede and Patzig concede, there is little direct evidence in the middle books that forms are predicated of particulars, but they take two very brief remarks from Z.8 to show that this is so.[52] The first is found at 1033$^a$30, where we meet with the claim that "the brazen sphere is a sphere"; the second comes a few lines later at 1033$^b$3, where we find the comment, "he makes this, which is a sphere."

To convince us of the stronger claim that form and composite enter into the essence-of relation, Frede and Patzig point to the fact that Aristotle regularly refers to form as "essence and *ousia*."[53] Presumably, they construe the regularity of joint reference as evidence that Aristotle did not see us as confronted with three different sets of things—forms, *ousiai*, and essences—but that he took substantial forms to exhaust the pool of essences and *ousiai*, so that there are no essences besides the forms that constitute the *ousiai* of ordinary objects. Further, Frede and Patzig seem to take the regularity of joint reference to suggest that a form is the essence and *ousia* of precisely the same thing or things, and since it is beyond question that form is the *ousia* of the concrete particular, it must be its essence as well.

It is certainly true that Aristotle likes to couple the terms 'essence' and '*ousia*' when he talks about form. They appear together so regularly that the expressions can come to seem like mere variants of each other. And in a metaphysical theory in which the Z.6 Identity Thesis is central, the tendency to use the terms 'essence' and '*ousia*' almost interchangeably is both natural and understandable. After all, that thesis tells us that the primary *ousiai* are necessarily one and the same in number as their essences, so to refer to a primary *ousia* is to refer to a fundamental essence. But the fact that Aristotle sometimes uses the terms 'essence' and '*ousia*' almost interchangeably is no evidence at all that substantial forms exhaust the pool of essences. We know from Z.4 that they do not, just as we know that form is not the only thing that functions as the *ousia* of concrete objects. The matter out of which a particular is made plays this role as well. What is true is that substantial forms exhaust the pool of fundamental essences and primary *ousiai*, and it is fundamental essences and primary *ousiai* that Aristotle means to single out when he calls form "essence and *ousia*."

Furthermore, it is true that, for each substantial form, there is some-

---

[52]Ibid., vol. 1, 40, 51, and vol. 2, 131–135.

[53]Ibid., vol. 1, 40–41. Frede and Patzig never express this point as explicitly as I do, but I think it is pretty clear that this consideration of usage represents a point of departure for their interpretation.

thing for which that form is both essence and *ousia*—the form itself. As we have seen, the idea that the essence-of and *ousia*-of relations must be reflexive in the case of fundamental essences and primary *ousiai* is central to the concepts of things that play those ontological roles. But it hardly follows from this fact that what plays the role of a primary *ousia* is the essence of everything for which it is the primary *ousia*; if Aristotle's joint use of the terms 'essence' and '*ousia*' has an eye only to the case where the relations are reflexive, that use is no indication whatsoever that a form bears both relations to all and only the same things.[54]

Indeed, Aristotle's own conception of essence makes it prima facie implausible even to entertain the hypothesis that form is the essence of familiar concrete particulars. The essence of an object is what to be consists in for that object. But concrete particulars are composites of matter and form, and this is not an accidental fact about them. It is *what* they are, so their essences have to reflect this. As we have seen, the Aristotle of Z and H seems to be pointing to universals that do, in the appropriate way, reflect what composites are when he refers to things that are form and matter "taken generally" (e.g., 1035$^b$27–30). Frede and Patzig, however, want to deny that the relevant references identify items that could constitute the essences of ordinary objects. The central piece of evidence they adduce here is the summary passage of Z.11 (1037$^a$22ff.), where Aristotle states that there is a formula or definition only of primary *ousia*.[55] Aristotle's example here bears on the term 'man', and he tells us that the term picks out something with a formula or definition only when it is used to refer to the soul. When it is used to pick out something incorporating matter, what it picks out, he claims, lacks a formula. Since essence is what is expressed by a definitional formula, Frede and Patzig take the passage to show that there is no essence expressed by substance terms in what I have called their mixed senses. And since something has to function as the essence of familiar objects, it is a short step to the conclusion that forms are the things that play this role.

---

[54]Once again, I should reiterate my response to the objection that the '*hechastou*' of 1032$^b$2 strongly suggests that a form is essence and *ousia* of the same thing. It may be that in this passage Aristotle is invoking a derivative sense of 'essence of' in which $x$ is the/an essence of $y$ just in case reference of $x$ is essential to the formula expressing what $y$ is. But it may also be that we do not have the expression 'essence of' here at all, but rather that the genitive has the force of identifying that in which something (the form) that is an essence (i.e., a fundamental essence) is or that of which it is a constituent. Likewise, I would argue that although 1043$^a$38–1043$^b$1 might seem to suggest that the essence of the composite is its form, the text is merely telling us that it is the forms of sensible substances that represent fundamental essences. The ensuing lines, I think, make this fairly clear.

[55]Frede and Patzig, *Aristoteles "Metaphysik Z,"* vol. 2, 189–192, 209–213.

Once again a careful reading of Z.4 is the tonic we need. That chapter shows us the elasticity of such terms as 'definition' and 'formula'. Pretty clearly, the Z.11 summary is putting these terms to a specialized use. The summary points back to the discussions of Z.10, where Aristotle attempts to show that form is susceptible of the kind of definition appropriate to what functions as primary *ousia* and fundamental essence. That kind of definition must express its definiendum in terms that involve a reference to no other entities, for what it picks out has to be what I have called an independently identifiable essence. In the Z.11 summary, Aristotle is restricting such terms as 'formula' and 'definition' to accounts that meet this rigorous standard. But it is a mistake to take Aristotle's denial here that substance-kinds have a definition of this sort as the outright denial that they have essence. The denial is merely an expression of the obvious point that the essences in question are not among the fundamental essences.

As we have seen, in H.3 (1043$^b$23ff.), Aristotle makes it perfectly clear that substance-kinds are definable, that there are essences associated with substance terms in their mixed senses. Indeed, in that chapter he uses the term 'definition' in another specialized sense. Given the sense operative in that context, nothing can have a definition that does not imply a prior predicative relationship between matter and form. No one, I take it, would find in the H.3 text evidence that forms lack essences. Neither should we take the Z.11 summary that Frede and Patzig make so critical to show that there are no essences associated with the substance-kinds of the *Categories*. In both cases, we have definition and essence. The respective essences, however, belong to different levels in the Z–H hierarchy of essences and, accordingly, there is a different kind of formula or definition appropriate in each case. In the case of forms, we have fundamental essences; consequently, our definition can make a reference to nothing but the form to be defined. Substance-kinds, on the other hand, are derived essences whose instances are neither primary nor *kath hauto* beings, so a different strategy is required in formulating what their to be consists in.

The H.3 text is not idiosyncratic. It expresses a view we meet over and over again in the physical and biological works and even in *Metaphysics* E.1, the view that the substance-kinds under which natural objects fall can be defined only by reference to both form and matter.[56] And, as we see in Chapter 7, the H.3 idea that there are essences involving both

---

[56] 1025$^b$28ff. See also *Metaphysics* K.7 (1064$^b$28ff.). Frede and Patzig insist that the view expressed in these two texts as well as many texts in the physical and biological writings is one Aristotle comes to reject in *Metaphysics* Z. See *Aristoteles "Metaphysik Z,"* vol. 2, 209–213.

form and matter looms large in the dialectic operative in the second half of H. In fact, Aristotle devotes all H.6 (the grand finale of Z–H) to the task of showing how the definition of substance-kinds by reference to both form and matter is consistent with the prephilosophical intuition that natural objects are genuine unities.[57] If we followed Frede and Patzig in denying definition and essence in the case of substance-kinds, we would be unable to make much sense of a major philosophical project of the middle books.

We do not, however, have to go beyond Z.10 and 11 to find compelling evidence that Aristotle believes substance-kinds to have definition and essence. In the course of showing that substantial forms are susceptible of the kind of definition required of things that play the role of a primary *ousia* and fundamental essence, the Aristotle of Z.10 reminds us of the contrast between substantial forms and their associated substance-species. The text is one we have met before, but it is worth quoting one more time:

> But *man* and *horse* and things like them that are said of particulars, but universally, are not *ousia* but a certain composite of this formula and this matter taken universally. (1035ᵇ27–30)

This text is hardly what one would have expected of a philosopher who questions the "real existence" of substance-kinds, for it is difficult to read the passage except as a formal pronouncement that there are universals that play the role of the substance-kinds of the *Categories*.

Frede and Patzig concede that the text initially seems to support the idea that there are substance-kinds, but they propose that we understand the passage as an anticipatory expression of what they take to be the Z.13 doctrine that nothing universal can be *ousia*.[58] They argue that, since Aristotle is denying that things like *man* and *horse* are *ousiai*, they do not exist at all; for since they are not accidents either they fail to fall under any Aristotelian category.[59] But, first, the term '*ousia*' is being used here as an abstract expression. Aristotle is denying, as my account

---

[57]See 1045ᵃ7ff. See also my discussion of these issues in Section III of Chapter 7.

[58]See *Aristoteles "Metaphysik Z,"* vol. 2, 189–192, for their discussion of this text. Frede and Patzig argue that, if we take the text to imply that kinds have essences, then it is difficult to explain how form and essence are related and how the form can be the essence of a member of the kind (see p. 189). But these difficulties arise only if we assume that (a) forms exhaust the pool of essences and (b) forms are essences of composite particulars. I take it that the text in question forces us to reject both assumptions. Forms constitute a proper subset of the set of essences—the subset consisting only of fundamental essences; and forms are their own essences, but not the essences of composite particulars. The species associated with those forms constitute the essences of the relevant particulars.

[59]Ibid., vol. 2, 246–247.

implies he should, that substance-kinds like *man* and *horse* are the *ousia* of the particulars of which they are predicated. There is no indication here whatsoever that Aristotle denies that these universals have their proper place in the categorial tree whose bottom nodes are occupied by concrete particulars and whose uppermost node is occupied by the universal *ousia* itself. Second, although the text denies that kinds constitute the *ousia* of anything, it is not clear that it tells us why this is so. If, however, we insist on finding reasons in the text, we are (as we see in the next chapter) ill advised to focus on the generality of *man* and *horse*. The more plausible story would focus on the passage's claims that *man* and *horse* are said of particulars and that they are compounds of form and matter. Finally, although this text does not explicitly refer to definition, it provides a fairly clear picture of just what the definitions of substance-kinds would look like and, hence, a good idea of the structure of their essences.

In the Z.11 criticism of the younger Socrates (1036$^b$21ff.), Aristotle makes explicit what is suggested in the Z.10 comments on *man* and *horse*. He tells us that the natural kinds under which concrete particulars fall can be defined only by reference to both matter and form. Frede and Patzig admit that, like the Z.10 text, this section of Z.11 initially appears to make a claim about substance-kinds that is incompatible with their interpretation. But they argue that Aristotle's response to the younger Socrates really bears on the definition of form, and once again they base their argument on their literalist reading of the Z.11 summary's claims about "formulas." Although they recognize that the definition of form must be matter-free identification, their actual analysis of Aristotle's response construes it as a proposal that the definition of the substantial form of a natural object "be executed in such a way that the definition of the form alone reveals that such a form can appear only in suitable materials."[60]

Some might find it difficult to understand how this is to be done; they might find it unclear how the definition of a form can exhibit the purity of independent identification required in the case of what is a primary and *kath hauto* being while at the same time expressing the fact that the form can appear only in the right kind of matter.[61] Without going into

---

[60]Ibid., vol. 2, 211–212.

[61]There are important issues here that are independent of the debate over the status of kinds and their treatment in Z.10–11. The key question focuses on the kinds of demands the requirement that the definition of a form be matter-free imposes on us. It is easy to be sympathetic with the Frede–Patzig claim that the definition of some natural forms must make some kind of reference to the fact that they are instantiated only "in suitable materials." Presumably, Frede and Patzig would insist that a formula making this minimal claim (without referring to any particular kind of matter) does not violate the condition of independent identifiability. I am inclined to agree.

this problem, we can agree, I think, that there is little point to the trouble Frede and Patzig make for themselves in their reading of this text. Since it is clear that the Aristotle of the middle books does not want to deny that substance-kinds are real existents, that they are susceptible of definitions, and that the essences expressed in such definitions constitute the essences of familiar particulars, there is no reason to deny that the force of the text is precisely what it initially appears to be. Aristotle is making a general claim about the kinds under which natural objects fall, the claim that we can identify their essences only by reference to both form and matter.

But even the weaker Frede–Patzig claim that forms are predicated of ordinary particulars is dubious. Whenever Aristotle gives his official tally of subjects and their metaphysical predicates, form is paired off with matter and with nothing else.[62] In the Z.10 ($1035^b27$–30) text where Aristotle identifies the universals that *are* essentially predicated of familiar particulars, those universals turn out to be kinds (like *man* and *horse*) and not forms. The context of that text is not one that allows us the freedom of supposing that, in addition, forms might be predicatively related to the relevant particulars, for the passage is meant to identify the critical differences between substance-kinds and the associated substantial forms that, up to this point in the chapter, Aristotle has been discussing. And the differences the passage points to include the facts (a) that kinds are not the *ousia* of anything, (b) that they include matter as well as form, and (c) *that they are said of particulars like Socrates.*

Still, Frede and Patzig claim that the two brief comments quoted earlier from Z.8 provide evidence that Aristotle would, in fact, endorse the idea that forms are predicated of the particulars whose forms they are. Before we examine the texts themselves, a couple of general observations are in order. The alleged pieces of evidence are exceedingly brief comments whose immediate context is the attempt to prove the ingenerability of form. It would be surprising were Aristotle, with no explanation whatsoever, to make that context the vehicle for expressing a view that is squarely at odds with the overall account of the rest of Z and H. There is also a larger context of which the proof of the ingenerability of form is a part; and that context *does* bear on the predicative status of form. Aristotle uses the comments on the ingenerability of form as a bridge to the claim that form is a "such" ($1033^b19$ff.). But that claim represents Aristotle's attempt to restrict the predicative range of form to the various parcels of matter that are its "thises." It is difficult to believe that, in the very passage meant to prepare us for the claim that form is

---

[62]Z.3 ($1029^a23$–24); Z.13 ($1038^b5$–6); and Θ.7 ($1049^a27$–36).

only a "such" for the "this" that is its matter, Aristotle is telling us that form is predicated of something other than matter.

Were we, then, to find in the relevant comments any suggestion at all that form is predicated of the composite, we would be prudent to construe the suggestion as an inadvertent slip rather than as an expression of genuine Aristotelian doctrine. In fact, the two texts Frede and Patzig point to provide no evidence whatsoever on this question. Although Aristotle does not express himself as carefully as he might,[63] the second of the two comments ("he makes this which is sphere"; 1033ᵇ3) is almost certainly meant as a remark about form rather than the composite. Aristotle has just identified the composite ("brazen sphere; (1033ᵇ1–2), and by a double use of 'this' he points to the two principles—matter and form—that have to enter into our account of the coming to be of the composite. The immediately succeeding comment (1033ᵇ3–6) is the clincher here; it tells us that if there is a coming to be of "this" we are off on an infinite regress. The referent of this third use of 'this' must be the second "this" mentioned in 1033ᵇ3, the form whose generability we can endorse only on pain of regress.

Things are a little less clear in the case of the 1033ª30 comment, for it does seem to suggest that the form expressed by the term 'sphere' is predicated of the composite picked out by the definite description 'the brazen sphere.' But the suggestion loses its appeal when we understand the comment in the context in which it is made:

> Just as he does not make the subject, the bronze, so he does not make the sphere, unless [he does so] by coincidence on the grounds that [*hoti*] the brazen sphere is a sphere and he makes that. (1033ª28–31)

Aristotle is formulating the thesis he goes on to prove, the thesis that form does not come to be. The comment that the composite (the brazen sphere) is a sphere occurs as part of a clause [introduced by 'unless' (*ei*

---

[63]Frede and Patzig would insist that I am overlooking the fact that the "this" of 1033ᵇ3 is something that is made. But, although he is a bit sloppy here, what Aristotle means to say is clear enough. We make the brazen sphere by taking this—the bronze—and making it into this—the sphere. This comes out in the very next line, where Aristotle goes on to deny that the "this" of 1033ᵇ3 is itself made. Aristotle is struggling in these lines to formulate the ingenerability thesis, and he attempts parallel reformulations over the next fifteen lines or so. These reformulations become progressively clearer. They also confirm the idea that the "this" of 1033ᵇ3 is the form. See, e.g., 1033ᵇ9ff., which gives us in order, once again, the composite, the matter, and the form and tells us that we make the composite by taking matter and introducing form into it. It is worth pointing out, one more time, that the use of 'this' to refer to form in this part of Z.8 does not have the kind of doctrinal force that the technical use of 'this' has later in Z.8. In this part of Z.8, the use of 'this' is that of a topic-neutral designator—a mere tag.

*me*)] in which Aristotle sets aside an objection that someone might raise against the thesis he is formulating. The comment does not represent a claim Aristotle himself necessarily endorses; it is part of a summary version of an argument one might take to show that form does, in fact, come to be. Pointing in the direction of the chunk of bronze, someone might say: "Look, that thing over there is a sphere. It is something that was made. Therefore, something that is a form—the sphere—was made. Therefore, a form came to be." There is much wrong with this argument, but Aristotle does not go to the trouble of sorting things out for us. He merely points to the kind of strategy required to handle the objection based on the argument. The reference to coincidence is meant to remind us of a distinction Aristotle draws elsewhere, that between coincidental unity/sameness and *kath hauto* unity/sameness.[64] That distinction presumably enables us to disarm the imagined objector.

Aristotle's notion of numerical unity/sameness of the *kath hauto* variety corresponds to our notion of numerical identity, but Aristotle claims that nonidentical objects can enter into the weaker relation of coincidental unity/sameness.[65] Our chunk of bronze, the sphere (in the sense of *the spherical object*), and the brazen sphere are three things that coincide in this way. They are coincidentally one/the same in the sense that, for a certain period of time, to point to one is to point to the other two. We can use the term 'is' to express both numerical identity (as when we say, "Cicero is Tully") and coincidental unity/sameness (as when we say, "That chunk of marble is the Pieta"). But, despite the fact that the two relations can be expressed by a single term, they differ in several ways. Most significant, the relation of coincidental unity/sameness is not governed by the indiscernability of identicals; consequently, inferences bearing on things that are coincidentally one/the same either fail outright or yield conclusions much weaker than their unwary proponents might hope for.[66] The argument of our imagined objector is a case in point. The objector takes the argument to show that the sphere has come to be; but, if sound, the argument only establishes the weaker conclusion that the sphere (i.e., *the spherical object*) or something (the chunk of bronze) that is a sphere is coincidentally one with something (the brazen sphere) that has come to be. That conclusion, however, presents no problem for the claim that form is ingenerable, and this is what Aristotle means to point out when he tells us that the argument

[64]See, e.g., *Metaphysics* Δ.6 (1015[b]16–35) and Δ.9 (1017[b]26–1018[a]3).

[65]An excellent account of the notion of accidental unity/sameness is found in Frank Lewis, "Accidental Sameness in Aristotle," 1–36.

[66]See, once again, Lewis, "Accidental Sameness," for a detailed discussion of these issues.

summarized in the conjunction following '*hoti*' supports a conclusion that holds only by coincidence.

But, then, we can suppose Aristotle to insist that the 1033ª30 comment Frede and Patzig point to requires disambiguation:

(7)    The brazen sphere is a sphere

can be read as

(7′)    The brazen sphere is *kath hauto* one in number with something (the chunk of bronze) that is a sphere

or as

(7″)    The brazen sphere is coincidentally one with/the same as something (the chunk of bronze) that is a sphere.

Frede, Patzig, and our imagined objector all construe the comment along the lines of (7′). That reading does imply that a form is predicated of a composite, but the very force of introducing the notion of coincidental unity/sameness here is to insist on the reading provided by (7″). That reading, however, does not imply that form is predicated of the composite. It merely tells us that the form is predicated of something (the matter) that is numerically different from but coincidentally one with/the same as the composite. And that claim is precisely what we expect from Aristotle's theory.[67]

So, despite the arguments of Frede and Patzig, we can rest content with the interpretation our explorations of Z and H have led us to. Substance-forms and substance-kinds both genuinely exist, but they belong to distinct explanatory levels. Kinds are predicated of composite particulars and constitute their essences. Substantial forms are the primary *ousiai*, but not the essences, of composites. They are predicated accidentally of the matter making up composites, but they are not predicated (either accidentally or essentially) of the composites whose *ousiai* they are.

[67]Another way of interpreting this text is to take Aristotle himself to be making the conjunctive claim in the *hoti* clause and to construe the preceding reference to coincidence as a reminder on his part of how we are to understand each component of the argument summarized in the *hoti*-clause. Like the reading I have given, this interpretation yields the result that the only sense in which the conclusion of the argument is true is one that makes it compatible with the thesis that form does not come to be; and, like my reading, this account has Aristotle insist that we understand the first conjunct of the *hoti* clause along the lines of (7″) rather than (7′).

# CHAPTER 6

# The Z.13 Thesis

I

No text from Z and H has received more attention than Z.13. The attention has its source in the assumption that Aristotle is arguing for a highly problematic thesis in this chapter. The thesis, we are told, is the claim that

(A)   No universal is *ousia*.[1]

---

[1]The expression I have translated as 'universal' is '*katholou legomenon*', which can also be translated as 'things said universally' or 'things said to be universals'. Michael Woods, "Problems in *Metaphysics* Z, Chapter 13," argues that the former is the correct translation and that Aristotle distinguishes between universals and things predicated universally. The arguments of Z.13, Woods argues, are not intended to show that universals cannot be *ousia* but only that things predicated universally cannot. As we have seen, Woods mistakenly identifies species and form; he holds that, while universals, things that are species/forms are not predicated universally, so Aristotle can consistently maintain both the Z.13 thesis and the view that form/species is *ousia*. I (along with others) have argued that the distinction Woods imputes to Aristotle has no firm textual basis. That point can, I think, be made simply by noting that the thesis of Z.13 is the answer to the question implied by 1028ᵇ34–36 and 1038ᵇ1–3, where '*katholou*' appears without any form of '*legomenon*'. The philosophical point Woods reads into the distinction is, however, interesting. Woods tells us that "to speak of a plurality of objects I need some means of marking off each member of the set from other things. I do this, according to Aristotle, by recognizing occurrences of certain forms in matter. Thus, I must already regard things as possessing the form before I can think of objects as a genuine plurality. Insofar as the statement that the form is predicated universally of its members implies the contrary of this, it is incorrect. Aristotle refused to say that *anthropos* was *katholou legomenon* because

That claim, however, initially appears incompatible with the conjunction of two other claims defended and developed in the middle books. Aristotle holds, we have seen, that

(B)   Form is *ousia*,

but he also holds that

(C)   Form is a universal,

and (A–C) constitute an inconsistent triad.

There are commentators who believe that Aristotle cannot escape the charge of inconsistency here, and they conclude that the doctrine of the middle books is, at bottom, contradictory.[2] Most commentators, however, have denied that the metaphysics of Z and H gives rise to contradiction, insisting either that Aristotle rejects one or more of (A–C) or that, when we spell out the precise doctrine that each of these claims abbreviates, the alleged inconsistency disappears. Thus we find com-

---

that would suggest that you could first distinguish individual substances and then notice that the predicate applied to them which supplied a basis for distinguishing them in the first place. With species in relation to genera, on the other hand, it is the other way around. The genus does not itself supply a basis for distinguishing species; the species are distinguished by the appropriate differentiae" (pp. 237–238). Species/forms are universals that are not predicated universally of individuals, whereas genera are universals that are predicated universally of their species. The idea that Z.13 might be attacking the view that genera are not the *ousia* of their logical subordinates is one I endorse in Section III, but I have doubts that Aristotle saw things the way Woods suggests. First, it is not clear that Aristotle would embrace the epistemological picture at work in Woods's account of recognition and individuation; if he would, it would be the species that provides the sortal principle Woods is after and not forms, so Woods's confusions about species and form appear to be significant. It is not the species, but the form that is *ousia*; hence, the universal that by Woods's account is not predicated universally is not even a candidate for status as *ousia*. Form, however, is a universal that by Woods's account is predicated universally, since it is predicated only accidentally of the independently identifiable parcels of matter constituting the individuals belonging to the associated species. So, when we get clear about the species/form distinction, it turns out that Woods's distinction between universals and things predicated universally is precisely the one Aristotle would not invoke here. Such a distinction would generate the consequence that forms are not *ousia*, but that species are; that consequence would have what serves as explanandum in Aristotle's account turn out to be explanans, and vice versa. For more on the Woods's account of Z.13, see James Lesher, "Aristotle on Form, Substance, and Universal: A Dilemma," *Phronesis* (1971), 169–178; Loux, "Form, Species, and Predication in *Metaphysics* Z, H, and Θ"; Alan Code, "No Universal Is a Substance: An Interpretation of *Metaphysics* Z.13 (1038ᵇ8–15)," *Paideia* (1978), 65–74; and Michael Frede and Gunther Patzig, *Aristoteles "Metaphysik Z,"* vol. 2, 245–246.

[2]For the charge of inconsistency, see Lesher, "Aristotle on Form, Substance, and Universals"; R. D. Sykes, "Form in Aristotle: Universal or Particular?" *Philosophy* (1975), 311–331; and Daniel Graham, *Aristotle's Two Systems*, chap. 9.

mentators who insist that, as accurate expressions of Aristotelian doctrine, (A) and (B) must employ different senses of the term 'ousia';[3] others who insist that the notion of universality at work in (C) is quite different from that operative in the Z.13 slogan (A);[4] others who see 'form' as ambiguous in (B) and (C); and still others who simply deny that (C) represents genuine Aristotelian doctrine.[5] Whatever their response to (A–C), commentators seem to be generally agreed that Z.13 and the immediately succeeding chapters have deeply significant implications for our interpretation of the overall theory of the middle books and that this section of the text must function as a critical constraint on our reading of Z and H.[6]

When we turn to Z.13, however, we find that things are a little less straightforward than these commentators would have us believe. That chapter incorporates a flurry of arguments. And although those arguments may individually conclude with a claim that might be summarized or abbreviated by some slogan such as "No universal is *ousia*," Aristotle presents us with the totality of arguments to support a different, weaker claim:

> It seems impossible that any universal [or, anything said universally] be *ousia*. (1038ª8–9)[7]

---

[3]See A. R. Lacey, "*Ousia* and Form in Aristotle," *Phronesis* (1965), 54–69.

[4]See Woods, "Problems in *Metaphysics* Z, Chapter 13"; Loux, "Form, Species, and Predication in *Metaphysics* Z, H, and Θ"; Frank Lewis, "Form and Predication in Aristotle's *Metaphysics*"; Rogers Albritton, "Substance and Form in Aristotle's *Metaphysics*," *Journal of Philosophy* (1957), 699–708; Jonathan Lear, *Aristotle: The Desire to Understand*, 284–291; Gerald Hughes, "Universals as Potential Substances: The Interpretation of *Metaphysics* Z.13," in Burnyeat et al., eds., , *Notes on Book Zeta*, 107–126; Loux, "*Ousia*: A Prolegomenon to *Metaphysics* Z and H"; D. K. Modrak, "Forms, Types, and Tokens in Aristotle's *Metaphysics*;" and Montgomery Furth, *Substance, Form, and Psyche*, 247–249.

[5]Those who see Aristotle as holding to a doctrine of individual forms might express their view either by reading a homonymy into 'form' as it appears in (B) and (C) or by denying that (C) is true. See Wilfrid Sellars, "Aristotle's *Metaphysics*: An Interpretation" and "Substance and Form in Aristotle," in *Philosophical Perspectives*, 73–124, 125–136; Joseph Owens, *The Doctrine of Being in the Aristotelian Metaphysics*, 223–227; A. C. Lloyd, *Form and Universal in Aristotle*; Michael Frede, "Individuals in Aristotle" and "Substance in Aristotle's *Metaphysics*," in *Essays in Ancient Philosophy*, 49–71, 72–80; Edwin Hartman, *Substance, Body, and Soul*, especially chap. 2; Terence Irwin, *Aristotle's First Principles*, especially chap. 12; Charlotte Witt, *Substance and Essence in Aristotle*, chap. 5; and Michael Frede and Gunther Patzig, *Aristoteles "Metaphysik Z,"* vol. 1, 48–57, and vol. 2, 241–263.

[6]A recent and very explicit expression of this view is found in the Frede–Patzig commentary. They begin their discussion of the chapter with the claim that "Chapter 13 is crucial for the interpretation of Book Z." *Aristoteles "Metaphysik Z,"* vol. 2, 241.

[7]For a criticism of the idea that '*eoike*' has the cautionary force I associate with it, see ibid., vol. 2, 244–245. Frede and Patzig point out correctly that Aristotle does make the unqualified claim that no universal is *ousia* in a number of places. I do not quarrel with the idea that the claim expresses genuine Aristotelian doctrine. The question is, Which

The arguments of Z.13 are not presented as proofs of a thesis, each of which Aristotle himself necessarily endorses, but rather as considerations that cumulatively explain the plausibility of a view that makes an initial claim on our credence. Indeed, when we examine the individual arguments of the chapter, we find that we cannot take all of them with the same degree of seriousness. At 1038$^b$15–16, for example, we meet with the claim that, since *ousia* is "that which is not said of a subject," no universal is *ousia*. Although the Aristotle of Z and H does not deny that subjects of predication have some claim to the title *ousia*, the argument of Z.3 is sufficient to make us cautious of attributing too much weight to any argument that depends on the subject criterion.[8] Likewise, 1038$^b$23–29 and 1039$^a$14–19 appear to argue that, since *ousia* is always a *tode* and never a *poion* or *toionde*, universals are not *ousiai*; but by Z.8 already we know enough of the shifting uses of the term '*tode*' to be wary of supposing that Aristotle himself would invoke the *tode*/*toinde* contrast as one that neatly and definitively divides things into two discrete sets.

Nor is it clear that the arguments of Z.13 all generate one and the same conclusion. Several of them seem to yield the conclusion that no universal can be the *ousia* of other things. At 1038$^b$31–1039$^a$2, however, Aristotle claims that to construe universals as *ousiai* is to run the risk of entanglement in the difficulties associated with the Third Man. But those difficulties arise only if we make certain very specific assumptions about universals, assumptions that have the force of treating universals not merely as the *ousia* of something else but as *ousiai* in just the sense in which concrete particulars are *ousiai*.[9]

Furthermore, there is evidence, internal to Z.13 alone, that Aristotle felt comfortable construing some universals as the *ousiai* of ordinary objects. At 1038$^b$21–22 the claim that *man* is the *ousia* of the particular men in which it is found appears to be treated as nonproblematic, and at 1038$^b$30–31 this tolerance seems to be generalized to cover all analogous cases. So the idea that *man* is the *ousia* of particular men is not challenged. What is challenged in these two passages is the idea that the genera under which *man* and analogous universals fall is their *ousia*.

At best, then, the arguments of Z.13 are taken to provide cumulative

---

doctrine? I find it significant that Aristotle's first statement of the claim is prefaced by the qualifier, as though he were warning us that the claim does not wear its force on its sleeve. See 1038$^b$34–35, which also seems to qualify the claim. This is the last general statement of the thesis, so both the opening and the final statements in Z.13 of what is thought to be the thesis Aristotle is proving in that chapter formulate the statement in a guarded way.

[8]For a discussion of what is right in the subject criterion, see Chapter 7.

[9]The contrast I have in mind here is that between '*ousia*' as an abstract term in the context 'the *ousia* of _____' and '*ousia*' as a concrete term.

evidence for the plausibility of one or more claims in a very general logical neighborhood. And although there can be no doubt that there is some claim in the neighborhood that Aristotle is willing to endorse, it would be hazardous to suppose that he would unequivocally and unconditionally assent to the bald claim that there is no sense in which something we might call a universal is *ousia*. In this connection the alleged thesis of Z.13 has the same status as a related "thesis" of the middle books. In both Z.13 and Z.16, the denial that universals are *ousiai* is paired with the claim that no *ousia* can have another *ousia* in it.[10] Although there certainly is a sense in which Aristotle endorses a claim abbreviated by that slogan, it is also true that there is a perfectly natural way of understanding the sentence "No *ousia* has another *ousia* present in it" such that Aristotle would unquestionably reject the slogan understood in that way.[11]

So there are grounds for questioning the idea that Z.13 is a secure repository of settled doctrine on a fixed thesis, and an examination of the vast body of literature on the chapter confirms these doubts. Commentators disagree about the interpretation of virtually every sentence in the chapter, they disagree about the structure of particular arguments in the chapter, and they disagree about the number of arguments the chapter contains.[12] Indeed, what one commentator construes as an argument for the thesis that universals cannot be *ousiai* another commentator construes as the dialectical commentary and elaboration of a proponent of the thesis that universals are *ousiai*.[13]

The idea, then, that Z.13 should serve as some sort of overarching constraint on our interpretation of the later theory of *ousia* is problematic and the suggestion that we cannot begin to delineate the main contours of Z and H until we have come to terms with the "theoretical"

[10]1038ᵇ29–30 and 1039ᵃ3–4; 1041ᵃ3–5.

[11]I am thinking of the idea that the substantial form of an ordinary concrete *ousia* both enters into its constitution and is its primary *ousia*. It is interesting that Frede and Patzig, who want to construe all the claims of Z.13 as definitive expressions of Aristotelian doctrine, concede the point I am making here. See *Aristoteles "Metaphysik Z,"* vol. 2, 258.

[12]Gerald Hughes nicely summarizes the situation: "Discussion of the thirteenth chapter of Book Z of Aristotle's *Metaphysics* can hardly be said to have reached any satisfactory conclusion. . . . The translation of some of the key sentences is in doubt . . . the precise force of some of the central arguments is not clear; and there is even a considerable difference of opinion about where Aristotle is putting forward his own views and where he is rehearsing the arguments of his (presumably Platonic) opponent" ("Universals as Potential Substances," 107).

[13]Consider, for example, the different accounts of 1038ᵇ18–30 as found in Ross, *Aristotle's Metaphysics*, vol. 2, 210–211; Woods, "Problems in *Metaphysics Z*, Chapter 13"; Hughes, "Universals as Potential Substances"; and Burnyeat et al., eds., *Notes on Book Zeta*, 128–135. I follow the fine-grained division of arguments found in Ross when I claim (a few pages hence) that there are at least seven arguments here.

contributions of this chapter, suspect. Chapter Z.13 just does not provide us with a firm basis for "fixing" the theory Aristotle wants to
develop in the middle books. A better strategy is to attempt to delineate
the Z–H account of *ousia* independently of this chapter and its immediate successors and, then, to attempt to make sense of this body of the
text in the light of the theory as so far delineated. At any rate, that is the
strategy I have invoked, and its ability to make sense of the claims of
those chapters is the best test of the strategy itself. I claim, then, that the
central themes of Z.13–.16 make clear sense against the backdrop of the
theory we have outlined in the past few chapters. Viewed in the light of
that theory, Aristotle's aims in those chapters are easy to identify and
explain. Indeed, this strategy provides us with an embarrassment of
riches, for what emerges is that there is not just one point we can attach
to the arguments of this section of the text. There are a number of
different concerns that we can reasonably associate with Aristotle's
remarks on the slogan that no universal is *ousia*, and it is extremely
difficult to be certain just which of those concerns is the main focus of
the various lines of argument we meet in Z.13–16. Indeed, in the light of
this underdetermination of the text, it is not unreasonable to suppose
that Aristotle did not associate a single force with the slogan but instead
saw it as a point of convergence for a number of quite different ideas. Of
course, the attribution of any particular set of intentions is hazardous
here; and I shall be satisfied if I can succeed in isolating a number of
concerns that are plausibly associated with the slogan and the main
arguments supporting it and are consistent with the overall theory of
the rest of Z and H. What I argue is that, although it is easy enough to
identify a number of interesting and important claims for which the
slogan of Z.13 is a natural vehicle, one claim we cannot read into Z.13
and its neighbors is the idea that the primary *ousiai* are particular forms,
each present in just one individual. It turns out that this is one reading
of Z.13 the text just does not support.

II

Although they are elaborated and developed in varying degrees, there
are at least seven different arguments for one or more claims abbreviated by the slogan of Z.13. They break down as follows:[14]

[14]As I indicated in the previous note, I take the fine-grained approach to Z.13, finding
more arguments for the slogan than Woods or Hughes do. Not much hangs on this, since
the arguments I attribute to Aristotle (and either Woods or Hughes do not) are not central
or pivotal. I am, however, inclined to think that seeing iii–v as separate arguments *given by*

   (i)    The Generalized *Idion* Argument: $1038^b9$–15
  (ii)   The Subject Argument: $1038^b15$–16
 (iii)   The Specialized *Idion* Argument: $1038^b16$–23
 (iv)   The *Tode/Toionde* (*Poion*) Argument: $1038^b23$–29 and $1039^a14$–19
  (v)   The *Ousia* in an *Ousia* Argument: $1038^b29$–30
 (vi)   The Third Man Argument: $1038^b30$–$1039^a2$
(vii)   The Unity of *Ousia* Argument: $1039^a3$ff.

As I have already suggested, (ii) and (iv) should be taken with a grain of salt,[15] and both (v) and (vi) have a fairly specialized thesis as their target. It is generally thought, however, that (i) must be accorded a special status in Aristotle's thinking, and for good reasons: the argument invokes a premise that we repeatedly meet in the middle books and elsewhere, it seems to play a role in (iii), and since it has a generality not associated with the other arguments it seems to provide the most serious threat of yielding a conclusion that can make serious trouble for Aristotle's overall theory. So let us look at the argument in some detail. Its text is as follows:

  (1)   The *ousia* of each thing is peculiar to it and does not belong to another.
  (2)   But the universal is common, for that is said to be universal which by nature belongs to many.
  (3)   Of which, then, will this be the *ousia*?
  (4)   for (it will be the *ousia*) of all or none.
  (5)   But it cannot be the *ousia* of all.
  (6)   If it will be (the *ousia*) of one, this one will be the others;
  (7)   for things whose *ousia* and essence are one are themselves one.

We can agree that (1) is a preliminary and abbreviated formulation of the premise we meet in (7). Step (2) is either a definition of the notion of a universal or a claim that follows from such a definition. Step (4) is a disjunctive premise, one disjunct of which is denied in (5). That denial is justified in (6) and (7), and the implicit conclusion of the argument is provided by the remaining disjunct of (4).

Let us try to set this argument out in greater detail. After telling us

---

Aristotle is the more natural reading of the relevant lines. See Burnyeat et al., eds., *Notes on Book Zeta*, 128–130, for partial support of the Ross view.

[15]Frede and Patzig, who take form to be a subject and who understand the force of the "this"/"such" contrast in a different way, see ii and iv as definitive arguments for the Z.13 thesis. See *Aristoteles "Metaphysik Z,"* vol. 2, 252 and 256. Our disagreement about these two arguments hinges on issues external to and independent of Z.13.

that a universal is something common to a plurality of objects, Aristotle presumably asks us to focus on an arbitrary universal *U*. He tells us that

   (a)   Either *U* is the *ousia* of all the objects in its associated plurality or *U* is the *ousia* of none of those objects.

The aim is to show that the first disjunct of (a),

   (b)   *U* is the *ousia* of all the objects in its associated plurality,

is false, and the method is that of reductio. We are to assume that (b) is true and to choose a sample object from the plurality mentioned in (b).[16] Call the sample object Sam. Step (b) assures us that

   (c)   *U* is the *ousia* of Sam;

But for any arbitrary object *x* such that *x* belongs to the plurality associated with *U* and *x* is distinct from Sam, (b) also guarantees that

   (d)   *U* is the *ousia* of *x*.

But since

   (e)   Things whose *ousia* and essence are one are themselves one,

it follows that

   (f)   Sam is one with *x*.

But by hypothesis

   (g)   Sam is not one with *x*.

Accordingly, we have to conclude that (b) is false and that

[16]I agree with Code that the argument proceeds by choosing a sample object in the interests of showing that (b) is false. To construe the antecedent of (6) as expressing the attempt on the part of Aristotle's opponent to put forward a third option [distinct from those expressed in (4)] has the result that Aristotle begs the question against the opponent in the consequent of (6). For more on (6), see not only Code, "No Universal Is a Substance," 69; but also Woods, "Problems in *Metaphysics* Z, Chapter 13," 218; Harold Cherniss, *Aristotle's Criticism of Plato and the Academy* (Baltimore: Johns Hopkins Press, 1944), 318–319; and Frede and Patzig, *Aristoteles "Metaphysik Z,"* vol. 2, 248ff. Although I agree with Code on the "sample object" interpretation of (6), we disagree on precisely how Aristotle's reductio proceeds; see "No Universal Is a Substance," 70–71.

(h)   U is the *ousia* of none of the objects in its associated plurality

is true. And since U was an arbitrarily chosen universal, the proof that (h) is true serves as a proof for the general claim summarized in the slogan of Z.13.[17]

The implicit justification for premise (a) is, I take it, found in the idea that a universal bears a single uniform relation to all the objects in its associated plurality, so let us call (a) the *uniformity assumption*. Premise (e) is sometimes called the uniqueness requirement,[18] but since that label might seem to beg the question in favor of one particular interpretation let us call it the *idion premise*. It is because of the critical role of this premise in the initial argument of Z.13 that I call the argument the Generalized *Idion* Argument.

Although this argument may strike us as straightforward, there are several distinct issues with respect to which the text leaves the argument indeterminate. Consider, first, the claim in (2) that a universal is by nature common to a plurality of objects. There is a one-many relation that Aristotle wants to insist on here. But which relation does he have in mind? The use of the term *'huparchein'* ('belong') suggests the relation is that of predication, so that for every universal U there is a plurality of objects a . . . n such that U is predicated of, and hence common to, all and only a . . . n. This reading of (2) is supported by a text from *De Interpretatione* 7, where Aristotle seems to be defining the universal as "that which is of such a nature as to be predicated of many subjects" (17ª38–39), and the idea that each universal is common to a plurality of objects in the sense that it is predicated of each object in the plurality is both natural and one we meet over and again in Aristotle.

If we agree that predication is what is relevant, we still have to ask about the generality of Aristotle's concern here. We might think, for example, that the concern is with all universals, so that the Generalized *Idion* Argument establishes that no universal can be the *ousia* of any object in its predicative range, whether that range is constituted by the

---

[17]Frede and Patzig see an ambiguity in *'oudenos'* (1038ᵇ13). As they read it, *'oudenos'* can mean 'none of the items in the associated plurality' or 'absolutely nothing', and they suggest that Aristotle seeks to establish the stronger claim that a universal can be the *ousia* of absolutely nothing. I see no reason for supposing that this is so. Indeed, unless we just assume that forms are individuals, there are compelling reasons for supposing that Aristotle would not have endorsed this stronger claim. It is not just my conviction that Aristotle construed forms as universals that leads me to reject the Frede–Patzig reading of *'oudenos.'* That term appears in the disjunction of 1038ᵇ12–13, where it is paired against *'panton'*. Since *'panton'* must be interpreted as 'everything in the associated plurality', we have no option but to restrict *'oudenos'* in the same way. See *Aristoteles "Metaphysik Z,"* vol. 2, 250–251, for the Frede–Patzig discussion of the alleged ambiguity.

[18]See Woods, "Problems in *Metaphysics Z*, Chapter 13," 217–218.

relation of essential predication or of accidental predication. Frequently, however, Aristotle uses the term 'universal' more narrowly, so that something is said to be universal with respect to a given plurality of objects just in case it is predicated of each such object essentially.[19] If it is this narrower use that is at work in 1038[b]9–15, then the Generalized *Idion* Argument has the more restrictive aim of showing that no universal can be the *ousia* of any of the objects of which it is predicated essentially. Sometimes we find Aristotle putting the term 'universal' to an even narrower use. There are contexts in which 'universal' is a stand-in for 'infima species'.[20] Were this use to be operative in Z.13, its aim would be that of showing that no species can be the *ousia* of any of its members. And there are contexts where 'universal' is used to refer only to genera.[21] In the case of genera, there are distinct sets of objects that might be viewed as the pluralities with respect to which it might be said to be common; there are the various particulars of which the genera are predicated as well as the species which are their immediate logical inferiors. Accordingly, if we believe Aristotle has this restrictive sense of 'universal' in mind here, then we can add several theses to the list of claims the Generalized *Idion* Argument might be taken to establish. Finally, if we agree that it is predication that constitutes the commonality of a universal in (2), we might want to ask whether the Z–H contrast between eliminable or analyzable and noneliminable or primitive predication is operative here. If we take Aristotle to be limiting his discussion to the two kinds of case of predication mentioned in Z.3 and Θ.7, and at the beginning of Z.13 itself [cases in which "the to be of the subject is different from that" (1029[a]22–23) of the predicate], then there is a further conclusion we can associate with the Generalized *Idion* Argument—that no accident is the *ousia* of any of the concrete particulars of which it is predicated and no substantial form is the *ousia* of any of the parcels of matter of which it is predicated. Last, there remains the possibility that the notion of commonality here is not that captured by the concept of predication, that Aristotle has some other as yet uncharacterized one-many relation in mind in (2).

So Aristotle's failure to identify the universals and associated pluralities he is interested in here leaves the range of the argument of 1038[b]9–15 unspecified. There are any number of theses he might be arguing for. And it is not just the notions of universality and commonality that are left open; Aristotle's formulation of the critical *idion*

---

[19]We meet with this use of 'universal' in B.3, for example; see 998[b]17 and throughout the *Posterior Analytics*.

[20]See Z.3 (1028[b]34), in which Aristotle uses 'universal' to refer to the species.

[21]See 998[b]14–16 and 1059[b]24–27.

premise is itself subject to several different interpretations. His second statement of the premise in (7) differs from the initial statement we meet with in (1) in incorporating a reference to the notion of essence. On this score (7), or (e), admits three quite different readings, which, at the risk of misleading, we can formulate as follows:

(e′)  (x) (y) (z) (If x is the *ousia* and the essence of y, and x is the *ousia* and the essence of z, then y and z are one)

(e″)  (w) (x) (y) (z) (If w is the *ousia* of y, and x is the essence of y, and w is the *ousia* of z, and x is the essence of z, then y and z are one)

(e‴)  (x) (y) (z) (If x is an essence, and x is the *ousia* of y, and x is the *ousia* of z, then y and z are one).

The text most naturally suggests the reading provided by (e′), but, in the absence of any statement to the contrary, (e″) and (e‴) remain possible (if slightly farfetched) readings of (7) or (e). But things are even more complicated. I have said that there is something potentially misleading in each of (e′), (e″), and (e‴). What is misleading is the assumption built into these three formulations that the first unity or oneness mentioned in (7) or (e) is numerical unity or unity in number. But Aristotle repeatedly reminds us that numerical unity does not exhaust the kinds of unity.[22] Things can be one in species and one in genus as well. Perhaps Aristotle has one of these forms of unity in mind here rather than numerical unity. The unity expressed in the consequent of each of (e′), (e″), and (e‴) is likewise open to interpretation in each of these different ways.

It is often claimed that the Generalized *Idion* Argument is one by which Aristotle makes real trouble for himself. It should be clear, however, that there is not just one argument unambiguously set out for us in 1038ᵇ9–15. The text gives us a general argument frame that can, quite consistently with Aristotle's formulation of the frame, be filled in to generate a whole host of different arguments with nonequivalent conclusions. To get any one argument for a given thesis, we must make several choices. As we survey the potential choices open to us here, we see that it is only if we are very selective in our reading of the text that we can conjure out of 1038ᵇ9–15 an argument that has any chance of causing trouble for the doctrine we have found in Z and H.

If the notion of universality operative in the argument is that of predication, then regardless of whether the predication Aristotle has in mind is essential rather than accidental predication, primitive or non-

---

[22]See Δ.6 (1016ᵇ32–1017ᵃ3) and I.1 (1052ᵃ29–35) for the distinction in question.

eliminable rather than derived or analyzable predication, generic rather than specific predication, or all forms of predication, then the argument has no force at all of calling into question any feature of Aristotle's doctrine. What the argument shows under this interpretation is that, whatever set of universals we focus on, no universal in the set can be the *ousia* of any of the objects in its predicative plurality. As we have seen, however, Aristotle wants to deny that his candidates for the role of primary *ousia* are predicated of any of the objects whose *ousia* they are. Depending on just which forms of predication we read into the Generalized *Idion* Argument, the argument shows that accidents cannot be the *ousia* of the particulars of which they are predicated, that genera and species cannot be the *ousia* of the particulars of which they are predicated, that species cannot be the *ousia* of their members, that genera cannot be the *ousia* of their species, or that substantial forms cannot be the *ousia* of the parcels of matter they inform. But Aristotle denies all these claims. He holds that a substantial form is the *ousia* of the particulars from the associated species, and he denies that forms are predicated of those particulars, insisting instead that a form is universal with respect to the parcels of matter making up those particulars. So, if the notion of universality here is that of predication, the Generalized *Idion* Argument is no threat at all to Aristotle's later theory of *ousia*. There is no inconsistent triad stemming from the central argument of Z.13, for that argument establishes not

(A)   No universal is *ousia*

but the weaker claim

(A')   No universal is the *ousia* of any of the objects of which it is predicated;

and (A') is not inconsistent with the conjunction of

(B)   Form is *ousia*

and

(C)   Form is a universal

as Aristotle understands (B) and (C).

The Generalized *Idion* Argument generates a conclusion that is problematic for the theory of the rest of Z and H only if the one-many relation tying a universal to a plurality of objects is something other than predication. But the suggestion that some other relation is operative here is highly implausible. In Aristotle, the notion of one thing's being universal with respect to other things is characteristically tied to the concept of predication. Although what, in any given context, Aristotle calls a universal can vary, his willingness to speak of anything as a universal with respect to a plurality of objects is regularly tied to talk about some predicative relation between the thing he is calling a universal and the objects constituting the relevant plurality. So to generate a problematic conclusion from the Generalized *Idion* Argument, we must suppose that the argument of 1038$^b$9–15 involves a completely uncharacteristic use of the term 'universal', we must suppose that this extraordinary use of the term 'universal' is imported into Aristotle's argument with no explanation whatsoever, and we must suppose that both these unlikely conditions obtain in an argument whose conclusion is flatly inconsistent with the rest of the doctrine of Z and H.

Furthermore, we must do what Aristotle fails to do—explain the notion of universality allegedly at work in the argument. It is difficult to know just what kinds of restrictions to place on the one-many relation supposedly at work in the argument of 1038$^b$9–15. Indeed, to get the desired result, we seem required to stipulate that, where one thing $x$ is predicated of the parcels of matter making up the objects $a \ldots n$, there is a relation tying $x$ to each of $a \ldots n$, and we have to suppose that that one-many relation is the one Aristotle has in mind here. Nothing in the text justifies this stipulation, but the stipulation is what is required if we are to get the result that Aristotle makes trouble for himself in Z.13. It is fairly clear, however, that it is not Aristotle who is making trouble for himself. We are the ones who are making trouble for Aristotle.

Even if we assume that this deviant use of the term 'universal' is operative in the Generalized *Idion* Argument, we still do not have all the materials in place to generate the result that the conclusion of the argument is inconsistent with the rest of Aristotle's theory. To ensure that the argument yields the conclusion that a substantial form cannot be the *ousia* of the particulars of the associated species, we must confront the ambiguity in the *idion* premise. As we have seen, that premise is subject to the three readings expressed by (e'–e'''). The most natural reading, we have said, is that provided by (e'). But to ensure that the argument of 1038$^b$9–15 has the desired consequence, we have to suppose that that reading is not the intended reading. Even if we suppose that some relation other than predication is operative here (that Aristotle has in mind a one-many relation covering the case of a form's relation to the associated particulars), the Generalized *Idion* Argument does not give us the consequence that a substantial form cannot be the *ousia* of the particulars of the associated species if the *idion* premise is given the most natural reading and taken to mean that things that have one and the same thing as *ousia* and essence are themselves one; for, although Aristotle holds that form is the *ousia* of ordinary objects, he denies that it is their essence. Their essence is that of the species. To get the desired conclusion, we must read the *idion* premise as (e″) or (e‴) suggest; these readings, we have said, are precisely those not naturally suggested by Aristotle's formulation of the *idion* premise.

To make the argument of 1038ᵇ9–15 problematic, then, we must assume that Aristotle is understanding the notion of universality in a completely uncharacteristic way, that this deviant notion of universality is introduced with no explanation whatsoever, that the explanation he would give is one that can be formulated only with an eye to generating a conclusion inconsistent with the rest of Aristotle's theory, and that the critical premise in the argument must be understood to mean something other than what Aristotle's formulation of it most naturally suggests it means. Each of these assumptions is individually hazardous; taken collectively, they constitute a pattern of interpretation that is indefensible. In its face, I can only repeat my earlier comment that, if we want to read problems into Z.13, they are not Aristotle's problems but problems of our own making. To argue this essentially negative point is not, however, to provide a coherent account of Z.13. What is required is a delineation of the kinds of philosophical concerns that might have motivated that chapter and its immediate successors. As I have suggested, the requisite account is not difficult to find. So let us turn to the task of explaining just which views Aristotle might have been interested in combating by way of the *Idion* Argument.

III

We want an account of Z.13 and, in particular, the Generalized *Idion* Argument that identifies a view that (a) might plausibly be expressed by the slogan that universals are *ousiai*, (b) Aristotle would have good reason to criticize, and (c) can be seen as a natural target of the *Idion* Argument. However we take individual passages in Z.13 and the following chapters, it is clear both that Aristotle finds something objectionable in the view abbreviated by the slogan and that he saw the Generalized *Idion* Argument as an important way of bringing out what is objectionable in the view.[23]

[23]Aristotle repeats the Z.13 slogan too often for us to assume otherwise; see 1040ᵇ26–27, 1042ᵃ21–22, and 1053ᵇ16–17.

We can begin to give a sense to the slogan if we look to the comments concluding the flurry of arguments of Z.13. Those comments are concerned with the related problems of the unity of *ousia* and the unity of definition (see 1038$^b$30–1039$^a$23). The idea that these problems are a central concern of Z.13 nicely fits the context, since Z.12 is concerned with that cluster of issues. In Z.12, however, Aristotle deals with problems about unity by shelving them. The strategy of Z.12 is to stipulate that the genus in a definition is not something over and above the universals that are its subordinates, that a genus is a mere determinable with no reality or conceptual content apart from the determinate expressions that are its subordinates. Intriguingly, we meet at 1038$^b$30ff. language strikingly similar to that in which (at 1038$^a$5–8) the stipulation of Z.12 was framed; even more intriguingly, the passage in question is one that is naturally read as expressing the implications of the arguments that precede it, as summarizing the upshot of rejecting the slogan Aristotle is concerned with.[24] Aristotle says:

> And in general it follows that if *man* and things said in the same way are *ousia*, nothing in their formula is the *ousia* of anything nor does it exist apart from them nor in anything else. I mean, for example, that there is not something that is animal over and above the particulars; and the same is true of whatever else is in their formula. (1038$^b$30–34)[25]

Aristotle goes on to relate the issue to questions about the unity of definition, but the similarity to the language of Z.12 by itself makes the connection. The point is that, if we construe genera as fully determinate entities with complete conceptual content in their own right, we can never explain how what is subject to definition can constitute what is genuinely one thing. Certainly concern about the unity of form is at the forefront here, but, as we see in the next chapter, Aristotle also wants to ensure that species provide us with concepts of genuine unities. It may, then, be that the arguments of Z.13 and surrounding chapters bear on the role of genera in definition generally. In any case, the slogan that universals are *ousiai* should be understood as the view that as fully determinate things with complete conceptual content in their own right

[24]One who wants to deny that the Generalized and Specialized *Idion* Arguments focus on different candidates for status as *ousia* might take the passage in question as expressing the upshot of the Specialized *Idion* Argument; but it is not unreasonable to think that the term 'universal' has an invariant reference across the two arguments. From 1038$^b$16 onward Aristotle is talking about genera, and there is no reason to suppose he has changed the subject at 1038$^b$16. He is talking about the same things that concerned him at 1038$^b$11–15 and is merely considering a new account of how those things (genera) might function as the *ousia* of their subordinates. At any rate, we have to understand the text this way if we assume the interpretation I outline in this section.

[25]For an expression of the same idea, see *Metaphysics* I.2 (1053$^b$16–21).

genera are the *ousia* of their immediate logical inferiors, and that by somehow sharing this content with their inferiors genera are responsible for the being of those inferiors.[26] Understanding the slogan in this light enables us to see Z.13 as the natural successor to Z.12, but it also enables us to see the discussion of Z.13 unfolding into the discussion of Z.14, where Aristotle focuses on idiosyncratic features of what he takes to be the most notorious example of a theory subscribing to the slogan, Plato's. In taking Aristotle to be attacking the view that genera have a determinate conceptual content that can be identified independently of any reference to their logical inferiors, we have Aristotle expressing an idea that one can find in texts as early as the *Categories* (e.g., 1b10–15).

If we take this reading of Z.13, then in the Generalized *Idion* Argument Aristotle is using the term 'universal' (as he does elsewhere) to refer to genera; the pluralities to which they are common are constituted by their immediate logical inferiors (certainly substantial forms; perhaps species as well). The view Aristotle is attacking is, then, one that mistakenly construes generality as the mark of the real. Whereas he holds that determinateness is the mark of the real, his opponent holds that, the more general a thing is, the more real it is, the more deserving of the title '*ousia*'. Further, his opponent claims that, since it is because genera are what they are that their logical inferiors are what they are, genera are the *ousia* of their inferiors.[27]

On this account, the *idion* premise is a kind of Identity of Indiscernibles principle for forms (and perhaps species), telling us that definables are individuated by the elements in their essence. The view Aristotle wants to counter is that genera give us the complete conceptual content of their immediate logical inferiors; his appeal to the *idion* premise has the force of pointing out that, since definables are individuated by their essences, the effect of assuming that genera exhaust the conceptual content of their logical inferiors is to preclude the possibility of there being more than one definable within a given genus. Since ex hypothesi

---

[26]For versions of this approach, see the accounts in Woods, "Problems in *Metaphysics* Z, Chapter 13"; Albritton, "Substance and Form in Aristotle's *Metaphysics*"; Lear, *Aristotle: The Desire to Understand*; Loux, "*Ousia*: A Prolegomenon to Z and H"; and Furth, *Substance, Form, and Psyche*.

[27]Frede and Patzig, *Aristoteles "Metaphysik* Z," vol. 2, 245–247, express doubts about attempts (such as those found in Hughes, "Universals as Potential Substances," and Woods, "Problems in *Metaphysics* Z, Chapter 13") to construe the Generalized *Idion* Argument as an attack on the idea that genera are *ousiai* and to support this view by suggesting some logical difference in the case of (a) the relation between a species and its members and (b) the relation of a genus and its subordinates or members. My proposed interpretation of the Generalized *Idion* Argument has it hinge, not on the uniqueness of the relation of a genus and its subordinates and/or members, but on the fact that genera lack the kind of completeness or determination required of a candidate for status as *ousia*.

each genus has more than one logical inferior,[28] we can conclude that a genus cannot be the *ousia* of all its logical inferiors. Given the uniformity assumption, we can conclude that a genus is the *ousia* of none of its logical inferiors.

There is, of course, an obvious response to this line of argument. The proponent of the slogan can concede that genera do not exhaust the conceptual content of their inferiors but insist, nonetheless, that they make an essential contribution to that content. Aristotle has the proponent of the view respond in just this way:

> But, perhaps, things are as follows: [the universal] cannot be the *ousia* in the way the essence is, but it can enter into this. For example, could not *animal* be in *man* and *horse*? (1038[b]16–18)

This response leads Aristotle into what, because of its more specific focus, I call the Specialized *Idion* Argument:

> Then it is clear that there is some formula of this; and it makes no difference whether this is the formula of everything in the *ousia*. For, nevertheless, this will be the *ousia* of something in the way that *man* is the *ousia* of the man in which it is, so that the same result will follow as before; for this [e.g., *animal*] will be the *ousia* of that as something peculiar to that in which it is. (1038[b]18–23)

This is a difficult passage. Aristotle is claiming that, despite all efforts, the theorist who construes generality as a mark of the real has failed to provide an account that does not succumb to the pitfalls associated with the view that a genus exhausts the conceptual content of its logical inferiors. But why should we think this? Well, the proponent of this view makes genera complete and fully determinate ways of being. But, then, genera cannot give us just a part of an essence, for if genera have the completeness and determinateness proposed for them, then we do not have to await the contribution of some further thing to have a complete and fully determinate way of being. We already have that in the genus taken by itself. Unfortunately, we have, for each genus, just one such way of being; that is, if we understand genera as the account suggests, the idea of adding something to a genus to generate a complete what it is to be is gratuitous. We already have in the genus something that qualifies as a complete what it is to be, and we have just one such what it is to be, and not many. So the attempt to formulate the view in terms of partial as opposed to complete essences fails. If we

---

[28]This is a definitional fact about genera. See *Topics* A.5 (102[a]31–102[b]3).

construe genera as the account suggests, then the notion of a complete essence emerges one level too early, and we have, once again, only one essence where we needed several.[29]

At this point, the theorist who wants to make generality the mark of the real might suggest that the logical inferiors of a genus are constituted by the addition of something like accidents to the complete way of being that is the genus, so that the logical inferiors are each a kind of complex of the genus and something modifying it. Fairly clearly, Aristotle has this kind of response in mind in Z.14 (1039ª34–1039ᵇ15) when he attacks the Platonic account of differentiae by pointing to a dilemma the account must face. He reminds us that the attributes that have to be added to a genus to generate its various logical inferiors are contraries. But, then, either the proposed account preserves its conception of the genus as one thing across its logical inferiors, in which case it is committed to the idea that a single object can simultaneously exhibit incompatible modifications, or it maintains consistency on this score by rejecting the central idea that there is one underlying mode of being common to all the logical inferiors.

IV

One plausible reading of the *Idion* Arguments, then, has Aristotle attacking the idea that a genus is the *ousia* of its logical inferiors. If we construe Aristotle as arguing this point, not merely for the genera entering into the definitions of substantial forms, but also for the genera under which species fall, then a corollary of the *Idion* Arguments is that genera cannot be the *ousia* of the particulars falling under a species. But what of the relationship between a species and its members? The most natural reading of the *idion* premise suggests an interpretation of the argument of 1038ᵇ9–15 that makes this relationship its central focus. The most natural reading of that premise, we have said, is provided by

(e′)　(x) (y) (z)　(If x is the *ousia* and the essence of y, and x is the *ousia* and the essence of z, then y and z are one).

If we endorse this reading, then we have to agree that the *Idion* Argument establishes, not the thesis that no universal is the *ousia* of the objects of which it is predicated, but the thesis that no universal is both the *ousia* and the essence of the objects of which it is predicated.

[29]See Frede and Patzig, *Aristoteles "Metaphysik Z,"* vol. 2, 253–256, for a somewhat different but compatible approach to this passage.

Understood in this light, the *Idion* Argument is quite naturally interpreted as bearing on the relationship between a species and its members. Provided that the notion of predication underlying the concept of a universal at work in the argument is not so restrictive as to exclude the case of essential predication, the relationship between a species and its members provides a clear case of one thing common to many. And since the species is the essence of its members, it is natural to suppose that an argument whose conclusion is most plausibly read to preclude a thing's being both *ousia* and essence of the things of which it is predicated has the relationship of a species to its members as its central focus.

But, apart from the details of Aristotle's theory, what reasons are there for supposing that the *idion* premise is true when it is understood as (e'), and what reasons are there for supposing that Aristotle would have had any interest in defending the premise understood in this way? In fact, Aristotle may have believed that Plato held a view that identified essence and *ousia* for one and the same set of objects; but there is more here. To reject (e') is to commit a mistake that involves what, from Aristotle's perspective, is a serious confusion of levels; it is a mistake that he would have been particularly interested in combating.

We can assume that the unity expressed in the consequent of (e') is unity in number. If we take it to be any weaker form of unity (such as unity in form or unity in species), the premise does not succeed in generating the contradiction required for the reductio in the *Idion* Argument. There is, after all, nothing problematic in two numerically distinct objects from the same species being one in form or one in species; this is just what we would have expected and wanted. So the idea at work in (e') is that it is impossible for numerically different things to have one and the same thing for their essence and *ousia*. But why should we suppose this to be true?

The focus in Z.13 is on candidates for status as primary *ousia*, so it is just assumed that a proponent of any view Aristotle is considering is prepared to argue that a given candidate for status as *ousia* provides us with a terminus to questions about why things are what they are. The assumption, then, is that a given candidate is construed as a primary *ousia*, as something that, while the *ousia* of other things, is its own *ousia*; it is its own *ousia* because it is the essence that it is. But if the essence in question is to be the essence of something that is its own *ousia*, then the essence must be one such that anything for which it is the essence is something that is what it is in its own right. It must be something such that nothing can have it for its essence unless it is what it is independently of anything else. But, then, the idea that anything that has something of this sort as its essence has something other than itself for its *ousia* is incoherent. In the case of anything that has an essence of this sort as its essence, the *ousia*-of relation must be reflexive. Anything that has as its essence something of this sort (what we earlier called a basic or fundamental essence) is its own *ousia* and its own essence. Hence, only one thing can have an essence of this sort as its essence and *ousia*, and that is just what the *idion* premise under the interpretation provided by (e') tells us. One consequence is that no universal that is the essence of a plurality of objects can be the *ousia* of any of those objects, so no species can be *ousia* of the things of which it is essentially predicated. Another consequence is that nothing that is the *ousia* of a plurality of objects can be their essence.

So there is another piece of genuinely Aristotelian doctrine that we can read into the *Idion* Argument. The point can be expressed in less technical terms, for the central idea here is that in the case of objects for which the request for an *ousia* explanation is legitimate the notions of essence and *ousia* belong to distinct explanatory levels. In the case of ordinary objects, the concept of what constitutes their essence is part of the framework we seek to explain when we attempt to identify their *ousia*. We begin with the fact that those objects are the kinds of thing they are or have the essences they do. Those essences give us the complete concepts of what to be consists in for those objects; to identify their *ousia* is to provide an account that explains why those essences are predicated of them. The account we provide identifies essences more basic than those whose predication we seek to explain and attempts to show how our original essences depend on or presuppose those more basic essences. So the notion of the *ousia* of this kind of object belongs to a framework one level below that of its essence; consequently, for an object of this kind, the essence-of and *ousia*-of relations must have distinct entities for their terms.[30]

The related ideas that the species or essences predicated of ordinary

[30]An objection that might be raised here (as well as elsewhere) is that, since Aristotle often uses the terms 'ousia' and 'essence' almost interchangeably, the claims I make here cannot be correct. Here, I would remind the reader of the discussions of Section VII of Chapter 5. As I concluded there, Aristotle does sometimes use the terms as variants on each other. However, in a metaphysical theory in which the Z.6 thesis is dominant, this is clearly understandable. That thesis tells us that the primary *ousiai* are necessarily numerically one and the same as their essences (the fundamental essences). So the primary *ousiai* just *are* the fundamental essences. But we must remember that any usage that treats 'essence' and 'ousia' as interchangeable involves an abbreviation. 'Essence' is an incomplete expression. We need to specify just what any potential referent of the term is an essence of; when Aristotle uses the term as a variant on 'ousia', he is referring to the fundamental essences, the essences of the substantial forms that are their own *ousia* and essence, and not to the essences of the composite particulars whose *ousiai* (but not essences) those forms are.

objects are not their *ousia* and that their *ousia* is not something predicated of them are thus not just incidental features of the later theory of *ousia*. They are expressions of the most fundamental structural features of that theory inasmuch as they represent the distinction between what, given the theory, needs to be explained and the ontological materials in terms of which we formulate the requisite explanation. If we agree that this is the point Aristotle is attempting to make in the *Idion* Argument, then we have to agree that the argument does not merely establish that species do not constitute the *ousia* of their members. It has the more general consequence that nothing predicated essentially of ordinary objects can be their *ousia*. Although they do so in varying degrees of specificity, the universals predicated essentially of familiar particulars provide us with object concepts for those particulars; accordingly, they are part of the framework which, by the lights of the later theory, stands in need of explanation. Therefore, they cannot enter into that explanation. Since giving that explanation is specifying the *ousia* for the objects making up the framework to be explained, universals predicated essentially of those objects cannot be their *ousia*. Generic kinds cannot, then, be the *ousia* of ordinary particulars, nor can they be the *ousia* of the species to which those particulars belong. The metaphysical relations of essential predication tying substance-kinds to their logical inferiors are all relations within the framework a theory of *ousia* attempts to explain, so those relations cannot enter into that explanation.

## V

Sometimes we are told that the thesis Aristotle is concerned to defend in Z.13 is that no universal construed as numerically one thing can be the *ousia* of a plurality of different things (where those things are either particulars or universals).[31] On this interpretation, Aristotle is concerned to show that the unity of a universal is not numerical unity but a different kind of unity, unity in form; accordingly, he uses the argument of Z.13 as an occasion to show that universals (whose candidacy for status as *ousia* he never questions) could not function as the *ousia* of other things were they construed as things that are each "one in number."[32] The *idion* premise, it is claimed, formulates precisely this insight

---

[31]See the very clear account provided in Henry Telloh, "Aristotle's *Metaphysics* Z.13," *Canadian Journal of Philosophy* (1979), 77–89. See also his "The Universal in Aristotle," 73.

[32]The expression 'unity in form' translates the same Greek expression as 'unity in species'. I use the former translation here for two reasons: first, it is the terminology of commentators such as Telloh who argue for this interpretation; second, the claim that a

by telling us that when we have a plurality of distinct objects, were their *ousia* to be something that is numerically one thing, those objects would themselves all be numerically one with each other. The conclusion we are supposed to be driven to, then, is that universals have formal rather than numerical unity.

The distinction between being one in number and being one in form certainly is a distinction Aristotle likes to make, and there are contexts in which he formulates the *idion* premise explicitly in terms of unity in number. Indeed, in Z.16 (1040ª17–18), he formulates the premise in just this way. Furthermore, there are several passages in which Aristotle tells us that, were we to construe what functions as *ousia* as something that is one in number, we could never explain how there can be numerically different things with the same *ousia*. Intriguingly, in both B.4 (999ᵇ27–1000ª4) and M.10 (1086ᵇ23–31) the analogy he invokes in support of this claim is reminiscent of the example used in Z.17 to show what identifying the *ousia* of a thing involves. He focuses on the relationship between syllables and their constituent letters and tells us that, if we were to treat each of the common principles of things as numerically one thing, we could not account for the fact that there can be different tokens of a single letter type and so could never generate the various syllables out of the letters that are their principles. So the idea that the notion of numerical unity is critical in the *Idion* Argument certainly seems plausible.

But is it? Well, it depends on how we put the point. If we take Aristotle to be saying that there is something objectionable in speaking of a single form as one in number and that the only notion of unity that applies here is unity in form, then we must confront the fact that in B.4 (999ᵇ24–27) he expresses serious reservations about the strategy of attributing only unity in form to first principles. But there is a more basic difficulty with this interpretation. It is difficult to understand what Aristotle would be saying if he were to be making the contrast between unity in number and unity in form central in his account of universals. In the case of particulars, the contrast between unity in number and unity in form has a straightforward application. Socrates and Plato are one in form; they are both men. But they are numerically different men and, so, not one in number. It is not, however, clear what the force of applying this contrast in the case of a single universal is. What would we be saying if we were to insist that the form *man* is not one in number

---

form is one in species suggests that there is a further species besides that under which particular composites fall. The term we meet in Aristotle is 'one in *eidos*', which permits either translation. Aristotle himself, I think, uses the expression in both senses.

but only one in form? Being one form, one universal is just what being one in number consists in for *man*.[33] The proposal that we withhold the expression 'one in number' in the case of universals looks like nothing more than an arbitrary stipulation precluding certain ways of talking; the metaphysical implications of a stipulation of this kind cannot be of any deep significance.

The fact remains, however, that Aristotle frequently claims that one of Plato's mistakes was to treat each of his Forms as numerically one thing, so the suggestion that Aristotle's talk about numerical unity is a vehicle for pointing to a mistake we might fall into in our attempt to identify *ousia* may, nonetheless, be correct. The mistake is not, however, one of saying that *man*, for example, is numerically one form. Aristotle himself has to concede this. Something else must be at work here, and a clue to the nature of the mistake is provided by the fact that Aristotle likes to link the Platonic mistake about numerical unity with what appears to be a different mistake on Plato's part, that of construing Forms as things that are individuals subject to the "this something" schema.[34] Perhaps there are not two different mistakes here but one.

We have seen that, for Aristotle, reference to both numerical unity and the "this something" schema always has an eye toward sortal predications. To speak of something as one thing is to construe it as subject to a counting procedure, and counting presupposes a measure provided by the appropriate sortal universal. Likewise, the applicability of the "this something" schema hinges on the predicability of a substance-kind. It may be, then, that when Aristotle criticizes Plato for taking Form to be something numerically one, something subject to the "this something" schema, and something that is an individual, he is claiming that Plato went wrong in supposing that a Form such as *man* is countable by precisely the same sortal or count noun as the individuals whose *ousia* it is supposed to be. The mistake, then, would not be that of construing Forms as each numerically one thing, but of misunderstanding how the concept of numerical unity applies to them. Not content with the idea that each Form is numerically one in the sense of 'numerically one form' or 'numerically one universal', Plato wanted to under-

---

[33]One might suppose that *Metaphysics* I.1 (1052ª30–36) tells us otherwise, but I think we better understand Aristotle if we take the apparent suggestion that the universal is itself one in kind to be a rough and ready gesture to what grounds our application of the expression 'one in kind'. See n. 43 for more on this text.

[34]See 143ᵇ30, 169ª31–36, 178ᵇ38–179ª10, 999ᵇ34–1000ª1, 1003ª10, 1033ᵇ19–24, 1039ª23–24, 1040ᵇ16–32, 1060ᵇ20–23, 1086ª29–30, and 1089ᵇ28–30. In these passages, we repeatedly meet the terms *'kath hechaston'*, *'tode ti'*, and *'hen arithmo'*. The fact that Aristotle uses now one, now another of these terms as though they were mere variants on each other suggests that he is accusing Plato of a single mistake when he invokes the three terms.

stand the numerical unity of Forms in terms of precisely the same sortal concepts whose applicability to the relevant individuals Form (as the *ousia* of those individuals) serves to underwrite. So the Form *man* turns out to be one more man, and the consequence is that a Form is not just the *ousia* of the individuals from the associated plurality but another *ousia* in just the sense that those individuals are each an *ousia*.[35]

If we read this cluster of ideas into the notion of numerical unity in terms of which (in both B.4 and Z.16) Aristotle formulates the *idion* premise, then the Generalized *Idion* Argument has a narrow but (given the precedent of Plato) important aim: to show that it is impossible for a universal construed as numerically one thing to be the *ousia* of each object in the associated plurality. The aim of the Specialized *Idion* Argument is to show that universals so understood cannot even be a component in the *ousia* or essence of more than one object. The case would be precisely like that of the letters and the syllables. Construed as further individuals, further items for which the appropriate substitution instance of the schema 'this *K*' holds true, our candidates for status as *ousia* could not enter into the constitution of more than one object. As Aristotle puts it in Z.16, universals construed in these terms could not occupy several distinct and discontinuous regions of space at a given time. The Form *man*, after all, is just another man, and nothing we can identify as "this man" can be in more than one place simultaneously.

Construing the *Idion* Arguments in this way enables us to make sense of a number of otherwise rather obscure points. First, we can see how the recently mentioned claim from Z.16 that each of Plato's Forms is restricted, at any given time, to exemplification in just one region of space might be something other than the question-begging assertion it initially seems to be. Second, we can find added force in the dilemma of Z.14. If a generic Form is numerically one thing in the sense of being just one more plant or one more animal, then the idea that one and the same Form simultaneously exhibits incompatible differentiating features certainly is problematic; the only recourse open to the Platonist in the face of this difficulty would seem to be the multiplication of plants and animals, so that each differentiating modification has a different plant or animal for its subject. Third, if we suppose that Aristotle understands

---

[35]For texts that suggest this interpretation, see 1038ᵇ33 and 1053ᵇ16–21. The idea at work here entails but is not entailed by what is often called the self-predication assumption. Although it is not implausible to suppose that, in the case of some universals, Aristotle held to the self-predication assumption, he would reject out of hand the idea that universals are countable by all the same sortals that serve as the count measure for the associated individuals. The species is *man*, but it is not one more man or one man among the many men.

Plato's view as making the relevant mistake about numerical unity, then we can understand better his contention in Z.15 ($1040^a8-1040^b4$) that the attempt to define a Form is no different from the attempt to define one of the individuals whose *ousia* it is. After all, if the Form is just another man, then attempts to identify those features of it that are necessarily uniquely individuating would seem to be subject to precisely the same kind of threat of reduplication that we confront in our attempt to identify in purely general terms a set of properties that might serve to individuate your run-of-the-mill man. Fourth, understanding the *Idion* Argument in this light helps explain why Aristotle would have thought that the familiar problems associated with the Third Man are relevant to the Z.13 thesis.[36] If what he is attacking is the view that universals are to be viewed as numerically one thing in this problematic sense, then the Third Man argument is, indeed, relevant. To generate the familiar regress associated with that argument, we have to make the assumption that the universal serving as the *ousia* of a batch of particulars is subject to the same system of sortal predication ('one man', 'this man') as the particulars making up the batch. That assumption creates a new batch of relevantly similar entities, and, when conjoined with the idea that for any batch of relevantly similar objects there is some entity outside the batch that underwrites the similarity, the assumption forces us to appeal to some further entity (one that,by the problematic assumption, again turns out to be subject to the original system of sortal predication) to play the role of *ousia* for the entities making up the new batch.[37] Fifth, understanding the Z.13 thesis as this interpretation proposes, we can appreciate Aristotle's inclination to associate the thesis that no *ousia* can be present in an *ousia* with the view he is attacking in Z.13–16, and we can see how he might have thought that his own criticism of the former thesis does not call into question his own view that his forms are somehow in the individuals they constitute. What is problematic in that thesis is not the idea that the universals that are the *ousia* of a thing enter into its constitution. What is problematic is coupling this innocent (and inevitable) claim with the idea that universals are subject to precisely the same framework of sortal predication as the individuals whose *ousia* they are. What results is the bizarre view that

---

[36]See $1038^b30-1039^a2$. It is interesting to read Aristotle's early comments on the Third Man argument in *De Sophisticis Elenchis* 22 ($178^b38-179^a10$) with this interpretation in mind.

[37]See, once again, Owen, "The Platonism of Aristotle"; Woods, "Substance and Essence in Aristotle"; Code, "On the Origins of Some Aristotelian Theses about Predication"; and Frank Lewis, "Plato's Third Man Argument and the 'Platonism' of Aristotle," for more on the Third Man argument.

our man Socrates has in him not only another man but also another animal; so we have a man in a man and an animal in the first man as well as the second.[38] Finally, understanding Aristotle's aims in this way, we get a clearer sense of what he means when he speaks of a Platonic Form as something over and above the individuals whose *ousia* it is and as something that is separate; he means that a Form such as *man* is just one more man to be added to our inventory of individual men, an item that is individuated by precisely the same boundary-drawing universal that collects particulars; we understand as well why in Z.13 Aristotle slides from the idea that no universal can be the *ousia* of other things to the idea that no universal can be an *ousia*. What is problematic in the view he is criticizing is just the idea that the things that are the *ousia* of individuals are to be construed as *ousiai* in precisely the sense the individuals themselves are.

More generally, seeing these themes about numerical unity and individuality as central to the argument of Z.13–16 provides us with the resources for understanding Aristotle's own conception of the relationship between his account of universals and that of Plato's. The surprising upshot, I think, is that Aristotle would have seen his own view as more Platonistic than Plato's. What I mean is simply that Aristotle has no doubts about the reality of universals. Despite changing views about the priority relations tying particulars and universals, Aristotle repeatedly tells us, from his earliest works onward, that there is no escaping the fact that there is "one thing predicated of many."[39] As he sees it, this is not a merely linguistic or conceptual fact about us and the way we happen to talk or think. It is a fact about the world that there are things that are predicated of many, things that recur; the phenomenon of universality is a brute fact that cannot be reduced to any more basic phenomena. From Aristotle's perspective, however, the irreducibility of this phenomenon is not one Plato could accept. He could not come to terms with the idea that the ultimate explanatory principles include things that are categorically different from the particulars into whose explanation they enter; rather than accept this fundamental dichotomy between particular and universal, Plato had to interpret universals as further particulars. Aristotle states this diagnosis elegantly in B.2:

> The sense in which we say the Forms are both causes and self-dependent substances has been explained in our first remarks about them; while the theory presents difficulties in many ways, the most paradoxical thing of

[38]Perhaps this is the idea underlying 1038$^b$29–30.
[39]See, e.g., *Posterior Analytics* A.11 (77$^a$5–9), A.24 (85$^a$31–35 and 85$^b$17–21), and B.19 (100$^a$7–9).

all is the statement that there are certain things besides those in the material universe, and that these are the same as sensible things except that they are eternal while the latter are perishable. For they say there is a man-himself and a horse-itself and health-itself, with no further qualification—a procedure like that of the people who said there are gods, but in human form. For they are positing nothing but eternal men, nor are the Platonists making the Forms anything other than eternal sensible things. (997ª34–997ᵇ12; Ross translation)

VI

There are, then, several different views we can associate with the slogan that no universal is *ousia*. Just which Aristotle actually intended we cannot say with certainty. Perhaps he viewed the slogan as one with a variety of targets, so that the force of the slogan shifts in the varying contexts in which we meet it. Perhaps, even in Z.13–16, there is not a single, fixed view that Aristotle is attacking, but rather a family of related views that he sometimes distinguishes for separate treatment and sometimes lumps together for common criticism.

Although I think there is more than one view we can plausibly see Aristotle as attacking in this section of Z, I do not believe that we can read the text as having the consequence so often associated with Z.13 in the literature on the middle books, the view that there cannot be a single form for the different members of a single species. On this score, I part company with a large number of commentators who see in the Z.13 thesis and the arguments supporting it the critical textual evidence for attributing to the later Aristotle the doctrine that numerically distinct members of a single species each have a numerically distinct substantial form.[40] So let me close my discussion of Z.13–16 by indicating why I think the attribution of a doctrine of individual forms cannot be made.

Allegedly, the single most important piece of evidence for this reading is the fact that Aristotle interprets the unity operative in the *idion* premise of the argument from 1038ᵇ9–15 as numerical unity. Proponents of this interpretation refuse to see the premise's use of the notion of a universal as subject to any of the restrictions we discussed in Section II; they do not take the joint reference to *ousia* and essence in the premise as having the implications we discussed in Section IV; and they do not understand Aristotle's use of the notion of unity as having the specialized anti-Platonic force we discussed in the previous section. They insist that the *idion* premise means just what it initially seems to

[40]See n. 5 for references to proponents of this interpretation.

mean, that it is impossible for numerically distinct things to have numerically one thing as their *ousia*, and they draw the conclusion that Aristotle construed the form of an individual as something unique to it, as something "that cannot belong to another."[41]

Quite apart from questions of the overall consistency of the theory of Z and H, there are problems with interpreting the *idion* premise in this way. First, defenders of the individual-form interpretation must provide a filler for the expression 'numerically one thing'. Given Aristotle's theory, the only sortal that does the job here is the term 'form'; the defender of individual forms must hold that in saying that a given individual has numerically one form for its *ousia* he/she is using the expression in such a way that, if confronted with another individual from the same species, Aristotle would agree that we have two forms. The idea presumably would be that the *ousiai* of the two individuals are themselves one in form but two in number. But the contrast between formal and numerical unity is one Aristotle characteristically reserves for concrete particulars, the things that have forms.[42] Aristotle would agree that, while numerically distinct men, two individuals are one in form; but he would not extend this contrast to the case of form itself. Different forms can, in some cases, be generically one; the form associated with horses is generically one with that associated with cats. But the idea that numerically different forms might themselves be one in form is difficult to fathom. Being one in form with something else is having the same form as that other thing, which drives us to the conclusion (consistent with Aristotle's actual usage) that the notion of formal unity is not one that applies to forms that are numerically different.[43]

But, if the defender of individual forms can make sense of the kind of contrast between numerical and formal unity required by his/her interpretation, he/she must confront the fact that, when it is interpreted in terms of strict numerical unity, Aristotle rejects the *idion* premise. In B.4 (999[b]22), for example, Aristotle tells us that it is unreasonable to suppose that numerically different individuals from the same species have

---

[41]See, especially, Frede and Patzig, *Aristoteles "Metaphysik Z,"* vol. 2, 241ff.

[42]See, e.g., $\Delta$.6 (1016[b]32–1017[a]3).

[43]Passage 1052[a]30–36 is no comfort to one who holds that forms can be numerically different yet one in form, since Aristotle shows no inclination in that text to permit that kind of pairing of diversity and unity. Indeed, when we reflect on the fact that throughout the early chapters of Book I Aristotle is concerned to counter a Platonic conception of universals as things that are each numerically one thing in the problematic sense explored in the previous section, we can appreciate his unwillingness, in that context, to speak of universals themselves as numerically one. It may, in fact, be precisely the concern to distinguish his account of universals from Plato's that underlies the problematic suggestion that the universal is only one in kind. To my knowledge, he nowhere else says this.

numerically different things as their *ousia*. The context is one in which, I would argue, he has in mind the Platonic idea that the Forms are countable by sortals applicable to the individuals whose *ousia* they are; Aristotle is canvassing all the options open to someone who endorses the idea. He appeals to the letter/syllable argument to show that what the Platonist calls one thing cannot be parceled out among the different individuals in the requisite way, and he argues that the idea that each individual from a species has a numerically different *ousia* is equally untenable. It is interesting that he denies ($999^b25$–27) that the appeal to the idea of unity in kind or form makes the view any more tenable, for the view in question is precisely the kind of view that would result from introducing individual forms into the doctrine of Z and H. And Aristotle explicitly rejects the view.

Why does Aristotle find the idea of numerically distinct things as the *ousia* of the various individuals from a single species unreasonable? He does not tell us in the B.4 passage, but it is not difficult to see just what is wrong with the idea that there are different things serving as the *ousia* of the various individuals from a given species. *Ousia* explanations are inherently general. To identify the *ousia* of an object is to identify that which serves as "the cause of the being of the thing." But to be for an individual just is to be a member of its proper species, which means that we need a single account for all the members of a given species. There is a single species-predicate that identifies what being consists in for all the members of a kind, and it is because a single form is predicated of distinct parcels of matter of one and the same sort that each is the kind of thing it is. The conditions of existence are perfectly general here: we have "one thing common to many" or "one thing predicated of many." As Aristotle sees it, this situation requires an explanation that itself points to "one thing common to many" or "one thing predicated of many."

If we set aside the issue of the correct interpretation of the *idion* premise and simply focus on the view that there are numerically distinct forms for the various individuals of a given species, we must conclude that it is a view the Aristotle of Z and H could not have held. The idea that there are individual forms in a given species is subject to either of two quite different interpretations. Either the forms in question differ only quantitatively, or there are qualitative features that differentiate them from each other. The latter interpretation would read a doctrine of individual essences into the middle books, so that Aristotle would hold the kind of view endorsed by Leibniz or, perhaps, Scotus.[44] But the idea that the substantial form associated with a given individual is essen-

---

[44]This seems to be the view of Terence Irwin, *Aristotle's First Principles*, 250ff.

tially different from that of another individual from the same species runs afoul of Aristotle's claim that individuals are indefinable. Form is essence, and essences are the things expressed by correct definitions, so if the forms associated with the various members of a species are qualitatively distinct there ought to be a definition for each member of the species. Aristotle, of course, insists ($1036^a2-7$, $28-29$) that there is definition only of the universal; as we have seen, Z.15 attempts to show why this is so. Aristotle gives us two reasons for the claim that no individual can be defined. A definition must express a necessary truth, so there cannot be definitions for merely transitory beings like ourselves; let the individual in question cease to exist, and the proposed definition is false ($1039^b20-1040^a7$). But even individuals whose nonexistence is impossible cannot be defined. As Aristotle sees it, what Leibniz later called the identity of indiscernibles does not hold true for individuals. No matter how extensive the set of general properties one identifies in one's attempt to provide an individuating characterization of an individual, it is always possible that there be some numerically distinct individual exemplifying all and only those properties ($1040^a8-1040^b4$). Both arguments seem to apply to the case of individual forms. Obviously, the second does; but so does the first, since it is implausible to suppose that a form that is necessarily unique to a given transitory individual has a career any more permanent than the individual in question.[45]

In any case, no defender of individual forms is likely to deny that the different forms associated with a given species agree in many of their features, that those forms have certain characteristics in common. Unfortunately, it is difficult to see how anyone who finds in the Generalized *Idion* Argument grounds for supposing that Aristotle endorsed a doctrine of qualitatively different individual forms can attribute to him

[45]Aristotle also holds to the more general view that all knowledge (including both definition and demonstration) is of the universal. Some commentators, however, see *Metaphysics* M.10 (especially $1087^a10ff.$) as evidence that the mature Aristotle wants to make particulars the objects of knowledge, and they attribute this allegedly new view to what they take to be the central doctrine of Z and H—that substantial forms are particulars. See, e.g., Charlotte Witt, *Substance and Essence in Aristotle*, 163–175, and Michael Frede and Gunther Patzig, *Aristoteles "Metaphysik Z,"* vol. 1, 54–56. The fact is, however, that Z.15 ($1039^b27ff.$) shows that the Aristotle of the middle books still subscribes to the old view. Furthermore, the focus of M.10 is not the idea that the principles and *ousiai* are universals, but rather that, while being universals, they are each numerically one (in the objectionable Platonic sense) and separate. After rejecting the view that the principles and *ousiai* have the ontological status Plato attributed to them, Aristotle has to confront the fact that any apprehension we might have of universals is derived from our apprehension of and (hopefully) applicable to the particulars we meet in our day-to-day commerce with the world. It is this fact that the distinction between potential and actual knowledge is meant to accommodate; and although the terminology of M.10 may be new, problems surrounding this dialectic hardly appear for the first time in M.10. See, e.g., *Posterior Analytics* B.19, *De Anima* Γ.6–7, and *Metaphysics* A.1.

the view that those forms share any of their features. The Generalized *Idion* Argument, we have to recall, is followed by the Specialized *Idion* Argument; we must construe whatever assumptions about unity and diversity we read into the Generalized *Idion* Argument as operative in the Specialized *Idion* Argument as well. After all, the latter argument shows that, in whatever sense it is impossible for universals to constitute the complete *ousia* and essence of a plurality of individuals, it is impossible for a universal to constitute part of the *ousia* and essence of that plurality. So, if the Generalized *Idion* Argument has the consequence that no two objects can have numerically one thing as their *ousia*, the Specialized *Idion* Argument has the consequence that no two objects can have in common even a part of their *ousia*. But, then, the proponent of the view that the individual forms associated with a given species differ qualitatively seems forced to attribute to Aristotle the view that the forms associated with a given species are radically different, that they do not share any of the features by which they are intelligible. The suggestion that Aristotle held that kind of view is simply outrageous.

The idea that the individual forms associated with a given species differ only quantitatively does not fare much better. As we have seen, the Z.6 Identity Thesis tells us that the things a theory construes as the primary *ousiai* have to be numerically one and the same with their essence. A consequence of this thesis is that a theory (such as that found in the *Categories*) that identifies a plurality of distinct objects with one and the same essence as candidates for the title 'primary reality' must be wrong—and a theory that tells us that numerically distinct forms qualitatively or essentially the same are the primary *ousiai* is a theory of just that sort.

Quite apart from conformity to the Z.6 thesis, an interpretation that attributes to Aristotle a theory construing numerically distinct yet essentially identical forms as the *ousia* of the various individuals of a species imputes to him a really bizarre piece of metaphysics. It suggests that, confronted with the question of how it is possible for a plurality of concrete individuals to be things of a single kind, Aristotle appeals to further individuals (now, presumably, abstract rather than concrete) and argues that our original individuals are things of a single kind because each has within it a constituent that is numerically different but one in kind with the counterpart constituents of the other individuals. Accordingly, he answers the original question by an account that prompts precisely the same sort of question, and the suggestion that we have reached the primary *ousiai* is likely to convince no one. It is clear that Aristotle must now appeal to the universal form or essence those individual forms all share if he is to forestall the kind of question that originally led him on the search after *ousia*, so the appeal to individual forms was otiose. Unfortunately, given its reading of Z.13, this interpretation precludes Aristotle from making the kind of theoretical use of the notion of general or universal form that the interpretation cannot avoid demanding of him.

If one approaches Aristotle from the perspective endorsed by defenders of individual forms, it is easy to be sympathetic with those who claim that the doctrine of Z and H is inconsistent. But I hope I have shown that we need not (indeed, cannot) read Z.13 in the way proponents of this interpretation suggest. It is easy enough to find any number of different claims that, consistently with the rest of Z and H, we can see Aristotle as attacking under the slogan 'no universal is *ousia*', and the text of Z.13 taken by itself does not even admit a reading that has the consequence that only individual forms can be the *ousia* of particular concrete objects.

We also have Aristotle's own testimony on this point. He tells us quite explicitly that there is one form for a given species:

> But when we have the whole thing, the "such" that is form in "these" flesh and bones, then we have Callias and Socrates. And they are different because of their matter (for that is different); but they are the same in their form; for the form is indivisible. (1034ᵃ5–8)

Although commentators tell us otherwise, this passage provides as secure a basis as we could hope to find for attributing to Aristotle the view that there is just one form across the species.[46] The form has

---

[46]William Charlton, "Aristotle and the Principle of Individuation," takes the passage to provide an account of our ability to distinguish cospecific individuals. As Charlton interprets Aristotle, it is by reference to the qualitative features of objects that have their source in matter that we manage to tell one from the other. For a critique of Charlton, see S. Marc Cohen, "Aristotle and Individuation," *Canadian Journal of Philosophy* (1984), supp. vol. 10, 41–65. I find myself agreeing with Cohen. Charlotte Witt takes the passage to explain how things with numerically different yet qualitatively indistinguishable forms differ qualitatively; see her *Substance and Essence in Aristotle*, 176–177. Frede and Patzig likewise reject the traditional reading of this passage; see *Aristoteles "Metaphysik Z,"* vol. 2, 146–148. They concede that Aristotle speaks "as if objects of a species shared the same *eidos*" and that he "expresses himself in a way that makes us suspect that we are dealing with numerically one and the same form"; but they claim that he does so "while obviously intending to insist that each one of these objects has an individual *eidos*" (p. 147). To support what they take to be so obvious, they point to the talk of generation at 1034ᵃ4 and support the idea that this talk implies individual forms by reference to Z.7 (1032ᵃ24–25) and Λ.5 (1071ᵃ27–29). They deny that '*tauto de to eidei*' (at 1034ᵃ8) implies individual forms, claiming that it is such a traditional and common (p. 147) piece of terminology that its use is neutral as between general and particular forms. They deny that 1034ᵃ7–8 implies that "objects of a species are distinguished *only* by their matter" (p. 147), and they interpret '*atomon gar to eidos*' to mean only that the individuality of a form can be expressed by its formula "since the formula used to designate the form of a thing as such remains the same for all the objects of a species" (p. 148). The Z.7 passage, however, is more naturally read as

different parcels of matter as its metaphysical subjects, and because those parcels of matter are different we have at one and the same time the numerically distinct predicative complexes that are Callias and Socrates. But those complexes are constituted by a single predicate, and that is not a fact about how we happen to talk or think. It is a brute fact about the world that one thing can be metaphysically predicated of many.

As straightforward as it is, we need not rely on this passage from Z.8 taken by itself. In Z.16 (1040ᵇ25–26), for example, after arguing that Plato's conception of universals as "thises," each numerically one in precisely the way that individuals are numerically one, has the consequence that no universal could be present in more than one place at a given time, Aristotle explicitly says that universals are found in more than one region of space at one and the same time. So, from Aristotle's perspective, the idea that there are things that simultaneously are predicative constituents of numerically distinct objects in distinct regions of space is not just nonproblematic; it is the kind of truism we appeal to in adjudicating between opposing accounts of universals.

The idea that it is in virtue of taking different parcels of matter as its metaphysical subjects that a single form can constitute the numerically distinct predictive complexes that are Socrates and Callias is likewise one that we meet in places other than Z.8. As early as B.4, the view is suggested. After denying that the *ousiai* of objects from a given kind are "many and different," Aristotle implies (999ᵇ23–24) that the correct account has the individuals whose *ousia* is the same differing in their matter. In Δ.6 (1016ᵇ32–33), where he explains how the expressions 'one in number', 'one in form/species', and 'one in genus' apply to concrete individuals, Aristotle tells us that things are one in number whose matter is one. In Δ.9 (1018ᵃ6–7), we meet with the claim that things whose matter is one are the same.[47]

It might be thought that the defender of individual or particular forms could accommodate the overwhelming textual evidence that matter is the principle of numerical plurality or diversity in a given species by

---

implying a doctrine of general forms; see especially 1032ᵃ25. And the Λ.5 passage permits a reading that does not imply individual forms. Further, it would be surprising were Aristotle, who has been using '*eidos*' throughout Z.7 and 8 to refer to form, to alter his usage without explanation and to employ '*eidos*' to refer to the species. Finally, the use of '*toionde*' and '*taisde*' at 1034ᵃ6 so clearly points back to the earlier Z.8 use of the "this"/ "such" distinction to express the idea that a form is something *general* that is predicated of a *particular* parcel of matter that it would be difficult to interpret Aristotle as saying anything other than what the traditional reading has him say. The contrast here is clearly that between constituents that are peculiar or proprietary and constituents that are common, and the force of the passage just is that matter is the *principium individuationis*.

[47]See also *Metaphysics* I.9 (1058ᵇ5–10) and the argument to show that there is a single universe in *De Caelo* A.9 (277ᵇ26–279ᵇ4).

claiming that matter diversifies not the cospecific individuals themselves but rather the cospecific forms associated with each. The idea would presumably be that it is because of its association with different parcels of matter that a single specific form is so multiplied that there are numerically different forms for the various individuals in the species.[48] Apart from the fact that this sort of view is nowhere suggested by the text, the idea that the diversification or multiplication of a given form has to await its predication of distinct parcels of matter precludes interpreting the numerically distinct individual forms resulting from that predication as the *ousia* of the individuals whose form they are. It is the form that is predicated of a parcel of matter that is the cause of the being of the composite particular; if individual forms presuppose the prior predication of a single form of the relevant parcels of matter, they can hardly play the required causal role. Since, on this view, it is the single prediversified form that must be construed as the *ousia* of the various members of a species, the account fails to avoid the alleged inconsistency involved in construing universals as *ousia* and saddles our ontology with a whole host of entities playing no theoretical role at all.

But if a doctrine of general forms is so naturally associated with the theory of Z and H, why have commentators read Z.13 in a way that calls this attribution into question? Well, there are texts which, if one takes this deviant reading of Z.13, might seem to support the idea that there are individual forms. In earlier chapters, we have seen some of these texts. We have already discussed the passage at the end of Z.6 in which Aristotle alludes to "the question whether Socrates and to be Socrates are the same" (1032[a]8), and we have seen that there is little in this allusion that would support a doctrine of individual forms. A passage that is sometimes linked with the Z.6 comment is the claim in Δ.18 that "Callias is *kath hauto* Callias and what it is to be Callias" (1022[a]26–27). Since the claim is made to illustrate the idea that the essence of a thing belongs to it *kath hauto*, the text might be read as supporting the idea that there is some essence that is unique to Callias. And since form is essence, the idea that it is the individual form that Aristotle has in mind might seem reasonable.[49] But the passage hardly requires this inter-

---

[48]Edwin Hartman says things that suggest he holds to this sort of account; see "Aristotle on the Identity of Substance and Essence," 552–553. See also Jennifer Whiting, "Form and Individuation in Aristotle," 3. Michael Frede and Charlotte Witt, on the other hand, take the individual forms of cospecific individuals to be diversified of and by themselves; see Frede, "Substance in Aristotle's *Metaphysics*," in *Essays in Ancient Philosophy*, 78, and Witt, *Substance and Essence in Aristotle*, 177–179. Obviously, their view is not subject to the difficulty I outline here.

[49]Henry Telloh, "The Universal in Aristotle," 72, and Michael V. Wedin, "Singular Statements and Essentialism in Aristotle," 81, both take 1022[a]26–27 to support a doctrine of individual forms.

pretation. Indeed, it is far more plausible to suppose that, when Aristotle speaks of the what it is to be for Callias, he has in mind the species *man*. After all, what it is to be for Callias is to be a man. Given the fact that in the Δ.18 catalogue of uses of the expression '*kath hauto*' we have no other entry covering the predication of a species of its members, we have no choice but to interpret the claim in this way.

Again, one might point to Aristotle's willingness to ask whether proper names from the category of *ousia* are homonymous in just the way general substance terms are as an indication that he held that there are individual forms that are at least candidate referents for a proper name in what we might call its pure as opposed to mixed sense.[50] But the passages in which the issue is raised (see 1037ª5–7) show no temptation on Aristotle's part to take this extension of the homonymy doctrine seriously. Indeed, it is pretty clear that when he mentions the extension he has in mind Plato's view that identifies the person with his/her soul. Had he known of the possibility of distinguishing the mixed and pure senses of substance words, Plato would certainly have been tempted by the idea that the name 'Socrates' is being used homonymously in "Socrates is thinking of the Acropolis" and "Socrates weighs 195 pounds," but Aristotle would have insisted that the Socrates who is thinking of the Acropolis is precisely the same metaphysical subject who has a propensity to being overweight.[51]

A related argument for particular forms claims that Aristotle construes forms as metaphysical subjects and insists that only individual forms can function as metaphysical subjects.[52] The evidence, however, that Aristotle took forms to be subjects at all is scant. In Z.3 (1028ᵇ36–1029ª7), he mentions form in connection with the subject criterion, but the point there is not that form is itself a metaphysical subject. The idea is the more innocent one that, against the background of the hylomorphic analysis, the subject criterion puts us in contact with contexts that include not just the familiar particulars of the *Categories* but their matter and form as well. In H.1 (1042ᵇ29), Aristotle again lists form under the heading provided by the concept of a subject,[53] but he is not thereby

---

[50]Wedin, "Singular Statements and Essentialism in Aristotle," interprets the proposed extension of the homonymy thesis to have this implication.

[51]See, e.g., *De Anima* B.2 (414ª4–18).

[52]See Michael Frede, "Substance in Aristotle's *Metaphysics*," *Essays in Ancient Philosophy*, 74–75; Daniel Graham, *Aristotle's Two Systems*, 233–234; Terence Irwin, *Aristotle's First Principles*, 206ff. and 252ff.; Charlotte Witt, *Substance and Essence in Aristotle*, 159–160; and Michael Frede and Gunther Patzig, *Aristoteles "Metaphysik Z,"* vol. 1, 37–38 and 52, and vol. 2, 37–40. It is not merely those who attribute a doctrine of individual forms to Aristotle who have taken the text to imply that form is a subject; see, e.g., Sheldon Cohen, "Aristotle's Doctrine of the Material Substrate," 188–189.

[53]Terence Irwin, *Aristotle's First Principles*, 211, takes Aristotle to be referring to form at

registering his endorsement of any novel metaphysical insight. The remark is part of a summary of the results of Z, one that points back to the discussion in Z.3 and should be understood in the theoretically noncommittal terms of that discussion. Finally, there is what I have called the Subject Argument of Z.13 itself, which runs as follows:

> Furthermore, *ousia* is that which is said of no subject; but the universal is always said of some subject. (1038$^b$15–16)

But this brief text hardly constitutes strong evidence that Aristotle believed in individual forms. First, he never claims that what in the first clause he refers to as *ousia* is form, whether construed generally or individually. Second, Aristotle himself does not necessarily endorse all the arguments outlined in Z.13; they are presented as considerations that cumulatively support the *apparent* truth of the claim that no universal is *ousia* (1038$^b$8–9). Third, in the light of the difficulties Z.3 points to, our own confidence in any argument that relies on the subject criterion should be guarded.

The fact is that, when Aristotle turns to the business of identifying the things that function as primitive or basic metaphysical subjects, he invariably lists just two: composite *ousiai*, which are subjects for their accidents, and matter, which functions as subject for its substantial form. Form, whether construed as general or particular, never appears in this inventory of basic metaphysical subjects.[54] At best, form's status as subject would be derived. The most we can say here is that form is a subject in the sense that it is that in virtue of which composite *ousiai* are subjects.[55] This derived sense of 'subject' would not, of course, require particular forms. Still, as far as I can determine, there is little evidence to support the claim that Aristotle is inclined to invoke even this derivative notion of subject in connection with form.

We have already seen the quite different idea that a doctrine of individual forms follows from Aristotle's comment that forms "are and

---

1038$^b$5–6. The contrast between essence and subject in the preceding line, however, makes this reading of '*tode ti*' highly problematic, and 1049$^a$27ff. decisively tells against it. In the latter passage, Aristotle repeats the distinction of 1038$^b$5–6 and makes it clear (by the use of '*soma kai psuche*') that he has in mind the composite when he speaks of the subject that is a *tode ti*.

[54]Z.3 (1029$^a$23–24), Z.13 (1038$^b$5–6), and Θ.7 (1049$^a$27–36). So, in two of the contexts (Z.3 and Z.13) where defenders of individual forms would have Aristotle construe form as a subject, he explicitly excludes it from his official list of things that are subjects.

[55]Frank Lewis suggests this sort of account in "Substance and Predication" (unpublished manuscript), chap. 13. Although Lewis defends the view that forms are universals, he is motivated to delineate a sense in which forms are subjects by the belief, which he shares with defenders of individual forms, that 1038$^b$15–16 expresses genuine and significant Aristotelian doctrine about form.

are not" without themselves coming into being or passing away. As we noted, that passage has a perfectly innocent reading; it cannot, in any case, be read in terms of individual forms without carrying the implication that, contrary to what Aristotle explicitly tells us, substantial forms do come to be and pass away.

Commentators sometimes point to the claim that form is subject to the "this something" schema as additional evidence for the attribution of individual forms to Aristotle.[56] The idea presumably is that there must be a single sense in which both the form and the concrete particular can be said to be a "this something" and that the concept of individuality or particularity is what gives us that sense; hence, individual forms. But Aristotle denies that form is a "this something" in just the way an individual member of the associated species is, and there is no evidence that Aristotle takes it to be an a priori constraint on his theory that form and individual be either separable or subject to the "this something" epithet in the same way. Indeed, the very structure of his theory as involving different levels of substance discourse suggests that they should not.[57]

Finally, a passage from $\Lambda.5$ is often cited as evidence of a doctrine of individual forms.[58] Aristotle tells us there that the causal factors incorporated in our account of different individuals from the same species must be one in kind but different in number; then he says:

> Your matter and form and moving cause are different from mine, but they are the same in their universal formula. (1071a28–29)

Initially this passage seems to be solid evidence that the Aristotle of $\Lambda$ holds to a doctrine of individual form; but that does not show that the Aristotle of Z and H does. There is good evidence that the two texts were written in different periods, and, given the difficulty of reading Z and H except in terms of a theory of general forms, any evidence we might have that the author of $\Lambda$ holds to individual forms is evidence

[56]See, e.g., Lloyd, *Form and Universal in Aristotle*, 38–39, and Frede, "Substance in Aristotle's *Metaphysics*," in *Essays in Ancient Philosophy*, 77–78.

[57]Frede and Patzig point to 1037a6–7 from Z.11 as evidence that Aristotle believed in individual forms; see *Aristoteles "Metaphysik Z*," vol. 1, 53. Aristotle tells us that *man* and *animal* are each compounds of form and matter treated universally, and Frede and Patzig argue that one cannot treat forms universally unless they are particulars. But for Aristotle it is the *to ex amphoin* that is treated universally. Certainly this is a natural way to put things if it is only the matter that has to be generalized, and the agnosticism Aristotle expresses in the very next sentence (1037a7–10) about the extension of the homonymy doctrine to the proper names of substances is certainly not what we would expect from a philosopher who is firmly under the conviction that substantial forms are particulars.

[58]See, e.g., Lloyd, *Form and Universal in Aristotle*, 6; Irwin, *Aristotle's First Principles*, 253; and Frede and Patzig, *Aristoteles "Metaphysik Z*," vol. 1, 52.

that Aristotle changed his mind on this point.[59] But the Λ passage need not be read as entailing that your substantial form and mine are numerically different. Aristotle's point is that the factors that play a causal role in your case must, taken as a whole, be different from the factors that play a causal role in my case. Aristotle lists three such factors. Provided that at least one factor differs in the two cases, we have the required diversity. And the fact is that your matter differs from mine. Just as we can be siblings with the same parents, so we can have the same form.[60]

It is not just particular texts that have led commentators to attribute a doctrine of individual forms to Aristotle. There is as well a general philosophical theme, one substantiated by reference to no particular text, that we are told (by such authors as Frede and Hartman) is central to Aristotle's conception of *ousia* and requires that each individual have its own form.[61] On this view, Aristotle believes that something must guarantee the identity of a concrete thing as the thing that it is. The matter that comes and goes over the career of a concrete individual does not provide the relevant principle of identity, so the form has to provide it. But a form common to all the members of a species does not give us a notion of identity over time for numerically different particulars.[62] Each must have its own principle of identity, one that makes each individual a distinct particular with a career and history of its own. So forms are individuals.

This line of thought brings together a host of different issues. Certainly, its proponents are right in denying that the numerical identity of the matter constituting a concrete object provides us with the kind of secure guarantor of identity over time they demand of Aristotle's theory; and when Aristotle insists that matter is a principle of individuation he is not suggesting that it ensures individual identity over time. Matter individuates only in the sense that at any given time the substantial form associated with a given species has, in the case of each individual in the species, a different parcel of matter as its metaphysical subject. So

[59]Jonathan Lear argues this point in *Aristotle: The Desire to Understand*, 275.

[60]For a different (but compatible) interpretation of the Λ.5 requirement on individuality, see Lesher, "Aristotle on Form, Substance, and Universals," 175.

[61]See Frede, "Substance in Aristotle's *Metaphysics*" and "Individuals in Aristotle," in *Essays in Ancient Philosophy*, and Hartman, *Substance, Body, and Soul* and "Aristotle on the Identity of Substance and Essence." I suspect that Terence Irwin is motivated by similar considerations; see *Aristotle's First Principles*, 252ff. See also Frede and Patzig, *Aristoteles "Metaphysik Z,"* vol. 1, 45. But not all defenders of individual forms agree that issues bearing on numerical unity over time are relevant to this debate; see, e.g., Witt, *Substance and Essence in Aristotle*, 144.

[62]In "Transtemporal Stability in Aristotlelian Substances, " Montgomery Furth suggests that identity of form (where this is interpreted as a general form) is a sufficient condition for numerical identity over time. In his comments on Furth's paper, "What Is It to Be an Individual?" *Journal of Philosophy* (1975), 647–648, Alan Code points to the difficulties surrounding this suggestion.

matter provides us with a principle of numerical plurality at a time. But the matter that makes up an individual and serves as subject for the form can be replaced. It can even happen that no portion of the matter that makes up an individual at one point in its career is identical with any portion of the matter that makes up that same individual at a later point in its career, and there is good reason to suppose that Aristotle appreciates this fact.[63] This is not to say that Aristotle is either a Heraclitean about identity over time or a mere conventionalist who takes questions of numerical identity to be settled by the considered judgments of the community at large. He believes that the matter making up an individual is replaced gradually and in an orderly fashion, and he believes that in the case of any individual it is possible to trace the matter that in its case serves as metaphysical subject of the form continuously through space and time. He does not, however, believe that the identity of a concrete particular over its career requires the persistence of a constituent that belongs uniquely to that particular. There is a single form that is, throughout the career of the individual, predicated of the continuous stream of matter that over time makes up the individual, but that form is common to all the members of the species. If we are not satisfied with the kind of continuity of matter Aristotle's account gives us and demand that each concrete particular incorporate a constituent unique or peculiar to it whose identity consists in something more than the possibility of tracing a continuous path through space and time, then Aristotle's response is that we are asking for more than the concept of an individual concrete thing can give us.[64] After all, there are no individual essences.[65]

[63]See *De Generatione et Corruptione* A.5 (321$^b$24ff.) and Hartman's discussion of the passage in "Aristotle on the Identity of Substance and Essence."

[64]One seriously misunderstands Aristotle's theory of the person if one argues that individual souls are required to ensure personal identity. See Code's discussion of this point in the last section of "Aristotle on Essence and Accident."

[65]Although Montgomery Furth has a firm grasp of the idea that all the members of a species share the same essence, his attempt to display the hylomorphic career of an individual over time suggests that, for any time $t$, any composite substance $s$, and any matter $m$ such that $s$ is made up of $m$ at $t$, it is a necessary truth that if $s$ exists at $t$ then $s$ is made up of $m$ and only $m$ at $t$; see *Substance, Form, and Psyche*, 279–284, especially the diagram on p. 283 which serves to explicate the symbol '7', a name for Socrates. That diagram strongly suggests what is false, that only at the cost of perishing or becoming someone else could Socrates have a material constitution different (even by a single cell) from that which he in fact had. This suggestion is not just false; it fails to capture Aristotle's views on these issues. Aristotle denies that there are any haecceities (features or clusters of features such that they are exhibited necessarily and necessarily uniquely by a particular composite *ousia*).

# CHAPTER 7

# The Completed Hierarchy of Essences and Two Problems

I

Before we began characterizing the main contours of the later theory of *ousia*, we found Aristotle suggesting that any theory attempting to isolate the primary *ousiai* and to delineate the system of priorities and dependencies in virtue of which its favored candidates play that role can be displayed as a theory of essences. The connecting link between the two enterprises is the familiar idea that there is no such thing as just existing or being, that the to be of a thing consists in its being *what* it is. Accordingly, the age-old enterprise of identifying the principles of being or the primary *ousiai* just is the enterprise of specifying the priorities and dependencies in virtue of which things are what they are or have the essences that they do. So a theory of *ousia* must be a theory of essence, and the system of priorities and dependencies it isolates must be something that can be expressed in terms of the kind of hierarchical framework or structure Aristotle proposes in Z.4–6. As he envisions it, that structure consists of a series of levels such that every essence occupies one and only one level in the hierarchy. At the basic or foundational level, there are essences that can be identified without reference to any other essences, and this requirement on the definitions appropriate in their case is just the reflection of the requirement that basic essences should presuppose or depend on no prior essences. These are the fundamental essences, and essences other than the fundamental essences occupy that lowest level in the hierarchy such that there is no essence at that level or any higher level which, in the relevant way, they presuppose or are identifiability-dependent on.

The fundamental essences are the essences of things that are (a) primary (things whose being what they are serves to explain why everything else is what it is) and (b) *kath hauta legomena* (things whose being what they are depends on nothing else), so they are the essences of the primary *ousiai*. In the case of a primary *ousia*, there can be no gap between an object and what it is, so the primary *ousiai* are necessarily one and the same with the things that are their essences. According to the theory outlined in the middle books, substantial forms are the primary *ousiai* and fundamental essences. Every substantial form is separable in formula or definition, so every substantial form is a *kath hauto legomenon*. And, since everything that is not a substantial form has for its *ousia* either a substantial form or something whose being what it is is ultimately analyzable in terms of the fact that some substantial form is the *ousia* of something else, substantial forms are the primary beings.

These fundamental essences are "suches" rather than "thises." They play their causal role as things predicated of matter, and they are predicated of matter only accidentally. Their being so predicated gives rise to entities of a new level of ontological complexity, for, as we have seen, substantial forms can be viewed as functions, functions that take as their arguments appropriate parcels of matter and have as their values particulars falling under substance-kinds. They are, as we put it, *tode ti*–forming functions. The essences of these new entities constitute the second level in our hierarchy. In dealing with this level, we might want to provide a fine-grained delineation of the structure and insist that the complications introduced by the physicochemical analysis of matter of various levels of complexity be reflected in the hierarchical ordering of essences. The fact is, however, that apart from occasional reminders that it is proximate matter that serves as the subject for a given substantial form, the Aristotle of Z and H tends to ignore these complications and to focus instead on the contrast between the case of familiar particulars (the primary realities of the *Categories*) and the case of their substantial forms. For the moment, let us follow Aristotle in this simplifying procedure.

We have, then, the essences of familiar particulars, the essences expressed by the definitions of their proper species. These are derivative essences. Their definitions, we have seen, must make reference to both the essence that is the appropriate form and the kind of matter that is its proximate subject. But if our definition of a substance-kind is properly to reflect the what it is to be for things of that kind, it must make reference to the ineliminable predicative nexus tying a form to its matter. This is so because the ordinary objects that belong to substance-species are things that come to be and pass away and things whose being what they are in between just consists in the fact that the appropriate form is predicate for the matter out of which they are composed; this fact must be written into their essences.

Unlike substantial forms, the essences we identify by definitions of this sort exhibit the distinctive features of sortal universals. Whereas the fundamental essences lack a built-in principle of individuation and are the forms of numerically distinct objects only because they are predicated of numerically distinct parcels of matter, the kinds under which composite particulars fall provide us with concepts of things, each of which is a particular instance of the kind distinct from other instances of that kind. Its members are subject to the "this something" and "one in number" schemata. But, since kinds are by nature things that can be essences of distinct objects, no object belonging to a kind can be one and the same with its essence. The kind or essence is, however, predicated *kath hauto* or essentially of its members; but the predicative tie is one that is subject to ontological analysis. The predication linking a substance-kind with one of its members is always analyzable in terms of the corresponding form-predication, and that predication holds only accidentally. Although the kind is the essence of its members, it is the matter and form that enter into the relevant form-predications that constitute their *ousia*; the form, of course, is their primary *ousia*. But, while the form is their primary *ousia*, it is an essence belonging to a level of ontological analysis at one remove from the familiar particulars whose being it serves to explain, and so it is not predicated of them.

The next level in the hierarchy of essences is constituted by the essences of accidents; here again, we may wish to provide a more fine-grained account to reflect the fact that essences of this level depend in more and less direct ways on essences of the second level.[1] Except for occasional gestures, however, the middle books have little to say about these essences after Z.5. But it is clear that, to the extent that Aristotle is willing to attribute a notion of essence to accidents, it is the notion of a derivative essence. To identify an accident, we must identify the kind of *ousia* that it is, in the end, the accident of. But, we have seen, the relationship between the essence of an accident and the essence of the substance-kind that is its proper subject is not easily pinned down. As we put it in our discussion of Z.5, in attempting to define an accident we never seem to get it just right. Either we fail to identify the kind of *ousia*

---

[1] I am thinking here of facts of the sort we noted earlier where, for example, the essence of a color is dependent on that of a surface, which, in turn is dependent on that of body.

on which the accident depends and we say too little, or we make the requisite identification and end up saying too much. So accidents have what I call defective essences, and this fact underlies Aristotle's caution in invoking the term 'essence' here. He insists, however, that if we are willing to speak of essence in this case we must construe the essence and the accident whose essence it is as one and the same. If we have defective essences, it is because the accidents whose essences they are are themselves defective entities; there just is nothing stable or determinate, nothing "substantial," that counts as what they are. At this third level in the hierarchy, then, we have essences and things that are not just derivative or parasitic but defective as well.

Since they are forms, accidents are "suches" or predicates whose metaphysical subjects are ordinary particulars falling under substance-kinds; they are predicated of these *ousiai* only accidentally. Like substantial forms, accidents can be viewed as functions. They take as their arguments familiar particulars, and they have as their values things like a sunburned man, a tired horse, and a large cow, things we have called complexes; with their emergence, we have the possibility of a new level of essence in the hierarchy.


II


When we delineate the main contours of Aristotle's later theory of *ousia* in terms of the idea of a hierarchy of essences, several questions emerge. I conclude my discussion of Z and H by focusing on two of these questions. The first bears on the place that matter occupies in the hierarchy; although doctrines from Θ are relevant to this issue, it is a question Aristotle never explicitly addresses in the middle books. The second stems from the derivative status accorded the essences of familiar particulars in the hierarchy; here we have a cluster of problems at the back of Aristotle's mind throughout Z and H and center stage in the concluding chapters of H.

We can get at the first problem by noting a gap in my articulation of the hierarchical structure, a gap I hastily and not very artfully covered over with the remark that, since the Aristotle of Z and H tends to ignore the complications resulting from his views about the various levels of analysis to which matter is susceptible, we can follow him in this simplifying procedure. This tendency conceals an important difficulty for the theory of the middle books. The difficulty surfaces when we attempt to provide for this truncated version of Aristotle's hierarchy the fine-grained analysis that properly displays the ontological structure of the proximate matter for the substantial form of an ordinary particular. So let us try to do this.

We have our man, George Bush, and his essence, that of the kind *man*. That essence presupposes the fundamental essence that is the human soul, but it also presupposes the essence or essences of the matter of which the human soul is predicated. Let us continue to suppose that this is the familiar pack of flesh and bones. The essences of these things, then, occupies a level intervening the basic level occupied by substantial forms and the level occupied by the essences corresponding to our familiar substance concepts, such things as the kind *man*. Since on Aristotle's physicochemical theory the parcel of flesh and the pack of bones are the kinds of stuff or thing they are, have the essences they do, only because some form is predicated of some parcel of matter of a more elementary kind, a new level of essence emerges, one intermediary between the fundamental level and that occupied by the essence of flesh and the essence of bones. Similarly, new levels of essence continue to emerge as Aristotle's physicochemical theory directs us to engage in further analysis.

The difficulty here is not that new levels keep emerging. That is just what we expected when we set out to present the fine-grained delineation of the structure. The difficulty comes out when we attempt to characterize the terminus of this series of physicochemical analyses. We can be certain that Aristotle would insist that after a finite number of steps the analysis has a terminus,[2] but to see the problems for Aristotle's account here let us consider the kinds of options open to him at the terminal point in the analysis.

One might follow the lead of such texts as *De Generatione et Corruptione* B.1 ($329^a24$–$329^b2$) and attribute to Aristotle the view that we do not reach the terminus here until we have carried out the requisite analysis for the four elements. The ultimate subject of predicates, then, turns out to be the prime matter we discussed in Chapter 2 and mentioned in later chapters. This is a matter which by "being bound up with a contrariety" ($329^a26$–27) (hot/dry, cold/dry, hot/wet, cold/wet) constitutes fire, earth, air, and water, and the grounds for supposing that there is a "common matter" here are strictly empirical. According to Aristotle, experience shows that "these bodies change into each other" ($329^a36$), so we must postulate a common subject of which the relevant pairs of contraries are predicated.

The suggestion seems to be that underlying the fact that the various parcels or quantities of the most elementary stuffs are the kinds of stuff

---

[2]E.g., see *Metaphysics* α.2 ($994^a1$–$994^b6$).

they are is the fact that the appropriate pairs of contraries are predicated of parcels or quantities of this common matter; predications like these represent the terminus in our analysis of the notion of what can serve as matter for substantial forms. Confronted with this account, we are irresistibly drawn to ask any number of questions. What, for example, is the force of speaking of "parcels or quantities of this common matter"? How can an account that takes the most elementary stuffs there are to be constituted by the predication of *qualitative* features like the hot, the cold, the dry, and the moist avoid construing accidents as prior to *ousia*? Aristotle tells us so little here that we just do not have the requisite materials for answering these questions.

If Aristotle has little to say about this common matter, his commentators have been more than willing to help him. Their philosophical reactions to the notion of an ultimate subject of change have shown a dramatic polarity. Some are positively captivated by the notion and insist that Aristotle's analysis requires that prime matter be the subject for every instance of unqualified coming to be or passing away.[3] Others have found this notion a philosophical embarrassment, arguing that it involves the unintelligible or incoherent idea that there is something that lacks all characteristics.[4] Both reactions, I think, are out of place. Aristotle makes it perfectly clear that what serves as matter for an unqualified coming to be is what is suited to play the role of proximate matter for the appropriate substantial form. He is explicit in telling us that this common matter is matter for the relevant pairs of contraries and, hence, is relevant only to the context of elemental change.

Aristotle also does not hold that the matter lacks all characteristics. He tells us that "it has no separate existence but is always bound up with a contrariety" ($329^a26-27$), so it always has some characteristic or other. If the objection is that any parcel of this common matter is bare in the sense that it could lose the qualitative features it actually possesses, then it seems to me that a response of Sheldon Cohen's is on target. Cohen points out that to criticize prime matter on this score is like accusing a man of indecent exposure on the grounds that, if he were to take his clothes off, he would be naked. Actually, the criticism is even more out of place than the accusation since, on Aristotle's account, it is not the case that when prime matter changes its clothes there is a time, however brief, when it is without any. The objection that prime matter

[3]See, e.g., Joseph Owens, "Matter and Predication in Aristotle," especially 196–197. See also Norbert Luyten, "Matter as Potency," in E. McMullin, ed., *The Concept of Matter in Greek and Medieval Philosophy* (Notre Dame, Ind.: University of Notre Dame Press, 1963), 106–107.

[4]See, e.g., Jones, "Aristotle's Introduction of Matter," 474–476.

is only contingently related to the relevant pairs of contraries is answered by Cohen's contention that this is just the price we pay to ensure the plasticity required of what is to play the role of subject for the mutual transformations of the most elementary stuffs.[5]

Indeed, it is easy to be sympathetic with Cohen's overarching claim that, taken by itself, Aristotle's conception of a common matter for the four elements is not philosophically absurd. But if the idea of a common matter for the qualitatively most elementary stuffs is not by itself crazy, it does not follow that it is an idea the Aristotle of Z and H should feel comfortable in endorsing. When we try to fill out Aristotle's brief remarks about this common matter, I think, we arrive at a notion that does not comport well with a theme central to the later (as well as the early) theory of *ousia*. Unless we assume that Aristotle is talking about prime matter in Z.3 (and this assumption, we have said, is dubious), we never find him explicitly saying that the common matter has nothing predicated of it essentially. Cohen makes a plausible case for the idea that some characteristics may well turn out to be predicated of this common matter necessarily.[6] It may, for example, be a de re necessity that this or that parcel of prime matter occupies some region of space. But de re necessity may be our notion of essential predication; it is unfortunately not Aristotle's. Aristotle countenances as essential predications only those that bear on what a thing is; the idea that prime matter is the subject underlying the most primitive substance-predications (those involving the predication of the relevant stuff-kinds of parcels or quantities of fire, earth, air, or water) seems to entail that, for any parcel or quantity of this underlying matter, there is nothing such that it is what that parcel or quantity is a parcel or quantity of. Clearly the relevant contrarities are not themselves predicated of their common matter essentially. It can survive the replacement of any one of the relevant pairs of contraries by another, so their predication cannot mark the matter out as what it is. And, in any case, Aristotle wants to deny that a form-predication can ever be other than accidental. But we have reached the bedrock of characterizations that might provide an essence for this matter; and if we deny that the contrarities provide it we seem forced to deny that it has any essence at all. There may be philosophers for whom the idea of something that is in its own right no kind of thing at all may not be troublesome, but the Aristotle of Z and H hardly seems to be one of them.

As we have seen, in Z and H (and probably even in the earliest

---

[5]Sheldon Cohen, "Aristotle's Doctrine of the Material Substrate," especially 176, 179.
[6]Ibid., 178–181.

works), Aristotle denies that there is such a thing as just being or existing. He insists on the essentialist interpretation of being or existing, where talk about the being of a thing is translated into talk about what it is. To be for a thing just is to be a thing of a certain sort or kind, so the legitimacy of talk about the being or existence of a thing hinges on our ability to identify the universal that answers the What it it? question for that thing. This essentialist interpretation of existence is not just one more thesis Aristotle happens to endorse, a thesis whose repudiation would leave everything else intact. The whole idea of a search after the primary realities is shaped and defined by this thesis. Aristotle's notion of a system or pattern of ontological priorities and dependencies makes little sense without it. So it is not a thesis Aristotle can repudiate without repudiating almost everything in the later (indeed, even the earlier) theory of *ousia*. It is, though, difficult to see how the idea that there *is* something that functions as matter for things of the most elementary substance-kinds does not involve a repudiation of this thesis. Such a repudiation of the thesis is no mere counterexample we can overlook. Confronting this matter, we are confronting something that is a first principle in the sense of a genuine starting point for explanation. The appeal to prime matter does not just involve a repudiation of the thesis, it represents the repudiation of essentialism for something that lies at the very foundation of our theory.

Is there nothing we might construe as essential predicate here? Not if we follow the literature on the topic. The characterizations we find there are pretty stark. We are told, for example, that in the case of this matter "there is nothing to halt the gaze of the intellect"[7] and that its only characteristic is that of "pure indetermination."[8] Aristotle never says such things; they represent supplements to and inferences from the scant and scattered remarks he makes. So perhaps we can find something that could serve as essence. The idea that the concept of matter itself provides the requisite essential predicate will not do. 'Matter' is an incomplete expression that needs to be filled out with a specification of just what its bearer is matter for; but once we provide the relevant specification, we have a predicate that expresses a thing's function or role rather than its essence. Likewise, the traditional claim that this matter is pure potentiality fails to provide the required *kath hauto* predi-

---

[7]Owens, "Matter and Predication in Aristotle," 192.

[8]Luyten, "Matter as Potency," 107. The idea that this matter is pure determinability or "pure potentiality" is often associated with the bizarre view that the most basic matter is the matter for all substantial forms, so that it can become anything. That idea is clearly not Aristotle's. In *De Generatione et Corruptione* B.1, it is "potentially perceptible body" (329[a]35), where this is a reference only to the elements.

cation. Like 'matter', 'potentiality' is an incomplete expression. We could specify what this matter is a potentiality for by saying that it is what is potentially fire, earth, air, or water. We might thereby open ourselves to the charge that we have built too much that is merely contingent into the proposed essence. Is it, after all, a necessary truth that there are just four elements or that they are mutually generated from each other? We might try to put things right here by saying that the matter in question is what is potentially the most elementary kinds of stuff. But still we must face the fact that this is a relational fact about the matter. Although the idea that a relational feature of a thing can constitute its essence is nonproblematic (and, according to the Aristotle of Z and H, inevitable) in the case of things from the accidental categories, the matter we are dealing with is something that is an ultimate principle of all composite *ousiai*; we read a relation into its essence only at the cost of making an accident prior in formula to *ousia*. In any case, there is something implausible in the idea that we identify the essence of a thing by identifying what it can become or can be. What a thing can become or be is not what it is in itself, we want to say, and we want to supplement the claim with the idea that things display the potentialities they do in virtue of what they actually are. So the two cannot be the same. It is doubtless this final insight that was the source of Aristotle's insistence that a form and its matter be definitionally independent, and the idea that prime matter has as its essence the potentiality for constituting the most elementary stuffs runs counter to this insistence. Finally, even this strategy of leaving open the specification of just which kinds of stuff are the most elementary kinds seems to build too much that is contingent into the essence of the common matter of *De Generatione et Corruptione* B.1. According to Aristotle's argument, it is only if there are several kinds of elementary stuff and those stuffs are subject to mutual or reciprocal generation and corruption that we must postulate a common matter. Although Aristotle's intuitions about what is necessary do not always correspond to ours, it is not clear that even he took these facts to be necessary; and, while Aristotle's notion of the necessary is broader than his notion of what belongs to an essence, nothing that is contingent can, in his view, be essential.

Aristotle himself flirts with the idea that the most basic matter is a familiar kind of stuff. Indeed, he sometimes uses the expression 'first matter' or 'prime matter' as a term marking whatever it is that turns out to be the most basic kind of matter. Thus in Θ.7 he says:

> But if there is something primary that is in no way said to be "thaten" with respect to something else, then this is prime matter. For example, if earth

is airy, and air (while not fire) is fiery, then fire is prime matter. (1049ª24–27)

We have here once again the appeal to the linguistic fact that when one thing is made out of another it is called "thaten" with respect to what constitutes its matter; if there is a kind of stuff such that it is not analyzable in terms of some prior matter and hence not called "thaten" with respect to anything else, that stuff is prime matter. The suggestion seems to be that perhaps something like fire could turn out, in this sense, to be prime matter. We need not take the suggestion to represent doubts on Aristotle's part about the phenomenon of reciprocal generation of the elements or even a serious suggestion about what could be the elementary stuff if there were just one. There are obvious problems with construing fire as the most elementary stuff which Aristotle chooses to ignore here: fire is hot and dry, and we are hard pressed to explain how it could maintain those features while taking on the characteristic features of water, the cold and moist. But the passage does suggest a willingness on Aristotle's part to concede that things could have turned out differently, that some story other than the one empirical observation forces us to tell in De Generatione et Corruptione B.1 could have been the right story.

And, as Cohen points out, we cannot in discussing all of this lose sight of the fact that the story Aristotle tells here is false.[9] And the story we (or rather our theoretical physicists) tell nowadays might prove false too. So let us pursue the idea that it is not the common matter of De Generatione et Corruptione B.1 that is, in the sense of Θ.7, prime matter, but that something else is; let us follow out the idea that this basic matter is something, like fire, with characteristic features of its own. It is consistent with this line of thinking that there be more than one kind of stuff that is an irreducibly basic kind of matter. From Aristotle's perspective, it would have to turn out that these different kinds of stuff never change into each other. But to simplify the discussion, we can follow the proposal of Θ.7 and suppose that more complex kinds of stuff all reduce to just one kind of elementary stuff.

What we should ask is just how this supposition would effect the doctrine of Z and H. Toward answering this question, let us suppose (as the proposal in Θ.7 does) that the basic structure of the rest of Aristotle's physicochemical account is preserved. We must recognize that our new candidate for status as prime matter would not itself have the internal structure of those more complex stuffs into whose constitution it ultimately enters. Although it is the doctrine that form does not come to be or pass away that receives pride of place in the middle books, Aristotle is firm in holding that an analogous doctrine applies in the case of matter.[10] The analogue has two sides. What functions as the proximate matter for a particular case of coming to be or passing away does not itself come to be or pass away as such in that change. What comes to be or passes away is the composite. But the proximate matter for a given substantial form can, in some other case of generation or corruption, come to be or pass away. Presumably, the same is true of whatever it is that functions as its matter. But at some point, Aristotle claims, there must be something that functions as matter but is like all substantial forms in being immune to generation and corruption. The matter in question is whatever it is that, in the $\Theta$.7 sense, is prime matter. So our chosen candidate for status as prime matter does not come to be or pass away, there is no matter prior to it that enters into its constitution, and, accordingly, there is no form that gives it its characteristic features. And it is not a form. So we have something that functions as matter that just is what it is in its own right. What it is (fire, in the $\Theta$.7 example) is not analyzable in more primitive terms; it seems to be a *kath hauto legomenon*. There is no explaining why it is what it is except by reference to itself, so it seems to be something that is its own *ousia*. Indeed, is it not its own essence as well? And since any account of why more complex things are what they are ultimately requires a reference to its being what it is, what the proposal of $\Theta$.7 seems to drive us to is the idea that form is not alone in being primary *ousia*. If the supposition of an unanalyzably basic matter with essential features of its own is correct, then form must share the privileged title of 'primary reality'.

So there is a dilemma here. Either we take as basic matter what Aristotle actually does seem to take, the common matter of *De Generatione et Corruptione* B.1, and then we seem forced to repudiate the essentialist thrust of Aristotle's metaphysical theory: there is something that just is without being any kind of thing at all, something that just is and for which "there is no saying what it is."[11] Or we suppose that the basic matter is something that has characteristic features in its own right, and then we must deny that everything other than form is what it is because form is what it is. We must hold that familiar particulars and the matter out of which they are made are what they are not just because forms are the essences they are but also because they are all

---

[10]It is fairly clear from 1033ᵃ29 and 1033ᵇ3–5 that the argument of Z.8 applies both to matter and form. See also 1069ᵇ35–1070ᵃ3.

[11]Dancy, "Aristotle's Second Thoughts," 373.

ultimately constituted by some stuff that is unanalyzably the kind of stuff or thing it is. Form shares center stage as primary *ousia*.

Perhaps, there is a way out of this dilemma. Perhaps we have misread the relevant texts, and the issue of a prime matter is just not one that confronts Aristotle in the way we have suggested. As we saw in Chapter 2, this is the thrust of one kind of interpretation of Aristotle's doctrine. The interpretation denies that Aristotle ever meant to endorse the idea of a single matter for the four elements. The literature surrounding this interpretation is substantial, and much of it is devoted to the necessary business of examining particular texts in their particular contexts. As I have already indicated, my own view is that those who construe Aristotle as endorsing the idea of a common matter for fire, earth, air, and water have had the better of this debate, and I have nothing to add to the exegetical controversy surrounding the issue. However, since our concern here is with the philosophical implications of the concept of matter, let us suppose that we can succeed in gerrymandering the texts to give the result that prime matter as traditionally understood is not the common matter for the four elements, and let us see what the prospects are that Aristotle can, on this supposition, escape our dilemma.

What is needed here is an account of the reciprocal generation of the four elements. All parties to the controversy agree that Aristotle believes in elemental change, and the foes of prime matter owe us an account of how elemental transformations occur. I know of only two such accounts, one presented in recent years by William Charlton and the other suggested in the late 1950s by Hugh King and found more recently in the work of Montgomery Furth. Charlton seems to think that Aristotle's chief goal in his analysis of change is to respond to the Presocratic (Parmenidean, to be more exact) worry that change requires that things come to be or pass away out of nothing; the root concern is that coming to be and passing away are, respectively, just "creation and annihilation." Charlton denies that Aristotle counters this anxiety by insisting that there is something that persists or remains throughout the whole process of a change.[12] He agrees that there is something we can call the subject of a change, something that underlies the change, but he thinks that this is merely what corresponds to our characterization of the thing that comes to be. And that, he holds, is merely a characterization of something that exists prior to the change. In some cases that thing may, under the appropriate description, persist through the change, but this is not an essential feature of change. According to Charlton, Aris-

---

[12]William Charlton, *Aristotle's Physics I and II*, 140, 77.

totle took it to be sufficient to counter the anxiety of his predecessors to show that there is a certain continuity in a change, that things do not just pop into and out of existence. He characterizes the kind of continuity Aristotle took to be sufficient here in the following terms:

> The idea, however, that if there is nothing which remains throughout a change, then things come to be out of or pass away into nothing, is mistaken. Between alteration on the one hand, and creation and annihilation on the other, there is a third possibility. If you have a glass jar from within which you have removed the air and everything else you can find; and you see a frog suddenly appear in it; then you might call that coming to be out of nothing. If you see a man sitting in a chair, and suddenly he has vanished irretrievably, and in his place is a pile of books which have never been seen or heard of before, you might be tempted to say that the man has passed away into nothing and, by a strange chance, the books have come into being out of nothing in the same place. But when the passing away of one thing is always and intelligibly attended by the coming to be of another, for instance when wood passes away in smoke and flames or a saucer of water passes away and the air is refreshed, then we do not say that the first thing has passed away into nothing, but into the second, and we say that the second has come into being, not out of nothing, but out of the first. Yet we cannot say that there is something which remained throughout and underwent these transformations, unless we can find some description under which this thing can be identified throughout.[13]

Accordingly, in the case of the mutual generation of the elements, we need not suppose that there is some persisting matter or subject before, during, and after the change. It is sufficient that there be an orderly transformation of the one into the other, so that where there was water there is now air, with no gap in between.

One might object that Charlton's characterization of Aristotle's proposed solution is actually a statement of the problem Aristotle was attempting to address in *De Generatione et Corruptione*, that is, that Aristotle saw that there is an orderly transformation from water to air with no gap in between and found this a source of puzzlement that only a philosophical theory of the process could dispel. But let us set this objection to the side as well as historical questions about the accuracy of Charlton's characterization of the Parmenidean anxiety or Aristotle's treatment of it. Let us focus instead on the philosophical question of the implications of the view Charlton attributes to Aristotle for the doctrine of Z and H. They are, I think, disastrous. A driving force behind the theory of *ousia* in the middle books is the idea that, in the case of things

---

[13]Ibid., 140.

that come to be and pass away, the ontological principles in terms of which we characterize their coming to be are principles that enter into our metaphysical analysis of those things once they have come to be. As we have seen, Aristotle just assumes that, if a thing of a certain kind can come to be only if some subject or matter comes to be something or other (comes to have some form predicated of it), then that thing's being a thing of that kind, after it has come to be, requires that the relevant predication continue to hold. If a composite oak tree ('oak tree' in the mixed product sense) can come to be only if some matter comes to have predicated of it the form oak tree ('oak tree' in the pure product sense), then the composite's being an oak tree (again, in the mixed sense), once it has come to be, has to rest on the fact that its matter is an oak tree (in the pure sense). If we sever the tie between the idea of a subject for change and the idea of that which persists through change, not only do we have recalcitrant texts (in which Aristotle seems to define the idea of a subject for change in terms of persistence) on our hands;[14] we also undermine the assumption that justifies the central insight of the middle books. There is little left to support the contention that familiar particulars are matter-form composites if the subject for their coming to be need not persist as subject for the appropriate form.

We cannot exempt, I think, even one kind of generation from the principle that the conditions requisite for a thing's coming to be something or other are the conditions for its being that once it has come to be. Elemental change cannot prove an exception to the general idea that change requires a subject and something that comes to be predicated of it, with that same predicative tie explaining why, after it has come to be, a thing is whatever it is. What makes the whole apparatus of species-predications and their corresponding form-predications work is that, where there is change, there must be a subject-predicate relation that holds as long as the state of affairs the change culminates in continues to obtain. This predicative relation is not something extraneous to our conception of matter and form; seen in the light of the context of coming to be and passing away, it just is what gives us any purchase we have on the matter-form relation.

So if Charlton's interpretation provides Aristotle with an escape from our dilemma, it is not one that Aristotle of Z and H would want to exploit. Although the account of King and Furth has much in common with Charlton's, it provides us, as Charlton's does not, a kind of picture of how, in the absence of an appeal to a common matter for the elements, Aristotle might have characterized the mechanics of elemental transformation. Their idea is that when one element is transformed into

[14]See, e.g., 192ᵃ28–29, 194ᵇ23–25, and 1069ᵇ3–8.

another there are two stuffs each characterized by a distinct pair of contraries.[15] As they see it, something actually does persist through elemental change—one of the contraries. Suppose that water becomes air. When this happens, the cold in the cold and the wet is replaced by the hot to give us the hot and the wet that is air. Thus the wet persists.

Let us ignore the fact that this account does not accommodate a kind of elemental change Aristotle seems to believe possible, that where both contraries are displaced by their opposites (see 331$^b$4–12), and focus instead on the way this interpretation would have us construe the contraries relevant to our analysis of the four elements. For the account to work, as I see it, the contraries have to be something like "thises" or quasisubstances rather than the "suches" or predicative entities they are more naturally construed as. There is, after all, nothing for them to be predicated of, since the elements are constituted by the contraries and nothing else. King seems to interpret them along the lines I have suggested, calling them dynamical forces.[16] In one respect, this analysis represents a kind of dividend for the account; as we mentioned earlier, our initial concern when confronted with Aristotle's account of the constitution of the elements is that, in taking notions like the wet, the dry, the hot, and the cold as constitutive (whether exclusively, as King suggests, or together with a common matter) of the four stuffs into which all composite *ousiai* are ultimately to be analyzed, Aristotle is suggesting a theory that requires us to analyze *ousia* in terms of notions that seem to fall under the accidental categories. That worry prompts the inference that he does not have in mind here our ordinary notions of qualitative attributes but some theoretical notions not to be analyzed in terms appropriate to items from the dependent categories. King's account points, however vaguely, in a direction that might clarify the kind of notion Aristotle is invoking in *De Generatione et Corruptione*.

But even if we reinforce the account with King's characterization of the contraries, the King–Furth account has serious shortcomings as an attempt to rescue Aristotle from our dilemma. In its treatment of the contraries as quasisubstances with a qualitative dimension of their own, the view seems too close to the proposal of Θ.7. There turn out, in this interpretation, to be four rather than one qualitatively determined force, stuff, or whatever. But the point we made apropos of the proposal that fire be prime matter holds here. The account would require that these four forces share center stage with substantial form. They would

[15]King, "Aristotle without *Prima Materia*," 376ff., and Furth, *Substance, Form, and Psyche*, 221–227.
[16]King, "Aristotle without *Prima Materia*," 378–379.

be *kath hauta legomena*, their own *ousia* and essence; they would each be an instance of something that is a primary *ousia*.

But would they be so generous as to share center stage with substantial forms? That is not clear, since this account of elemental change once again forces us to countenance a kind of coming to be and passing away that is not subject to characterization in terms of the ontological apparatus that the analysis of Z and H requires us to apply to every coming to be. On this score, the account of elemental transformations that King and Furth attribute to Aristotle is the counterpoint to the account Charlton reads into the text. Whereas Charlton's account of elemental change has Aristotle dispersing with a persisting subject for the predication of a form, King and Furth have Aristotle doing without predicates.[17] As they see it, the only factors involved in elemental transformations are the quasisubstances (Furth calls them a "third kind of subject") that are the contraries; in an almost Empedoclean spirit, we generate the elements from each other by a process akin to what Aristotle in *Physics* A.4 (187ª32) calls "combination and separation." Quite apart from the fact that throughout the middle books Aristotle repeatedly denies that this kind of additive process is sufficient to generate anything with a genuine unity, this account has Aristotle deviate from a pattern of analysis in the characterization of change that the doctrine of Z and H presupposes is universally applicable.

So revisionist readings of Aristotle's doctrine of elemental transformation do not help us out of our dilemma. This is not surprising, since the idea that there must be a matter that is in its own right no kind of thing seems to be inevitable in a theory that takes primary *ousia* to be something that is predicated of something else. If we believe that we can reiterate for our original subjects for form-predications and their successors the form of analysis into which they enter *and* we hold that the only thing that is what it is in its own right is something that exists only as predicated of something else, then we are inevitably led to the idea that there is a bedrock subject for predication that is in its own right no kind of thing at all; that is the idea of prime matter as traditionally construed.

As I have said, the Aristotle of Z and H never confronts this issue. He does make the occasional concession that the things functioning as proximate matter for our original form-predications are themselves analyzable in terms of notions like bile, the sweet, and the fat. But we are

---

[17]A complication here is that Furth also seems to make the spatial regions inhabited by contrarieties something like subjects for the contraries; see *Substance, Form, and Psyche*, 221.

given no idea of the kind of story these concessions require,[18] so we cannot be sure how the Aristotle of Z and H would respond to the dilemma we have posed for him. What is clear, however, is that, within the context of a theory that makes all essential characterizations turn on things accidentally predicated of something else, the idea that there is an ultimate subject for the most elementary characterizations of substance does not square with the essentialist insight that to be for a thing is just to be essentially some kind of thing. The later theory thus gives rise to a problem that the discussions of Z and H simply fail to resolve.

III

If the middle books fail to address the first of the two problems we associated with Aristotle's hierarchy, they give considerable attention to the second. We can get at this problem if we recall that, within the hierarchy Aristotle proposes, the essences of composite particulars turn out to be derivative essences and the particulars whose essences they are, derivative entities. That leads us to ask whether the theory of Z and H is not one that calls into question the reality of the framework of common sense championed in the *Categories*. After all, what the account tells us is that, when we reach the most basic level of ontological characterization, the familiar particulars of common sense are gone; the kinds under which those particulars fall and which constitute their essences have no application; and the logical features distinctive of those kinds are displaced by structures bearing little resemblance to them. Confronted with these claims, it is difficult not to interpret the overall pattern of *ousia* explanations delineated in Z and H as a reductionist strategy, one that identifies for us the genuinely real objects and shows us how the objects and concepts constitutive of the common-sense framework are mere constructions out of the genuinely real objects.

If we are inclined to characterize the later theory in these terms, we are likely to see it as a piece of radical reductionism; for the reduction it seems to recommend is not a mere case of replacement, so that there are things in the framework of common sense that are identified with more basic things in the fundamental framework and there are concepts or

---

[18]See, e.g., 1044[a]15–20. It may be that Aristotle would respond to the dilemma by way of his distinction between potential and actual being. The idea would be that the "to be is to be some kind of thing" formula is meant to hold only for things that actually are. But if we take this line, we need an account of the 'there is' in 'there is prime matter', and I am not certain what account Aristotle would be prepared to provide here.

universals in our familiar framework replaced by concepts or universals in the more basic framework. In fact there are no things in the more basic framework corresponding to the particulars of common sense, and there are no concepts that in any straightforward sense replace the kinds that dominate the discourse of the marketplace.[19] What corresponds in the fundamental framework to the particular man or horse of *Categories* 5 is not a thing at all. What we have instead is the obtaining of a certain state of affairs. Where, in the framework of common sense, we had our man Socrates, we now have the fact that a certain form is predicated of a certain parcel of matter. There is no longer a "this," but, as Aristotle likes to tell us, a "this in a this"; and the predicative tie here is noneliminable. On this score, we might think, we go wrong if we take Aristotle's talk of composites to involve the substitution of a more basic or fine-grained entity for a grosser, unanalyzed entity. Aristotle's talk of composites is not talk about entities at all, but a shorthand way of abbreviating a complicated recipe in which predicative relations between distinct entities are pivotal. In the same way, we might contend, the claim that ordinary objects are predicative complexes should not be understood to involve a transframework identification of objects, but as a warning that no such identification is possible. What in the framework of common sense are construed as things or objects or subjects in the basic framework are represented only in terms of the obtaining of certain predicative relations or states of affairs.

And just as there are no things in the basic framework corresponding to familiar particulars, the fundamental framework seems to refuse to recognize universals corresponding to our familiar substance-kinds. Here, again, it is tempting to claim that we misconstrue Aristotle if we take his talk about "the form and the matter taken generally" ($1035^b29$– $30$) to represent the attempt to identify universals in the more basic

---

[19]A formal account of the reductive strains in Z and H is provided in Frank Lewis, "Form and Predication in Aristotle's *Metaphysics*." Although I agree with virtually everything Lewis has to say in his account, I worry that he pushes the reductive side of Z and H too far. He insists that the accidental predication of a form of its matter and the accidental predication of an accident of an individual composite exhaust the forms of predication in Z and H. If the focus is on unanalyzable or primitive forms of one-many predication, this claim is correct. But if we stress it too much, we run the risk of overlooking the fact that there are two distinct frameworks operative in Z and H and that Aristotle claims that, within the framework of commonsense particulars the paradigmatic predicative relation is that found in species-predications. *Within that framework*, Aristotle wants to say, the relationship between an individual and its species holds a privileged status. It is true that species-predications are analyzable in terms of form-predications, but that truth is a claim about the relationship of two different frameworks and not a claim in the framework of common sense. For more on the reductive strain, see Furth's discussion of H.2 in *Substance, Form, and Psyche*.

framework that play the role of sortals. What he is saying, we might claim, is that kind talk represents a generalization of particular instances of the predicative discourse on which the particulars of common sense are founded; just as the form-predications in question do not yield things that replace our ordinary particulars, the generalization of the patterns at work in those predications do not give us concepts of things that, in any simple way, replace our familiar kind concepts.

So the account of Z and H can strike us as a piece of radically reductive metaphysics, one that calls into question the status of the framework of common sense. After all, the objects constituting the underlying framework are supposed to be the most real things, and the concepts and structured connections Aristotle associates with that framework are supposed to provide us with the resources for giving a complete characterization of those things and the ontological relations into which they enter. That might seem to suggest that our talk about common sense particulars is, at best, a convenient shorthand for more complicated claims that could, in principle, be formulated exclusively in the austere vocabulary of the underlying framework. Indeed, it might even be taken to imply that the characteristic claims of common sense represent a distortion of the sober metaphysical truth; for, although we can provide complicated recipes that take us from the claims of the underlying framework to the claims of common sense, it is not difficult to think of the framework of the agora as one that falsifies reality. It objectifies or posits objects where the underlying framework refuses to do so. It tells us that there are particular things or concrete objects where the underlying framework would have us see only the holding of a relation between a form and its matter or the obtaining of a predicative state of affairs, and it converts the generalization of these structures into what it construes as concepts expressing essences. Further, it confers on the objects and concepts it manufactures a special status, treating those objects as though they are the most real things and those concepts as though they give us insight into what is most real about those objects. In the face of the apparent reduction Aristotle outlines in the middle books, all this can strike us as misleading, as a potentially dangerous gerrymandering of sober metaphysical truths. At best, the framework of common sense can seem superfluous; at worst, a distortion.

This assessment of the common sense framework stands in stark opposition to the account provided in the *Categories* and related works. Although we have tended to characterize that account in technical terms by reference to the subject criterion, the doctrine of essentialism, and the Unanalyzability Thesis, we cannot lose sight of the fact that the formal machinery associated with the account is motivated by and represents the expression of an underlying intuition about the validity of the common sense picture of the world. In its fundamental features, Aristotle believed, that picture is accurate. The objects constitutive of the framework are genuine realities and its substance-predicates, universals that enable us to identify just what their reality consists in.

The apparent conflict here is not merely one between a cherished view and a later account that seems to displace it. If there is a genuine tension between these two frameworks, we cannot be disinterested or impartial observers of the conflict. We have a stake in the conflict because for beings like ourselves there is something inescapable in the intuitions motivating the early theory of *ousia*. Our own metaphysical status is tied up with questions about the validity of the common sense framework of the *Categories*. If the familiar particulars constitutive of that framework are not genuine realities, then neither are we; if the kind concepts central to the framework are, at best, mere constructions out of other more basic concepts, then the very notion of a person becomes suspect.

We seem no have no choice, then, but to endorse the metaphysical implications of our familiar picture of the world. From Aristotle's perspective, this fact is not merely a locus for the kind of existential anxiety that we in the twentieth century have become all too familiar with. As he sees things, a theory that calls into question the phenomena it set out to explain calls itself into question, and the phenomena that the theory of Z and H seeks to explain are paradigmatically exemplified by species-predications, predications whose proper linguistic expression tells us that there really are things that fall under concepts or universals adequate to provide their essences. If, then, the upshot of Z and H is that there is something misleading or distorting in the beliefs to which the phenomenon of species-predication gives rise, then the theory of the middle books itself is one we have reason to question.[20]

This methodological precept that a theory must preserve the common sense beliefs whose truth it seeks to explain has its roots in Aristotle's most deep-seated beliefs about the world and our place in it. We are part of what Jonathan Lear calls an "harmonious" world, a teleological world that implants in us a "desire to understand" that world and provides us with the epistemic resources to achieve this end.[21] The commonsense beliefs we find inescapable constitute an essential part of the epistemic

---

[20]For a discussion of this methodological precept, see G. E. L. Owen, "*Tithenai ta Phainomena*," reprinted in J. M. E. Moravcsik, ed., *Aristotle* (Garden City, N.Y.: Doubleday, 1967), 167–190.

[21]See Lear's very perceptive remarks in *Aristotle: The Desire to Understand*, chaps. 1 and 3.

tools for providing the kind of account of the world that world leads us to seek. In a world of the sort Aristotle envisioned, the kind of conflict or tension we have been characterizing cannot be irresolvable. If the theory of Z and H is to be a correct account of the fundamental features of the world, then it must be possible to preserve the central insights motivating the theory of the *Categories*.

And the fact is that the Aristotle of Z and H shows every indication of wanting to preserve them. Throughout Z and H, he tells us that, although form is the *ousia* of ordinary particulars, those particulars themselves deserve the title '*ousia*'. Despite the fact that the framework of common sense rests on a more fundamental framework, the objects constitutive of that framework are genuine realities. Furthermore, although he construes them as composites, Aristotle denies that familiar particulars are just heaps or constructions. He insists that they are genuine unities, and he construes it as a constraint on any account of their fine-grained structure that it has just this result. Despite his contention that we cannot take the subject criterion as providing the whole story about which things we should call *ousiai*, he insists that there is something right in that criterion. We must supplement the criterion with the idea that the notion of a fundamental essence provides us with a guide in our attempt to identify the realities. As we saw at the end of Chapter 1, however, this idea was already a theoretical demand implicit in the privileged status the theory of the *Categories* attributed to the infimae species under which familiar particulars fall. The *Categories* idea that in virtue of being subjects for their kinds and the attributes that happen to characterize them those particulars are candidates for status as *ousia* is one the Aristotle of Z and H endorses. Furthermore, he is at pains to preserve the privileged status of the species under which familiar particulars fall. He repeatedly tells us that those universals are subject to definition, so that there are genuine essences associated with them. Indeed, no sooner has he provided his final statement of the pattern of reduction relating form-predications to species-predications than he underlines this claim about the definability of concepts proper to ordinary particulars.[22] He is obviously concerned to counter an interpretation one might be tempted to read into those patterns of reduction, that only universals proper to the underlying framework provide us with concepts of the what it is to be for realities. The rest of H is concerned with the task of showing just how, despite the reductive patterns central to the theory of Z and H, the substance-species of the *Categories* provide us with concepts of things that are at once genuine realities and genuine unities, and a pivotal theme in this enterprise is

[22]See 1043$^b$23–1044$^a$14, especially 1043$^b$28–33.

one that we met as early as Z.4, that our substance concepts stand in sharp contrast to universals that are mere constructions.

So the Aristotle of Z and H is not merely concerned to show how our beliefs about familiar particulars falling under substance-species rest on a more fundamental level of discourse in which form-predications play the central role. He is equally concerned to show that the structural features of the later theory do not call into question our intuitions about the reality and unity of those particulars and the integrity of the framework of substance-species under which they fall. Indeed, an underlying assumption of Z and H is that, if this kind of reconciliation of frameworks is not possible, the later theory itself has to be rejected. Unless the Aristotle of Z and H can come to terms with the Aristotle of the *Categories*, his claims have no chance of being true.

The fact that both Aristotles have their say in Z and H is something other commentators have noticed. Some, ignoring or simply missing the deep differences between the early and later theories of *ousia*, have failed to recognize the challenge of the task Aristotle sets for himself on this score.[23] Others, misreading and exaggerating those differences, have argued that the enterprise is bound to fail and that, at bottom, the doctrine we meet in Z and H is an inconsistent mix of early and late views.[24] They claim that the fact that Aristotle wants both to apply and to withhold the "this something" schema in the case of form, the fact that he seems to say both that form is separable and that only the composite is separable, and the fact that he insists both that *ousia* is invariably particular or individual and that form is universal represent contradictions that result from the attempt to assimilate frameworks that are ultimately incommensurable. Both views, it seems to me, fail to appreciate the subtleties of the middle books. The novel account of substance-predication in Z and H does involve a potentially problematic form of analysis; the attempt to delineate that account while preserving the insights of the early theory of *ousia* represents a major philosophical challenge. On the other hand, Aristotle fully appreciates the nature of this challenge and is sensitive to the demands it places on him. Whether or not the reconciliation of frameworks ultimately succeeds, Aristotle is not an ignorant bungler who fails to appreciate the differences in those frameworks.

[23]I am thinking of commentators who see the differences between the approach of the *Categories* and that of the middle books not as differences in doctrine but as differences in methodology, so that we have a set of logical claims and a set of metaphysical claims with no genuine inconsistency. See, e.g., Joseph Owens, "Aristotle on Categories," *Review of Metaphysics* (1960), 78–90, and *The Doctrine of Being in the Aristotelian Metaphysics*.
[24]This idea is one of the central claims of Daniel Graham's *Aristotle's Two Systems*.

## IV

The project of reconciling the two frameworks, I have suggested, is the focus of the later chapters of H. The role of H.6 is paramount in this enterprise. Aristotle would, however, claim that throughout Z and H he has prepared us for this project; many of the central claims of the middle books are formulated with an eye to this problem and its ultimate resolution. So before we confront directly the closing chapters of H, it would be well to call in review those features of the account as so far presented that provide us with grounds for thinking that the central insights of both the earlier and the later theories can be preserved in a single coherent package.

The most obvious efforts in this direction are to be found in the cluster of ideas surrounding the "this"/"such" contrast of Z.8 and the element/principle contrast of Z.17. Both contrasts appear in contexts designed to show that an ontological theory that reads an internal structure into ordinary objects is not inevitably committed to construing them as mere aggregates or collections of more basic entities. The contrasts serve as vehicles for expressing the distinctive categorial features of matter and form. Aristotle suggests that those features are such as to ensure that despite (indeed, because of) their hylomorphic structure the familiar particulars of the *Categories* are genuine unities and not, as he likes to put it, mere heaps.

The central idea, we have said, is that matter and form are entities of distinct ontological types. Matter has a kind of completeness that form lacks. It is a potential object of singular demonstrative reference, a "this," and hence something suited to play the role of metaphysical subject. It is the kind of thing that can, within the context of a recipe for objects of a certain kind, be listed among the nameable ingredients out of which objects of that kind are made. Form, however, is a predicable entity, and its proper linguistic expression is by way of general terms which, despite appearances to the contrary, do not divide their reference. Form is not a "this"; it is "how" something that is a "this," a parcel of matter, is. It is not something that, in the context of a recipe, is just another item in the list of ingredients; rather, it is what is expressed by the set of directions specifying how the various ingredients are to be put together.

So hylomorphic structures are more than heaps or aggregates. An ordinary object is not a "this plus this" or a mere assemblage of ingredients. To capture the structural features distinctive of the constitution of an ordinary object, we must say that the materials composing it are such and such, that its ingredients are put together such and such. And although the "how" the matter is or the "how" the ingredients are put together is not a complete entity that can be a singular subject of predication for other things or enter into a list of such subjects, it has a fully determinate conceptual content, one that can be identified independently. Indeed, Aristotle claims that it is the only kind of thing such that what it is can be identified without reference to what other things are. When, in the case of any particular form, we specify just what it is, we find that its determinate conceptual content is precisely the sort required: it is the how some parcel of matter of the appropriate sort must be, the way ingredients of the right kind must be put together, if that matter or those ingredients are to constitute a particular of the associated substance-species. As we put the point earlier, substantial forms are *tode ti*–forming functions. Given appropriate parcels of matter as their arguments, they have particular instances of the associated substance-kind as their values. So forms are just the kind of thing that give us the genuine unities that the particulars of the common sense framework are.

Another set of themes whose formulation has an eye to the tension between the later theory of *ousia* and the intuitions motivating the early theory is the pair of claims about levels we find in the thesis that matter is "thaten" and the thesis that form is not predicated of individuals. Although Aristotle claims that the composite is "not said to be that, but thaten" (1033$^a$5–6) because of the poverty of our language, we have seen that he likes to exploit this linguistic accident to make the point that the matter constituting an individual does not compete with it for status as subject of predication. Matter is a metaphysical subject, but it is a subject of a different level or within a different framework. In the same way, the idea that the species associated with a form rather than the form itself is predicated of the individual members of the species underlines the need to distinguish the framework we seek to explain from the framework in terms of which it is explained. Although form is a universal, the metaphysical subjects constituting its predicative plurality belong to a level of ontological analysis at one remove from the individuals for which the species provides an essence.

So Aristotle wants to counter the idea that the pattern of *ousia* explanations identified in Z and H calls into question either the status of familiar particulars as genuine subjects of predication or the status of their species as object concepts or essences. There are two distinct frameworks, each with its own proper metaphysical subjects and universals. Matter is a basic metaphysical subject and form, its predicate within the framework of form-predications; but neither matter nor form play those roles in the framework of common sense. That is a framework constituted by familiar particulars and their substance-kinds. Within that framework, those particulars are our paradigmatic subjects and their species, our paradigmatic essences.

Confronted with the assurances provided by this pair of claims about levels, we cannot resist pointing out that although there are distinct frameworks here Aristotle insists that one is more basic than the other. And, while we may concede that we confuse the frameworks or assimilate one to the other only at the risk of category mistake, we want to remind Aristotle that the framework of form-predication provides us with metaphysical subjects that are prior to those of the commonsense framework of the *Categories* and that only its universals are essences whose conceptual content is not reducible to that of prior essences. Aristotle certainly would not deny these facts, but he would insist that there are respects in which particulars falling under substance-kinds have a better claim to status as realities than the matter or form in terms of which we explain their status as members of those kinds.

Certainly, this is one of the themes Aristotle associates with the thesis that neither matter nor form come to be or pass away. As we have seen, there is a contrast implicit in that thesis. The factors in terms of which we explain a particular case of generation or corruption do not themselves come to be or pass away in that change. What comes to be or passes away is the composite particular. The point of the contrast is to highlight what, in our discussion of Z.8, we called the factual autonomy of the individual composite *ousia*. Individuals are, so to speak, out there for us to confront and interact with. They have careers with a beginning and an end, and those careers form a chapter in the history of the everyday world. In a sense that is easy to grasp but difficult to define rigorously, they have a kind of independence that the form and matter entering into their analysis fail to exhibit. Taken in isolation, the substantial forms of natural objects are not among the denizens of the world. Their being requires their instantiation, and that, in turn, requires a metaphysical subject of which they can be predicated. Their proper mode of being, then, is that dependent kind of being of something that is inherently a predicate. What constitutes the matter of a particular natural object can, under some descriptions, appear as a thing in its own right. But so appearing, it is not playing the role of matter for a form. It has, so to speak, jumped up a level and is now taking its place among the metaphysical subjects constitutive of the framework of particulars under substance-species. And Aristotle is always quick to point out that, when the matter that was once constitutive of a given individual jumps levels in this way, it is never an instance of a kind whose members exhibit the structural, functional, behavioral, or organizational complexity of the individual whose matter it can be.[25]

So, although the Aristotle of Z and H claims that there is a straightforward sense in which the matter and form entering into the constitution of familiar particulars are prior to those particulars, this priority (following Aristotle, we can call it priority in formula or essence) must be measured against a kind of factual or existential priority properly associated with ordinary natural objects.[26] Focusing on either kind of priority might lead us to invoke the term *'ousia'*. The former priority invites the use of the expression as an abstract term to express the idea that matter and form are the *ousia* of concrete particulars and that form is their primary *ousia*, whereas the latter priority suggests the use of the term in its concrete form to yield the claim that the individual objects of the natural world that come to be and pass away are *ousiai*. This is precisely the kind of result that the generalization of the doctrine of the homonymy of substance words to the term *'ousia'* itself would lead us to expect. Because form is the primary *ousia* of a concrete object, that object is itself an *ousia*.

The idea that the concrete particular has a kind of factual or existential priority over form comes out as well in Aristotle's treatment of the notions of "this something" and separability. We have seen that he claims that the applicability of the term *'ousia'* itself hinges on our willingness to apply the terms 'this something' and 'separate', and he insists that both expressions have an application in the case of the form and the composite. But, although commentators have frequently denied this, Aristotle does not claim that either expression applies univocally to both. When we recall once again that the term *'ousia'* itself is used homonymously in the two cases, we have to agree that this is precisely the result we should expect. Aristotle never rigorously defines for us the notion of separateness supposed to be applicable to the composite. My own view is that he has a fairly general idea in mind here, one not sharply distinguished from the cluster of ideas associated with the "this something" epithet.

The "this something" epithet applies to the composite in the sense

---

[25]See, e.g., Z.16 (1040$^b$5–15), where the claims of matter and the parts of concrete objects for status as *ousia* are challenged.

[26]Although the account Aristotle provides is clear on the kinds of priority it assigns the component concepts in the theory, the metatheoretical remarks Aristotle makes on the term 'priority' do not always reflect the nuances of his actual account. Neither the discussion of priority in *Categories* 12–13 nor the entry on priority in *Metaphysics* Δ.11 makes the kinds of distinctions that accurately reflect the subtleties operative in either the earlier or later theories of *ousia*.

that some instance of that schema is true of it. Each concrete thing is a particular instance of its substance-kind and, so, something we can refer to as "this *K*." Being a member of its species is just what to be consists in for a concrete object. The species, in turn, is predicated essentially of a plurality of such particulars. Accordingly, its logic is the individuative or sortal logic that Aristotle ever more successfully comes to articulate. Substance-kinds enable us to distinguish particulars of one species from those of another, and they provide us with principles for distinguishing and counting particulars within a single species, both at a single time and at different times. So, in virtue of being a member of its species, a concrete object is a particular distinct from all other particulars. It is this distinctness, I think, that Aristotle has in mind when he says that the concrete individual is separate.[27] Composite particulars are things that can be distinguished from other things in the world about us and consequently can serve as subjects for the predication of accidents. Accordingly, each can be thought of as something with a history of its own. Each concrete thing can be viewed as what Donald Morrison calls an individual "center of ontological influence" with its own "distinct ontological boundaries."[28] Accordingly, each has the kind of factual autonomy we mentioned earlier.

So the themes Aristotle marshalls in highlighting the priority he claims for the composite constitute a kind of seamless web; Aristotle himself likes to call attention to the relations among these themes. In H.1 ($1042^a29-31$), he tells us that it is because the composite has a career with an identifiable beginning and end that it has the kind of separateness in existence that both its form and matter lack. In Z.8 ($1033^b19-22$), he ties the idea that the composite comes to be and passes away to the idea that it is what is subject to the "this something" epithet in its primary use.[29] In I.1 ($1052^b15-17$), he implies that it is in virtue of being

[27]I see an intimate connection between the idea that a concrete thing is separate and the idea that it is something we can characterize, for appropriate *K*, as "this *K*" and "one *K*." Here I remind the reader of the discussion in the previous chapter on Aristotle's claims that Plato took his Forms to exhibit numerical unity. Those claims are often made in the context of the view that Plato separated the Forms.

[28]See Donald Morrison, "Aristotle on Separation," *Oxford Studies in Ancient Philosophy* (1986), 125–157. Morrison's is a very perceptive and sensitive treatment of the notion of separation, much of which I agree with. I do not, however, agree that the claim that form is separable in formula is a "cheat" (p. 126). I see it as an essential component in the theory of *ousia* explanations and in the account of essences as constituting a structured framework with a secure foundation. Further, I do not think that Aristotle had just a single notion that he invariably associated with the notion of separation. Accordingly, I think that we can accept Morrison's insights without rejecting the claims made by Gail Fine in "Separation." See the interchange between Fine and Morrison in *Oxford Studies in Ancient Philosophy* (1985), 159–165 and 125–157.

[29]Ross misleads us here in translating '*tode ti*' in these passages as "this." The contrast

instances of universals that provide principles or measures for counting that particulars have their own identifiably distinct spatial locations, and he tells us that our ability to identify, distinguish, and count particulars hinges on this fact. Substance-kinds draw boundaries around their instances, both spatial and temporal boundaries; because particular composites are so marked out, they are, as Aristotle likes to put it, separate in an unqualified sense.[30]

But the cluster of themes surrounding the idea that the composite is separate and subject to the "this something" schema is simply inapplicable in the case of form.[31] Substantial forms are not particulars and so cannot be individual subjects for the metaphysical predication of other things; unlike substance-kinds, they are not predicated essentially of anything but themselves. A form is how its matter is, not what it is; consequently, it does not exhibit the sortal logic of substance-kinds. It does, however, have a determinate conceptual content, and that content can be identified without reference to anything else. Accordingly, we can say that form is separable in formula. And the content we can independently identify is the right content. It is a content such that in virtue of its being predicated accidentally of the appropriate matter there are individual members of substance-kinds, things to which the relevant instantiations of the "this something" schema apply. As we put it earlier, form is a *tode ti*–forming function, which suggests a derivative sense in which form is subject to the "this something" epithet.

The idea that form is separable in formula is the familiar one that, if it is to be the primary reality, form must be a fundamental essence, one that can be defined without reference to other essences. And the idea

---

between Aristotle's use of '*tode ti*' to pick what comes to be and his use of '*tode*' as a neutral referring device at 1033[b]2, 13, and 19 is lost if we do not provide a different translation of the two uses.

[30]Again, I remind the reader of Aristotle's tendency to assimilate the ideas expressed by such terms as 'this something', 'one in number', 'individual', and 'separate'. Although we might in certain contexts be able to distinguish the ideas he associates with these terms, he often uses them as mere variants on each other, as though they represented alternative linguistic devices for expressing a network of ideas that cannot be separated sharply from each other. See, e.g., 999[b]33–35, 1003[a]5–12, 1003[b]25–32, 1029[a]28, 1039[a]30–33, 1037[b]27, 1040[b]5–10, 1042[a]26–32, 1052[b]15–16, 1060[b]22, 1086[a]34, 1086[b]26, and 1087[b]34–1088[a]14.

[31]Frede and Patzig, however, disagree. They seem to believe that the form and composite are both subject to the *tode ti* schema and separate in one and the same sense; see *Aristoteles "Metaphysik Z,"* vol. 1, 38–40, and vol. 2, 49–52. Since they see the connection between the *tode ti* schema and the notion of a particular instance of a species, their claim that the schema is univocal is perplexing. Furthermore, I find it puzzling that they point to H.1 (1042[a]29) to show that the form exists separately. They take the addition of "according to formula" to be a mere restriction on the claim that form exists separately, but pretty clearly the addition is meant to contrast the kind of separateness forms have (separateness in formula) with the kind of separateness composites have (separateness in existence) and not to introduce a new form of separateness in existence.

that form is "this something" is tied up with its status as the primary *ousia* of things to which instances of the "this something" schema in its primary sense are applicable. But, then, Aristotle's insistence that both form and composite be separable and subject to the "this something" schema brings out the two dimensions of priority underlying the use of the term '*ousia*' in the two cases. Form has the priority in essence its role in *ousia* explanations requires; composite particulars have the kind of factual or existential priority that makes them the central point of focus in our everyday commerce with the world.

V

Throughout the middle books Aristotle is concerned to show that the intuitions about the reality and unity of familiar particulars that motivated the early theory of *ousia* can be preserved in the face of the general theory of *ousia* explanations delineated in Z and H. In H.6, he confronts the issue a final time. It is significant, I think, that he devotes the final chapter in what is clearly a treatise in its own right to this problem. The implication is that, unless we can silence once and for all the claim that the theory of Z and H calls into question the validity of the common-sense framework, the aims of the middle books will not be achieved.

Aristotle begins the discussion of H.6 by referring to the familiar problems about definition:

> Now a definition is one formula not by a bond [or] in the fashion of the *Iliad*, but by being of one thing. Well, then, what is it that makes *man* one? Why one and not many, like both animal *and* twofooted—especially, indeed, if there are, as some say, a particular animal-itself and twofooted-itself? Why aren't those themselves man and the men will 'be' by participation, not in *man*, not in one, but in two, animal *and* twofooted, and generally man wouldn't be one but more than one, animal and twofooted? (1045$^a$12–1045$^a$19; Furth translation)

Initially this strikes us as the problem we met in Z.12 and the logical works. Certainly the language and example are reminiscent of those texts. Definition involves a reference to a genus (*animal*) and a differentia (*two-footed*), so how can what we define be one thing? The fact is, however, that the focus of H.6 is quite different from that of Z.12, and the problem Aristotle confronts here has no analogue in the discussions of Z.12 or earlier texts such as the *Posterior Analytics* and *De Interpretatione*. Whereas the central concern of Z.12 was the unity of substantial form, here Aristotle discusses problems stemming from the definition of the species. Although the logical writings were, unlike Z.12, concerned with the definition of the species, the theoretical background of the discussion of definition in the *Posterior Analytics* and *De Interpretatione* was such that the strategies Aristotle could appeal to there in coping with problems about the unity of definitions were precisely those at work in Z.12. Given the new theory of form-predication, however, those strategies are now seen to be insufficient to put to rest anxieties about the definition of substance-kinds.

That the terms 'man' and 'animal' are being used here in H.6 in their mixed product senses to signify substance-kinds is, I think, clear. First, the passage I have quoted follows a passage in which Aristotle states that he intends to address the same problem considered in H.3's discussion of definition;[32] there he focuses on the view that there is an analogy between the problem of the unity of definition and the problem of what makes a number (apparently composed as it is of several units) one thing. Although that discussion closes with reflections on the case of form, reflections that are repeated and developed in H.6 itself, that case is considered precisely because it does not present us with a problem of unity. Indeed, the discussion of the analogy is in a context where Aristotle uses the term 'definition' in a specialized and very restrictive sense in which it does not apply to the formula of a form but only to the case where we seek to identify the essence of a species. As he puts it, he is concerned only with the case in which "the formula—the definitory one—signifies "something of something," and the one must play the role of matter and the other of form" ($1043^{b}31$–32; Furth translation). Second, the passage immediately following the one we have quoted repeats the H.3 reference to matter and form by telling us that, in the case we are concerned with, "one part is matter and the other, form" ($1045^{a}29$).

If the concern is with the definition of the species, the issue we are addressing is one with complexities that are simply not operative in the problem confronted in either Z.12 or the logical writings. Although the discussion of Z.12 has as its focus the definition of form rather than the species, it shares with the discussions of definition in the logical works certain assumptions about the relationship between a genus and its differentia. In both contexts, that whose definition we are concerned with (the form in Z.12; the species in *Posterior Analytics* and *De Interpretatione*) is something held to be subject to no ontological analysis. The

<hr />

[32]I take $1045^{a}7$–8 to be an unambiguous reference to H.3, especially to $1043^{b}32$ff. My understanding of the relationship between Z.12 and H.6 is similar to that found in Edward Halper, "*Metaphysics* Z.12 and H.6," but Halper and I differ on the interpretation of the two chapters, especially in our accounts of H.6.

discussions of the logical works are carried out against the backdrop of the Unanalyzability Thesis, and the Z.12 discussion assumes that each substantial form is paradigmatically a unity. The task in both contexts, then, is to show how the facts of definition are consistent with the unity of the thing being defined. The problem is that, whether the object of definition be the form or the species, our definition makes reference to both a genus and a differentia, suggesting that we are defining an aggregate of separate things rather than something that is one in its own right. In both contexts, we can show that the plurality is only apparent by pointing to the fact that genera are not independently identifiable universals with a determinate conceptual content of their own but mere determinables whose content can be identified only by reference to their determinate expressions in the universals that are their logical inferiors (substantial forms in Z.12; species in *Posterior Analytics* and *De Interpretatione*).

But, whereas in dealing with the case of the species the Aristotle of the logical writings can deny that the items mentioned in its definition are distinct things one of which is said or predicated of the other, the Aristotle of Z and H cannot avail himself of this claim. For, whatever status he ascribes to the genera under which substance-species fall,[33] the Aristotle of Z and H is committed to the idea that species are "this form and this matter taken universally" (1035$^b$29–30). Talk of substance-kinds is, by the lights of the middle books, a generalization on the patterns of discourse expressing particular form-predications. So, in the case of substance-species we do have one thing said or predicated of another; the relation here is that of accidental predication, where the "to be of the subject is different from that of" the predicate. And the fact is that the Aristotle of Z and H seems inclined to associate the matter expressed in a species with the genus found in its definition and the form with the differentia.[34]

The opening lines of H.6 identify a new problem whose resolution calls for new strategies, but the problem is narrower than the cluster of

---

[33]The treatment he wants to provide is outlined in I.8 (1057$^b$35–1058$^a$8), where the genera under which species fall likewise turn out to be mere determinables. The problem, however, is that the fact that we have form said of matter in the species precludes Aristotle from appealing in this context to this feature of substance-genera in the way he does in Z.12 in the case of the genera under which substantial forms fall.

[34]I take it that this idea is implicit in 1035$^b$29–30. We must concede that species are defined by way of genus and difference, and if the 1035$^b$29–30 point about matter and form is true we must find a way to reconcile these two approaches to the definition of a species. The idea comes out more explicitly in 1043$^b$29–33 and receives final statement in 1045$^a$20ff., which, taken with the immediately preceding comment on the unity of man, implies the association of matter and genus, form and differentia.

issues that Aristotle actually confronts in H.6. A close look at the passage shows that it prepares us for a discussion bearing on issues broader than those associated with the unity of definition. The reference to individual men at 1045ª18 suggests a concern as well with the unity of concrete particulars, and almost immediately Aristotle shifts the discussion from the case of the species to that of the particular by focusing on the phenomenon of coming to be. Problems about the unity of definition and the unity of the particular are not separate issues but a single problem viewed from different perspectives. After all, what we define when we identify the essence that is a species is simply what to be consists in for the particulars of which the species is predicated essentially. Similarly, when a particular comes to be, what it comes to be is a member of its proper species. As we have seen, the conditions required for a particular's coming to be a thing of a certain kind are precisely those required for it to be a thing of that kind once it has come to be. Talk about a species is just a generalization of talk about the conditions that must be satisfied if its members are to be what they are.

The opening passage also suggests (in the use of '*esontai*' at 1045ª18) a concern, not just with the notion of unity, but the notion of being as well; and the chapter's later reflections on unity go hand in hand with analogous claims about being.[35] The concern, I take it, is the familiar one that if a thing is made up of more basic things then its status as a being is suspect. If an ontologist has already entered into his/her inventory of the "real beings" the matter and form entering into the constitution of a thing, then adding the composite itself to that inventory would appear superfluous. But this concern about the reality of a composite, about its status as a further entry in the ontologist's census of beings, is not really a problem separate from that of the unity of the composite. It is the worry that what is composite is nothing more than an aggregate of its constituents or components that prompts concerns about its status as a genuine being or reality, but it is this same concern that leads us to question the unity of a composite. Indeed, earlier in H.6 Aristotle formulates the problem of unity by asking what the cause is of there being one thing in the case of "things having a number of parts, and where the totality isn't like a heap, but the whole is something besides the parts." (1045ª8–20; Furth translation).

So although H.6 opens with a discussion of the unity of definition, its focus is much broader. It seeks to accommodate the full range of concerns about the validity of the framework of commonsense particulars

---

[35]See 1045ª36–1045ᵇ7, where the focus on being is clear.

in the light of the later theory of *ousia*. Aristotle's initial attempt at responding to those concerns is found in the following passage:

> Plainly then for those who pursue defining and formulating as they are accustomed, it's not possible to answer and solve the aporia; but if, as *we* formulate it, there is on the one hand matter and on the other form, and the one potentially and the other actually, then the topic of investigation would no longer seem an aporia. For this aporia is the same even if the definition of *cloak* were: *rounded bronze*; for then this name would be a sign of the formula, so that the topic of investigation is: what's the cause of the unity of the rounded and the bronze. But then it's clear there's no aporia any longer, because the one [aspect] is matter, the other is form. Then what's the cause of *this*, namely of what is potentially [something] *being* actually [so], aside from the maker, in the case of things where there is genesis? For there is no other cause of what is potentially sphere being actually sphere, but this was the essence for whichever of the two it is. (1045ᵃ20–32; Furth translation).

This is a puzzling passage. In making the shift from the problem of the unity of definition to the unity of the composite particular, Aristotle tells us that, since the components or constituents making up a composite are matter and form, the original aporia disappears. He seems to claim that the reason our perplexities are dispelled when we focus on matter and form is that the potentiality/actuality distinction goes hand in hand with the matter/form distinction. Presumably, then, it is the fact that the concepts of potentiality and actuality are applicable here that serves to dissolve the problem about unity, so that if the focus is on the coming to be of a composite, all that is required to explain how what comes to be is one thing is the efficient cause or agent initiating the change that is the coming to be of the composite.

Commentators have taken the appeal to the potentiality/actuality distinction to represent Aristotle's last word on the problem of unity. Having assimilated the problem of genus/differentia complexity in the definition of the species to the problem of matter/form complexity, they claim, Aristotle is satisfied that he has sufficiently accommodated the unity of ordinary objects falling under substance-kinds with the reflection that matter just *is* potentially whatever it becomes; that it *is* potentially what it actually will be. There are problems with this sort of interpretation of H.6. For one thing, it is not clear what the assimilation Aristotle seems to be suggesting here comes to. The idea that the differentia and the form are one and the same thing is familiar enough. But what of the relation between the genus and the matter? Is Aristotle saying that the genus and the matter (the matter taken generally, I presume) are identical? Or is it rather that the genus term somehow expresses or signifies the matter? Or is the relation even looser so that what we have is a kind of analogy where the determinability of a genus is to be understood by analogy with the potentiality of matter? Aristotle does not answer these questions, but surely one would have thought that, were the assimilation in question to represent Aristotle's final resolution of the problem of unity, he would have done more to tell us just what the cash value of the assimilationist strategy is.

There is a still more pressing difficulty with this interpretation of H.6. The interpretation puts the full weight of the account of unity Aristotle is supposed to be providing on a unity he wants to read into the relationship between what is potential and what is actual. But as Richard Rorty points out, that unity just does not provide the discriminations Aristotle needs if he is to give a successful account of the unity he associates with the individual members of substance-species.[36] The distinction between the potential and the actual can be applied in cases where Aristotle wants to deny the relevant unity. Reflection on Aristotle's favorite example of a count noun not expressing a genuine substance-kind, the term 'cloak' as defined in Z.4, brings out the point. As we have seen, Aristotle's concern in introducing this term is to point out that the unity of an *ousia* is not the kind of unity hinging on the merely conventional fact that we have a single count noun true of that object and others. Were we to introduce the term 'cloak' as an abbreviation for the complex expression 'white man', we would not thereby succeed in specifying a kind of thing. The unity required by a genuine substance concept, Aristotle tells us, would be missing. Nonetheless, for any white man the account of unity this interpretation reads into H.6 seems to apply; for prior to his becoming white, the man is potentially what he will actually be—white.

If we take the potentiality/actuality distinction to carry the full weight of the argument of H.6, it seems, we have Aristotle delineating a kind of

---

[36]See Richard Rorty, "Genus as Matter: A Reading of *Metaphysics* Z–H." For an opposing view, see Charlotte Witt, *Substance and Essence in Aristotle*, 126–142. Witt believes that Aristotle's appeal to the actuality/potentiality distinction represents his final word on the problem of unity. In her attempt to contrast the application of the act/potency distinction to the cases of substantial and accidental change, Witt insists that, in the case of *ousia*, it belongs to the essence of whatever serves as matter for a given form that it be a potentiality for that form and concludes that matter and form are "two ways of being the substance, rather than two beings" (p. 141). But even if we were to agree with Witt that this strategy would solve the problem of the unity of the composite, we could not overlook two problems with her account. First, Aristotle claims that, even in the case of *ousia*, the relationship between a form and its matter is *kata sumbebekos*. Second, Aristotle explicitly denies that the potentiality for actualization by a given form is written into the essence of whatever serves as matter for that form. See *Physics* Γ.1 (201ª31–34) and *Metaphysics* K.9 (1065ᵇ25–28).

unity far too broad for his own purposes, which are to isolate the unity of things like a certain man and a certain horse. It is possible that the interpretation is right and that Aristotle's resolution of the problem of unity just falls short of our expectations, but I am inclined to think otherwise. It is significant, I think, that as soon as he has pointed to the potentiality/actuality distinction, Aristotle invokes the term 'cloak'. Although he gives the term a different definition ('round bronze') from that it had in Z.4, the connections with the use of that term in Z.4 can hardly have escaped him. Though the brazen sphere frequently does function as a model for the constitution of substantial unities, the unity of brazen spheres is no closer to the unity he wants to read into substance-species, on the one hand, and their instances, on the other, than the unity operative in the case of white men. In introducing the term Aristotle suggests as much.[37]

But if the appeal to the potentiality/actuality distinction is not Aristotle's last word on the problem of unity, what is? A quick reading of the rest of H.6 might make us suspicious of the idea that Aristotle has any more to say on the issue; after pointing out that since form lacks all composition no problem can arise in its case, Aristotle reiterates the perplexity the question of unity caused his predecessors. (1045ᵃ36–1045ᵇ17). Then he concludes the chapter by summarizing how his own account deals with the issue:

> But, as has been said, the final matter and the shape are the same and one, [the one] potentially, the other actually, so that investigating what's the cause of unity and being one is similar; for each thing is 'some one', and what is 'potentially' and 'actually' are after a fashion one, so that there is no other cause—besides that, if any, which brought about the movement from potentiality to actuality. And such things as have no matter are all simpliciter 'just what is some one'. (1045ᵇ17–24; Furth translation)

This passage strikes us as a mere restatement of the first attempt to deal with the problem of unity. The claim that the composition we are concerned with is that of matter or potentiality and form or actuality coupled with a loosely formulated suggestion that the potential and the actual are one is supposed to be sufficient to convince us that a problem that vexed his predecessors does not arise within the context of Aristotle's theory. If anything, this passage is less helpful than the passage it restates, since the problematic role of the potentiality/actuality distinction is even more prominent here.

---

[37] I take *"esti gar haute he aporia he aute kan ei . . ."* to suggest that the case of *cloak* is not a case of a genuine substance-kind.

But perhaps we are missing something in the two passages, for there is a suggestion that we have not tried to come to terms with. In both passages, Aristotle seems to be suggesting that there is no need for a special cause of or a special explanation for the unity of the composite. The idea is, I take it, that once we have assembled all the materials required to explain why, in the case of any particular coming to be, this or that sort of thing comes to be, the unity of what comes to be is not a further fact that needs to be explained. Once we have marshaled the resources provided by Aristotle's account in terms of the notions of matter, form, potentiality, actuality, and efficient or agent cause and applied them correctly to explain why a thing of the relevant kind comes to be, we have done all the explaining there is to be done. There is not another thing, namely, why the thing that has come to be is one thing, that needs to be explained. The explanation for that has presumably already been provided.

Why should we think that this is so? Well, in his discussion of the unity of form midway through the chapter (1045$^b$6), Aristotle reminds us of a fact we have overlooked throughout our discussion in the past few sections, the fact that being and unity are not genera. We have been talking blithely throughout this section of the chapter about the unity and reality of the composite oblivious of the fact that, for Aristotle, there is no such thing as just being or just being one thing. I take it that this fact represents a critical presupposition of the line of argument developed in the two passages we have been discussing. There is no such thing as just being; to be is to be a member of a substance-kind. Nor is there such a thing as just being one thing apart from a sortal universal that provides us with a measure for a counting procedure. But, if the change we are seeking to explain is a genuine case of generation, then what comes to be is something like a man, a dog, or a geranium: one man, one dog, one geranium. But to be a man, a dog, or a geranium is what to be consists in for things of these kinds; being one man, one dog, or one geranium is what being one thing amounts to for them.[38] If, using the materials Aristotle's theory provides us, we have adequately explained how something like these things has come to be, we have explained all that there is to explain. There are no further ontological facts (such as the fact that the thing is real or one) that remain to be explained.

Aristotle makes this point in even stronger terms in *De Anima* B.1 (412$^b$6–9), where he tells us that "we can dismiss as unnecessary the

---

[38]See *Metaphysics* Γ.2 (1003$^b$26–29) and I.2 (1054$^a$13 ff.), where Aristotle tells us that *one man* and *a man* are not separated or distinguished in coming to be and passing away.

question whether the soul and body are one." Such a question "is meaningless" since "unity has many senses (as many as 'is' has), but the most proper and fundamental sense of both is the relation of an actuality to that of which it is the actuality."[39] As in H.6, the point here is not that it is because their internal structure can be characterized in terms of the potentiality/actuality distinction that there is no problem about the unity of living beings. The idea is rather that living beings that can, in fact, be characterized by that distinction fall under universals that represent the paradigmatic concepts in terms of which we give sense to talk about unity and being—substance-kinds (like *oak tree, giraffe,* and *man*). Any theory (such as the one provided by Aristotle) that successfully explains how these sortals apply to concrete particulars has, eo ipso, solved the problem of unity.

Aristotle would also argue that his own theory has solved the problem in a way that does discriminate between the individual man of the *Categories* and the individual cloak of Z.4. He would concede that a man agrees with a cloak in owing his existence to a metaphysical predication that holds only accidentally, but he would insist that, since a man is a thing that comes to be and passes away (that a man is, as we put it nowadays, a merely contingent being), the situation could not be otherwise. He would insist that the predication on which a man's existence depends or in which it consists is different from that underlying the existence of the cloak of Z.4. The former, but not the latter, has as its metaphysical predicate a substantial form; and substantial forms, Aristotle wants to say, are *tode ti*–forming functions. Taking the appropriate parcels of matter as their arguments, they yield as their values individuals falling under substance-kinds; and those kinds constitute the fundamental concepts in terms of which we give content to attributions of existence and in terms of which we individuate, count, and reidentify the familiar objects making up the everyday world. So, although Aristotle would concede that anything satisfying the definition of *cloak* given in Z.4 is a cloak and is one cloak among others, he would remind us that to be a cloak just is to be a man that happens to be white and that to be

---

[39]The point here is that, where the actuality is a substantial form (like the soul) predicated of its proximate matter (the body), that actuality is precisely the kind of actuality whose predication grounds the existence of particulars in their proper substance-species; and those species give us the sortals that give content to the notion of being and provide paradigmatic measures for counting and hence for claims that this or that is "one K." Substance sortals, then, represent the determinates for the central or focal use of 'being' and 'one' within the category of *ousia*. So there is an explanation for the being and unity of sensible substances, that provided by the apparatus of form-predication. That apparatus explains why a thing is a member of its substance-species, and that membership in turn gives sense to attributions of existence and counting procedures as they bear on the sensible substance in question.

one cloak is to be one man that is white. He would contend, then, that any unity or existence attaching to cloaks is parasitic on the unity and existence of men, but he would deny that the kind *man* presupposes, in the same way, any further kind to do its work in giving content to attributions of existence or in functioning as a measure for counting procedures. It is a universal that is fundamental to the business of carving up the world; it owes its foundational role here to the fact that its applicability rests on the predication of a substantial form.

So, for Aristotle, there are no special problems about the unity and reality of the composite objects constitutive of the commonsense framework of particulars.[40] Indeed, although Aristotle himself permits and encourages us to pose these questions throughout Z and H, his final verdict is that they represent worries about what is really a pseudo-problem based on a misunderstanding of the logic of 'being' and 'one'. Since there is no such thing as just being or just being a thing and no such thing as just being one thing, the very questions we have been trying to formulate throughout this chapter do not represent genuine philosophical questions that admit of straightforward answers. The being of an object is its being what it is, an instance of its species; the unity of an object is being one instance of that species. If we agree that Aristotle's theory of form-predication successfully explains the phenomenon of species-predication, then we must agree that the framework of *ousia* explanations he develops in the middle books has no force whatsoever to undermine the unity and reality of concrete particulars. Indeed, if the theory is successful in explaining how these particulars are men, dogs, and geraniums, it has guaranteed the applicability of the only notions of reality and unity that make any sense in their case.

So the theory of Z and H does the work we want it to do. But it requires us to do our work, for if it is to give the results it promises, it has to be applied correctly. That requires that we know *where* to invoke

---

[40]An interesting feature of Z and H is Aristotle's treatment of the grand question, What is Being? As he points out in Z.1 (1028ᵇ2–7), this is the question his predecessors posed and he will try to answer in Z and H. In that context, the question is transformed into the question, What is *ousia*? But that is still an imposing and impressive question. By the time we get to H.2, however, our grand question turns out not to have any very grand answers. What looks like a search for some very impressive general pronouncements about reality, unity, and the like has as its terminus very particular, very detailed answers of a humble sort, those provided by particular form-predications. Aristotle pretends to play the game of the great speculative metaphysician, but in the end he tells us that the only answers we can give to the questions they sought to answer (or better, to the questions that replace those questions) are quite humble and very specific claims about *how* parcels of matter are. Parmenides and Plato would surely not have been happy with these results, believing, no doubt, that some sort of trick had been played on them or that their whole enterprise had been ridiculed. Such, I take it, is the cost of misunderstanding the logic of 'to be' and 'one'.

its pattern of *ousia* explanations. We have to know, for example, that *man* is a genuine substance sortal and that *cloak* is not; that geraniums are *ousiai* and that hoplites are not. We have to know, in short, which universals provide us with essences for ordinary objects; we have to be able to distinguish universals that provide answers to the What is it? question posed of ordinary objects from those that enable to say how those objects are. But knowing these kinds of things is just knowing our way around the framework of the *Categories*. The later theory of *ousia* is not just compatible with the insights of the early theory; it presupposes them.

# Bibliography

Ackrill, J. L. *Aristotle's Categories and De Interpretatione*. Oxford: Oxford University Press, 1963.

——. "Aristotle's Definitions of *Psuche*." *Proceedings of the Aristotelian Society* 73 (1972–73), 119–133.

Albritton, Rogers. "Substance and Form in Aristotle's *Metaphysics*." *Journal of Philosophy* 54 (1957), 699–708.

Alexander of Aphrodisias. *In Aristotelis Metaphysica Commentaria*. ed. M. Hayduck. Berlin, 1891.

Allen, R. E. "Individual Properties in Aristotle's *Categories*." *Phronesis* 14 (1969), 31–39.

Annas, Julia. *Aristotle's Metaphysics Books M and N*. Oxford: Oxford University Press, 1976.

——. "Individuals in Aristotle's *Categories*: Two Queries." *Phronesis* 19 (1974), 146–152.

Anscombe, G. E. M., and Peter Geach. *Three Philosophers*. Oxford: Basil Blackwell, 1963.

Aquinas, Thomas. *In Aristotelis Metaphysica*. ed. M. R. Cathala and R. M. Spiazzi. Turin, 1950.

Balme, D. M. *Aristotle: De Partibus Animalium I and De Generatione Animalium I*. Oxford: Oxford University Press, 1972.

Bambrough, Renford, ed. *New Essays on Plato and Aristotle*. London: Routledge and Kegan Paul, 1965.

Barnes, Jonathan. *Aristotle's Posterior Analytics*. Oxford: Oxford University Press, 1975.

——. *Complete Works of Aristotle: The Revised Oxford Translation*. 2 vols. Princeton: Princeton University Press, 1984.

——, M. Schofield, and R. Sorabji, eds. *Articles on Aristotle*. 4 vols. London: Duckworth, 1975–79.

Bergmann, Gustav. *Meaning and Existence*. Madison: University of Wisconsin Press, 1959.
———. *Realism*. Madison: University of Wisconsin Press, 1967.
Blackwell, Richard. "Matter as a Subject of Predication in Aristotle." *Modern Schoolman* (1955), 19–30.
Bogen, James, and James E. McGuire, eds., *How Things Are*. Dordrecht: Reidel, 1985.
Bolton, Robert. "Essentialism and Semantic Theory in Aristotle." *Philosophical Review* 85 (1975), 514–544.
Bonitz, Hermannus. *Index Aristotelicus*. Berlin, 1870.
Bostock, David. "Aristotle on the Principles of Change in *Physics* I." In Schofield and Nussbaum, eds., *Language and Logos*, 179–196.
Brennan, Sheilah O'Flynn. "Substance and Definition, Reality and *Logos*: *Metaphysics* Z–H." *New Scholasticism* 59 (1985), 21–59.
Bruschwig, J. "La forme, predicat de la matiere?" In Pierre Aubenque, ed., *Etudes sur la Metaphysique d'Aristote*, Paris, 1979.
Buchanan, Emerson, *Aristotle's Theory of Being* (Greek, Roman, Byzantine Monographs 2). Cambridge, Mass., 1962.
Burnyeat, Miles, et al., eds. *Notes on Book Zeta of Aristotle's Metaphysics*. Oxford Study Aids in Philosophy, Sub-Faculty of Philosophy, Oxford University, 1979.
Chappell, V. C. "Aristotle's Conceptions of Matter." *Journal of Philosophy* 70 (1973), 679–696.
Charlton, William. "Aristotle and the Principle of Individuation." *Phronesis* 17 (1972), 239–249.
———. *Aristotle's Physics Books I and II*. Oxford: Oxford University Press, 1970.
———. "Prime Matter: A Rejoinder." *Phronesis* 28 (1983), 197–211.
Cherniss, Harold. *Aristotle's Criticism of Plato and the Academy*. Baltimore: Johns Hopkins University Press, 1944.
———. *Aristotle's Criticism of Presocratic Philosophy*. Baltimore: Johns Hopkins University Press, 1935.
Code, Alan. "The Aporematic Approach to Primary Being." *Canadian Journal of Philosophy*, supp. vol. 10 (1984), 41–65.
———. "Aristotle on Essence and Accident." In Richard E. Grandy and Richard Warner, eds., *Philosophical Grounds of Rationality*, 411–444. Oxford: Oxford University Press, 1983.
———. "Aristotle's Response to Quine's Objections to Modal Logic." *Journal of Philosophical Logic* 5 (1976), 159–86.
———. "No Universal Is a Substance: An Interpretation of *Metaphysics* Z.13 (1038$^b$8–15)" *Paideia* 7 (1978), 65–74.
———. "On the Origins of Some Aristotelian Theses about Predication." In Bogen and McGuire, eds., *How Things Are*, 101–131.
———. "The Persistence of Aristotelian Matter." *Philosophical Studies* 29 (1976) 357–367.
———. "What Is It to Be an Individual." *Journal of Philosophy* 75 (1978), 647–648.
Cohen, S. Marc. "Aristotle and Individuation." *Canadian Journal of Philosophy*, supp. vol. 10 (1984), 41–65.
———. "Essentialism in Aristotle." *Review of Metaphysics* 32 (1979), 387–405.
———. "Individual and Essence in Aristotle's *Metaphysics*." *Paideia* 7 (1978), 75–85.
Cohen, Sheldon. "Aristotle's Doctrine of the Material Substrate." *Philosophical Review* 93 (1984), 171–194.
Cooper, John. "Aristotle on Natural Teleology." In Schofield and Nussbaum, eds., *Language and Logos*, 197–22.

Cousin, D. R. "Aristotle's Doctrine of Substance, Part I." *Mind* 42 (1933), 319–339.
——. "Aristotle's Doctrine of Substance, Part II." *Mind* 44 (1935), 168–185.
Dancy, Russell. "Matter: Aristotle and Chappell." *Journal of Philosophy* 70 (1973), 698–699.
——. "On Some of Aristotle's First Thoughts about Substance." *Philosophical Review* 84 (1975), 338–373.
——. "On Some of Aristotle's Second Thoughts about Substances: Matter." *Philosophical Review* 87 (1978), 372–413.
——. *Sense and Contradiction: A Study in Aristotle*. Dordrecht: Reidel, 1975.
Driscoll, John. "*Eide* in Aristotle's Earlier and Later Theories of Substance." In O'Meara, ed., *Studies in Aristotle*, 129–159.
Duerlinger, James. "Predication and Inherence in Aristotle's *Categories*." *Phronesis* 15 (1970), 179–203.
Fine, Gail. "Separation." *Oxford Studies in Ancient Philosophy* 2 (1984). 31–87.
——. "Separation: A Reply to Morrison." *Oxford Studies in Ancient Philosophy* 3 (1985), 159–65.
Frede, Michael. *Essays in Ancient Philosophy*. Minneapolis: University of Minnesota Press, 1987.
——, and Gunther Patzig. *Aristoteles "Metaphysik Z."* 2 vols. Munich: Verlag C. H. Beck, 1988.
Frege, Gottlob. "Function and Concept." In Peter Geach and Max Black, eds., *Translations from the Philosophical Writings of Gottlob Frege*. 21–41. Oxford: Basil Blackwell, 1966.
——. "On Concept and Object." In Peter Geach and Max Black eds., *Translations from the Philosophical Writings of Gottlob Frege*. 45–55. Oxford: Basil Blackwell, 1966.
Furth, Montgomery. "Aristotle on the Unity of Form." In Matthen, ed., *Aristotle Today*, 77–102.
——. *Substance, Form, and Psyche: An Aristotelian Metaphysics*. Cambridge: Cambridge University Press, 1988.
——. "Transtemporal Stability in Aristotelian Substances." *Journal of Philosophy* 75 (1978), 624–646.
——, ed. and trans., *Aristotle: Metaphysics Books Zeta, Eta, Theta, Iota*. Indianapolis: Hackett, 1985.
Gotthelf, Allan. "Aristotle's Conception of Final Causality." *Review of Metaphysics* 30 (1976), 226–254.
——, and James Lennox, eds. *Philosophical Issues in Aristotle's Biology*. Cambridge: Cambridge University Press, 1987.
Graham, Daniel. "Aristotle's Discovery of Matter." *Archiv fur Geschichte der Philosophie* 66 (1984), 37–51.
——. *Aristotle's Two Systems*. Oxford: Oxford University Press, 1988.
——. "The Paradox of Prime Matter." *Journal of the History of Philosophy* 27 (1987), 475–490.
Grayeff, Felix. *Aristotle and His School*. London: Duckworth, 1974.
Grene, Marjorie. "Is Genus to Species as Matter to Form?" *Synthese* 28 (1974), 51–69.
Halper, Edward. "*Metaphysics* Z.12 and H.6: The Unity of Form and Composite." *Ancient Philosophy* 4 (1985), 146–159.
Hamlyn, D. W. *Aristotle's De Anima II and III*. Oxford: Oxford University Press, 1968.
Happ, H. *Hyle: Studien zum Aristotelischen Materiebegriff*. Berlin: De Gruyter, 1971.
Hare, J. E. "Aristotle and the Definition of Natural Things." *Phronesis* 24 (1979), 168–179.

Haring, E. S. "Substantial Form in *Metaphysics* VII." *Review of Metaphysics* 10 (1956–57), 308–332, 482–501, 698–713.
Hartman, Edwin. "Aristotle on the Identity of Substance and Essence." *Philosophical Review* 85 (1976), 545–560.
——. *Substance, Body, and Soul.* Princeton: Princeton University Press, 1977.
Heinaman, Robert. "Non-Substantial Individuals in the *Categories*." *Phronesis* 26 (1981), 295–307.
Hintikka, Jaakko. *Time and Necessity: Studies in Aristotle's Theory of Modality.* Oxford: Oxford University Press, 1973.
Hughes, Gerald. "Universals as Potential Substances: The Interpretation of *Metaphysics* Z.13." In Burnyeat et al., eds., *Notes on Book Zeta*, 107–126.
Hussey, E. L.. *Aristotle's Physics Books III and IV.* Oxford: Oxford University Press, 1983.
Irwin, Terence. "Aristotle's Discovery of Metaphysics." *Review of Metaphysics* 31 (1977), 210–229.
——. *Aristotle's First Principles.* Oxford: Oxford University Press, 1989.
Jaeger, Werner. *Aristotle: Fundamentals of the History of His Development.* trans. Richard Robinson. Oxford: Oxford University Press, 1948.
Jones, Barrington. "Aristotle's Introduction of Matter." *Philosophical Review* 20 (1975), 146–172.
Kahn, Charles. "On the Theory of the Verb 'To Be'." In Milton Munitz, ed., *Logic and Ontology*, 1–20. New York: New York University Press, 1973.
——. *The Verb 'Be' in Ancient Greece.* Dordrecht: Reidel, 1974.
King, Hugh R. "Aristotle without *Prima Materia*." *Journal of the History of Ideas* 17 (1956), 370–389.
Kirwan, Christopher. *Aristotle's Metaphysics Books Δ, Γ, and E.* Oxford: Oxford University Press, 1971.
Kosman, L. A. "Substance, Being, and *Energeia*." *Oxford Studies in Ancient Philosophy* 2 (1984), 121–49.
Kung, Joan. "Aristotle on Thises, Suches, and the Third Man Argument." *Phronesis* 26 (1981), 207–247.
——. "Can Substance Be Predicated of Matter?" *Archiv fur Geschichte der Philosophie* 60 (1978), 140–159.
Lacey, A. R. "*Ousia* and Form in Aristotle." *Phronesis* 10 (1965), 54–69.
Lear, Jonathan. *Aristotle and Logical Theory.* Cambridge: Cambridge University Press, 1980.
——. *Aristotle: The Desire to Understand.* Cambridge: Cambridge University Press, 1988.
Lee, E. N., A. P. D. Mourelatos, and R. M. Rorty. eds. *Exegesis and Argument: Studies in Greek Philosophy Presented to Gregory Vlastos.* Assen: Von Gorcum, 1973.
Lesher, James. "Aristotle on Form, Substance, and Universal: A Dilemma." *Phronesis* 16 (1971), 169–178.
Lewis, Frank. "Accidental Sameness in Aristotle." *Philosophical Studies* 42 (1982), 1–36.
——. "Form and Predication in Aristotle's *Metaphysics*." In Bogen and McGuire, eds., *How Things Are*, 59–83.
——. "Plato's Third Man Argument and the 'Platonism' of Aristotle." In Bogen and McGuire, eds., *How Things Are*, 133–174.
——. "Substance and Predication." Unpublished manuscript, forthcoming, Cambridge University Press.

——. "What Is Aristotle's Theory of Essence?" *Canadian Journal of Philosophy*, supp. vol. 10 (1984), 89–131.

Lloyd, A. C. "Aristotle's Principle of Individuation." *Mind* 79 (1970), 519–529.

——. *Form and Universal in Aristotle*. Liverpool: Francis Cairns, 1981.

Locke, John. *An Essay Concerning Human Understanding*. 2 vols. ed. John Yolton London: Dent, 1947.

Loux, Michael J. "Aristotle on the Transcendentals." *Phronesis* 18 (1973), 225–239.

——. "Form, Species, and Predication in *Metaphysics* Z, H, and Θ." *Mind* 88 (1979), 1–23.

——. "*Ousia*: A Prolegomenon to *Metaphysics* Z and H." *History of Philosophy Quarterly* 1 (1984), 241–266.

——. *Substance and Attribute*. Dordrecht: Reidel, 1978.

——. "Towards an Aristotelian Theory of Abstract Entities." *Midwest Studies in Philosophy* 11 (1986), 495–512.

Lukaciewicz, J. "The Principle of Individuation." *Aristotelean Society Supplementary Volume* 27 (1953), 69–82.

Luyten, Norbert. "Matter as Potency." In McMullin, ed., *The Concept of Matter*, 102–113.

McMullin, Ernan, ed. *The Concept of Matter in Greek and Medieval Philosophy*. Notre Dame, Ind.: University of Notre Dame Press, 1963.

Matthen, Mohan. "The Categories and Aristotle's Ontology." *Dialogue* 17 (1978), 228–243.

——. "Individual Substances as Hylomorphic Complexes." In Matthen, ed., *Aristotle Today*, 151–176.

——, ed. *Aristotle Today*. Edmonton: Academic Printing and Publishing, 1986.

Matthews, G. B., and S. M. Cohen. "The One and the Many." *Review of Metaphysics* 21 (1967–68), 630–635.

Modrak, D. K. "Forms and Compounds." In Bogen and McGuire, eds., *How Things Are*, 85–99.

——. "Forms, Types, and Tokens in Aristotle's *Metaphysics*." *Journal of the History of Philosophy* 17 (1979), 371–381.

Moravscik, J. M. E. "Aristotle on Predication." *Philosophical Review* 76 (1967), 80–96.

——, ed. *Aristotle*. New York: Doubleday, 1967.

Morrison, Donald. "Separation: A Reply to Fine." *Oxford Studies in Ancient Philosophy* 3 (1985), 167–173.

——. "Separation in Aristotle's *Metaphysics*." *Oxford Studies in Ancient Philosophy* 3 (1985), 125–157.

Nussbaum, Martha. *Aristotle's De Motu Animalium*. Princeton: Princeton University Press, 1978.

O'Meara, Dominic, ed. *Studies in Aristotle*. Washington: Catholic University of America Press, 1981.

Owen, G. E. L. "Aristotle on the Snares of Ontology." In Bambrough, ed., *New Essays on Plato and Aristotle*, 69–95.

——. "Inherence." *Phronesis* 10 (1965), 97–105.

——. "Logic and Metaphysics in Some Earlier Works of Aristotle." In Owen and During, eds., *Aristotle and Plato in the Mid-Fourth Century*, 163–190.

——. *Logic, Science, and Dialectic*. Ithaca: Cornell University Press, 1986.

——. "Particular and General." *Proceedings of the Aristotelian Society* 79 (1978–79), 279–294.

——. "The Platonism of Aristotle." In Barnes, Schofield, and Sorabji, eds., *Articles on Aristotle*, vol. 1, 14–34.

——. "*Tithenai ta Phainomena*." In Moravscik, ed., *Aristotle*, 167–190.

——, and I. During. *Aristotle and Plato in the Mid-Fourth Century*. Goteburg: Studia Graeca et Latina Gothaburgensia 11, 1960.

Owens, Joseph. "Aristotle on Categories." *Review of Metaphysics* 14 (1960), 73–90.

——. *The Doctrine of Being in the Aristotelian Metaphysics*. Toronto: Pontifical Institute of Medieval Studies, 1957.

——. "Matter and Predication in Aristotle." In Moravscik, ed., *Aristotle*, 191–214.

Page, Carl. "Predicating Forms of Matter in Aristotle's *Metaphysics*." *Review of Metaphysics* 39 (1985), 57–82.

Popper, Karl. "The Principle of Individuation." *Aristotelian Society Supplementary Volume* 27 (1953), 97–120.

Quine, W. V. O. *Word and Object*. Cambridge: MIT Press, 1960.

Regis, Edward. "Aristotle's Principle of Individuation." *Phronesis* 21 (1976), 157–166.

Robinson, H. M. "Prime Matter in Aristotle." *Phronesis* 19 (1974), 168–88.

Rorty, Richard. "Genus as Matter: A Reading of *Metaphysics* Z–H." In Lee, Mourelatos, and Rorty, eds., *Exegesis and Argument*, 393–420.

——. "Matter as Goo: Comments on Grene's Paper." *Synthese* 28 (1974), 71–77.

Ross, W. D. *Aristotle's Metaphysics*. 2 vols. Oxford: Oxford University Press, 1924.

——. *Aristotle's Physics*. Oxford: Oxford University Press, 1936.

——. *Aristotle's Prior and Posterior Analytics*. Oxford: Oxford University Press, 1949.

Russell, Bertrand. *Logic and Knowledge*. ed. R. C. Marsh. London: George Allen and Unwin, 1956.

Schofield, Malcolm. "*Metaphysics* Z.3: Some Suggestions." *Phronesis* 17 (1972), 97–101.

——, and Martha Nussbaum, eds. *Language and Logos: Studies in Greek Philosophy Presented to G. E. L. Owen*. Cambridge: Cambridge University Press, 1982.

Sellars, Wilfrid. *Philosophical Perspectives*. Springfield, Ill.: Charles Thomas, 1967.

Smith, J. A. "*Tode Ti* in Aristotle." *Classical Review*, 35 (1921), 19.

Sokolowski, Robert. "Matter, Elements, and Substance in Aristotle." *Journal of the History of Philosophy* 8 (1970), 263–288.

Solmsen, Friedrich. "Aristotle and Prime Matter." *Journal of the History of Ideas* 19 (1958), 243–252.

——. *Aristotle's System of the Physical World*. Ithaca: Cornell University Press, 1960.

Sorabji, Richard. *Necessity, Chance, and Blame*. Ithaca: Cornell University Press, 1984.

Stahl, Donald E. "Stripped Away: Some Contemporary Obscurities Surrounding *Metaphysics* Z.3 (1029ª10–26)." *Phronesis* 26 (1981), 177–180.

Strawson, P. F. *Individuals: An Essay in Descriptive Metaphysics*. London: Methuen, 1959.

Sykes, R. D. "Form in Aristotle: Universal or Particular?" *Philosophy* 50 (1975), 311–331.

Telloh, Henry. "Aristotle's *Metaphysics* Z.13." *Canadian Journal of Philosophy* 5 (1979), 77–89.

——. "The Universal in Aristotle." *Apeiron* (1980), 70–78.

Waterlow, Sarah. *Nature, Change, and Agency in Aristotle's Physics*. Oxford: Oxford University Press, 1982.

——. *Passage and Possibility*. Oxford: Oxford University Press, 1982.

Wedin, Michael V. "Singular Statements and Essentialism in Aristotle." *Canadian Journal of Philosophy*, sup. vol. 10 (1984), 67–88.

Weidemann, Hermann. "In Defense of Aristotle's Theory of Predication." *Phronesis* 25 (1980), 76–87.

White, Nicholas. "Aristotle on Sameness and Oneness." *Philosophical Review* 80 (1971), 177–97.

——. "The Origins of Aristotle's Essentialism." *Review of Metaphysics* 26 (1972), 387–405.

Whiting, Jennifer. "Form and Individuation in Aristotle." *History of Philosophy Quarterly* 3 (1986), 359–377.

Wiggins, David. *Sameness and Substance*. Cambridge: Harvard University Press, 1980.

Williams, C. J. F. *Aristotle's De Generatione et Corruptione*. Oxford: Oxford University Press, 1982.

Witt, Charlotte. *Substance and Essence in Aristotle*. Ithaca: Cornell University Press, 1989.

Woods, M. J. "Problems in *Metaphysics* Z, Chapter 13." In Moravscik, ed., *Aristotle*, 215–238.

——. "Substance and Essence in Aristotle." *Proceedings of the Aristotelian Society* 75 (1974–75), 167–80.

# Index

*Library of Congress Cataloging-in-Publication Data*
Loux, Michael J.
    Primary ousia: an essay on Aristotle's Metaphysics Z and H /
Michael J. Loux.
        p.  cm.
    Includes bibliographical references and index.
    ISBN 0-8014-2598-0 (alk. paper)
    1. Aristotle.   Metaphysics.   Book 7-8.    2. Metaphysics—Early
works to 1800.   I. Title.
B434.L68   1991
111'.1—dc20
                                                        90-25775